Women into the
Unknown

Women into the Unknown

A Sourcebook on Women Explorers and Travelers

MARION TINLING

GREENWOOD PRESS ————————————————

New York • Westport, Connecticut • London

G
200
.T55
1989

Library of Congress Cataloging-in-Publication Data

Tinling, Marion.
    Women into the unknown : a sourcebook on women explorers and
travelers / Marion Tinling.
      p. cm.
    Bibliography: p.
    Includes index.
    ISBN 0–313–25328–5 (lib. bdg. : alk. paper)
    1. Explorers, Women—Biography. I. Title.
G200.T55   1989
910′.88042—dc19   88–18677

18069780

British Library Cataloguing in Publication Data is available.

Library of Congress Catalog Card Number: 88–18677
ISBN: 0–313–25328–5

First published in 1989

Greenwood Press, Inc.
88 Post Road West, Westport, Connecticut 06881

Printed in the United States of America

The paper used in this book complies with the
Permanent Paper Standard issued by the National
Information Standards Organization (Z39.48–1984).

10 9 8 7 6 5 4 3 2 1

Copyright Acknowledgments

The following authors and publishers have kindly given permission to quote passages from copyrighted material.

John Murray (Publishers) Ltd., for Daisy Bates, *The Passing of the Aborigines* (1938); for Freya Stark, *The Zodiac Arch* (1968), *Perseus in the Wind* (1948), *Beyond Euphrates* (1951), *The Valleys of the Assassins* (1934), *The Lycian Shore* (1956), *Riding the Tigris* (1959), and *The Minaret of Djam* (1970); and Dervla Murphy, *Wheels within Wheels* (1979), *Full Tilt* (1965), *Tibetan Foothold* (1966), *In Ethiopia with a Mule* (1968), and *On a Shoestring to Coorg* (1976).

Dervla Murphy for her works, listed above, published by John Murray.

The American Geographical Society for Louise A. Boyd, *The Fiord Region of East Greenland* (1935).

Macmillan & Company for Stephen Gwynn, *The Life of Mary Kingsley* (1933).

David Higham Associates Ltd., for Ella Maillart, *Cruises and Caravans* (London: J. M. Dent, 1942) and *The Land of the Sherpas* (London: Hodder & Stoughton, 1955).

Ella Maillart for her *Turkestan Solo* (London and New York: Putnam, 1935), *Forbidden Journey* (London: W. Heinemann, 1937), and *The Cruel Way* (London: W. Heinemann, 1947).

Jonathan Cape for Duff Hart-Davis, *Peter Fleming* (1974) and Peter Fleming, *News from Tartary* (1930).

Methuen & Co. Ltd., for Margery Perham, *Colonial Sequence, 1930 to 1949* (1967).

Faber & Faber Ltd., for Margery Perham, *African Apprenticeship* (1974).

Alfred A. Knopf, Inc., for Elizabeth Marshall Thomas, *The Harmless People* (1959) and *Warrior Herdsmen* (1965).

To my beloved sister May,
for all she has done for me in our lives.

CONTENTS

MAPS
DELINEATED BY THOMAS TINLING

1
Africa

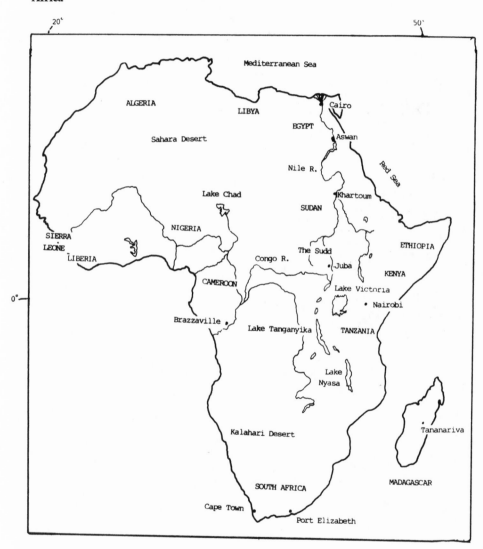

2
Northern Asia

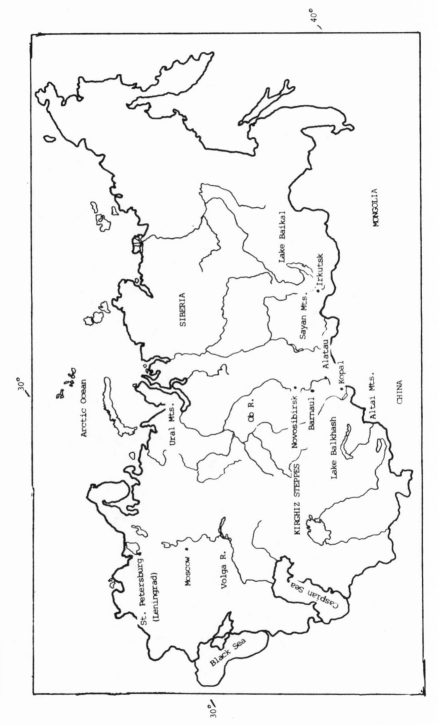

3

China and Mongolia

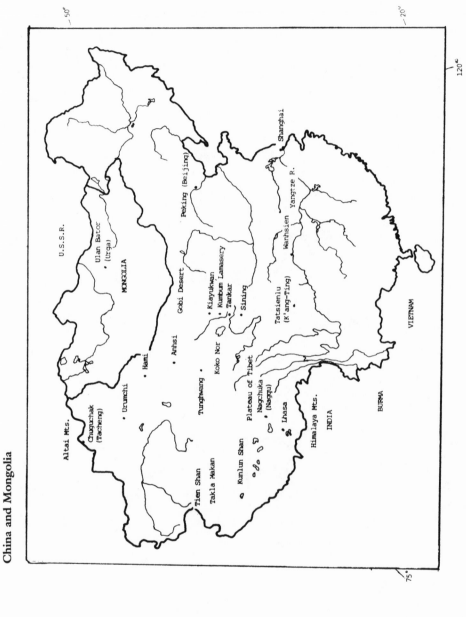

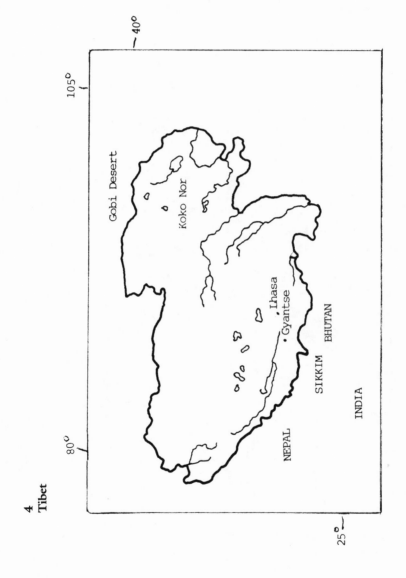

4
Tibet

105° 40°

Gobi Desert

Koko Nor

Lhasa
Gyantse

80° 25°

NEPAL

SIKKIM

BHUTAN

INDIA

5
Near and Middle East

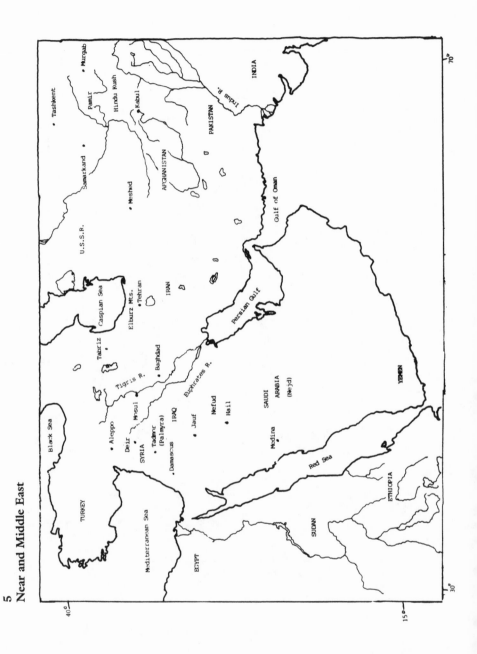

6
The Nile

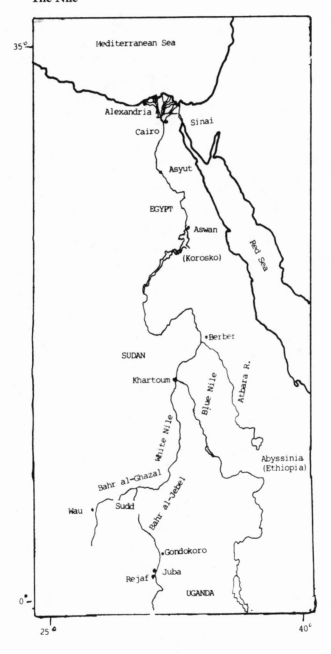

35°

Mediterranean Sea

Alexandria

Cairo

Sinai

Asyut

EGYPT

Aswan

(Korosko)

Red Sea

•Berber

SUDAN

Khartoum

Blue Nile

Atbara R.

White Nile

Abyssinia
(Ethiopia)

Bahr al-Ghazal

Bahr al-Jebel

Wau •

Sudd

•Gondokoro

Rejaf •   Juba

UGANDA

0°

25°

40°

7
Australia

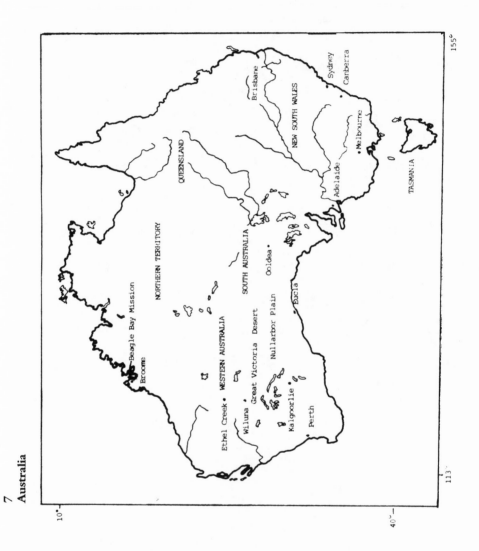

9
South Sea Islands

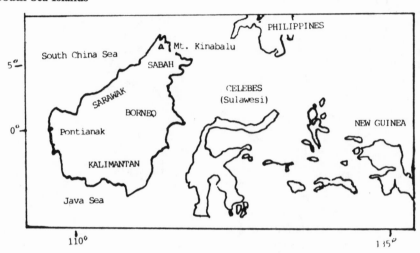

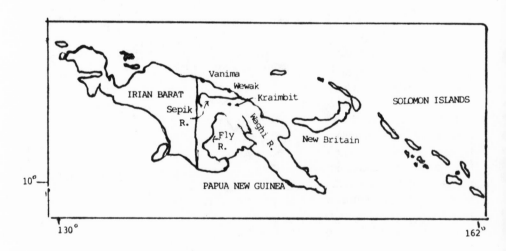

INTRODUCTION

The questing spirit is not confined to one sex, yet among explorers women are comparative newcomers. Few women were able to travel outside of their own countries before the eighteenth century. Indeed, until the time of the Second World War, the average middle-class woman had little of the freedom and self-assertion men took for granted. In addition to social restraints, lack of money limited women's opportunities for travel. The early male explorers had wealthy patrons; later they were sponsored by geographical societies. Both sources of support were long denied to women.

A surprising number of women, nevertheless, had enough initiative and fortitude to visit lands marked "unexplored" on maps, lands inhabited by those whose color, speech, and habits were strange and new. Some went with husbands, and a few carried on the work as widows. Others were able to finance and lead their own expeditions, earning as they went by lecturing, teaching, or writing. In the last century and a half, women have traveled all over the two hemispheres, from jungle to mountain. They have lived with Pygmies in Africa and with Bedouins in Arabia. Some collected and photographed wild animals; others climbed the most challenging mountains; not a few studied plants in hidden corners of the world. They investigated the lives and customs of peoples hitherto unvisited. Their lectures and writings not only brought pleasure to the stay-at-home, but carried new ideas to the rest of the world and even helped influence public policies. A number added significantly to geographical knowledge, and some gave their names to places on the maps.

What motivates a man or woman to leave the comforts of home to venture into possible danger and certain hardship? The old male reasons for exploration—conquest, acquisition of wealth, and imperialism—are out of favor, and today different reasons are given for travel. Some wish to take the benefits of Christianity or modern technology to other lands. Some want to study plants or wildlife. Others are interested in uncovering the remains of ancient civilizations.

Many are devoted to preserving a vanishing culture or to protecting the world's environmental balance. A few confess they want simply the thrill of discovery, or just the fun of being on the open road. The testing of one's strength and ability to survive is a sufficient motive to others.

For women, in particular, the reasons seem very personal. The need to escape stultifying Victorian social restrictions impelled some to travel abroad. It is worth noting that not a few of the earliest English traveling women were wealthy and titled; Dorothy Middleton's *Victorian Lady Travellers* was aptly named. Many made their escape only after they were freed from family responsibilities and when they were far from young.

Did the escapees see themselves as liberated women? Were they motivated by a desire to show that a woman can do whatever a man can do? Annie Peck carried a "Votes for Women" pennant to a mountain top. Fanny Bullock Workman was photographed on a Himalayan peak with a newspaper headed "Votes for Women." Grace Gallatin Seton was a strong believer in woman suffrage. On the other hand, Gertrude Bell was a founder of the Anti-Suffrage League. Almost all commented on the low status of women in countries they visited, yet they did not see themselves as pioneers for feminism. They were drawn by curiosity and attracted by the color and excitement of foreign lands.

News stories and reviews of travel books by women were often patronizing, their writers disparaged as "globe-trotteresses." Women were not admitted to the Royal Geographical Society (R.G.S.), the bastion of English male explorers, until many years after its founding. A suggestion made in 1847 to accept some female members was met with a chilling report that "This is not deemed expedient at the moment." In 1860, when John Speke suggested that honorary membership be given to the African explorer Alexine Tinne, the idea was allowed to fall to the ground.

A break came in 1892, when Isabella Bird Bishop had returned from her second long trip to the Far East and May French Sheldon from leading an expedition into East Africa. The council of the R.G.S. admitted fifteen women, including these two, as well as Kate Marsden, who had ministered to the lepers in Siberia. Seven more women were admitted before the gates were firmly closed in 1893, not to be reopened until 1913. Today a satisfying proportion of the Fellows of the Royal Geographical Society are female.

The Explorers Club in New York was even slower to open its doors to the female sex. In 1925 four women travelers, indignant at being excluded from explorers' and adventurers' clubs and the opportunity to discuss common problems and the joys of travel, organized the Society of Woman Geographers. Acceptance into its ranks was an honor from the beginning and remains so today.

Women's perceptions of travel and discovery differ from those of men, and their explorations add a new dimension to knowledge. Women have been able to talk to the women of other cultures where men were forbidden to do so. In general, women show less interest in politics and the introduction of European ideas and technology than do men. They observe more closely the rhythm of daily life—birth, marriage, child-rearing, death, and household economy. These matters, so much a part of every woman's life, are basic and universal, enduring through all political changes.

The ability of women to add to our knowledge of countries once almost unknown and still little understood by the European world is unquestioned. Dozens of women now work in Antarctica as research scientists, medical doctors, and administrators. In the last decade, numbers of women have chosen wilderness living as forest technicians, wildlife specialists, and other callings that take them far from cities. No longer can exploration be considered an exclusively male field.

A word on the scope of this volume. It was impossible to include biographies of more than a small sample of the many women who have been and are explorers. Nor was it easy to decide who is and who is not an explorer. I looked for women who went into unknown territory, sought new information, and brought back fresh ideas; women who had some conception of what to expect, and whose minds were open enough to accept different points of view. They were willing to absorb the atmosphere of a country and to experience fully the lives and emotions of other peoples. The most successful tried to speak the language of those they visited, to eat the local food, and to live pretty much as the natives did. While a few were unable to rid themselves of religious and racial prejudice, not one was unchanged by exposure to the world beyond her own circle. All kept some account of the things they saw. Many were publicly recognized and honored for their contributions.

Limitations of space dictated the omission of several whole categories of travelers: mountaineers, sea voyagers, air and space travelers, underseas explorers, and most round-the-world travelers—all of whom deserve special books of their own. Women who simply resided for a time in a foreign country were generally omitted. Among these were many missionaries, probably the first European women to go into foreign lands, as well as several famous Englishwomen who chose to live abroad.

For every man or woman who is able to leave a sheltered life and step into an unknown world, there are thousands who are tied to a job or domestic responsibilities. They are the armchair travelers, to whom travel accounts offer vicarious adventure. Because the narrative of exploration is necessarily autobiographical, it brings the housebound reader immediately into the traveler's world. It both entertains and informs, adding geographical and historical breadth to personal adventure.

Each of the biographical sketches includes a chronological listing of the subject's travel writings and a bibliography of the chief biographical sources. Only women who wrote in English or whose books were translated into English were included, although this decision unfortunately eliminates many renowned travelers. Except for a very few, all the biographees wrote at least one travel account. Ynes Mexia, a Mexican-American botanist, never published a book, but she left accounts of her travels in manuscript. Harriet Chalmers Adams also never completed a book, but her many articles in the *National Geographic* chronicle her travels. Recent scholarship has uncovered for the first time the stories of several early travelers. Florence Baker's story was known only from her husband's books until her diary was published in 1972, a hundred years after the event. Little was in print of Alexine Tinne's travels until Penelope Gladstone's *Travels of Alexine* appeared in 1970. While a few of the women have been the subjects of full-length biographies, for others only the barest biographical information could be found.

The writers were strong, independent women. Most led busy lives in addition to their travels, and some were noted for other accomplishments, but they appear here primarily in their roles as travelers and writers of travel literature.

To bridge the gap between the explorers treated here and others worthy of study, an annotated list of travel books by women is included. The number of such books is very large and only those I judged to be most interesting and valuable have been listed. In general, Americans and Europeans describing travel in their own countries have been omitted.

The tale of early exploration, wonderful as it may be for the homebound reader and as background for the traveler, cannot serve as a guide to what can now be seen and experienced. Nor can a map of the country traversed long ago substitute for one that is up to date. The maps supplied are a compromise between the country described and present geographical reality. Few regions of the earth remain today as they were in the eighteenth, nineteenth, or early twentieth centuries. The names of places have changed; the modes of travel are different; road builders and engineers are continually busy remaking the face of the earth itself.

Some say the world is so changed that areas to be explored no longer exist and that travel is not the challenge it once was. True, travelers need no longer subject themselves to the hazards faced by the earlier explorers. Modern communication systems can monitor and rescue one who is injured or falls ill far from medical help. Insecticides and vaccines, protective lotions and dark glasses, lightweight clothing and equipment, as well as changes in the countries visited, make the lot of today's traveler much easier than before. As for areas of exploration, the fact is that many parts of the world and many aspects of life remain to be investigated and described. This is true especially in the field of human beliefs and customs, the very field to which women explorers are drawn and in which women are particularly good observers.

Contemporary explorers may be dropped into wild places by airplane, but once there they must walk jungle paths to find tribes whose ways of life differ widely from those familiar to the American or European. Women today willing to go as explorers rather than as tourists may experience the same exhilaration and satisfaction in travel as their predecessors who dared to step into the unknown.

BIOGRAPHIES

HARRIET CHALMERS ADAMS
1875–1937

Harriet Chalmers Adams was the first president of the Society of Woman Geographers. When the society was founded in 1925, Adams was one of the best-known women explorers of America. She had been in every Latin American country, had crossed Haiti in the saddle, and had visited almost every land that had ever been under the dominion of Spain or Portugal, following the trail of Columbus and the conquistadors. From 1907 on, few years had passed without an article or two from her pen, most of them published in the *National Geographic* magazine. She lectured widely, helping to dispel her North American listeners of prejudicial views of South America. As a war correspondent for *Harper's* magazine in 1916 she was the only woman allowed to visit the trenches in France. In 1925, when she began her presidency of the society, she had just returned from a trip through Spain and Morocco.

Her enthusiasm and wide friendship among other women travelers gave the Society of Woman Geographers the spark it needed to attract nationally- and internationally- recognized women geographers and those who had done distinguished work in the allied sciences. The organization still flourishes in Washington, D.C., where Adams made her home for many years.

Harriet Chalmers was born on October 22, 1875, in Stockton, in the San Joaquin Valley of California. Her father, Alexander Chalmers, was an engineer from Edinburgh who had come to the west coast in search of adventure, crossing the plains with an ox team. In California he met and married Frances Wilkins, whose father came from New Hampshire in the days when California was part of Mexico. Harriet heard from her grandfather stories about the Spanish conquerors and explorers of Mexico and South America, and her father, a traveler and adventurer at heart, gave the child her first taste of exploration. She was only eight, she recollected, when her father tossed her into a saddle and set off for a trip through the state of California, "and that journey made me over, from a domestic little girl . . . to one who wished to go to the ends of the earth and to see and study the people of all lands.'' Her mother and sister "found their pleasure at some resort, but dad and I preferred to mount a horse and gallop away to some wild mountain range which we had never before visited" (Jacksonville, Fla., *Sunday Times Union*, May 10, 1914). Father and daughter explored widely in California's Sierra Nevada. She had no formal schooling after the age of eleven but was taught by her parents and private teachers.

When in 1899 Harriet married Franklin Pierce Adams, an electrical engineer from her hometown, she found someone equally enthusiastic about travel, and the following year they went to Mexico on an engineering survey. This taste of a different yet oddly familiar culture fired their interest in further exploration, and at Christmas time, 1903, they started on a three-year tour of South America, during which they covered over 40,000 miles and crossed the cordilleras of the Andes four times. They went into the jungles where rubber was being collected and to the mines. They visited Tiahuanaco in the Bolivian Andes, the oldest town in America, and sailed on Lake Titicaca, the Lake of the Clouds. They went to Cuzco, sacred to the Quechuas, where they marveled at the ancient stone walls and buildings left by the Incas and deplored the domination of the Catholic priests.

One of the first of Harriet's many articles for the *National Geographic* describes their experiences in the Andean highlands:

> Those were long days in the saddle, with little food and less water. We knew the river water to be impure, as the sewage of Cuzco flows into it, and the brooks are also contaminated as they pass through the villages. At night we slept on the ground, wrapped in our blankets, at times finding shelter in a ruined temple, as there are many lesser ruins throughout the Valley of Yucay. We met no travelers save the highland Indians, and picked up a few words of their tongue. I felt that we had left civilization far behind. Even the Spanish colonial days faded. We were in the old Peru.
>
> To know a country and a people, one must leave the highway and live near to Nature. We traveled much in the saddle on this great elevated plateau—over a thousand miles on a single journey—and gradually my standpoint changed. I started as an outsider, having little real sympathy for the Quichuas and Aymaras, little understanding of the history and environment which has made them the sullen, lifeless folk they are. In time I grew, through study and observation, but more through sharing the life, half-Andean myself, and find, in looking back over years of travel in South America—years in which we visited every country—that my greatest heart interest lies in the highlands of Peru and Bolivia. (*National Geographic* 19, Sept. 1908, p. 618)

Her favorite country was Peru. "Perhaps it is because there is hardly a foot of that marvelous land that I have not journeyed over and then, too, Peru is the richest in interest historically" (*San Francisco Chronicle*, Oct. 27, 1907).

During their long days on horseback, Harriet first rode sidesaddle but soon switched to riding astride. She wore a short skirt of khaki or corduroy, a jacket, high boots, and a sombrero. At one point a pack mule fell over the edge of a steep trail and carried with it her trunk, containing their entire spare wardrobe. When she herself fell into a torrent of water, she had to borrow various articles of clothing from friendly English miners deep in the Andes. She donned the doctor's bathrobe, the superintendent's underwear, and the engineer's slippers. All hairpins lost, she wore her hair in a braid. She mourned the loss of her Pond's cold cream, which protected her face from the dry air.

They met llama trains carrying goods and learned to anticipate their coming and scramble out of the way, for the trains pushed everything else off the trail. However, they had reason to be grateful to the woolly llamas, for once the animals saved their lives. Traveling alone, they were far from shelter when night came on, and at the great altitude the nights were freezing cold. They saw a herd of llamas settled down for the night and crept among them, nestling into their warmth and sleeping cozily through the night.

Harriet became intensely interested in the Indians, survivors of a once proud and powerful race. Their poverty and the bleakness of their lives were distressing. Men, women, and children chewed coca continually. "It degrades the race and dulls their minds but it makes the world look bright to the user" (*San Francisco Chronicle*, Oct. 27, 1907).

In 1908 Franklin joined the staff of the Pan American Union and remained with this organization as editor and counselor until 1934. When he could not accompany Harriet on many of her subsequent travels, she went by herself and managed well.

> I've wondered why men have so absolutely monopolized the field of exploration. Why did women never go to the Arctic, try for one pole or the other, or invade Africa, Thibet, or unknown wildernesses? I've never found my sex a hinderment; never faced a difficulty which a woman, as well as a man, could not surmount; never felt a fear of danger; never lacked courage to protect myself. (*New York Times*, Aug. 18, 1912)

Harriet did not confine herself to travel in rural South America but visited the cities also and became acquainted with the women, who were beginning to take up the professions of medicine and law and teaching. In a 1916 article on "The Women of the Other Americas," Adams wrote:

> If you had told me that I would meet Peruvian girls who could beat me at tennis, and Argentine women whose gowns would out-dazzle New York's; hear a Venezuelan girl of twenty speak eloquently on social reform, and have a tooth filled by a woman dentist in Chile, I would not have believed it. . . . The time has come for the women of the Americas to know one another. We can lead the way in much we have been long in learning—courage to ignore traditions which hinder progress; a bigger view of things that mean world betterment, efficiency, sanitation. (*Ladies Home Journal*, Oct. 1916, p. 15)

Her lectures were popular, and she could be counted on to give the newspapers good headlines. Reporters were amazed that this petite woman, elegantly dressed, could have roughed it in wild countries. She brought back photographs, many taken herself, and illustrated some of her talks with stereoptican slides. One story described an attack by vampire bats in the Amazon jungle. In the night she, who slept on the ground outside a hut, heard a curious sound, "like the purring of many cats," and saw weird black creatures, like monstrous birds, crossing to the open door. When she awoke, she looked at the men sleeping on the floor of the hut. "There were wounds in their throats, breasts and necks. They were breathing with difficulty. I shook the men and called my husband frantically. Finally, they opened their eyes." The bites of the bats, she explained, were really not dangerous, but they drew enough blood to leave the victims dazed and weak (*New York Times*, Aug. 18, 1912; *Ladies Home Journal*, Nov. 1916).

She was convinced that Asians settled the Americas. She followed "trails which lead to the sources of the aboriginal South American, and that has led me to Siberia, along the Gobi desert in China, down into the sacred lands of India, perhaps the beginning of all races" (Jacksonville, Fla., *Sunday Times Union*, May 10, 1914). In the 1920s she went to Sanlúcar de Barrameda, Spain.

It was when I began reading, in Spanish histories, of New World colonization that this port first came to my notice. . . . Columbus sailed from San Lucar on his third voyage to the Americas. . . . I have followed Magellan around the world—through Fuegian waters, across the western ocean, to that lonely coconut-fringed island of the Philippines where he lies. . . . Only those who know and love Spanish America and those parts of our own country which once belonged to Spain can fully appreciate all this one sleepy little port has meant to the Western World. (*National Geographic* 46, Aug. 1924, pp. 199–204)

The Geographical Society of Philadelphia elected Harriet a corresponding member in 1911; in 1913 the Sociedad Geografica de La Paz made her a *corresponsal* member; and in the same year the Royal Geographical Society of London elected her a Fellow.

The first serious accident Harriet suffered while traveling occurred in 1927, when she was in the Balearic Islands. She fell from a sea wall and broke her back. Rescued by fishermen, she spent the next two years strapped to a board and was told that she could never walk again. She recovered and went to Spain, North Africa, and Asia Minor for seven months. In 1930 she was in Ethiopia, a guest at the coronation of Emperor Haile Selassie I.

In 1933, after Franklin Adams retired, he and Harriet spent several years in Europe. She retired as president of the Society of Woman Geographers that year. She died in Nice, France, on July 17, 1937; Franklin died three years later. Both were buried in Stockton. Harriet's family gave her scrapbooks and her books to her hometown public library, and a group of Stockton admirers have formed the

Harriet Chalmers Adams Society to preserve her memory. The book on Peru, on which she had been working, was never completed, leaving as her only literary heritage the articles in popular magazines and in the *National Geographic*.

BIBLIOGRAPHY

Works by Harriet Chalmers Adams

"Picturesque Paramaribo." *National Geographic* 18 (June 1907): 365–73.
"East Indians in . . . Trinidad." *National Geographic* 18 (July 1907): 485–91.
"Along the Old Inca Highway." *National Geographic* 19 (Apr. 1908): 231–50.
"Peru's Unknown Montana." *Tropical and Subtropical America* 1 (May 1908): 167–72.
"Some Wonderful Sights in the Andean Highlands." *National Geographic* 19 (Sept. 1908): 597–618.
"Cuzco." *National Geographic* 19 (Oct. 1908): 669–89.
"Kaleidoscopic La Paz." *National Geographic* 20 (Feb. 1909): 119–41.
"The First Transandine Railroad from Buenos Aires to Valparaiso." *National Geographic* 21 (May 1910): 397–417.
"A Solenodon Paradoxus Brandt." New York Zoological Society *Bulletin* 41 (Sept. 1910).
(With Franklin Adams) "The Liberation of Bolivia." *Review of Reviews* 47 (Jan. 1913): 67–78.
"Snapshots of Philippine America." *World's Work* 28 (May 1914): 31–42.
"Iguazu, Niagara's Mate." *Bulletin of the Pan American Union* 39 (Sept. 1914): 364–77.
"Sidelights on Latin-American Trade." *World Outlook* 1 (Nov. 1915).
"Pathfinders and Placemakers." *World Outlook* 2 (Apr. 1916): 2.
"The Women of the Other Americas." *Ladies Home Journal* 33 (Oct. 1916): 15, 102–110.
"Sliding off the World's Roof." *Ladies Home Journal* 33 (Nov. 1916): 13, 86–90.
"Wonderful Falls of Iguazu." *The Sister Republics* (Dec. 1916).
"In French Lorraine." *National Geographic* 32 (Nov. 1917): 499–518.
"Rio de Janeiro in the Land of Lure." *National Geographic* 38 (Sept. 1920): 165–210.
"Grand Canyon Bridge." *National Geographic* 39 (June 1921): 645–50.
"Volcano-girded Salvador." *National Geographic* 41 (Feb. 1922): 188–200.
"A Longitudinal Journey thru Chile." *National Geographic* 42 (Sept. 1922): 219–73.
"Our Andean Adventures." *Wide World* (Mar. 1924): 461–70.
"Adventurous Sons of Cadiz." *National Geographic* 46 (Aug. 1924): 153–204.
"The Truth about Spain and Primo de Rivera." *Review of Reviews* 71 (Jan. 1925): 69–72.
"Across French and Spanish Morocco." *National Geographic* 47 (Mar. 1925): 327–56.
"Altitudinal Journey through Portugal." *National Geographic* 52 (Nov. 1927): 567–610.
"Barcelona, Pride of the Catalans." *National Geographic* 55 (Mar. 1929): 373–402.
"Cirenaica, Eastern Wing of Italian Libia." *National Geographic* 57 (June 1930): 689–726.
"Madrid out of Doors." *National Geographic* 60 (Aug. 1931): 225–56.

"River-encircled Paraguay." *National Geographic* 63 (Apr. 1933): 385–416.
"Madeira the Florescent." *National Geographic* 66 (July 1934): 81–106.
"European Outpost: The Azores." *National Geographic* 67 (Jan. 1935): 34–66.

Works about Harriet Chalmers Adams

Adams, Mildred. "Up and Down the World." *The Woman's Journal* n.s. 15 (Jan. 1930): 12–14.
Brown, C. B. "Far-traveled Woman." *Sunset* 36 (Apr. 1916): 39.
Downing, Margaret B. Article in Jacksonville, Florida, *Sunday Times Union* (May 10, 1914).
Howard, Eric, article in a series, "Famous Californians," *San Francisco Call-Post* (June 16, 1923), reprinted in *Stockton Daily Herald* (June 19, 1923).
In Memory of Harriet Chalmers Adams. Washington, D.C.: Society of Woman Geographers, 1938.
Lawrence, Walter F. "A Lady of Pan-America." *Midpacific Magazine* (Aug. 1913).
Notable American Women, 1607–1950. Edited by Edward T. James and others. Cambridge, Mass.: Harvard University Press, 1971.
"South America through a Woman's Eyes." *San Francisco Chronicle* (Aug. 12, 1906): 8.
Tisdale, Blanche. "California Woman's Saddle Trip through Central and South America." *San Francisco Chronicle* (Oct. 27, 1907): 3.
———. "A California Woman among the Indians of Patagonia and Tierra del Fuego." *San Francisco Chronicle* (Nov. 3, 1907).
Wharton, Elna H. "A Woman Turns Geographer." *The Forecast, America's Leading Food Magazine* (July 1930).
An obituary appeared in the *New York Times*, on July 18, 1937.

Clippings of a number of articles by and about Adams, plus some unidentified items from magazines and newspapers, can be found in the Harriet Chalmers Adams scrapbooks located in the Stockton–San Joaquin County Public Library in Stockton, California.

DELIA DENNING AKELEY
1875–1970

Delia Denning Akeley made her explorations a tie between the world of Equatorial Africa and the American museum visitor. First with her husband, Carl F. Akeley, and then alone, she visited Africa a number of times between 1905 and 1929 to collect specimens of its wild animals for the great American natural history museums. She is represented today in the museums of Chicago, New York, Brooklyn, and Newark. In addition to hunting big game, she studied the Pygmies of the Congo and brought back to America many native objects and thousands of photographs of African life. These, with her lectures, books, and articles, made the exotic African world known to the American public.

She was the first Western woman to cross the African continent, from the Indian Ocean to the Atlantic, at the head of her own expedition, a lone woman with only native guides and porters. She proved that in a dangerous country at a dangerous time a woman could travel in safety armed with little more than courage and a sympathetic understanding of the Africans.

Little is known of Delia Akeley's early life. She was born on a farm near Beaver Dam, Wisconsin, the daughter of Patrick and Margaret Denning, probably on December 5, 1875. The ninth child in the family, she was christened Delia Julia, but early in life acquired the nickname Micky and a reputation as an Irish scrapper. At thirteen she ran away from home and never saw her parents again. Not until many years later did she seek any contact with her relatives. She reached Milwaukee and was befriended by a man named Reiss, who found her a job and later married her. This part of her life, also, was swept under the rug in Delia's memory; she believed that her real life began when she met Carl F. Akeley, a sculptor at the Milwaukee Art Museum. She helped Akeley experiment with taxidermy in the preparation of lifelike animal specimens for museums. When he was offered a job at the Field Museum of Natural History in Chicago, Delia went along as his assistant. They were married in 1902.

Before Carl Akeley's time, museums had displayed crudely stuffed animals in stiff poses against painted backgrounds or surrounded by artificial foliage. He perfected methods that made the animals look more lifelike and the backgrounds more realistic. Although the first exhibit he and Delia produced for the Field Museum won him fame, he was not satisfied with it. He felt that if he could go to Africa he could learn more about elephant behavior, collect specimens, study their habitats, and make truly representative wildlife groupings. He had spent five months on a hunting safari in Africa in 1896. Now the museum commissioned him to return there to collect specimens for a new exhibit, and Delia was allowed to go along "to collect butterflies and birds."

They arrrived in Kenya in 1905, hired porters and collected provisions at Nairobi, and set off for the Athi Plain. Mickey soon found that collecting birds and butterflies was not to be her role. For self-defense she had to learn to handle a gun, and before long she was hunting game along with Akeley.

They spent almost eighteen months in East Africa, moving from one camp to another, with a large body of native porters and all the equipment needed for living in the bush and for photographing, hunting, and preserving elephant specimens. Among those they collected, two were brought down by Delia, a spectacular achievement for a beginner and a woman. Mickey learned to respect and fear the mighty beasts, and she proved her mettle in the long marches through rough terrain in the tropical heat. She loved the country, enjoyed Akeley's interest in the hunt, and was exhilarated by the thrill of the chase. In addition to her elephants, she contributed to the final museum collection nineteen other animals and many interesting birds.

They saw enough in Africa to realize that much of its wildlife was doomed to extinction by big-game hunters and white settlers. Public information about many species depended on museum collections such as they were providing. When the American Museum of Natural History asked them to collect elephants, they packed up and moved to New York City in 1909, leaving later that year for Africa. Akeley sought an elephant family group, two bulls, a cow, and a calf. He insisted that they be perfect specimens. The hunt took them two years and carried them over many miles of the veldt and mountain jungle.

Again, Mickey was thrilled by the African life, but Akeley began to suffer from a series of illnesses—including spirillum fever, black-water fever, meningitis, and "impoverished blood." She nursed him through them all, spending sleepless nights when he was too ill to be entrusted to the care of black servants. She tried to persuade him to go out to Nairobi for medical help, but Carl seemed obsessed with his quest for the elephants. It took so long that the museum ran out of funds, and the Akeleys sold their New York farm. On one hunt, they were attacked by an elephant they had shot but not killed. At twenty yards, Akeley fired at the screaming, charging elephant, Mickey following with quick shots from her smaller gun. As the huge bull fell, Delia dropped to the ground. "I want to go home," she said, "and keep house for the rest of my life!"

They did not go home, and worse was to follow. While Delia was at a base camp packing for a trip to the high country, where they had seen signs of elephants, Akeley went off with a few porters to take pictures. After three days two of the porters who had been with Akeley returned and said the master had been caught by an elephant. Frantic, Delia prepared medical supplies, constructed a litter, and urged the frightened and mutinous porters to set off before daybreak to reach her wounded and possibly dying husband. She dispatched messengers to have a doctor sent and, by almost superhuman efforts, reached Akeley. For three months Mickey was nurse to her husband as well as supervisor of the safari and its provider of food, hunting birds and small game for the men.

She never hunted for pleasure, shooting only in self-defense, for food, or to acquire needed specimens. She was much interested in animal behavior, especially that of the primates. What she lacked in scientific training she compensated for by close observation and a capacity for understanding. She watched the baboons and found them remarkably like humans in their family groupings. She was sure that they conversed with each other, and she experimented in talking with them. She captured and made a pet of a beautiful vervet, which she named J. T. and which was to have a profound influence on her life.

In November 1911, Mickey and Akeley were welcomed home as hero and heroine. Akeley began to prepare a monumental display, Africa Hall, for the American Museum of Natural History in New York City. They settled in an apartment near Central Park, along with J. T., who had a room of his own. Carl had been jealous of Delia's affection for the little monkey even before they had reached home, and he was not quite as charmed as was she by its antics. It was noisy, mischievous, and destructive, as well as amusing. Delia never punished J. T. She was interested in his near-human behavior, but she knew he was a wild animal and would not understand human discipline.

She kept him for almost nine years; as he matured his playful bites became dangerous and his disposition changed. One day he bit her on the ankle so badly that surgery was needed, and she was in bed for three months. Later, after J. T. bit her savagely on the wrist, Delia admitted that the little monkey was too dangerous to keep, and arrangements were made to take him to the Washington, D.C., zoo.

Mickey's infatuation with the animal undoubtedly contributed to a deterioration of relations between the Akeleys. When the First World War broke out, Delia left to work in England and France, doing canteen duty. Soon after her return Akeley went again to Africa, this time without Mickey.

Akeley had met Mary Lee Jobe, a graduate of Columbia University, president of a camp for young people and a wilderness explorer who had traveled in the Canadian mountains. She began to take Mickey's place in Carl's affections, and in 1923 the Akeleys were divorced. A little over a year later Akeley married Mary Lee and took her with him to Africa, where he died in 1926. Mary Akeley buried him, wound up the expedition, and returned to complete Africa Hall. Somehow Delia's great contribution to Akeley's work was ignored. Akeley's will, written in 1921, left everything to his second wife.

By 1924 Delia had won a commission from the Brooklyn Museum of Arts and Sciences to collect wildlife specimens in Africa. She combined this mission with a plan of her own to study a primitive tribe. She was convinced that a woman alone, without armed escort, could live in the villages, make friends with the women, and secure authentic information concerning their tribal customs and habits.

She was almost fifty, a slender, elegant woman looking very scholarly with her white hair and pince-nez. Newspapers made much of the contrast between her femininity and the rough and dangerous country into which she would be going. Delia had no illusions about the dangers, but she relied on her experience, accumulated during her trips with Akeley, to carry her mission to success.

She went first to Kenya and ascended the Tana River to get her museum specimens. She traveled with five dugout canoes and a party of native porters. As they paddled, the men sang, loudly and joyfully. The noise of their coming made sure of a welcoming party at every settlement. The songs told all about the white woman and where she came from and where she was going and much else, for the Africans loved to exaggerate and the more important they made her seem, the more was their own reflected glory. Women appeared on the river bank, adorned with palm fronds and blossoms. Musicians came with reed flutes and drums. Almost always the people danced, not to entertain her but out of the sheer joy of living. The river journey lasted ten weeks, during which time Delia was kept busy. She hunted and preserved the specimens, took photographs and developed the negatives, and kept a journal.

At San Kuri, where rapids made the river unnavigable, Delia paid off her canoemen. The next part of the trip was to be across the Somali desert between the Tana and Ethiopia. Although it was closed territory, under military rule, Delia was allowed to proceed on her way without escort. The caravan marched by moonlight to avoid the heat of the day, and Delia hunted in the evening and early mornings. At Muddo Gashi, a military post which she reached after three "unforgettable months," the officers were astonished that she had been safe from the Somali tribesmen, who had just killed one of their men. Forbidden to proceed farther, she turned south and reached Meru, northeast of Mount Kenya. From there she sent her museum collection to America.

She was now free to search for a primitive tribe. She knew that the natives of Kenya and Uganda had been changed by contact with Europeans; to find people untouched by their influence she would have to go far into the jungle. She wanted to look for the Pygmies, about whom little was known except what misinformation had filtered out through travelers, missionaries, and officials. The little people were elusive, apt to vanish into the jungle without a trace when white men came near them. She learned that Pygmies could be found in the Ituri Forest, in the Belgian Congo (now Zaire).

She hired twenty-five porters and another eight men to carry her *tepoi*—a chair swung between two large bamboo poles. She tried to observe the amenities of civilized life in her jungle travels, taking along a silver tea service, a tablecloth, and a rubber bathtub for her nightly bath. The men set up her camp and prepared her meals, although she often cooked or baked bread, pies, or cakes in a primitive oven. She thought it worth the effort to have such luxuries in the jungle, "because one often suffers from the strange concoctions prepared by badly trained native cooks." She had suffered an attack of food poisoning while on the Tana River and lay for two days too ill to move, while her fatalistic porters discussed the division of her clothes if she were to die.

In many places she stayed in government rest houses, which she was to find almost without exception to be so filthy and flea infested that it was torture to stay in them. Indeed, she found much to dislike in the Congo, and as she traveled through the dense vegetation she began to feel oppressed and to wonder whether she was wise to pursue her search for the little people.

The first Pygmy family she met was brought to her camp by a friendly Walese sultan. She gave them salt and tobacco and a red balloon, which caused a furor and established her as having some magic power. When she wished to photograph the family she was surprised to see them line up and pose, and she realized that they were used to being trotted out for travelers for a slight remuneration, shared with the sultan. To see the primitive tribe she had to go deeper into the forest.

At last she came upon a group of Pygmy women dancing. They fled at her approach, but her men persuaded some of them to come back; Delia sent a message to their sultan that her visit was not official and that she had brought wonderful gifts. A Pygmy guided her into the rain-soaked, fog-filled forest, along with ten of her men carrying her supplies, food, and presents. Her men looked as fearful as she felt as they tripped over vines and creepers, following an indistinct trail. Weary, aching, and discouraged, she stopped at midday and made camp for the night, almost hoping for an excuse to turn back. But as soon as a fire was made and a hearty meal was eaten everyone felt better. The men joked about their difficulties of travel and brought out musical instruments, sang, and danced.

The next day a penetrating whistle, answered by a drum tattoo, indicated that they were in Pygmy land. Some thirty men, women, and children stood about, silent and unsmiling, holding elephant spears, clubs, and bows and arrows. The sultan sat on a stool drinking palm wine. Nothing was said and no one approached the visitors. Finally the sultan reached out and touched Delia's hand, smiled, and pointed to the stool beside him. He gave her wine in a broken gourd. She pretended to drink and passed the gourd to her servant, who cheerfully drained the cup.

For the next several months she lived with the Pygmies, shared in their hunting, observed their daily lives, and watched their revels. She taught them the childish game of jump the rope, using vines in lieu of rope. She witnessed a birth and was surprised to find that at birth the babies are of normal size. They seemed to stop growing at a certain age, and the average height of the adults was four feet. She was sure that the theory that they were stunted by malnutrition was wrong, for she found them healthy, happy, well-nourished people, free from disease. They decorated their bodies for special occasions but did not mutilate themselves as other Congo tribes did.

Delia began to realize that the Pygmies were not as isolated from the rest of the country as had been suspected. They knew what was going on, and one of the reasons they kept themselves so carefully hidden was their fear of the white man. Ever since the Belgians had taken power in the Congo, the Pygmies had watched the white man's power grow over their black neighbors. They feared that the black soldiers hovering near the forest trails were tools of the whites, sent to decoy them from their homes and force them to work in the fields and in the mines.

She herself was disgusted at the treatment of the Africans, who were forced to carry heavy loads and to build roads and railroads, while guards kept them to their tasks with whips, all for the profit of white men far away in comfortable homes and offices, who knew nothing of the country or its people. (The Congo natives would not gain independence until 1960.)

After she left the Pygmies, Delia continued her travels, but she was worn out and ill. It was time to leave Africa. Her collection had reached the United States safely: Thirty specimens of game animals, some extremely rare, went to the Brooklyn Museum, and almost 200 artifacts went to the Newark Museum in New Jersey. Delia made one more trip to Africa, in 1929, and visited the Pygmies, but she was driven out by torrential rains. She left no account of the journey. Between 1928 and 1930 she wrote about J. T. and about her African adventures in two books and numerous articles. She gave lectures and became a member of the Society of Woman Geographers.

In 1939 she married an old friend whom she and Akeley had known in Chicago, Dr. Warren G. Howe. They had a home in Vermont and another in Florida. He died in 1951, and Delia remained in Florida, in comfortable circumstances, until her own death on May 22, 1970.

She had loved Africa. She had been concerned about the changes she saw taking place as white hunters reduced the wildlife, settlers cleared the jungle, and white men tried to "improve" the natives. Above all, she showed that a sympathetic interest in people, no matter how alien, led to understanding and friendship.

BIBLIOGRAPHY

Works by Delia Akeley

"Report on the Museum's Expedition to Africa." *Brooklyn Museum Quarterly* 12 (July 1925).
"Among the Pigmies in the Congo Forest." *Brooklyn Museum Quarterly* 13 (Jan. 1926).
"Monkey Tricks." *Saturday Evening Post* 199 (Sept. 18, 1926): 36–39.
"Baboons." *Saturday Evening Post* 199 (Jan. 15, 1927): 12–13.
"Jungle Rescue." *Collier's* 81 (Feb. 11, 1928): 10.

"The Little People." *Saturday Evening Post* 200 (Mar. 3, 1928): 16–17.
"Crocodiles." *Saturday Evening Post* 201 (July 28, 1928): 34–40.
"*J.T., Jr.*" *The Biography of an African Monkey.* New York: Macmillan, 1928.
"Table from an Elephant's Ear." *Mentor* 17 (May 1929): 33–34.
"Elephants in the Fog." *Century* 119 (Oct. 1929): 120–29.
"On Wings of Fire." *Saint Nicholas* 57 (Jan. 1930): 159–64.
Jungle Portraits. New York: Macmillan, 1930.
"My First Elephant." In *All True! The Record of Actual Adventures That Have Happened to Ten Women of Today.* New York: Brewer, Warren & Putnam, 1931.

Works about Delia Akeley

Akeley, Carl. Notes in *American Museum Journal* (Feb. and Dec. 1912), on expeditions shared with Delia.
———. "Elephant Hunting in Equatorial Africa with Rifle and Camera." *National Geographic* 23 (Aug. 1912): 779–810.
———. *In Brightest Africa.* Garden City, N.Y.: Doubleday, 1920.
National Cyclopedia of American Biography. New York: J. T. White, 1888–date, vol. 57 (1977): 325–26 (under "Delia Howe").
"No Feminism in Darkest Africa." *Literary Digest* 89 (May 15, 1926): 54. An interview.
Olds, Elizabeth Fagg. *Women of the Four Winds.* Boston: Houghton Mifflin, 1985, pp. 71–153. Olds used Delia's unpublished journals and letters and personal recollections of friends and relatives to produce, for the first time, a full and accurate biography, with a bibliographical note on sources.
Parker, C. B. "Off to New Adventures." *St. Nicholas* 57 (Jan. 1930): 188–89.
Rittenhouse, Mignon. *Seven Women Explorers.* Philadelphia: Lippincott, 1964, pp. 58–78.
Searl, H. H. "In the Service of Science." *Woman Citizen*, n.s. 10 (Dec. 1925): 17.
"Woman of the Week: Delia Akeley." *News Review of Macmillan Company*, Feb. 22, 1932.
An obituary appeared in the *New York Times*, on May 23, 1970.

LUCY ATKINSON
fl. 1820–1863

Lucy Atkinson astonished her nomadic companions as she raced her horse on the Kirghiz steppes. She astonishes us with an engaging tale of adventures in remote parts of Asiatic Russia. From 1848 to 1853 she traveled from St. Petersburg to Irkutsk near Lake Baikal. She was accompanied by her artist husband, Thomas Witlam Atkinson, and then by her infant son, who was born in the Altai Mountains and was named for the mountain under which he was born. She rode wild horses caught from the herd, some, perhaps, never before mounted. Three times a day, when she could manage it, she bathed in icy mountain streams—and dipped her hardy little son into the water also. When they reached a city or town with other European residents, Lucy dressed in the latest fashion from St. Petersburg and attended gay parties. Traveling with a special passport from Emperor Nicholas I, the Atkinsons were provided with Cossack guards and were entertained by Russian nobility. In the steppes they were the guests of nomadic tribes, who guided them from one encampment to the next.

Ten years after her return to England Lucy published *Recollections of Tartar Steppes and Their Inhabitants*. Based on letters written to a friend in St. Petersburg, it is a fresh and absorbing account of travel in a country almost unknown to English readers in Atkinson's time and almost as unknown to many today. Those who travel the Trans-Siberian Railroad view it from train windows, but the railroad was built long after Lucy traversed the land. Her book, out of print for over a century, was reissued in 1972 and is again available to lovers of travel literature.

Lucy Atkinson was born an Englishwoman, although her birthplace and even her maiden name are not known. The title page of her *Recollections* gives the author's name as "Mrs. Atkinson." Its brief introduction tells us that, as she came of a large family and had to support herself from an early age, she went to St. Petersburg and for eight years remained in the family of a General Mouravioff, superintending the education of his daughter.

Mouravioff was governor general of eastern Siberia. In 1846, while in his household, Lucy became acquainted with Thomas Witlam Atkinson, an English architect who had abandoned his profession to travel about sketching scenes of nature. He was ready to start on a sketching trip to Siberia and was making arrangements to obtain a Russian passport that would enable him to cross the borders of the empire without being stopped at every government post. It is probable that he was a guest of the Mouravioff family.

Atkinson returned to St. Petersburg after a year of travel and claimed Lucy as his bride. The wedding took place in the house of the governor of Moscow, a relation of the Mouravioffs. Shortly afterward the Atkinsons began their travels together.

Before leaving Moscow they met with many Russians whose relatives had been involved in the Decembrist Conspiracy of 1825, when some of the Russian aristocracy and educated bourgeoisie sought to prevent the accession of Nicholas I. All had been exiled to Siberia and many remained there. The Atkinsons were given tokens of remembrance to carry to husbands, fathers, and brothers. Each family wished to have the travelers dine with them. "There was a melancholy interest in these gatherings," Lucy wrote. "It was only by a knowledge of the circumstances which had sent their friends into exile, and the difficulty of making any confidential communication to those so dear to them, that I could understand their anxious desire to detain us; nor shall I ever forget the parting and the blessing which they bestowed upon us" (*Recollections*, p. 3).

On February 22, 1848, the couple left Moscow, tucked, with their belongings, into a sledge, under two heavy bearskins. It was necessary to travel in winter when the snow was on the ground and at night before the sun had melted it. Four horses, their bells tinkling, were used to draw the sledge and were changed at each post station. Where the road was bare of snow, the driver took his own path through the forest. "There was something to me novel and wild in this ride," said Lucy. "I hailed the first dawn of day with delight, having slept but little during this my first night on the great Siberian road" (*Recollections*, p. 7). They stopped the second night at Nizhni Novgorod (later renamed Gorki) and next day dined with Prince Ourusoff, governor of the town.

They spent two weeks in Ekaterinburg (now Sverdlovsk), a mining center in the Ural Mountains where they watched men cut and polish gems. Lucy was given a rifle and pistol and practiced shooting each day, for they expected to travel in country where wolves, if not unwelcoming tribesmen, might attack them. They visited the "principal persons" in the town, many of whom Thomas had met on his previous visit. All tried to frighten Lucy with stories of misfortunes that had befallen other travelers in the regions to which she was going.

At Jaloutroffsky, a town off the post road, they met the first of the exiles, a relative of the Mouravioff family, for whom they had a gift. He sent for the other exiles in the neighborhood. Although they missed their families and friends at home, Lucy saw that they enjoyed much more freedom than they could have had in Russia—for instance, freedom of speech. "They fear nothing; the dread of exile has no terrors for them. But what they have not, is liberty to go where they please'' (Recollections, p. 25). The authorities here were lenient and allowed the gentlemen who were fond of the chase to hunt wherever they wished.

The travelers spent some time in Barnaul, a town of about 10,000 on the Ob River. It was the center of all the gold mining operations of the Altai Mountains and the site of a large silver smelting works, staffed by Russian engineers. Lucy's former status as a governess did not detract from her popularity among the Russians. "I immediately felt at home," she said, "and as though I had known them for years" (Recollections, p. 44). Dancing, fireworks, and picnics made life enjoyable during her short stay.

The Atkinsons soon were on the road again and, at the end of the post road, exchanged the sledge for horses. Lucy had been told that she could not use her sidesaddle because the horses were not accustomed to such a saddle and it was out of the question to use one in the mountains. She must ride astride. She was thankful for the advice when she encountered the ledges of rock they had to ride on; the mountains were almost perpendicular down to a river, boiling and foaming a thousand feet below. Her first night sleeping under the stars was another new experience. "The feeling was a strange one; sleeping in a forest, the water rippling at my feet, and surrounded by men alone" (Recollections, p. 55). The next night she arranged for a shelter to be erected to give her privacy to undress. When Thomas told her he had been in the habit of sleeping among the wandering tribes without taking off his clothes, she advised him that he would be healthier if he undressed at night.

Her first few days of riding tired her so much that she had to be helped off her horse and for several minutes could not stand. Determined to "conquer this weakness," she forced herself to walk. At one point, in ascending a rocky path, her horse stumbled, but she kept her seat and pulled him up, thus gaining the respect of the Kalmuck guides, all expert horsemen.

The travelers were bitten by mosquitoes, drenched with rain, and almost carried away by the swift streams they had to cross. Such hardships meant little to Thomas, who had experienced them on his former expedition, and Lucy's delight in the country compensated for any difficulties.

They visited the Altin Kool (Golden Lake) and spent eleven days being paddled about the lake in native canoes. At times they were in grave danger from sudden storms, as there were few places on the shore to find shelter. The Kalmucks, however, were good boatmen. Thomas found many enchanting views to sketch. They traveled down the Biya River to Sandyp, thence to the Katun River, near the border of Mongolia. It was a journey of three weeks, over high mountains. They were rewarded by a sunset view of Belukha, the highest peak in the Altai Mountains, "looking like a ruby encircled by diamonds" (Recollections, p. 74).

In September they started the hardest part of their journey, across the Kirghiz steppes to Kopal, a new fortress close to the Chinese border. They traveled first by carriage, then organized an expedition by horse and camel, accompanied by their Cossacks and Kirghiz tribesmen.

"What wild-looking fellows they appeared," Lucy wrote of their guides, who had "a good deal of good nature in the countenance; their Asiatic costume is exceedingly picturesque and beautiful, the shawls tied round their waists are by no means to be despised" (*Recollections*, p. 87). The men wore several robes, some as many as four or five, and high-heeled boots.

The Kirghiz women helped in the work of packing and tried to persuade Lucy that she would not be able to stand the journey through the desolate and little-inhabited wastes. But, she says, "I started on this journey, with the intention of accompanying my husband wherever he went, and no idle fears shall turn me; if he is able to accomplish it, so shall I be. I give in to no one for endurance" (*Recollections*, p. 88). What the women had observed and what concerned them was that Lucy was pregnant.

On the steppes they stayed in Kirghiz yurts. Their hosts slaughtered lambs, which they served with dried fruits. The Atkinsons carried their own samovar and brewed tea for almost every meal, sharing it with their hosts. The couple—and their plates, spoons, knives, and forks—were of great interest to the Kirghiz. "But what struck them most with astonishment," says Lucy, "was the attention paid me by Mr. Atkinson, as our sex is looked upon by the Kirghis as so much inferior to the 'lords of creation' " (*Recollections*, p. 92).

After many days of riding over rocks and sand hills in the heat, without finding water or a place of shelter, Lucy began to think her Kirghiz friends had been right about the country. Following a ride of a full day and half of the night, she pleaded to be allowed to rest. Her husband spread a fur on the ground, covered her with his robe, and gave her a drink of rum. Shortly she recovered and went on, but two hours later had to dismount and walk. Not until morning dawned did they reach a camp. For two days, they had had no food and no water except a watermelon. The women carried her into a yurt, rubbed her hands and feet, and gave her tea. Somewhat refreshed, the travelers rode still farther to a larger encampment, where they were expected. Even here they rested only a day. On September 20, thirteen days after the beginning of the arduous journey, they reached Kopal.

Two weeks later, on November 4, Lucy was delivered of a son, whose premature arrival, according to the doctor at Kopal, was "caused by excessive exercise on horseback." It was the young doctor's first confinement case, and he thought the child would not live beyond seven days. The baby was not only tiny but, even in his mother's eyes, ugly. They named him Alatau, for the mountain above Kopal, and Tamchiboulac, "a dropping-spring, close to which he was called into existence" (*Recollections*, p. 106).

Fortunately a house had been erected for them. They moved into it before it was finished and just a week before the birth. Lucy had prepared no clothes for the child, who had to be wrapped in his father's shirt. She made little caps and nightdresses from other spare garments. The women of Kopal thought she should swaddle the boy. "I assured them," said Lucy, "it was not customary in England." One friend was so insistent that Lucy consented, and the woman began to bind him. "But he very shortly showed her that he was a true Briton, and was not going to stand any such treatment, for he fought bravely, so much so that the bandaging was given up. Looking innocently into my face, she exclaimed, 'How very odd! I could not have believed it, had I not seen it; what a difference there is between English and Russian children' " (*Recollections*, p. 143). Alatau was a good child, never fussy except when a storm was coming. His mother thought he "was as good as a barometer on the road."

They were on the road again when the baby was but six months old. He was a good traveler and the delight of all their hosts. "The sultans wished to keep him: they declared he belonged to them; he was born in their territories, had been fed by their sheep and wild animals, ridden their horses, and had received their name; therefore he belonged to them, and ought to be left in their country to become a great chief" (*Recollections*, p. 152). Not being able to persuade the Atkinsons to give up their first-born, the sultans gave him marvelous presents—silk, lambs, goats to ride, and the promise of a stud of horses and attendants. "He is to be envied, lucky boy! Why was I not born a boy, instead of a girl?—still, had it been so, I should not have been the fortunate mortal I am now—that is, the wife of my husband and the mother of my boy. But, I pray you," joked Lucy, "do not make them acquainted with my feelings; they are both capable of taking advantage of the knowledge you would impart" (*Recollections*, p. 153).

Before Christmas they were back in Barnaul. Lucy reports that they were so much changed in appearance that their friends hardly recognized them. Both were thin and haggard, and "Mr. Atkinson was in a terrible plight, his boots had been patched and mended with the bark of trees" (*Recollections*, p. 206). After a few months' rest, they went back to their wandering. They established headquarters in Irkutsk and traversed many miles while Thomas made his sketches and collected information on the botany, geology, and mineralogy of the region. They did not return to England until 1854 when Alatau was ready for school.

In 1857 Thomas published his *Oriental and Western Siberia: A Narrative of Seven Years' Explorations and Adventures in Siberia, Mongolia, the Kirghis Steppes, Chinese Tartary, and Part of Central Asia*. A detailed and fascinating story of travel, the book is illustrated with engravings made from his sketches. It was well received, particularly in the United States, and Thomas was in demand for lectures. He was made a member of the Royal Geographical Society and the Geological Society. In 1860 a second work appeared: *Travels in the Region of the Upper and Lower Amoor and the Russian Acquisitions on the Confines of India and China*.

As far as Thomas's readers knew, however, neither Lucy nor Alatau existed. Although Atkinson described journeys on which his wife was a companion and mentions incidents in which she was involved, she is not mentioned once in either book. He sketched the Alatau Mountain and the dropping-spring for which his son was named, but the living child was ignored. One critic believes Atkinson deliberately suppressed information that might have detracted from his own fame as a traveler. Perhaps, however, it was only a matter of keeping his private life private.

What Lucy thought of her husband's books and his leaving her out of them is unknown, but, shortly after his death in 1861, she decided to supply the missing bits of his travels by publishing a selection of the letters she had written on her journeys. Of Thomas's books she said, "There is little allusion in them to the adventures we encountered during those journeys, and, especially, there is no mention of the strange incidents which befell myself, often left alone with an infant in arms, among a semi-savage people, to whom I was a perfect stranger" (*Recollections*, Preface).

Of Lucy Atkinson's later life, we know almost nothing, only that, in 1863, she was granted a civil list pension of a hundred pounds a year.

BIBLIOGRAPHY

Work by Lucy Atkinson

Recollections of Tartar Steppes and Their Inhabitants. By Mrs. Atkinson. London: Murray, 1863. New impression, with an introduction by A. G. Cross, London: Cass, 1972. Quotations in the text are from the 1972 edition.

Work about Lucy Atkinson

Cross, A. G. Introduction to Atkinson's *Recollections of Tartar Steppes and Their Inhabitants*. London: Cass, 1972.

FLORENCE VON SASS BAKER
ca. 1841–1916

Florence von Sass Baker spent nearly eight years in north and central Africa with her explorer husband, Samuel White Baker, and with him was the discoverer of Lake Albert, a source of the Nile River, and of Murchison Falls. She underwent some of the most frightening and painful travel experiences any woman has ever been called upon to bear, and all out of devotion to Sam, her lover and husband. In his accounts of his two African expeditions, he gave her full credit for her extraordinary hardihood and devotion in sharing with him every difficulty.

The first journey they shared, from 1861 to 1865, was one of geographical exploration in search of the source of the Nile. Samuel was not the first English explorer to undertake the search—he was preceded by John Speke, Richard Burton, and James Grant—but he was certainly the first to be accompanied by a wife. On his return to England he described his discoveries to the Royal Geographical Society and caused a sensation when he introduced Florence, a beautiful twenty-four-year-old girl, hitherto unknown to his family and friends, as his wife and the companion of his travels.

The purpose of the second journey into the Nile basin, from 1869 to 1873, was to abolish the slave trade, which existed there in its most barbarous and organized form. The khedive of Egypt appointed Sam governor general of the Equatorial Nile Basin, gave him the title of pasha, and financed a large expedition for a period of four years. Since almost every businessman and government official was involved in the profitable slave trade, which was, in fact, the economic base of the country, he met opposition at every step. Against almost impossible odds, he succeeded in extending the khedive's authority to near the Equator and struck the first blow at the infamous trade. Again, Florence— by this time Lady Baker, for Sam had been knighted in 1866—was with him throughout the journey.

The Bakers' story adds mystery and romance to travel and adventure. Samuel first met Florence in 1858 in Widdin, a Turkish fortress in the Balkans. He had been on a hunting trip with an Indian maharajah, when the boat in which they were traveling down the Danube struck ice and had to be abandoned. The two men attended a slave auction, where Baker impulsively bought a white slave, Florence. She was about seventeen, a golden-haired, dark-eyed beauty. He was thirty-seven, a widower with four children in England. Certainly he did not want a slave. His purpose in buying Florence was simply to rescue her, but he promptly fell in love with her and she with him.

If she told him any details about her origins or her previous life, he never divulged them, nor did she. It was supposed that her whole family had been massacred during the 1848 revolutions in Europe and that a family retainer had cared for her afterward. How she became a captive of Turkish slavers is unknown. It is quite evident that she was not an uneducated peasant. She spoke German and Hungarian and later learned Arabic and English with ease. She knew how to organize a household and was an expert seamstress and a competent nurse. Above all, she had common sense—better sense than Sam, on some occasions— and a way of defusing dangerous situations that got the couple out of trouble a number of times during their travels.

They lived together in Bucharest and later in Costanza, where Baker supervised the construction of a railway from the Black Sea to the Danube. He did not mention Florence in his letters nor during his few visits home, and seems to have taken the railway job as an excuse to remain out of England. He was a wealthy sportsman, of a good, but untitled, English family. He belonged to a distinguished London club and had friends in the best social circles. He had lived and hunted in Ceylon and elsewhere. When the railway opened in 1860, he was still not quite ready to take Florence to England, and he began to think about African exploration.

He had read with interest about the discovery and naming of Lake Victoria by fellow Britons Speke and Burton. He wrote to his family that he would not be home for some time: "A wandering spirit is in my marrow"—and he was off for central Africa, with Florence by his side.

In April 1861 they left Cairo in a *dahabeah*, a small sailing houseboat, which would carry them up the Nile toward their goal, Gondokoro and beyond. They left the boat at Aswan and crossed the desert, traveling on camels with a great deal of baggage, to Berber. Instead of proceeding up the Nile toward Khartoum, they decided to spend some time exploring the Nile tributaries of Abyssinia, giving themselves time to become acclimatized, hunt, and learn Arabic.

Sam, unlike many explorers, was quite willing to settle among the people he visited and get to know them. At a place called Sofi they built a house, set up their traveling beds, and remained for five months. Florence made hunting clothes for Sam, short trousers and a short-sleeved shirt of the heavy cotton woven by the natives, which Sam dyed brown with mimosa juice. With them he wore gaiters he made from gazelle leather. She made a similar outfit for herself, for she had no hesitancy about wearing trousers for riding. Sam used the skins from animals he had killed to make moccasins. One of his pastimes was sketching and he was able to illustrate his books with sketches of scenes, including one of Florence riding a camel, one of himself with a full black beard wearing the homemade suit of clothes, many of natives wearing no clothes at all, and a few making fun of his own mishaps while shooting.

After spending a year in this manner, they resumed their travel up the Nile, stopping at Khartoum to outfit their expedition. Khartoum, the ethnic line between black Africa and the Arab Middle East, was a filthy town and the center of the vicious slave trade. They hated the town.

The Baker expedition was large, with twenty-one donkeys, four camels, four horses, and a mountain of stores. Sam recruited forty-five men as an escort, for whom he designed smart uniforms. He hired a sailing boat and two barges, with forty boatmen, and on December 18, 1862, the fleet set off on its journey up the Nile, with the Union Jack flying from its masts.

John Speke was again in Africa, somewhere around the Equator, accompanied by James Grant. Since Speke and Grant had not been heard from for over a year, Baker saw himself as rescuing the explorers and becoming a hero. His ambition and his drive were to be severely tested, as was the ability of Florence to withstand the hardships of African travel.

With them was Saat, a black boy about twelve years old, who had escaped the slavers, been taken in by missionaries, then left to shift for himself. He appeared at Florence's feet one day in Khartoum and begged to be hired as a servant. He proved to be one of the most faithful and valuable members of the expedition, and they grew very fond of him. He was not the only black child Florence took into her heart during her African sojourn, though she could not really warm up to the adults and once, in her frustration, announced that she hoped never to see a black face again. Sam's attitude toward the Africans was typical of his race and his day. He regarded them as human, but somehow less so than whites. He thought they would be better off under white protection than left to their own tribal arrangements.

The expedition reached Gondokoro about six weeks after leaving Khartoum. The town was nothing but an odorous string of camps, occupied for about two months of the year by ivory traders, after which time it was deserted while the boats and cargo returned to Khartoum and the traders departed for the interior. It had once been a mission station, and the ruins of the brick buildings and a neglected lemon grove remained.

The traders did not welcome private travelers, particularly Englishmen who might report on their slaving activities. Nor were the tribes to the south friendly to white men. Baker's own escort, composed of Arabs, was found to be less than reliable. It was clear that his plan to proceed into the interior was possible only if he could go under the protection of the traders. One trader, Andrea de Bono, was due to arrive from the south with a large armed escort. After leaving his ivory and slaves in Gondokoro, he would return southward.

De Bono arrived, and with him, to Baker's great joy, were Speke and Grant. They had had a terrible journey and were thin, feverish, and ragged. But they had succeeded in skirting Lake Victoria and had found where the Nile flowed from it. Baker remarked somewhat sadly, "Does not one leaf of the laurel remain for me?"*(The Albert N'yanza,* I, 103). Speke produced a map and suggested that he try to find a lake to the west of Lake Victoria called the Luta N'zige. The Nile flowed into it and then out again. They had not been able to see all they wished because of obstacles put in their way by the monarch of Bunyoro.

Baker decided to undertake the search for the lake. A fateful decision, it led to two years of wandering, anxiety, difficulties and fatigue for the couple. They were misled and cheated by the traders and attacked by Africans. The baggage animals died, their food supplies failed, and they had fevers and ran out of medicines. Many of their party died. Unable to keep or find porters, they had to abandon most of their possessions. After nine months they reached Kamrasi, monarch of Bunyoro, whose permission and assistance were needed to approach the lake. Kamrasi took all he could get from them in the way of presents and held them prisoners for a long time, refusing them food or guides. Finally, he promised both, on the condition that Baker leave Florence with him!

Baker held his pistol two feet from Kamrasi's chest and threatened to blow him to extinction if he repeated his request. Florence gave the monarch her opinion in a flow of angry Arabic, which was translated faithfully and loudly by their woman interpreter. Kamrasi meekly apologized, saying that exchanging wives was meant as a gesture of friendship. He then provided food and an escort and allowed the Bakers to leave. On the path, Florence suffered sunstroke, followed by brain fever, and for many days lay in a coma. Baker watched her night and day, expecting her death at any time, and was overjoyed when one morning she opened her eyes "and they were calm and clear. . . . The gratitude of that moment I will not attempt to describe" (Baker, *The Albert N'yanza,* II, 90).

On March 14, 1864, Baker saw the lake (now called Lake Albert)—a great sheet of water stretching before him. Florence was still so ill that she could barely totter to the shore. He rushed down to the water and drank of it, overcome with emotion. He named the lake Albert N'yanza, for Queen Victoria's late consort.

The homeward journey was a continual trial. They got crude canoes from fishermen to take them north along the shore of the lake. Their canoe was charged by a hippopotamus and lifted half out of the water. They discovered a great falls, which Baker named Murchison Falls, for the president of the Royal Geographical Society. At length they reached Kamrasi's kingdom again but were marooned there until they met with a slave caravan with which they could travel. When they reached Gondokoro in February 1865 they had long been given up as dead.

In September they reached Suez. Here they stayed in an English hotel, drank ale, of which Sam had dreamed while suffering fever in the jungle, and slept on clean sheets.

"Had I really come from the Nile Sources?" Sam asked himself. "It was no dream. A witness sat before me; a face still young, but bronzed like an Arab with years of exposure to a burning sun; haggard and worn with toil and sickness and shaded with cares, happily now passed; the devoted companion of my pilgrimage to whom I owed success and life—my wife" (*The Albert N'yanza*, II, 357–58).

They spent a fortnight in Paris, where they bought some fashionable clothes and recovered their health and strength. They entered London without fanfare and were quietly married on November 4, 1865.

The news that Sam's children had now a stepmother (but not the details of the marriage) was broken to the family. As might have been suspected, they were not overjoyed, especially his sister, Min, who had been bringing up his girls. She thought she should continue to do so and that Sam and Florence should have a separate establishment in London. The disagreements, however, were kept within the family. Though a few tongues might wag, London was delighted with Florence.

Sam had been at work on his book describing the expedition, based on his diary and notebooks, even before they reached Suez. The book was published less than six months after their return. Entitled *The Albert N'yanza*, it was a great success. It was soon followed by *Exploration of the Nile Tributaries of Abyssinia*. The Royal Geographical Society had bestowed their gold medal on Sam before his return. Queen Victoria knighted him, although, having heard disquieting rumors about Florence, she refused to have her presented.

Florence soon won over Sam's family, especially the eldest daughter, Edith, who was only a few years her junior. She took her place as the head of a large household as to the manor born, and she was on the best of terms with Sam's old shooting companions, including the Prince and Princess of Wales. She spoke English well, although always with a slight accent. She was thoroughly anglicized and would undoubtedly have been content to settle into English country life with Sam forever. But Sam was restless.

Ismail, the khedive of Egypt, found the notorious slave trade embarrassing to his country. He proposed a project to suppress the trade in the equatorial provinces, to annex the provinces south of Gondokoro, to establish a regular commerce, and to open to navigation Lakes Victoria and Albert. Sir Samuel Baker was asked to head the project. Baker accepted the offer, which carried unlimited power, a salary of forty thousand pounds, and the title of pasha. Florence, of course, was to accompany him on the expedition.

Baker laid out approximately nine thousand pounds on articles necessary for the expedition, selecting every item personally in London: cloth, blankets, scarves, handkerchiefs "of gaudy colors," clothing, tools, and food for four years for the European party. This party included Lady Baker, Sam's nephew Julian (an engineer), a doctor, a storekeeper and interpreter, a secretary, several shipwrights, a lady's maid for Florence, and a manservant for Sam. They took two twin-screw steamers, which were divided into sections to be transported by camel across the desert and reassembled later.

The transport consisted of sixty-four vessels, including nine steamers. Sam was offered a force of 1,645 troops, including a Soudani regiment and an Egyptian regiment, and the necessary firearms, medicines, and provisions.

Unfortunately, the arrangements did not work out as planned, due to the passive resistance of those whose interests would be affected by the suppression of the slave trade. Delays, shortages, and the deficiencies of the troops threatened the expedition at the outset. But the greatest difficulty was the Nile itself. It had become blocked with masses of vegetation. "The entire river became a marsh, beneath which, by the great pressure of water, the stream oozed through innumerable small channels. In fact, the White Nile had disappeared" (Baker, *Ismailia*, p. 33). The slave traders had found another route, the Bahr Giraffe, and Baker's party proceeded up this river. However, it was necessary for the men to cut canals through the dense mass of vegetation. For many days they hacked their way along, towing the boats and finding clear lakes from time to time, until they reached a spot where progress was no longer possible. The whole expedition returned to the Nile to wait until the end of the rainy season, when the river would be high.

On the river bank Sam built a town, named Tewfikia, which they would occupy for six months until they could proceed to Gondokoro. They planted crops, and Sam drilled his bodyguard, called the Forty Thieves. As soon as he reached the Nile, he had surprised several boatloads of slaves and freed them all, pleasing the blacks but incurring the bitter animosity of the traders.

Florence lived on the *dahabeah*, with a small household of servants she had dressed in neat uniforms and trained to perform all the domestic tasks. She kept a diary, written in English, which was found among the family papers a hundred years later and was published as *Morning Star*. It adds a curious Victorian tone to Sam's more detailed and vigorous story. Florence speaks of the freed slaves as being "so happy"; of the donkeys when unloaded after many days on the boats as "so happy" to have a good roll. When any of the party was indisposed, she records that he was "not quite the thing." She was glad when they traveled because then Sam had to be with her and she was not left alone with her monkeys. "I have a dear parrot," she writes, and a mongoose, "all very nice creatures." Her maid, although she had read the account of their previous African journey, decided that Africa was much worse than she had expected, and she longed to go home. Sam's man also wished to go home, and the two left together.

In December it was thought to be possible to try to get through the Sudd again, and the camp was dismantled. Four months later, on May 19, 1871, Florence wrote from Gondokoro to "darling Edith" that they had arrived after a fearful struggle "dragging a flotilla of 59 vessels including a steamer of thirty two horse power over high grass and marshes." Gondokoro they found completely destroyed. "The whole country is in a state of the wildest anarchy owing to the acts of the ivory and slave traders" (*Morning Star*, p. 87).

They rebuilt the town and named it Ismailia. Getting provisions for some 2,000 people was a problem. The Baris, the local natives, refused to sell cattle or grain. Baker first attempted diplomacy and presents, and when that failed he sent his troops out with firearms to subdue the tribes and to confiscate cattle and grain. All the commanders of the troops, as well as the men themselves, hated the life and petitioned to return to Khartoum. Sam gave permission for all who were sick or disabled to go back, and while he was temporarily absent over a thousand left with thirty-eight of the boats.

Baker was discouraged but persistent. He set off for the south with Florence, Julian, the Forty Thieves, and a small force, plus a herd of cattle and sheep. In Bunyoro their old enemy, Kamrasi, had been succeeded by his son, Kabarega, who was every bit as difficult to deal with. Baker, with his firm belief that Turkish rule was much better for the ignorant natives than anything Kabarega had to offer, managed to offend the young monarch. Near Kabarega's palace in Masindi Baker built "Government House" and hoisted the Ottoman flag. Kabarega was not grateful for having his empire taken over and being appointed a governor under the Turks, and the Bakers soon discovered that the sultan could command a very large army against their small party. Sam decided to march to Rionga, Kabarega's rival, who was stationed seventy-eight miles away on the Nile.

It was less a march than a nightmarish flight, for they could get no escort, no animals, and no food. Fortunately, Florence had stored away six chests of flour, and this sustained the party as they struggled on foot, constantly harassed by natives who hid in the brush and threw spears at them. "Everybody would have been killed without Papa, but he managed everything so well," Florence wrote to Sam's daughter (*Morning Star*, p. 43). It is inconceivable that, had Kabarega wished the Bakers killed, he could not have done so. He merely wanted them out of his country.

The party reached the Nile, built a stockade, and made canoes and rafts to cross the river. They sent a message to Rionga, who went through a ceremony of blood brotherhood with Sam. Before they entered Patiko, the Forty Thieves donned their uniforms and marched into the town in style. In spite of having to carry everything through the jungle, they seem to have retained the uniforms, tools, and a good many other things with which to make an impression.

They remained six months at Patiko, which Florence considered a paradise. The tribesmen were friendly. They reached Khartoum at the end of July; once again, they had been believed dead.

Sam felt he had accomplished his mission. True, he had not been able to get the steamers to the lake. Nor had the Sudd been completely cleared. Also, he had left much bad feeling, although he and Florence are still thought of rather fondly among some of the tribes. Near Juba, an obelisk commemorating many of the early travelers includes the name of Florence Baker. Sam's grandnephew visited, a hundred years later, the area in Uganda traversed by the Bakers in 1864 and provided a corrected map of their route for the Royal Geographical Society (*Geographical Journal* 131, Mar. and Dec. 1965). He visited a son of Rionga and renewed the ties of blood brotherhood.

Sam's book about the last journey, *Ismailia*, was published in 1874. The Bakers settled down at Sandford Orleigh, a large house on the river Teign. They were to travel again, but never in Africa, and never in rough country. Sam died in 1893, Florence not until 1916.

BIBLIOGRAPHY

Work by Florence Baker

Morning Star: Florence Baker's Diary of the Expedition to Put Down the Slave Trade on the Nile, 1870–73. Edited by Anne Baker. London: William Kimber, 1972.

Works about Florence Baker

Baker, Samuel. *The Albert N'yanza, Great Basin of the Nile*. London: Macmillan, 1866.
———. *Exploration of the Nile Tributaries of Abyssinia*. Hartford, Conn.: O. D. Case, 1868.
———. *Ismailia*. London: Macmillan, 1874.
Brander, Michael. *The Perfect Victorian Hero: Sir Samuel White Baker*. Edinburgh: Mainstream, 1982.
Cox, James A. "Samuel and Florence Baker." In *Into the Unknown: The Story of Exploration*. Washington, D.C.: National Geographic Society, 1987, pp. 219–25.
Dictionary of National Biography. London: Smith, Elder, 1st supplement (1901), vol. 1, pp. 101–105 (under "Samuel White Baker").
Hall, Richard. *Lovers on the Nile: The Incredible African Journeys of Sam and Florence Baker*. New York: Random House, 1980.
Middleton, Dorothy. *Baker of the Nile*. London: Falcon, 1949.
Moorehead, Alan. *The White Nile*. New York: Harper, 1960, pp. 78–98.
Mozans, H. J. *Woman in Science*. New York: Appleton, 1913, p. 374.
Oliver, Caroline. *Western Women in Colonial Africa*. Westport, Conn.: Greenwood Press, 1982, pp. 3–49.
Rittenhouse, Mignon. *Seven Women Explorers*. Philadelphia: Lippincott, 1964, pp. 36–57.

DAISY BATES
1863–1951

Daisy Bates spent much of her lifetime—a full half of the twentieth century—working among the Australian Aborigines. Living with them in the bush, she studied the customs and legends of many different groups and interpreted to other Australians the natives' ways and needs. She tried to make the passing of the Aborigines as humane as possible, for she was convinced that they could not survive civilization.

Although she was wrong about their eventual extinction, Bates is remembered in Australia for her championship of the natives. Her articles brought the Aborigines to the attention of anthropologists, who came to Australia to study their culture. To some she was a heroine, to others a rather charming eccentric. She was appointed Honorary Protector of Aborigines at Eucla, but the post carried no salary. In the press she was known as Kabbarli, the White Grandmother of Ooldea, and as the Great White Queen of the Never Never. In 1934 she was made a Commander of the British Empire. Her papers are in the National Library in Canberra and numerous other depositories. Monuments were erected to her at two of her former camps, Pyap and Ooldea.

Bates was Irish by birth and British by affection. She was born in county Tipperary on October 16, 1863, and named Daisy May O'Dwyer. At the age of twenty-one she visited Australia. Fascinated by the sturdy pioneers who settled the country, she lost her heart to a strong and handsome cattle drover, John Bates. Their marriage proved a mistake. Bates was an easygoing rover, no match for his energetic bride, and she found his lifestyle boring. He never settled down, and they lived in a series of hotels and in the homes of friends. Ten years after her arrival in Australia, Daisy put her eight-year-old son Arnold in a boarding school and left for England, determined not to return until Bates had found a home for them. Due to an Australian bank failure, she had barely enough money for her passage.

She found work in London with W. T. Stead, editor of the *Pall Mall Gazette*.

She admired Stead and learned much from him. She had been in England five years when news came that the Australian bank would refund part of her deposit, enough to pay her way home. At the same time, Bates wrote that he and their son were looking for property in Western Australia. Just then Daisy read a letter in the *Times* alleging that white settlers were cruel to the Western Australian natives. A loyal daughter of the Empire, she could not believe the accusations. She went to the *Times*, told them she was going to Australia, and offered to investigate the charges and report her findings. Although she had lived in Australia from 1884 to 1894, she had barely noticed those the Australians called blackfellows, and she had no idea of doing more than investigating the charges of exploitation.

It happened that on the voyage out Daisy met an Italian priest, who told her of a Trappist monastery at Beagle Bay which ministered to the Aborigines in northwest Australia. After visiting among the natives of the west coast near Broome for six months, learning much about them and proving to her own satisfaction that the charges of exploitation by whites were untrue, she found an opportunity to visit the monastery. Although it was strictly forbidden for any woman except a queen to enter the walls, the abbot granted a dispensation in favor of Daisy and gave her his own bag bed and seaweed pillow.

The monks lived in Spartan simplicity and great poverty. Their monastery was to be evaluated, and, unless the Trappists could show improvements amounting to several thousand pounds, the land would revert to the government. Daisy, the few priests, and those Aborigines who could be persuaded to work spent four months rebuilding, weeding, planting, and surveying the land, thus saving it for the monks. In the process, they taught their guest much about the natives, and she learned more by talking to them and observing their ways.

The members of the Nyool-nyool tribe there were half clothed and half civilized. Most of them had had their two front teeth knocked out, and some wore bones through their noses. They practiced infant cannibalism. They slept in the bush, their beds a hollow in the sand where fire had burned to warm the ground. Despite efforts by the monks to Christianize the natives, they retained most of their customs, including the pernicious habit of lending their wives to the Asiatic pearl fishers on the coast, a practice that spread disease and was pure misery to the women.

The women had little status. "The secrets of life, the laws of life, are in the hands of men," wrote Bates. In the economy of camp life, they came behind the dogs. "There is no glorification of maternity, no reverence of woman as woman, in the dark mind of the aboriginal. . . . Apart from her physical fulfillment of certain dominant needs, a woman is less than the dust" (Bates, *Passing of the Aborigines*, p. 28).

Even though this first experience with the natives was shocking, Daisy felt impelled to make a systematic study of Aboriginal beliefs and customs. She spent her time riding through the countryside, camping with the Aborigines, sharing her food with them, and making friends with the old men. She learned from them about the complicated social system of the whole northern region. Whatever she saw was carefully recorded in her notebooks. She learned to think with the native's mentality and to talk in his language. She began to compile a dictionary of the various dialects.

John Bates had found a home for them, a cattle station on Roebuck Plains. However, the property did not belong to him. He managed the station. He had bought another piece of 183,600 acres on Ethel Creek in the Windell area of Western Australia, which Daisy named Glen Carrick. It was not stocked and had no house. In order to raise money and stock the place, Daisy decided to drive 770 Herefords from the Broome area to Glen Carrick. For six months she and John, with Arnold, now twelve, and eight men drove the cattle over a thousand miles. She began the drive with high hopes and enjoyment, but soon the noise, the heat, the heavy dust, and the waywardness of the cows, every one of them "surpassing the Irish pig in contrariness," wore her down. They reached Glen Carrick safely, except for 200 cattle that had somehow been lost, the very 200 with which she had planned to stock their own place. The others were sold at a profit. Daisy recovered her strength but not her regard for John. In her account of the cattle run, she omitted to mention his presence. From that time on, she saw very little of him.

She went to Perth, where she spent the winter socializing. She met the visiting Duke and Duchess of York (later King George and Queen Mary) and joined the Women's Club. She lectured to local clubs and became engrossed in what she now felt would be her life work, a study of the country's first inhabitants. She read books on the Aborigines and on anthropology. Her articles and talks established her as an authority on the natives.

Western Australia's registrar general, who had for some time wished to record the Aboriginal customs and language, appointed Daisy in 1904 to work on the project, with a stipend of eight shillings a day. She was given an office and access to the work of previous students. She was to compile a volume given the ambitious title of "A Short Authentic Historical Record of the Habits, Customs and Language of the Aboriginal Natives of This State." She corresponded with anthropologists, including Andrew Lang in England and R. H. Mathews of Australia, and she sent questionnaires to government employees throughout the state in order to collect local vocabularies. But she grew restless in office work and felt that the information coming in from her inquiries was inexact and confused. She proposed going out to the surviving natives at Maamba Aboriginal Reserve in Cannington, established in the 1890s, to record the legends and languages at first hand.

Here she lived for two years with the remnants of the Bibbulmun, the largest homogeneous group in Australia, who had lived in the Perth area. She described them as the finest group; they were not cannibals (as were the central tribes) and they did not practice infanticide, except, when twins were born, one was sacrificed. They had only one deity, a serpent god which dominated the earth and punished evil. They used stone tools and dressed in kangaroo skins. The people wandered from place to place, using shelters made of boughs, killing game and small animals and digging roots for food.

The coming of the white men in 1829 had begun the process of change. The land was fenced; sheep, horses, and cattle grazed over the grasslands, obliterating the natives' food and hunting grounds. White men's laws got the natives in trouble, and white men's diseases cut down their ranks. According to Daisy, it was not the settlers' cruelty but their kindness that had led to the current unhappy state of affairs. The whites established schools and hospitals, gave out rations, and set up missions, but the natives were being destroyed by civilization.

Daisy set out on a pilgrimage of the old camping grounds, seeking what was left of the people—all old, all government pensioners or beggars. She felt it important to record their myths, poetry, and beliefs before it was too late. In one camp she found natives who had contracted measles. The white doctor told Daisy that the hospital was overflowing with patients and that the natives would have to stay in their camp; Daisy would have to nurse them. The infection spread, and she alone nursed and fed the victims. She became known as a healer, attracting patients from other camps. During this time she cut her own wood and carried her own water, for she would not ask a native to work for her.

Daisy's celebrity was enhanced by an eccentricity of dress. She continued to wear the costume that had been fashionable when she had been a young woman in Victoria's England: a white blouse, a stiff collar and tie, a dark skirt and coat over corsets and petticoats, and black shoes and stockings. She added a brimmed hat with a veil and gloves. She wore this garb for the rest of her life, through two world wars, until she died at an age close to ninety. And she wore it not only in the city but also while traveling on foot in 106-degree heat and camping in the bush, cooking over an open fire, and tending to sick natives. She kept dozens and dozens of gloves, which she wore as protection against infections. "Immediately on my return from the annointment of sores," she wrote, "both gloves and hands have been steeped in boiling water" (*Passing of the Aborigines*, p. 215).

Occasionally she went to the city to attend functions at Government House, meetings of the Association for the Advancement of Science, or gatherings of the Perth Women's Club. On these occasions, she would stay in the best hotels and appear elegantly dressed and coiffed. Fastidious to a degree, she sat as straight as a ramrod. Her conversation was witty and intelligent.

Partly due to Daisy's work, interest in the Western Australian Aborigines was spreading. In 1910 two anthropological expeditions arrived in Perth, one from Cambridge University and one from Sweden, to undertake field work. Daisy was delighted when she was made a special commissioner to accompany the Cambridge group, but she found that the anthropologists condescended to her as a woman and an amateur and suggested that her researches be included in their reports rather than appear as a separate publication.

This suggestion did not suit Daisy at all. She would not have the book on which she had been working for years doomed to the status of an appendix to someone else's work. Because of her refusal, as well as changes in the government, and then World War I, her appointment was terminated, and the government dropped plans to subsidize publication. When she applied for a position as Protector of Aborigines, she did not get it, for the flimsy reason that it involved risks too great for a woman.

Daisy was left with no job and no income, except for what she could earn by writing. She could not look to John Bates for help. Though still married, she had begun to refer to him as "my late husband." As a matter of fact, he lived until 1935. Arnold was planning to be married and had ceased to be a significant part of her life. She sold Glen Carrick and then the property in Perth where she had planned to build a home for her old age.

The Australian press continued to write of her in glowing terms, and she had good friends. One of them invited her to occupy a home near Eucla, on the southern coast near the border between Western and South Australia. Here, she could study and carry out her duties as Honorary Protector of the Aborigines at Eucla, a post to which she was appointed in 1912. The natives, at least, took her position seriously and called her their "Queen government." After a short time, she moved from the friend's cottage to a lonely water hole at Jeegala Creek, where she pitched her tent and began to explore the Nullarbor Plain. She learned from the natives the skills of tracking and hunting. They gave her the "Freedom of their Totems," making her custodian of the sacred totem boards, holding for them "the mystery of life." She was so thoroughly accepted into the society of the Aborigines that she was allowed to watch the long, weird rituals of the initiation of the men. As she watched, she showed "no quiver of timidity, or of revulsion of feeling, or of levity" because she was thinking with her "black man's mind" (*Passing of the Aborigines* p. 25).

Daisy lived in other camps, one at Wirilya, near Yalata, and another in the sandhills of Ooldea, near the new Trans-Australian Railway Line. This was her home for sixteen years. She had an eight-by-ten-foot tent for living and sleeping, an upturned tank which she used as a library, and a bough shed with a ladder to the roof which she used as an observatory. She loved the stars, the birds, and the solitude.

The Aborigines respected her privacy, waiting outside her camp for attention, some of the newcomers "shyly flitting about among the trees" before daring to come close. Her prediction of the gradual breakdown of tradition was coming true. The black men gave up their customs and taboos. Most were dirty, ill fed, diseased. They needed her.

Her own living, she said, never cost more than ten shillings a week—bread, powdered milk, sugar, rice, butter, jam, and tea, with dried potatoes and a few fresh vegetables, made up her diet. Friends sent her delicacies, which she traded for flour and tea for her people. She learned to make dampers—biscuits made from flour and water—and to eat some of the native foods, such as roasted witchetty grubs and baked goannas. Though the money she earned from her writing did not reach far, she proudly refused charity.

As she nursed the old and the sick, she worked at her typewriter, turning out articles for newspapers and scientific periodicals and carrying on a voluminous correspondence. Hopes for publication of her research still haunted her, but she refused any suggestion of collaboration. The work was never published, and she eventually sold her papers to the National Library in Canberra.

Ernestine Hill, an Australian admirer, visited Daisy in her tent. She wrote a series of articles about her, using some of the dramatic stories Daisy had told her. An opera was written about Daisy. In 1933 she was invited to Canberra to discuss plans for the future of the Aborigines. In 1934 came her highest honor, when she was made a Commander of the British Empire, and 1938 saw the publication of Daisy's *The Passing of the Aborigines: A Lifetime Spent among the Natives of Australia*. A popular collection of her writings on the Aborigines, it was published first in England, and it became a European best-seller.

In spite of these successes, Daisy's last years were spent in poverty. Her life among the natives had been sometimes dangerous and often lonely. She had not always eaten well and was once hospitalized for malnutrition. She suffered from "sandy blight," an affliction of the eyes, and she lost her vision for long periods. As she grew older, she could no longer live in a tent. She was dependent on friends, for she had given all she had to buy food and medicines for her people. She died quietly in a suburban rest home in Adelaide on April 18, 1951.

BIBLIOGRAPHY

Works by Daisy Bates

"Possibilities of Tropical Agriculture in the Nor'west: The Beagle Bay Mission Experiments." *Journal* of the Western Australia Department of Agriculture (*Journal* WADA) 4 (July–Dec. 1901): 6–13.

"From Port Hedland to Carnarvon by Buggy." *Journal* WADA 4 (July–Dec. 1901): 183–202.

"Brands Act of Western Australia." *Journal* WADA 7 (Jan.–June 1903): 184–90.

"Rabbit Drive in Riverina." *Journal* WADA 7 (Jan.–June 1903): 111–15.

Letter in London *Times*, May 1904.

"The Marriage Laws and Some Customs of the Western Australian Aborigines." *Journal* of the Victoria Branch, Royal Geographical Society of Australasia (*Journal* RGS) 23 (1905): 36–60.

"Notes on the Topography of the Northern Portions of Western Australia." *Journal* RGS 23 (1905): 18–36.

"Fanny Balbuk-Yooreel, the Last Swan River (Female) Native." *Science of Man* n.s. 13 (1911): 100–1, 119–21.

"Measles in Camp." *Science of Man* n.s. 14 (1913): 31–32, 51–52, 67–68.

"Aboriginal Names of Places." *Science of Man* n.s. 14 (1913): 74–76.

"Social Organization of Some Western Australian Tribes." *Report* of the Australian Association for the Advancement of Science, Melbourne meeting, 1913, pp. 387–400.

"Aborigines of the West Coast of South Australia: Vocabularies and Ethnographical

Notes." *Transactions and Proceedings* of the Royal Society of South Australia 42 (1918): 152–67.

"Ooldea Water." *Proceedings* of the Royal Geographical Society of Australasia, South Australia Branch 21 (1919–1920): 73–78.

"Ngilgi, an Aboriginal Woman's Life Story." *Western Australian* (1935).

The Passing of the Aborigines: A Lifetime Spent among the Natives of Australia. London: Murray, 1938. Second edition, Melbourne: Heinemann, 1966. Quotations in the text are from the 1938 edition.

Bates contributed to Arthur Mee's *Children's Newspaper*, the *Adelaide Register*, the *Australasian*, *Cassier's Magazine*, the *Western Mail*, the *Western Australian*, and other papers.

Works about Daisy Bates

Allen, Alexandra. *Travelling Ladies*. London: Jupiter, 1980, pp. 156–89. Includes a bibliography.

Hill, Ernestine. *Kabbarli: A Personal Memoir of Daisy Bates*. Sydney: Angus & Robertson, 1973.

Holmes, Winifred. *Seven Adventurous Women*. London: Bell, 1953, pp. 155–76.

International Dictionary of Women's Biography. Edited by Jennifer S. Uglow and Frances Hinton. New York: Continuum, 1982.

"Kabbarli." *Salt* (Nov. 23, 1942): 18–23.

Mee, Arthur. "Friend of a Dying Race." *Desiderata* (Nov. 1938) abridgement.

Salter, Elizabeth. *Daisy Bates, "The Great White Queen of the Never Never."* Sydney: Angus & Robertson, 1971. Also published as *Daisy Bates*. New York: Coward, McCann & Geoghegan, 1972. Includes a bibliography of manuscript and printed sources.

Wilson, Barbara Ker. *Tales Told by Kabbarli: Aboriginal Legends Collected by Daisy Bates*. Sydney: Angus & Robertson, 1972.

An obituary appeared in the London *Times*, on Apr. 20, 1951.

Bates manuscripts and papers are located in the National Library of Australia in Canberra, the J. S. Battye Library of Western Australian History in Perth, the Barr Smith Library in Adelaide, the Mitchell Library in Sydney, the University of Queensland Library in Brisbane, and the State Library of Victoria in Melbourne.

GERTRUDE BELL
1868–1926

Gertrude Bell was a traveler, mountaineer, scholar, archeologist, statesman, and museum founder. Between 1900 and 1914, she explored the Middle East, the cradle of ancient Persian and Mesopotamian civilization. She learned to speak, read, and write Persian and Arabic. During her years in southwest Asia, she formed a wide acquaintance among the sheiks and rulers of the Arab countries. While away from her English home, she wrote long and entertaining letters to her family, which they treasured and later published. She also kept journals and wrote books about her travels, chief among them *Syria: The Desert and the Sown* (1907), *Amurath to Amurath* (1911), and *Palace and Mosque at Ukhaidir* (1914). She was made a Commander of the British Empire and a Fellow of the Royal Geographical Society.

World War I ended her travels, but for the rest of her life Gertrude worked in the Middle East, her knowledge and understanding of the desert peoples contributing to the changes she had herself foreseen. She predicted the breakup of Asiatic Turkey, the rise of Arab autonomies, and even a union of Arab states.

Gertrude Margaret Lowthian Bell was born in county Durham, England, on July 14, 1868, daughter of Sir Hugh Bell, an ironmaster, and granddaughter of a baronet. She was educated at Queen's College and won high honors in history at Lady Margaret Hall, Oxford. Though hedged about by the usual social restrictions imposed on Victorian women, she accepted them without protest, and even gave way to her parents' objection to marriage to a man she loved. After she was at length free to travel alone into areas previously unvisited by Europeans, she remained a loyal daughter, always consulting her parents about her plans and deferring to their wishes. A discreet, self-respecting, and respected Englishwoman, she represented her nation with pride and met other nationalities and tribes with respect.

She first visited the Middle East in 1892. Her uncle, Sir Frank Lascelles, was appointed to the British embassy at Tehran, the capital of Persia, and Gertrude went there with his family. The beautiful house provided for the ambassador was a delight to Gertrude, who immediately nicknamed it the Garden of Eden. Here she and the first secretary, Henry Cadogan, spent happy hours reading poetry together, and soon she wrote to her parents for permission to be engaged. They thought Cadogan unsuitable, his debts too heavy and his future uncertain, and they arranged for her to travel home escorted by a cousin. Cadogan died not nine months later.

Gertrude's series of essays on Persia was published anonymously in 1894 as *Safar Nameh: Persian Pictures, A Book of Travel*. She herself did not think well of the book, but it gave the reader a sense of the beauty and romance of that historic land. Bell returned to the Middle East in 1899, established herself in Jerusalem, and took daily lessons in Arabic. She had studied the history of the Holy Land, and she took several short journeys to visit the inheritors of its traditions and culture.

In the spring and early summer of 1900 she managed to circumvent the Turkish authorities to visit the Druses, whom she found to be "cultivated, civilised human beings," straight-speaking people (*Letters of Gertrude Bell*, p. 83). The head of the tribe, Yahya Beg, made her welcome, shared his meal with her, and arranged for guides to show her some of the archeological sites she wished to see. She thought him an extraordinarily handsome man, "the most perfect type of the Grand Seigneur" (*Letters of Gertrude Bell*, p. 83). Another short journey took her to the ancient city of Palmyra, which she thought was the loveliest city, next to Petra, she had seen in the country.

In Europe, meanwhile, she had spent time mountain climbing in the Alps and had established herself as one of the foremost women climbers. She traversed the Schreckhorn, the Finsteraarhorn, and the Engelhorn. On one occasion, trapped by a blizzard, she spent two nights on the Finsteraarhorn, one without shelter. During two journeys around the world with her brother, she traveled through the United States, India, Burma, and China. Everywhere in the British Empire, Gertrude had connections with important people. She stayed in embassies and was entertained by the ruling classes. Yet she had a genuine interest in meeting the indigenous people and in studying the customs of each area.

Her first long expedition in the Middle East began in January 1905. Her account, in *Syria: The Desert and the Sown*, opens with her intense excitement on starting out:

> To those bred under an elaborate social order few such moments of exhilaration can come as that which stands at the threshold of wild travel. The gates of the enclosed garden are thrown open, the chain at the entrance of the sanctuary is lowered, with a wary glance to right and left you step forth, and, behold! the immeasurable world. The world of adventure and of enterprise . . . an unanswered question and an unanswerable doubt hidden in the fold of every hill. . . . So you leave the sheltered close, and, like the man in the fairy story, you feel the bands

break that were riveted about your heart as you enter the path that stretches across the rounded shoulder of the earth. (*Syria*, pp. 1–2)

She journeyed through Syria and Cilicia to Konya. She had made many friends in the Arab world, and each one had relatives in the desert who were happy to entertain the traveling Englishwoman of high rank and to furnish escorts for the next part of the journey. Accompanied by three muleteers from Beirut and a cook-escort, Mikhail, she visited nomads in their tents and sheiks in their palaces. She heard the gossip of the desert, gave medical help to people far from doctors or hospitals, and investigated ancient archeological sites. She found many ruined temples and dwellings and was shown Roman coins found while ploughing.

The trip was not without danger. The Turkish government was sending troops to Yemen to quell an insurrection. The tribesmen suffered from the wholesale commandeering of their camels and mares. The tribes themselves were enemies, one to another, and only the strict rules of hospitality protected the travelers. "The word 'guest' is sacred from Jordan to Euphrates," Bell found, hospitality being "extended to all comers, no matter how inopportune" (*Syria*, p. 33). As the caravan approached a village of the Beni Sakhr, her muleteer, a Druse, was warned that they might kill him. Mikhail, however, was equal to the occasion. He changed the man's name from Muhammad to Tarif, a name used by the Christians. "So we converted and baptized the astonished Muhammad," said Bell, "before the cutlets could be taken out of the frying pan" (*Syria* p. 43).

At one time, men firing shots approached the party. Bell's guide wound his cloak about his left arm and waved it as a flag of truce while he and Gertrude rode slowly forward. "The firing ceased," she wrote; "it was nothing after all but the accepted greeting to strangers, conducted with the customary levity of the barbarian" (*Syria*, p. 74).

She began to see the desert with the eyes of the nomads. To them, the land was not a desert or a wilderness but "a land of which they know every feature, a mother country whose smallest product has a use sufficient for their needs" (*Syria*, p. 60).

When the Syrian part of the journey was finished, Bell and Mikhail looked back on their adventures:

> At the end I said: "Oh Mikhail, this is a pleasant world, though some have spoken ill of it, and for the most part the children of Adam are good not evil."
> ... "Listen, oh lady," said Mikhail, "and I will make it clear to you. Men are short of vision, and they see but that for which they look. Some look for evil and they find evil; some look for good and it is good that they find, and moreover some are fortunate and these find always what they want. Praise be to God! to that number you belong ... and again many times shall you travel in Syria with peace and safety and prosperity, please God!"
> "Please God!" said I. (*Syria*, pp. 336–40)

Bell was happy to have seen the uplands east of Jordan because she suspected that a generation or so later it would be scattered over with villages, mills, and even roads. *Syria: The Desert and the Sown* derived its title from Omar Khayyám's description: "The strip of herbage strown that just divides the desert from the sown" (*The Rubaiyat*, Edward Fitzgerald translation, verse 11). Gertrude's purpose was "to write not so much a book of travel as an account of the people I met or who accompanied me on my way, and to show what the world is like in which they live and how it appears to them" (*Syria*, Preface).

At Alexandretta she parted company with Mikhail, who had, in spite of his charms, proved irresponsible. She found another escort, Fattuh, who was a treasure and became a lifelong friend. He served her faithfully through the rest of her travels, and she, in turn, saw that he got needed medical care. He took entire charge of pitching camp, preparing meals, and choosing the places where she would sleep. In one village she was invited to use a chamber in a house, but when Fattuh saw the fleas he diplomatically told the host that he had already pitched the tent and arranged the lady's bed.

She became more and more interested in the archeological remains of the ancient dwellers of the land, and as she continued the journey toward Konya, she saw many more archeological sites. The Ottoman government cared nothing for the Moslem traditions, but in the mosques of Konya she found learned men who talked to her of the past. "I enjoyed my hours among those beautiful ghosts of the glory of Islam," she wrote to her family. "My best friend is a dancing Dervish; and Konia contains the mother house of the Dervishes" (Burgoyne, *Gertrude Bell*, I, 220).

Here, too, she met Professor (later Sir William) Ramsay, an archeologist with whom she was to conduct some excavating and to collaborate on a book entitled *The Thousand and One Churches*. The expedition began in 1907, and took her for two months into the Karadag to study the Byzantine and Christian remains. After spending some time with Ramsay and his wife and son, Bell continued the work alone, measuring, drawing the plans of the buildings, and photographing the sites.

Before the book appeared in 1909, she was off on another expedition, from Aleppo along the Euphrates to Hit, Karbala, and old Babylon to Baghdad—which she had not yet visited—and up the Tigris back to Konya. On this journey she first saw the great castle at Ukhaidir (colloquially called Kheidir), a great example of the architecture of a bygone age:

> Of all the wonderful experiences that have fallen my way, the first sight of Kheidir is the most memorable. It reared its mighty walls out of the sand, almost untouched by time, breaking the long lines of the waste with its huge towers, steadfast and massive, as though it were, as I had at first thought it, the work of nature, not of man. . . . Whether it was a Lakhmid palace or no, it was the palace which I had set forth to seek. It belongs architecturally to the group of Sassanian buildings which are already known to us, and historically it is related to the palaces,

famous in pre-Mohammadan tradition, whose splendours had filled with amazement
the invading hordes of the Bedouin, and still shine with a legendary magnificence,
from the pages of the chroniclers of the conquest. (*Amurath to Amurath*, pp. 140–
41)

She began with zeal to photograph and measure the great halls and chambers,
but she had sent her caravan on to Karbala, allotting only one day to this part
of the journey, and they needed their provisions if they were to remain for the
measurements and filming she now deemed necessary. Fattuh saved the situation
by riding through the night—a dangerous trip—to Karbala, returning with the
caravan and fresh provisions, including a bag of oranges for Gertrude.

Some twenty families of refugees from Nejd inhabited the ruins. They had
moved from Jauf because "we were vexed with the government of Ibn er Rashid"
(*Amurath to Amurath*, p. 144). They welcomed the "lady Khan" and shared
their scant supplies with her. For days she remained here, completing her drawings, reveling in the work, hard and dusty as it was, and enjoying the hospitality
of the Arabs.

Some days after they had resumed their travels, she heard a disturbance in
the night and awoke to find that robbers had made off with her money, her
servants' clothes, and her saddlebags, which contained her priceless notebooks,
the results of four months' work.

The chief of the Kurdish tribes, who was sent for, came to her camp with
twenty armed men. Next, the Kaimmakam of Midyad was notified, and he sent
fifty foot soldiers. "By the third day," wrote Bell, "there was no person in the
country-side, except, I believe, myself, against whom a charge of complicity
had not been raised" (*Amurath to Amurath* pp. 321–22). The affair caused
everyone so much distress that she would have called off the hunt, except that
the notebooks were of such great value to her.

Then everything mysteriously reappeared on a rock above the camp. Nothing
was missing except some money, which was subsequently refunded to Bell by
the Ottoman government. The soldiers went to a village, which had been suspected from the first, to find that every inhabitant had left it, thus fixing the
blame but losing the culprits. Gertrude rode after the soldiers to ask for a universal
amnesty, blaming herself for not having kept a watch over the camp during the
nights.

Her story of the journey through Asia Minor was published in 1911 as *Amurath
to Amurath*. Critics thought it too much laden with architectural detail, but it is
also an absorbing account of desert travel. By the time it appeared, Bell had
returned again to Ukhaidir for three more days of work. This time, she crossed
the desert directly from Damascus to Baghdad. Her book, lavishly illustrated
with drawings and photographs, was published in 1914 as *Palace and Mosque
at Ukhaidir*.

She was, for a time, weary of traveling and glad to be at home in England.
She joined the anti-suffragists. And she fell in love, but the man she loved, and

who loved her, was married. She could not break up the marriage, so she turned away from the possibility of happiness and, toward the end of 1913, started off for another Middle Eastern trip. She wanted to visit Hail, in the Nejd district of central Arabia, which was, for the moment, said to be peaceful. In contrast to previous trips, she started this one with a heavy heart. "I want to cut all links with the world, and that is the best and wisest thing to do," she wrote to an old friend (Burgoyne, *Gertrude Bell*, I, 284).

It turned out to be a difficult and exhausting trip. The report that all was peaceful was untrue. For many days, the caravan was in danger from warring tribes. At one point, Bell confided to her journal that she was deeply depressed and wondered whether the adventure was, after all, worth the candle. There were few archeological sites to examine, and she thought herself a fool to enter these wastes where nothing could be accomplished.

Hail itself gave her a sinister impression, and there she had the one really trying experience of all her travels. Because the Emir Ibn er Rashid was away, she was put up in his beautiful summer palace until he returned. Though treated well, she found herself a virtual prisoner there for eleven days. Ibrahim, the emir's representative, refused to honor a letter of credit and she was without money. She was not allowed to leave the palace to visit the town without an invitation and an escort.

Tiring of this game, she demanded a private audience with Ibrahim, told him she would stay no longer, that the withholding of her money caused her great inconvenience, and that she wanted an escort to the Anezeh borders. She was refused. After a few more days, she spoke "with much vigour" to one of the eunuchs "and ended the interview abruptly by rising and leaving him." After dark, the eunuch arrived with a bag of gold and full permission for her to leave when she liked. "Why they have given way now, or why they did not give way before, I cannot guess" (Burgoyne, *Gertrude Bell*, I, 300–1).

Her journey ended at Damascus in May 1914. No book resulted from this journey, yet it was one of the more important of her trips. The president of the Royal Geographical Society said her journey was "a pioneer venture which not only put on the map a line of wells, before unplaced or unknown but also cast much new light on the history of the Syrian desert frontiers under Roman, Palmyrene, and Ummayad domination" (*Letters of Gertrude Bell*, p. 289). She also brought back political information about the house of Rashid and the rival power of the Ibn Sauds. The society awarded Bell its gold medal in recognition of her achievement. The information was soon to be of inestimable value to her country for, within weeks of her return to England, World War I broke out, and Arabia was a theater of war.

As a recognized authority on the peoples of Mesopotamia she was recruited by the British government to serve with a newly formed Arab intelligence bureau in Cairo. Then she served as assistant political officer in Baghdad. When the old Turkish dominions were being divided after the war, Bell became Oriental secretary to the civil commissioner in Baghdad. She was influential in the establishment of Iraq as a new state, with Faisal, leader of the Arab revolt, as king. She created and directed the Iraq Museum, where a room was named for her. When she died in her Baghdad home on the night of July 11–12, 1926, she was the honorary director of antiquities for Iraq. She was buried with high military honors in the country she had adopted as her home.

BIBLIOGRAPHY

Works by Gertrude Bell

Safar Nameh: Persian Pictures, a Book of Travel. London: Bentley, 1894. Published anonymously. Later editions, under Bell's name, were entitled *Persian Pictures,* including one with a preface by Sir E. Denison Ross. New York: Boni & Liveright, 1928.

"Alps of the Dauphiné." *Nineteenth Century* 47 (Feb. 1900): 330–38. Same article in *Living Age* 224 (Mar. 24, 1900): 780–87.

"Turkish Rule East of Jordan." *Nineteenth Century* 52 (Aug. 1902): 226–38.

"Islam in India—a Study at Aligarth." *Nineteenth Century* 60 (Dec. 1906): 900–8.

"Note on a Journey through Cilicia and Lycaonia." *Revue Archéologique* 7 (1906–1907).

Syria: The Desert and the Sown. London: Heinemann, 1907. Another edition, London: Heinemann, 1919. Other editions were entitled *The Desert and the Sown.* Quotations in the text are from the 1919 edition.

(With Sir William Ramsay) *The Thousand and One Churches.* London: Hodder & Stoughton, 1909.

"Palace in the Syrian Desert." *Quarterly Review* 212 (Apr. 1910): 339–68.

"Mount of the Servants of God." *Blackwood's* 188 (Sept. 1910): 354–55.

"Churches and Monasteries of the Tur Abdin." *Amida* (1910). Reprinted, London: Pindar Press, 1982.

"Damascus." *Blackwood's* 189 (Apr. 1911): 539–49. Same article in *Living Age* 269 (May 27, 1911): 538–46.

"Asiatic Turkey under the Constitution." *Blackwood's* 190 (Oct. 1911): 425–40. Same article in *Living Age* 271 (Nov. 4, 1911): 259–70.

Amurath to Amurath: A Study in Early Mohammadan Architecture. London: Heinemann, 1911.

"Post-road through the Syrian Desert." *Living Age* 280 (Feb. 7 and 21, 1914): 329–43, 458–69.

Palace and Mosque at Ukhaidir. Oxford: Clarendon Press, 1914.

The Arabs of Mesopotamia. Basrah, Iraq: Government Press, 1917. Published anonymously; includes Bell's "Asiatic Turkey."

The Civil Administration of Mesopotamia. London: H. M. Stationery Office, 1920.

The Letters of Gertrude Bell. Selected and edited by Lady Florence Bell. London: E. Benn, 1927. Another edition, London: E. Benn, 1947. Quotations in the text are from the 1947 edition.

The Earlier Letters of Gertrude Bell. Collected and edited by Elsa Richmond. New York: Liveright, 1937.

The Arab War: Confidential Information for General Headquarters. London: Golden Cockerel, 1940.

Gertrude Bell: A Selection from the Photographic Archive on an Archaeologist and Traveler. Compiled by Stephen Hill. Newcastle upon Tyne, England: University of Newcastle upon Tyne, 1976.

Works about Gertrude Bell

Bodley, Ronald Courtenay. *Gertrude Bell.* New York: Macmillan, 1940.

Brittain, Vera. *The Women at Oxford: A Fragment of History.* London: Harrap, 1960, pp. 73, 76–77, 248.

Burgoyne, Elizabeth. *Gertrude Bell, from Her Personal Papers.* London: E. Benn, vol. I, 1958; vol. II, 1961.

Dictionary of National Biography, 1922–1930. London: Oxford University Press, 1937, pp. 74–76.

Europa Biographical Dictionary of British Women. Edited by Anne Crawford and others. London: Europa, 1985.

Ffrench, Yvonne. *Six Great Englishwomen.* London: Hamilton, 1953.

Forbes, Rosita. "Two Women Contend for a New 'Eden' in the East." *New York Times Magazine,* Feb. 7, 1926, pp. 9, 22.

Goodman, Susan. *Gertrude Bell.* Leamington Spa/Dover, England: Berg, 1985.

Harrison, Marguerite. "Gertrude Bell, a Desert Power," *New York Times Magazine,* July 18, 1926, p. 12.

Hill, Stephen. "Gertrude Bell." *Antiquity* 50 (Sept.–Dec. 1976): 190–93.

International Dictionary of Women's Biography. Edited by Jennifer S. Uglow and Frances Hinton. New York: Continuum, 1982.

Kann, Josephine. *Daughter of the Desert: The Story of Gertrude Bell.* London: Bodley Head, 1956.

Ladies on the Loose: Women Travellers of the 18th and 19th Centuries. Edited by Leo Hamalian. New York: Dodd, Mead, 1981, pp. 134–35.

Lives of Today and Yesterday: A Book of Comparative Biography. Edited by Rowena K. Keyes. New York: D. Appleton, 1931, pp. 132–44.

Mallowan, Max. "Gertrude Bell." *Iraq* 38 (Autumn 1976): 81–84.

Ridley, Maurice R. *Gertrude Bell.* London and Glasgow: Blackie, 1941.

Robins, E. "Impressions of *The Desert and the Sown,* and *Amurath to Amurath.*" *Fortnightly* 95 (Mar. 1911): 470–92.

Sackville-West, Victoria. *Passenger to Teheran.* London: L. & V. Woolf, 1926, pp. 58–62.

Sitwell, Edith. *English Women.* London: W. Collins, 1942, pp. 45–46.

Tabor, Margaret Emma. *Pioneer Women.* Third series. London: Sheldon Press, 1930, pp. 94–122.

Tibble, Anne. *Gertrude Bell.* London: A. and C. Black, 1958.

Winstone, H. V. F. *Gertrude Bell.* London: Jonathan Cape, 1978. A full scholarly assessment of Bell's work, with a bibliography.

Obituaries appeared in the London *Times,* on July 13, 14, and 15, and in the national newspaper of Iraq, *Al Alam al Arabi,* on July 14, 1936.

Bell manuscript and archival material is located in the University Library of Newcastle upon Tyne. Winifred Donkin's catalogue was published by the university in 1960. The Royal Geographical Society also possesses Bell archives.

ISABELLA LUCY BIRD BISHOP
1831–1904

Isabella Lucy Bird Bishop was the most popular woman traveler of Victorian England. The publication of her *Six Months in the Sandwich Islands* in 1875, followed soon afterward by *A Lady's Life in the Rocky Mountains*, won her many admirers and readers in both hemispheres. The books are still being published and read with pleasure. Not that Isabella courted fame. She was never happy in the world of society, paying visits, leaving cards, and indulging in gossip. Her idea of bliss was to be alone in a wilderness. From Hawaii she wrote:

> This is the height of enjoyment in travelling. I have just encamped under a *lauhala* tree, with my saddle inverted for a pillow, my horse tied by a long lariat to a guava bush, my gear, saddle-bags, and rations for two days lying about, and my saddle blanket drying in the sun. Overhead the sun blazes, and casts no shadow; a few fleecy clouds hover near him, and far below, the great expanse of the Pacific gleams in a deeper blue than the sky. Far above, towers the rugged and snow-patched, but no longer mysterious dome of Mauna Kea; while everywhere, ravines, woods, waterfalls, and stretches of lawn-like grass delight the eye. . . . The novelty is that I am alone, my conveyance my own horse; no luggage to look after, for it is all in my saddle-bags; no guide to bother, hurry, or hinder me. (*Six Months in the Sandwich Islands*, p. 237)

"This is a blessed country," she ends, "for a lady can travel everywhere in absolute security." She found absolute security, despite dangerous and frightening episodes, in almost all of the places she was to visit over the next years. She traveled in Australia, New Zealand, Hawaii, the United States, and Canada; with her first visit to Japan, she became fascinated with the East and subsequently went to Malaya, Korea, northern India, Kurdistan, Persia, and China. Her last long journey, taken at the age of seventy, was a thousand-mile ride across Morocco. She was among the first group of women accepted as fellows of the Royal Geographical Society in 1892. In nine travel books she reported on the people, the flora and fauna, and the politics of the places she visited. She illustrated them with engravings from her own sketches and later with photographs, taken on the spot and developed by dipping the film in a river using the night as her darkroom. She had in full measure the characteristics that make a great explorer—curiosity, perseverance, and courage.

Isabella Lucy Bird (for she was not Mrs. Bishop until she was fifty) did not strike her friends as able to rough it, to climb into the crater of a volcano, to ride through tropical storms day after day, to put up in flea-ridden caravansaries, or to subsist mainly on rice and water. She was less than five feet tall, and throughout her childhood, indeed much of her life, she was subject to a myriad of ailments. When her physician suggested a sea voyage as a method to regain health, he surely did not mean for her to gallop about on a horse (astride, no less) or climb mountains in a blizzard, but that is what she did, and that is what brought her strength and blooming health.

She was born on October 15, 1831, in Yorkshire, the daughter of a Church of England clergyman, and for her first four decades she was so imbued with evangelical Christianity that ever afterward she could not rid herself of the feeling that all other religions were base superstitions. She was also a true Englishwoman, convinced that the spread of English institutions and manners was a great good, without which most people were savages—a view that she found difficult to reconcile with her admiration of other and older civilizations.

She had one sibling, Henrietta (Hennie), for whom she had a deep emotional attachment. Her first books of travel were based on the lengthy letters she wrote to Hennie. Their father, Edward Bird, died in 1858, their mother, Dora Lawson, in 1866, and subsequently— between journeys—the sisters lived together in Edinburgh and in Hennie's cottage at Tobermory, on the island of Mull.

In 1850 Isabella had an operation to remove a spinal tumor. It was only partially successful and left her still an invalid, suffering from insomnia and depression. Perhaps her doctor had enough insight to realize that her problems stemmed from a strong personality at odds with an enfeebling environment; at any rate, he prescribed travel. In 1854 the Reverend Bird gave his daughter a hundred pounds and permission to stay away as long as it lasted. She made it last through the sea voyage and through several months of land travel in eastern Canada and the northeastern United States.

When she came home she was much better and had the materials for her first book, *The Englishwoman in America*, but as many other Englishwomen, including Fanny Wright, Frances Trollope, and Harriet Martineau, had visited America and had published their own views, Isabella's book did not make much of a stir. She said in her preface that she had read most of the published American travels and went to the States "with that amount of prejudice which seems the birthright of every English person," but that she found those prejudices gradually melted away: however, she then added that "the noble, the learned, and the wealthy have shrunk from the United States," leaving it to be peopled by those whose only possession was "stalwart arms."

Back at home, in the same old environment, Isabella's aches and pains returned. She went on other trips, once to the United States, where she studied the religious revival of 1858, again to Canada, where she helped settlers who had, with her assistance, emigrated from the West Highlands. She visited the Outer Hebrides and in 1871 took a trip to New York and the Mediterranean but was too ill to leave the ship.

The turning point was her visit to Hawaii, which she knew as the Sandwich Islands, in 1872. She remained for six months.

> During that time the necessity of leading a life of open air and exercise as a means of recovery, led me to travel on horseback to and fro through the islands, exploring the interior, ascending the highest mountains, visiting the active volcanoes and remote regions which are known to few even of the residents, living among the natives, and otherwise seeing Hawaiian life in all its phases. (*Six Months in the Sandwich Islands*, Preface)

She had taken charge of her own life at last, and her pattern of travel from that time on was set. Even the fortuitous beginning of the visit was to be repeated, with decisions taken on the spur of the moment to go where she had not planned to go. She stopped at Honolulu because a young man on the ship from New Zealand to San Francisco became dangerously ill. His mother, the only other woman on the ship, persuaded Isabella to disembark with her to get medical attention for the youth. This led to invitations to visit plantations, and she went to several of the islands. She was sorry that she had not had time to read up on the islands beforehand, but she soon remedied that, and her book includes much Hawaiian history and politics. It is, however, her graphic descriptions of the luxuriant plants, the glorious cascades, the fearful volcanoes, and the happy-go-lucky natives, as well as the westernized kings and queens of the islands, that make the book good reading.

On her way home, Isabella, alone on her horse, visited Lake Tahoe in California, then went on to the Rocky Mountains and headed for Estes Park in Colorado. Her adventures and misadventures in reaching that destination included terrifying rides through blizzards when her eyelids froze shut, some months snowed in with two young men in a mountain cabin, and a near love affair with a mountain desperado. These adventures provided the material for *A Lady's Life in the Rocky Mountains*, published in 1879. In Hawaii she had been persuaded to ride astride instead of sidesaddle (which ended her constant backache) and to dress in what she called her Hawaiian riding dress, trousers under a full skirt. She took her western saddle afterward with her and became a notable rider, able to handle almost any horse—and she met with many dreadful ones on her subsequent trips. In Colorado she had an especially fine mare, Birdie, who carried her sure-footedly through mud, snow, and ice.

When she went to Japan in 1878, she could no longer get along without a servant who could speak the language to arrange for transport, shelter, and food, for it was her intention to eschew those places chosen by tourists and to follow unbeaten tracks into the lesser known regions. She found Ito, an unprepossessing youth of eighteen, "the most stupid-looking Japanese that I have seen" (*Unbeaten Tracks in Japan*, I, 51), but he had worked with a botanist and knew how to dry plants; he could cook, he could write English, and he could walk twenty-five miles a day. She hired him with some trepidation, but he was found to be faithful and intelligent and "I doubt whether I could have obtained a more valuable servant and interpreter" (*Unbeaten Tracks in Japan*, I, 318). At the end of their many miles of travel and adventure, Ito said he was sorry it was over. She was, too.

The most unusual part of the eighteen-month trip was a visit to the so-called hairy Ainu, aborigines who lived in Hokkaido. They were quite different from the Japanese in physical build, in language, and in customs, which Isabella took great care to ask about, recording their explanations. The men had luxuriant long black hair and beards, and some had much body hair. They were hospitable, gentle, and courteous. She found them strangely captivating:

> They have no history, their traditions are scarcely worthy the name, they claim descent from a dog, their houses and persons swarm with vermin, they are sunk in the grossest ignorance, they have no letters, or any numbers above a thousand, they are clothed in the bark of trees and the untanned skins of beasts, they worship the bear, the sun, moon, fire, water, and I know not what, they are uncivilisable and altogether irreclaimable savages, yet they are attractive, and in some ways fascinating, and I hope I shall never forget the music of their low, sweet voices, the soft light of their mild, brown eyes, and the wonderful sweetness of their smile. (*Unbeaten Tracks in Japan*, II, 74)

Isabella did not find in Japan the Oriental splendor others had written about. Although it had many beauties of nature, the Japanese empire did not measure up to her expectations. It was "founded on an exploded religious fiction, . . . scepticism rampant among the educated classes, and an ignorant priesthood lording it over the lower classes; an Empire with a splendid despotism for its apex, and naked coolies for its base . . . appropriating the fruits of Christian civilisation, but rejecting the tree from which they spring" (*Unbeaten Tracks in Japan*, I, 306). But the people in the interior she found gentle and courteous, "so much so, that a lady with no other attendant than a native servant can travel, as I have done, for 1200 miles through little-visited regions, and not meet with a single instance of incivility or extortion" (*Unbeaten Tracks in Japan*, I, 7).

After leaving Japan, Isabella made short visits to Hong Kong, Canton, Saigon, and Singapore. She visited a prison in Canton and wrote a chilling description of its cells, its tortures, and its executions. In Saigon she wandered about for most of a day in the Annamese section, got herself invited into one of the houses, and was so footsore that she had to take off her shoes and bandage her feet with handkerchiefs before she could find a jinrikisha.

In Singapore she learned that a Chinese steamer was to sail for Malacca and was invited to go along to visit the Malay States. "I was only allowed five minutes for decision," she wrote, "but I have no difficulty in making up my mind when an escape from civilisation is possible" (*The Golden Chersonese*, pp. 108–9). The country was "practically under British rule" and was, moreover, so little known that no maps existed of the interior—just Isabella's kind of country. Armed with introductions to officials, she visited the states of the western peninsula, Sungei Ujong, Selangor, and Perak. For five weeks she enjoyed herself to the utmost—she rode elephants, got acquainted with monkeys, and regained the health she had lost in Japan's heat and dampness.

She returned home in time to benefit from the publicity following the publication of *A Lady's Life in the Rocky Mountains*. Her book on Japan was finished and was sent to her publisher, John Murray; but, while she was writing *The Golden Chersonese*, her beloved Hennie died, a victim of typhoid.

The quiet, stay-at-home Hennie had been the pivot of Isabella's far-flung circuit, and her loss was a terrible blow. Hennie's physician, Dr. John Bishop, who had been a good friend to both sisters, had as early as 1877 proposed marriage to Isabella. She could not see herself in a domestic role and had gently refused him; however, after Hennie died, Bishop renewed his proposal and was accepted. They were married in the spring of 1881. The marriage ended after only five years, when the good and gentle doctor died, another great sorrow for Isabella and, at the same time, a deliverance from ties that would keep her at home.

Whenever she had talked with her husband of traveling again, her thoughts had turned to China and the mysterious country between China and northern India. Now, wanting to memorialize her sister and her husband in the form of medical hospitals somewhere in the Far East, she planned to visit Asia again. By the summer of 1888, she was reading books about the Far East and assembling an outfit for traveling.

She went to India, where she established the Henrietta Bird Hospital in Amritsar and the John Bishop Memorial Hospital in Srinagar. She traveled for two months in Kashmir, half the time on a houseboat, half on horseback, then visited Lesser Tibet (Ladakh). She rode an Arabian horse, Gyalpo. Though he was the terror of the camp, with "no kinship with humanity," Isabella loved and trusted him. Escorted by a missionary well known to the Tibetans, she was able to visit monasteries and to learn something of the native life. Though much of the trip was hard and dangerous, she came through with no worse mishap than the loss of a horse (not Gyalpo), which drowned in crossing a rampaging river, and two broken ribs suffered when they pulled her from the flood.

Once again, chance brought Isabella to visit an unexpected region. In Simla she met Herbert Sawyer, a major in the Indian Army, who was about to go to western Persia and offered to escort her to Tehran. Although she much preferred to travel alone, Isabella was told she could not go alone to Persia, so she cheerfully accepted Sawyer's offer. It was a mistake. It was midwinter, bitterly cold. They had to take shelter in filthy caravansaries. Her guide, Hadji, was completely unreliable. Isabella suffered from cramps brought on by the severe cold. The food was abominable. They arrived at the British residency in Tehran "scarcely able to stand," and Isabella lay down in her clothes and slept until four in the morning. After a rest, they continued their journey into the Bakhtiari country. The weather turned fine, the desert was beautiful. But the major and Isabella were not entirely compatible, and she was not sorry to part company with him at Borüjerd, where Sawyer's work was finished. For the next six months, she led her own caravan, riding another favorite horse, Boy, across Kurdistan.

In Syria Isabella witnessed the results of brutal attacks by the Kurds on Armenian and Syrian peasants, and when she got back to England she spoke out about it, writing articles for the *Contemporary Review* on the atrocities. She was invited to dine with William Gladstone, who listened to her sympathetically, and she was asked to speak to a House of Commons committee on the Armenian question.

Her books had brought her much publicity, and she was lionized by society. She was made a fellow of the Royal Scottish Geographical Society and then of the Royal Geographical Society in London. She gave talks on the advancement of foreign missions, especially medical missions, for she had seen the desperate needs of the un-Christianized world. But three years at home, where she felt rootless, was enough. She was growing stout and continued to have many physical problems, but she longed to get away from social obligations, to be alone and free. She had had a peep at central Asia, but she had not yet been there. Why not combine her interest in Christian missions and her curiosity about the Asians and go back to the East?

She left for Yokohama at the beginning of 1894, armed with two cameras. She spent four months in Korea and was at first unimpressed, but after several visits its charms grew on her. She went in a sampan up the river Han to the Diamond Mountains and returned by land, riding some of the worst ponies yet encountered. In the mountains, she visited the Buddhist monks who had been exiled from the cities and, in spite of her contempt for Buddhism, she enjoyed their courtesy and gentleness, and she reveled in the beauty of the country.

Caught in the opening salvos of the Sino-Japanese war, she had to leave Korea, but soon she was in Mukden photographing Chinese troops on their way to Korea. With all the tenacity of a foreign correspondent, Isabella watched the course of events as the Japanese took over the country. She traveled north as far as Tok-Chon, where she found the country devastated by the war, and felt that Korea was hopeless and helpless, tossed about by certain great powers, whose only hope was to be taken in hand by Russia.

Since the vast expanse of China still lay unexplored, as far as Isabella was concerned, in January 1896 she set off for Shanghai, determined to travel up the Yangtze Valley as far as she could go. The trip began on a sampan, which was rowed up the river and dragged over innumerable cataracts by hordes of hard-working coolies. At Wanhsien she left the river valley and went north into Szechwan, carried in a bamboo chair. She caught sight of the mountains. "Why should I not go on, I asked myself, and see Tibetans, yaks, and aboriginal tribes, rope bridges, and colossal mountains, and break away from the narrow highways and the crowds, and curiosity, . . . of China proper?'' (*The Yangtze Valley*, II, 69).

She did go on, although officials did their best to dissuade her and she had just had the most dreadful experience in all of her travels. In Liang Shan Hsien a howling mob attacked her as a ''foreign devil.'' She managed to get into an inn, where she was put into an upper room, completely dark. The mob pursued her and tried to set the room on fire and to batter down the door. She was sitting with her revolver in her hand ready to shoot the first men who broke through, when soldiers were sent to disperse the mob and guard her through the night. In the morning, all was quiet and she went peacefully on the journey, though bruised and shaken by the experience. Afterward, Isabella carried the revolver concealed in a bag and ready to hand. She never had to use it, but she was again subjected to insults and pelted with missiles before being rescued. At Lo-Kiachan she was struck on the head by a stone, knocked insensible, and suffered a concussion. She felt ''a mortifying inclination to cry.''

In the mountains she visited the Mantze, people who shared with the Tibetans the Buddhist religion, a jolly and healthy people, where she was pleased to see that women and men were on a basis of perfect equality. She had one bad experience when the caravan was trapped in a blizzard climbing a mountain pass and all suffered from ''pass poison.'' But they recovered and she felt that the beauty of the mountains compensated for all the pain.

She forgave the Chinese for the rough treatment, though she said she could never forget the dreadful howling of the mob, and she conceded that there was ''a certain lovableness about the people.'' She recognized that China had ''an elaborate and antique civilisation which yet is not decayed, and which, though imperfect, has many claims to our respect and even admiration'' (*The Yangtze Valley*, I, 20).

She left the East for the last time in 1897, and her book on China appeared in 1900. The Boxer Rebellion subjected foreign missionaries in China to far worse treatment than she had ever received. Many of them were murdered and others were driven out of the country. English readers were much interested in Bishop's view of China.

Isabella's last expedition, to Morocco, did not result in another book; though she came back invigorated, she soon succumbed to a number of health problems and for her last years could do little but dream of travel. She died in Edinburgh on October 7, 1904.

BIBLIOGRAPHY

Works by Isabella Bird Bishop

As Isabella Bird

The Englishwoman in America. By I. B. London: Murray, 1856.
The Hawaiian Archipelago: Six Months among the Palm Groves, Coral Reefs, and

Volcanoes of the Sandwich Islands. London: Murray, 1875. Also published as *Six Months in the Sandwich Islands.* Honolulu: University of Hawaii Press, 1964. Quotations in the text are from the 1964 edition.

A Lady's Life in the Rocky Mountains. London: Murray, 1879.

Unbeaten Tracks in Japan: An Account of Travels in the Interior Including Visits to the Aborigines of the Yezo and the Shrines of Nikko and Ise. London: Murray, 1880.

The Golden Chersonese and the Way Thither. London: Murray, 1883.

As Isabella Bird Bishop

"Shadow of the Kurd." *Review of Reviews* 59 (May–June 1891): 642–54, 819–35.

Journeys in Persia and Kurdistan, Including a Summer in the Upper Karun Region and a Visit to the Nestorian Rayahs. London: Murray, 1891.

"Marriage System of Tibet." *Review of Reviews* 7 (May 1893): 471.

Among the Tibetans. New York: Revell, 1894.

Korea and Her Neighbors: A Narrative of Travel, with an Account of the Recent Vicissitudes and Present Position of the Country. New York: Revell, 1898.

"Education in China: An Elementary School." *Critic* 35 (Oct. 1899): 921–25.

"Asia's Great Need." *Missionary Review* 23 (June 1900): 426–29.

Chinese Pictures. London: Cassell, 1900.

The Yangtze Valley and Beyond: An Account of Journeys in China, Chiefly in the Province of Sze Chuan and among the Man-Tze of the Somo Territory. London: Murray, 1900.

Works about Isabella Bird Bishop

Adams, William Davenport. *Celebrated Women Travellers of the Nineteenth Century.* London: Sonnenschein, 1883.

Allen, Alexandra. *Travelling Ladies.* London: Jupiter, 1980, pp. 225–56.

Barr, Pat. *A Curious Life for a Lady: The Story of Isabella Bird, a Remarkable Victorian Traveler.* Garden City, N.Y.: Doubleday, 1970.

———. *Deer Cry Pavilion: A Story of Westerners in Japan.* New York: Harcourt, Brace & World, 1969.

Cook, Mrs. J. "Traveller and Friend of Missions." *Missionary Review* 28 (July 1905): 501–3.

Dictionary of National Biography. London: Smith, Elder, 2nd supplement, 1912, vol. I, pp. 166–68.

International Dictionary of Women's Biography. Edited by Jennifer S. Uglow and Frances Hinton. New York: Continuum, 1982.

Ladies on the Loose. Edited by Leo Hamalian. New York: Dodd, Mead, 1981, pp. 169–84.

"Life of Isabella Bird Bishop." *Blackwood's* 180 (Dec. 1906): 821–30.

Middleton, Dorothy. *Victorian Lady Travellers.* London: Routledge & Kegan Paul, 1965, pp. 19–53.

Miller, Lurie. *On Top of the World: Five Women Explorers in Tibet.* London: Paddington Press, 1976, pp. 71–99.

Pierson, A. T. "Mrs. Bishop on Protestant Missions in China." *Missionary Review* 23 (Sept. 1900): 675–79.

Rittenhouse, Mignon. *Seven Women Explorers*. Philadelphia: Lippincott, 1964, pp. 135–56.

Sprague, Marshall. *A Gallery of Dudes*. Boston: Little, Brown, 1966. The section on Bishop, "Love in the Park," also appeared in *American Heritage* 18 (Feb. 1967): 8–13, 80–85.

Stewart, A. G. "Recollections of Isabella Bishop." *Blackwood's* 176 (Nov. 1904): 698–704. Same article in *Living Age* 243 (Dec. 10, 1904): 683–87.

Stoddart, Anna M. *The Life of Isabella Bird (Mrs. Bishop) Hon. Member of the Oriental Society of London*. London: Murray, 1906.

Tabor, Margaret. *Pioneer Women*. Third series. London: Sheldon Press, 1930, pp. 35–64.

This Grand Beyond: Travels of Isabella Bird Bishop. Edited by Cicely Palser Haveley. London: Century, 1984.

Van Thal, Herbert. *Victoria's Subjects Travelled*. London: Barker, 1951, pp. 34–47.

Williams, Constance. *The Adventures of a Lady Traveller*. London: Sunday School Union, 1909.

Obituaries appeared in the London *Times*, on Oct. 10, 1904, and in the *Geographical Journal* 24 (July–Dec. 1904): 596.

LADY ANNE BLUNT
1837–1917

Lady Anne Blunt was the granddaughter of Lord Byron, the poet, and the wife of Wilfrid Scawen Blunt, poet, traveler, and diplomat. Shortly after their marriage in 1869, Wilfrid resigned from the diplomatic service, and in the following years the couple traveled much in the eastern Mediterranean region. In the winter of 1877–1878 and again in 1879–1880, they visited the Bedouin tribes of Arabia.

Circumstances obliged them to travel at times without escorts or interpreters, relying on guides provided by their native hosts. They wore Bedouin cloaks and turbans, rode camels or mares, and partook of the hospitality of the desert dwellers. They made friends with the Bedouins, sympathized with them, and grew attached to many.

Lady Anne was the scribe of their travels; she produced two books of graphic description, illustrated with her own excellent sketches, of life among the nomads of Arabia. She was a plucky, jolly person, an excellent companion on journeys that were often hard and dangerous.

Particularly fascinated by, as well as knowledgeable about, Arabian horses, the Blunts brought back from their travels the first of what became a noted stud, named, from their English country home, the Crabbet Stud.

Lady Anne Isabella Noel was born on September 22, 1837, the daughter of the first earl of Lovelace and the Honorable Ada Augusta Byron, who was Lord Byron's daughter by Baroness Wentworth. She grew up in wealth and comfort, and she is described as having "lots of brains." Lady Anne and her husband Wilfrid had a son, who lived but four days, and then a daughter. Three years after their marriage, Wilfrid succeeded to his brother's estates at Crabbet Park, Sussex, and then they began to travel.

Their 1877–1878 trip took them from the port of Alexandretta to Deir, thence down the Euphrates to Baghdad, and back again across the desert. It is described in her first book, *Bedouin Tribes of the Euphrates*, which was based on Wilfrid's diaries and notes. The Blunts knew something of the East from previous trips and knew some Arabic when they chose the Euphrates valley and Mesopotamia as the objects of the journey. At the Royal Geographical Society, they could find no detailed maps later than 1836. In addition to a paucity of information, there was much misinformation about the danger of plague and the possibilities of getting lost in a vast, uninhabited, unfriendly desert.

It was a time of political confusion, when the country was under Turkish rule, but the Turks, engaged in a Bulgarian war, had little control over the Bedouins. War between the desert tribes was part of their way of life, and authorities, unable to protect travelers, tried to discourage them by tales of brigandage. But Lady Anne and Wilfrid, as determined as they were courageous, were bent on seeing Arabia and those who lived there.

At the beginning of the trip, they thought themselves unlucky to be held up by heavy rains for a month at Aleppo; however, their host, the British consul Skene, had had many years of experience of Eastern life. "In him we found at last an intelligent sympathizer with our love of adventure, which the rest of our world had been at such pains to discourage; and we owe it to him that our vague scheme of spending the winter in the neighborhood of Bagdad took definite shape." He told them much about Bedouin life and manners, "things at which we had hitherto looked with the half-contemptuous ignorance with which the European world regards them, but which we now found set before us under a new and fascinating light" (*Bedouin Tribes*, pp. 36–37).

The left bank of the Euphrates, they were told, was controlled by the Shammar Bedouins, who exacted tribute from the tribes of Mesopotamia; the right bank, by the Anezeh, who held the whole of the Syrian desert. These two great tribes were constantly at war, and travelers could get caught in the cross fire of raiding parties. Many tributary shepherd tribes lived peaceably in the desert. Skene was on good terms with the Anezeh and could give them letters of introduction to the sheiks. The Blunts wished to join the Anezeh in their annual migration toward the Nejd in central Arabia.

They had a tent made in accordance with Lady Anne's design, bought horses, hired a cook and other servants, and laid in provisions. Hanna, the cook, was a fat Syrian Christian who proved to be an excellent servant; he delighted in the preparation of the fowl brought down by Wilfrid's gun and the huge truffles found in the desert. Not for the Blunts were the tables and chairs, white table-cloths, rubber bathtubs, and impedimenta with which other English travelers loaded their camels. They slept on the ground, with an oilskin, a carpet, and a quilt underneath, an eiderdown, another carpet and oilskin on top. They ate sitting on the ground, using their fingers, sometimes sharing a common dish with the Bedouins, and apparently refused none of the foods offered them, including roasted grasshoppers and hyena meat.

Their eastward journey began on January 9. During the next month, they met with plenty of adventure and some hardship. They arrived in Baghdad in a rainstorm, after slipping about in the mud of the river bank. "At last the City of the Caliphs loomed through the driving rain," wrote Lady Anne, "a grimy and squalid line of mud houses rising out of a sea of mud. Even the palm groves looked draggled, and the Tigris had that hopeless look a river puts on in the rain" (*Bedouin Tribes*, p. 140). They were made welcome at the British residency, where they changed into dry clothes and were served a pleasing dinner at a table spread with a cloth and decked with knives and forks, flowers, and fruit.

In spite of such civilized pleasures, they did not much care for the city and "our first thought, on arriving at Bagdad, was how to get out of it" (*Bedouin Tribes*, p. 149). They explained to the resident that they were not traveling to amuse themselves or to see the sights—they cared little for the archeological remains of ancient civilization—but to get introductions to the Shammar. He suggested that they deal with the Turkish officials, but after reflection Wilfrid decided to bypass the pasha, for they had been held up interminably at Deir by a pasha determined to keep them out of the desert. Instead, they planned to slip away, without asking leave of any authorities, and head north toward Mosul in search of the Shammar people and their sheik, Faris.

"We are starting," wrote Lady Anne, "rather like babes in the wood, on an adventure whose importance we are unable to rate," toward an unknown country where there were no towns, no markets, no guard houses (*Bedouin Tribes*, p. 157).

She and Wilfrid had a serious talk about what they were to do in case of a *ghazu*, a tribal raiding party. They were well armed and thought their small caravan could resist as many as fifteen or twenty men. If they met a larger party, it would be useless to resist, and "if they refuse to listen to terms of capitulation, we shall have to abandon the camels and baggage to their fate, and trust to our mares to carry us out of the difficulty. . . . the Arabs only care about plunder, and the utmost misfortune that could happen to us, if captured, would be to be stripped of some of our clothes, and left to find our way on foot to the nearest inhabited place—not a cheerful prospect, certainly, but still not altogether desperate" (*Bedouin Tribes*, pp. 165–66).

They did not run into any *ghazus*—at least not for some time—and they did find the camps of the Shammar. The Blunts were rather shy on their first visit to a Bedouin sheik, but Skene had told them the etiquette of an Arab reception. They entered the largest tent, and Wilfrid said loudly, "*Salaam aleykoum*," to which everyone answered in the same loud voice. The tribesmen, who had very likely never seen a European, rose to their feet, spread carpets, and brought camel saddles—the only furniture found in most tents—and talked for about half an hour, by which time the Blunts' guide had pitched their own tent nearby.

Each tribe knew the probable whereabouts of others, and most of them provided escorts for at least part of the way when they were told what the travelers wanted. Thus the Blunts were passed from one camp to another and finally found the man they sought. On March 14, Lady Anne wrote: "We are with Faris. I write it with some pride, when I think how many 'impossibilities' once stood in our way" (Bedouin Tribes, p. 226).

Faris, the sheik, had been expecting them; news travels in the desert. He greeted them and offered the hospitality of his tent. Anne thought him most attractive and said "I think we have at last found that thing we have been looking for, but hardly hoped to get a sight of, a gentleman of the desert" (Bedouin Tribes, p. 228). Their first impressions of the sheik were reinforced during their few days with Faris, and before they parted he and Wilfrid swore eternal brotherhood with "an oath as impressive as those of our marriage-service, and considered quite as binding by those who take it" (Bedouin Tribes, p. 237).

The travelers were obliged to leave the Shammar, in spite of invitations to remain forever if they liked, for they had agreed to meet Skene by a certain date at Deir. When they arrived in Deir, however, the consul was not there, and nobody knew where he was or when he would return. As he had been expected to help them reach the Anezeh, far to the south, the Blunts waited for some days. Again, the Turkish official tried to scare them with tales of robbers, waterless wastes, and so forth, but, as Lady Anne observed, they had never yet been prevented from going where they had a mind to. By a stroke of good fortune, they met a young man from Tadmor, "a very fine-looking young fellow, with an outspoken manner which impressed us favorably" (Bedouin Tribes, p. 262). He was returning to his home and could guide them that far. He was Mohammed Ibn Aruk, son of the sheik of Tadmor, of a family descended from the prophet Taleb, originally from a village in Nejd. He was planning to go there the following year in search of a wife from his own people.

In the end, Mohammed accompanied them not only to Tadmor but all the way across the western plain to the tents of the Anezeh. The missing consul caught up with them on the way, bringing with him two fine mares, one a chestnut they had purchased at Deir, the other a white mare which Skene had purchased for them. Anne was very pleased with the white mare and described her as having "the most extraordinarily beautiful head ever seen, with the sweetest of tempers" (Bedouin Tribes, pp. 287–98). The two horses were later brought home to England as part of the Crabbet Stud.

The Blunts visited numerous tribes, some wealthy (in terms of their camels, sheep, and horses); others poor, but all hospitable. They found Jedaan, head of the Anezeh. Wilfrid and Mohammed swore eternal brotherhood, and Mohammed promised to go with them the following year to the Nejd. On April 16, they came to the end of their journey at Damascus, where they were dismayed by the rude behavior and attitude of visiting English couples. "We were not prepared for the vast change a winter spent among the Arabs would make in our tastes, our prejudices, and our opinions" (Bedouin Tribes, p. 359).

They were in England for a few months and at the approach of winter set off on the proposed visit to the Nejd, which was the name given to the whole of central Arabia. Lady Anne's account of this trip was entitled A Pilgrimage to

Nejd, the Cradle of the Arab Race. According to Wilfrid, the Nejd was to the Arabs "what Palestine is the the Jews, England to the American and Australian colonists." Anne regarded the project as "an almost pious undertaking" (*A Pilgrimage*, p. x).

They faced a thousand-mile journey. The first station was to be Jauf, four hundred miles away from Damascus, where Mohammed hoped to find relatives and acquire a suitable bride. Then they would cross the Nefud, two hundred miles of a red sand desert, to reach Jebel Shammar, the metropolis of the Arab race, and Hail, the home of the Emir Mohammed Ibn Rashid.

Mohammed of Tadmor did not know the way, nor did anyone else in Damascus; again, they went from tribe to tribe, asking directions and hiring new guides and servants from time to time. The faithful Hanna was again with them as cook, and Anne rode the white mare, Sherifa. Of course, she rode sidesaddle.

Lady Anne had the misfortune to wrench her knee, but, whereas a lesser woman would have turned back or at least rested until it was better, she rode on. Soon they had a disagreeable adventure. They had felt so comfortable among the desert dwellers that they had relaxed their guard. They were resting some way from their caravan when horsemen rode up. Wilfrid, who recognized that they were under attack, hastily mounted his horse, but Anne was hampered by her injury and the deep sand. She was knocked down by a spear, and Wilfrid was struck with Anne's unloaded gun, which a horseman had grabbed. He struck Wilfrid's head with such force that the stock was broken. Fortunately, he had on heavy clothes and a turban bound with thick rope, which saved him from serious injury.

Anne cried out, "I am under your protection," the usual form of surrender, and Wilfrid dismounted. The attacking party, amazed that their captives were Europeans and that one was a woman, agreed to accompany them to their caravan, not far away, and it soon developed that the horsemen were from a friendly tribe, and all was peaceful. "Arabs are always good-humored, whatever else their faults, and presently we were all on very good terms, sitting in a circle on the sand, eating dates and passing round the pipe of peace. They were now our guests" (*A Pilgrimage*, I, 103–5).

After the party had crossed the Nefud, they began to hear tales that made them somewhat anxious about their possible reception at Hail, for the residents were of a tribe unfriendly toward Christians. "No European nor Christian of any sort had penetrated as such before us to Jebel Shammar." Ibn Rashid, for all they knew, might be ill-disposed toward them, and without his protection they ran a risk in entering Hail (*A Pilgrimage*, I, 193). "We intend to tell Ibn Rashid that we are persons of distinction in search of other persons of distinction" and then produce presents and wish him a long life (*A Pilgrimage*, I, 205). They were so enchanted with the desert and the Jebel Shammar that "Wilfrid declares that he shall die happy now, even if we have our heads cut off at Hail" (*A Pilgrimage*, I, 208).

They were well received, provided with a house, and shown the emir's mares.

"I was almost too excited to look, for it was principally to see these that we had come so far" wrote Anne (*A Pilgrimage*, I, 225). She visited the harem, where she found the women to be uninteresting. "They have no idea of amusement, if I may judge from what they said to me, but a firm conviction that perfect happiness and dignity consist in sitting still" (*A Pilgrimage*, I, 232–33).

After several days of hospitality at Hail, the visitors sensed a "mystification." On their fifth day, they were not invited to the evening meal; the presents of game ceased, and they were given camel meat instead of lamb; the soldier escorts were replaced by a slave boy. They discovered that young Mohammed's head had been turned by the handsome reception given him as an Ibn Aruk by the emir, and he had somehow given the impression that he had taken the Blunts under his protection, that the camels and horses of the caravan were his property, the servants his people. Casting the Europeans thus in a secondary role made the Blunts' relations with the emir not only embarrassing, but positively dangerous. When they got to the truth of the matter, explanations were made to the court, and friendly relations were resumed, but the rapport between Wilfrid and his blood brother was disturbed. To Anne, "the incident was a lesson, and a warning, a lesson that we were Europeans still among Asiatics, a warning that Hail was a lion's den, though fortunately we were friends with the lion. We began to make our plans for moving on" (*A Pilgrimage*, II, 21).

A large group of Persians who had made a pilgrimage to Medina was encamped just outside the walls of Hail waiting to continue their journey to their homeland. The Blunts joined them for safety on the road to Meshed. Mohammed had told them how three branches of his family had settled, during the eighteenth century, in different parts of the desert; they had long ago lost all contact with each other. At Jauf he had been successful in finding relatives and also an attractive young woman who agreed to become his wife. He planned to return the following year to claim her. The sheik of the lost third branch of the family heard that a relative was visiting Hail and sent out a party to find him. The Blunt caravan by chance met this party in the desert as they went toward Meshed, and they changed their plans to pay a visit to Mohammed's new-found relatives. When they rejoined the pilgrims, they found them very short of food. The Blunts were better provided for but had little food for the camels.

The last part of the journey was very difficult; when they reached Meshed, they were at the end of their money, strength, and patience. They refitted for the journey to Baghdad, where, "by a strange fatality we arrived once more in floods of rain, and where, again, we were welcomed in the hospitable four walls of the Residency" (*A Pilgrimage*, II, 106).

"Here, if we had been wise," added Lady Anne, "our winter's adventures would have ended too." But they were persuaded to continue by land to India, where Wilfrid had agreed to make a report on the feasibility of building a railroad from Tigris to the Persian Gulf. They had difficulties from the beginning in getting servants, and much of the trip was sheer misery. They suffered from rain, sandstorms, illness, treachery, and blackmail, and, for the last part of the journey, they had almost no help in loading the camels. They ended the month's weary journey at Bushire. "When we arrived at the door of the Residency, the well-dressed Sepoys in their smart European uniforms . . . refused to believe that such vagabonds, blackened with the sun, and grimed with long sleeping on the ground, were English gentlefolks" (*A Pilgrimage*, II, 232).

Lady Anne told her brother that Wilfrid would never go any land journey again. He did travel again, but never in caravan.

The couple bought a forty-acre garden near Cairo which contained the shrine of a local saint, Sheik Obeyd. Here they spent the winters, dressed in Bedouin robes, gardening and working together on the translation and versification of Arabic literature. Wilfrid's experiences in the Arab world and in India had a profound influence on his attitude toward imperialism; he became an outspoken critic of England's colonizing, which he thought not only mistaken but a grave danger for the future. So obsessed was he with this topic that he alienated many of his friends.

Lady Anne and Wilfrid also began to feel tension, and they separated in 1906 when Wilfrid left Sheik Obeyd forever. The Blunts were reconciled later but were not reunited until just two years before Lady Anne's death. She died at Sheik Obeyd on December 15, 1917, within months of succeeding to the barony of Wentworth. In addition to her two travel books and some fine watercolors, she left careful records and paintings of the horses in the Crabbet Arabian Stud, which she and Wilfrid owned jointly.

BIBLIOGRAPHY

Works by Lady Anne Blunt

Bedouin Tribes of the Euphrates. London: Cass, 1879; New York: Harper, 1879.
A Pilgrimage to Nejd, the Cradle of the Arab Race. London: Murray, 1881. Reprinted, London: Cass, 1968. Quotations in the text are from the 1968 edition.

Works about Lady Anne Blunt

Assad, Thomas J. *Three Victorian Travellers: Burton, Blunt, Doughty*. London: Routledge & Kegan Paul, 1964.
Dictionary of National Biography, 1922–1930. London: Oxford University Press, 1937, pp. 84–86 (under "Wilfrid Scawen Blunt").
Freeth, Zahra, and H. V. F. Winstone. *Explorers of Arabia*. New York: Holmes & Meier, 1978, pp. 269–89.
International Dictionary of Women's Biography. Edited by Jennifer S. Uglow and Frances Hinton. New York: Continuum, 1982.
Ladies on the Loose: Women Travellers of the 18th and 19th Centuries. Edited by Leo Hamalian. New York: Dodd, Mead, 1981, pp. 134–45.
Longford, Elizabeth. *A Pilgrimage of Passion: The Life of Wilfrid Scawen Blunt*. London:

Wiedenfeld and Nicolson, 1979. Reviewed in *Geographical Journal* 146 (July 1980): 304–5.

Upton, Peter, *Desert Heritage: An Artist's Collection of Blunt's Original Arab Horses.* London: Skilton & Shaw, 1980.

Van Thal, Herbert. *Victoria's Subjects Travelled.* London: A. Barker, 1951, pp. 48–54.

MARGARET BOURKE-WHITE
1904-1971

Margaret Bourke-White was a world-class photographer who traveled around the world on journalistic assignments. She went to Russia to record on film the great industrial construction that began the Five-Year Plan. She traveled in Europe before World War II, and she was in Moscow when the Nazi invasion began. She covered the events of the war in Africa, Italy, and Germany. During the collapse of imperial rule in India, she was in the Punjab, where she photographed Mahatma Gandhi. She returned later to cover the great, tragic migration of Moslems and Hindus after the partition of Pakistan. She visited South Africa and ever afterward hated diamonds and gold, equating them with the exploitation of black people. She covered guerrilla warfare in Korea.

In America, she photographed the ravages of the great drought in 1934 and the Dust Bowl refugees, and with Erskine Caldwell she wrote about poverty in the rural South. Wherever there was a great human upheaval during the 1930s through the 1950s, she was there.

She contributed the cover and the lead article in the first issue of *Life*, on November 23, 1936, and for some twenty years was one of the magazine's prime photojournalists. Her travels, recorded in pictures, articles, and books, gave the public graphic information about world events. She worked during the first years of the great pictorial magazines, *Fortune*, *Life*, and *Look*, before television provided world news. It was a time when readers were hungry for information about what was happening worldwide, a time of expanding knowledge and increased understanding, as well as increased friction, between the peoples of different countries. Bourke-White has been called a mirror of her times.

Margaret Bourke-White took the first part of her hyphenated name from her mother, Minnie Bourke, and the second from her father, Joseph White. She was their second child, born on June 14, 1904, in New York City. She was quite young when the family moved to Bound Brook, New Jersey, where she spent her childhood. Her father, whom she admired greatly, introduced her to the world of machines, specifically printing presses, which occupied his time and mind almost to the exclusion of everything else. He was also an amateur photographer, which perhaps influenced Margaret's choice of a career. Her mother taught her to be fearless and to work hard. Together, they fostered her interest in natural history.

Margaret entered Columbia University in 1921, where she planned to study herpetology. By the time she had graduated from Cornell University, however, she had decided to be a photojournalist. She started by concentrating on machines and industrial buildings in Cleveland and Detroit. Her striking series picturing steel mills was so impressive that Henry Luce offered her a job on *Fortune* at its inception in 1930. When Luce founded *Life* six years later, she worked for both magazines.

Fortune offered her the first opportunity to combine photography with travel abroad when the magazine sent her to Germany in 1930 to photograph German industry. She knew that American engineering firms were being hired to build the dams and mills Russia needed to change overnight from an agricultural to an industrial economy. No foreign photographer had been allowed to document this great change, and Margaret wanted to be the first. She expanded her trip to include Russia. It took weeks to get a visa, and once in the country there were endless bureaucratic delays. She finally reached the industrial centers and took monumental pictures of the new industries, including the construction of Dnieper Dam. She found that her fascination with machinery was shared by the Russians. She knew little about politics, but she loved the people and sympathized with their great hopes for the future. Her first book, *Eyes on Russia*, celebrated the energy and enthusiasm of the workers, but it was mainly a story of industry and machines—tractors, dams, and power. "Machine worship was everywhere," she wrote. The Russians "looked on the coming machine as their Saviour; it was the instrument of deliverance" (*Portrait of Myself*, p. 95).

An assignment to cover the 1934 drought and its victims in the American midwest caused Margaret to view humanity from a new viewpoint. She had never seen "people caught helpless like this in total tragedy." It jolted her "into the realization that a man is more than a figure to put into the background of a photograph" (*Portrait of Myself*, p. 134). She began to watch for the impact of events on human beings.

She wanted to combine her pictures with the words of a writer who could portray America as it really was. By good fortune, she was able to work with the great southern writer, Erskine Caldwell. They drove an automobile through the South, photographing sharecroppers and their bare cabins, a poor church where evangelists stirred impoverished whites into emotional frenzy, a chain gang doing road work. The book she and Caldwell produced, *You Have Seen Their Faces*, made publishing history. Its strong portrayal of an almost unknown segment of American life had an impact on the public's conception of tenant farming and in time influenced legislation.

Margaret and Erskine went to Czechoslovakia in 1938 and wrote a book together, *North of the Danube*, on the people of its small villages, recently freed from serfdom and tragically soon to be overrun by the Nazis.

In 1939, Margaret married Caldwell. He had pursued her whenever they had been apart during those two years with telegrams addressed to Honeychile or Child Bride; the courtship had been followed with great interest by the entire press. She resisted marriage, partly because an earlier marriage during her college days had caused so much emotional distress, but mainly because she felt that her life was so full of change, stress, and excitement that she needed to have an inner core of tranquility. Having to consider the needs and feelings of another person all the time, she feared, would destroy that inner peace and take away her freedom. But Caldwell and the public thought she ought to marry, and they prevailed. The couple bought a home in Darien, Connecticut. They collaborated on another book, *Say, Is This the U.S.A.*, a report on the state of America, which was published in 1941.

The Caldwells were in Russia that year. Germany broke the nonaggression pact and invaded Russia. Margaret photographed falling bombs from her hotel balcony in Moscow. Erskine broadcast the news live to American radio. After they returned to the United States, where both had lecture tours booked, they went off in different directions. When America entered the war, Margaret volunteered her services and was accredited to the Air Force as a correspondent. Erskine went to Hollywood. The marriage ended in divorce.

Margaret covered the war in uniform, always in the most dangerous spots she could get into. On her way to North Africa, when her ship was sunk, she spent almost a day in a crowded lifeboat, tossed about on a rough sea, before being rescued by a destroyer. She was allowed to go on a bombing mission over the Tunis airfield, taking pictures as the bombs hit, driving the German forces out. She never thought of the expedition as a mission of death. "The impersonality of modern war has become stupendous, grotesque," she wrote later. It was dangerous, but that thought, too, was pushed into the back of her head (*Portrait of Myself*, p. 226).

In Italy she was with the troops in Cassino, photographing artillery barrages and staying in a fourteenth-century monastery with some fifty monks and some combat engineers. Often the only correspondent present at some crisis, Margaret sent memorable combat pictures to *Life* and the American public. At the end of the war, she was with the first Allied troops to enter Buchenwald. "I saw and photographed the piles of naked, lifeless bodies, the human skeletons in furnaces, the living skeletons." Her camera seemed a frail barrier between her and the horror in front of her (*Portrait of Myself*, pp. 258–59).

Her major assignment after the war was in India. She met and photographed Gandhi and traveled with him. Her most difficult pictures were of the Moslem massacre of Hindus in Calcutta, shots of dead bodies with vultures feeding on them. It was a horrid sight, the ultimate result, she thought, of racial and religious prejudice. She returned to India when Gandhi was assassinated, and she photographed his funeral. She schooled herself to draw a veil over her feelings while she worked. Her pictures of the endless flow of refugees, some fleeing, some entering Pakistan, are unforgettable.

At home, she settled into her Connecticut hillside and wrote of India. Her writing had become more and more important to her. It gave her a chance to sort out the impressions that came crowding in while on the road, a period of quiet to make sense of the events in which she had been involved. She was at the height of her professional career, financially and emotionally secure. A very attractive woman, she had many friends and a number of devoted lovers.

In 1950 she went to the Union of South Africa to do a photo essay on its people and its problems. She went into a gold mine and brought back wonderful shots of the miners deep in the tunnels, but she had suffered great distress from the heat and she knew the miners were exposed to the heat and poor air every day. When they were released from the mine, the black workers slept in concrete barracks, locked in at night. Margaret hated the terrible injustice of the pass system. Then she went down into a diamond mine, in a bucket lowered by cables, and for some frightening minutes dangled twenty-five feet below the surface when the machine jammed. She saw vineyards where little children worked, being paid in wine! It made her as angry as she had ever been. Except for a chapter in her autobiography, she could not bring herself to write about her experiences in that unhappy state.

Margaret had always had such perfect coordination that she was able to walk on steel beams far above ground and to perch on high places to get her incredible shots. In 1951, however, she experienced the first signs of a curious malady, a loss of muscular control which made her stumble and interfered with her camera work. The condition was diagnosed as Parkinson's Disease, a brain malfunction which is progressive and irreversible. Two operations and much physical therapy helped somewhat. She herself was news as her long, brave fight against the disabilities of her disease became known. In 1969 the medication L-Dopa was available for the first time, but it was too late for her. She died on August 27, 1971, in a hospital in Stamford, Connecticut.

BIBLIOGRAPHY

Works by Margaret Bourke-White

Eyes on Russia. New York: Simon & Schuster, 1931.

"Silk Stockings in the Five–Year Plan." *New York Times Magazine*, Feb. 14, 1932, p. 4.

"Making Communists of Soviet Children." *New York Times Magazine*, Mar. 6, 1932, pp. 4–5.

"Russian Audiences." *New York Times Magazine*, Mar. 13, 1932, pp. 8–9.

"Where the Worker Can Drop the Boss." *New York Times Magazine*, Mar. 27, 1932, pp. 8, 23.

"A Day's Work for the Five–Year Plan." *New York Times Magazine*, May 22, 1932, pp. 8–9.

"A Day in a Remote Village of Russia." *New York Times Magazine*, Sept. 11, 1932, pp. 7, 16.
"Dust Changes America." *Nation* 140 (May 22, 1935): 597–98.
"Photographing This World." *Nation* 142 (Feb. 19, 1936): 217–18.
(With Erskine Caldwell) *You Have Seen Their Faces*. New York: Viking, 1937.
————. *North of the Danube*. New York: Viking, 1939.
————. *Say, Is This the U.S.A.* New York: Duell, Sloan & Pearce, 1941.
"Moscow a Week before the Nazi Invasion Began." *Life* 11 (Aug. 11, 1941): 17–27.
"Moscow Fights off the Nazi Bombers and Prepares for a Long War." *Life* 11 (Sept. 1, 1941): 15–21.
"How I Photographed Stalin and Hopkins in the Kremlin." *Life* 11 (Sept. 8, 1941): 25–29.
"Muscovites Take up Their Guns as Nazi Horde Approaches Russian Capital." *Life* 11 (Oct. 27, 1941): 27–33.
"A Trip to the Front." *Life* 11 (Nov. 17, 1941): 33–39.
"Photographer in Moscow." *Harper* 184 (Mar. 1942): 414–20.
Shooting the Russian War. New York: Simon & Schuster, 1942.
"Women in Lifeboats." *Life* 14 (Feb. 22, 1943): 48–50+.
They Called It "Purple Heart Valley": A Combat Chronicle of the War in Italy. New York: Simon & Schuster, 1944.
"India's Leaders." *Life* 20 (May 27, 1946): 101–107.
"Dear Fatherland, Rest Quietly": A Report on the Collapse of Hitler's "Thousand Years." New York: Simon & Schuster, 1946.
Halfway to Freedom: A Report on the New India. New York: Simon & Schuster, 1949.
"Shooting from a Whirlybird." *Life* 32 (Aug. 14, 1952): 140.
"Savage Secret War in Korea." *Life* 33 (Dec. 1, 1952): 25–35.
"Tomorrow's Inland Seaports." *Fortune* 52 (Aug. 1955): 92–101.
"Majestic Migration." *Life* 40 (Apr. 30, 1956): 10–11.
(With John La Farge) *A Report on the American Jesuits*. New York: Farrar, Straus & Cudahy, 1956.
"The Best Advice I Ever Had." *Reader's Digest* (June 1957): 60–62.
Portrait of Myself. New York: Simon & Schuster, 1963.
The Taste of War. Edited by Jonathan Silverman. London: Century, 1985. Contains her *Shooting the Russian War*, *"Dear Fatherland,"* and *They Called It "Purple Heart Valley."*

Works about Margaret Bourke-White

"Bourke-White's Twenty-Five Years." *Life* 38 (May 16, 1955): 16–18.
"Brave Story Retold: Bourke-White's Ordeal Makes a TV Play." *Life* 48 (Jan. 11, 1960): 78–79.
Brown, Theodore. *Margaret Bourke-White, Photojournalist*. Ithaca, N.Y.: Cornell University, Andrew D. White Museum of Art, 1972.
Contemporary Authors. Detroit: Gale Research, 1922-date, permanent series 1: 76–77.
Crotty, Elizabeth Ann. "Margaret Bourke-White as Seen from the Perspective of Selected Photographs, Writings, and Associates." Master's thesis, Syracuse University, 1978.
Current Biography. New York: H. W. Wilson, 1940–date, annual vols. 1940, 1971.

Fanizzi, Ken. "Margaret Bourke-White, Chronicler of History." News workshop. New York University, Department of Journalism, n.d.

Goldberg, Vicki. *Margaret Bourke-White: A Biography*. New York: Harper & Row, 1986. Based on interviews and exhaustive research.

Hancock, Elise. "Margaret Bourke-White (1904–1971)." *Cornell Alumni News*, Apr. 1972.

Liberty's Women. Edited by Robert McHenry. Springfield, Mass.: Merriam, 1980.

"Life's Bourke-White Goes Bombing, Photographs U.S. Air Force Attack on Tunisia." *Life* 14 (Mar. 1, 1943): 17–23.

Midcap, Lucille Scott. "Margaret Bourke-White, the Photojournalist and the Woman." Master's thesis, University of Florida, 1976.

Mydans, Carl. "Unforgettable Margaret Bourke-White." *Reader's Digest* 101 (Aug. 1972): 69–74.

Sherburne, E. C. "Lady Not-in-a-Rut." *Christian Science Monitor* (May 29, 1943): 5.

Siegel, Beatrice. *An Eye on the World: Margaret Bourke-White, Photographer*. New York: F. Warne, 1980.

Silverman, Jonathan. *For the World to See: The Life of Margaret Bourke-White*. New York: Viking, 1982.

Webster, E. R. "Tells the Story of Our Times in Photographs." *Independent Woman* 34 (Mar. 1955): 85–87.

An obituary was published in the *New York Times* on Aug. 28, 1971.

Bourke-White manuscripts are located in the George Arents Research Library, Syracuse University, and in the archives of *Time*.

LOUISE ARNER BOYD
1887–1972

Louise Arner Boyd planned, headed, and financed seven expeditions into the Arctic regions. Her fascination with the icebound world began as the hobby of a wealthy, socially prominent San Francisco suburbanite and progressed to serious scientific explorations sponsored by the American Geographical Society. As a woman and a nonscientist, her entrance into the world of Arctic exploration was depreciated by specialists, but in the end her contributions were widely acknowledged.

During World War II, Boyd's photographs, oceanographic surveys, and charts of the Greenland-Spitsbergen area were of inestimable value to the United States, and she was requested to hold off publication of her findings, which might have given the Germans an advantage, until after the war.

A portion of Greenland is named Louise Boyd Land. She was honored by the scientific community, by the governments of several countries, and by universities. She was a valued member of the Society of Woman Geographers. At the age of sixty-eight, she was the first woman to fly over the North Pole, in a plane chartered by the Louise A. Boyd North Pole Expedition.

In San Rafael, California, just north of San Francisco, the beautiful home of Louise Boyd, Maple Lawn, still stands, surrounded by spacious grounds. It was built in the 1850s by Louise's maternal great-grandfather, Ira Cook, who amassed a tidy fortune during the California Gold Rush. It is now the home of an Elks Club lodge. Next to it is Boyd Park, a large area given to the city of San Rafael in memory of Louise's two brothers, who died when they were in their teens. Around the corner is the former carriage house, now the office and museum of the Marin County Historical Society. Louise was born here on September 16, 1887, to John Franklin and Louise Cook Arner Boyd.

Her brothers, John Franklin, Jr., and Seth Cook, suffered from rheumatic fever; the latter died in 1901; the former in 1902. Their parents, too, were in poor health. Louise alone of the family seemed strong and healthy. In spite of the aura of illness in the household, she managed to live an outdoor life, learning to ride and shoot at the family ranch near Danville, California. She was educated at private schools, made her debut in 1907, and was active in Bay Area social life. In 1910 she and her parents traveled for a year in Europe and Egypt. In the 1918 influenza epidemic, Louise helped nurse patients, beginning a lifelong interest in the work of the Red Cross. Her father died in 1920, just a year after the death of his wife, leaving Louise mistress of the estate and heir to the family wealth.

She succeeded her father as head of the Boyd Investment Company of San Francisco. Soon after his death, she visited France and Belgium, touring in a chauffeured motor car with a woman companion. Four years later, she chose a less traveled part of the world to visit, and from the deck of a Norwegian tourist vessel she glimpsed for the first time the Arctic regions, a sight that was to determine her future. "Some day," she remarked, "I want to be way in there looking out instead of looking in" (San Francisco *Independent-Journal*, Aug. 22, 1959).

In her first book, *The Fiord Region of East Greenland* (1935), Louise describes the thrill of the Arctic:

> Far north, hidden behind grim barriers of pack ice, are lands that hold one spell-bound. Gigantic imaginary gates, with hinges set in the horizon, seem to guard these lands. Slowly the gates swing open, and one enters another world where men are insignificant amid the awesome immensity of lonely mountains, fiords, and glaciers. (*The Fiord Region*, p. 1)

She collected maps and photographic equipment, and she invited a few friends to go with her to Franz Josef Land in the summer of 1926, having taken some training from Francis de Gisbert, an expert on the polar regions. She chartered a Norwegian sealer, the *Hobby*, which had just returned from a voyage to Spitsbergen with supplies for the explorers Roald Amundsen and Lincoln Ellsworth. As it was being refitted for Boyd, the captain remarked, "Some American woman wants to see ice" (*New York Times Magazine*, May 1, 1938).

The *San Francisco Chronicle*, which kept the Bay Area au courant with Miss Boyd's social activities, reported her presentation to England's King George and Queen Mary in June 1925, and a year later, on July 31, 1926, it noted the trip to Franz Josef Land. Under the headline "San Francisco Woman in Arctic Hunt," it remarked that the expedition "will hunt polar bears, sea horses and other Arctic animals." When Boyd returned, she brought the skins of eleven polar bears and three seals (the "sea horses") and said that hunting polar bears was "one of the most interesting sports I have ever engaged in" (*San Francisco Chronicle*, Nov. 21, 1926). She took thousands of feet of film and about seven hundred photographs. The only hint of scientific interest was her description of the flowers growing in sheltered spots. She was quoted as saying "I have got the Arctic lure and will certainly go north again" (*San Francisco Chronicle*, Sept. 2, 1926).

Two years later she did go again, chartering the same ship and planning more hunting. When she arrived in Norway, she learned that Amundsen, who had been searching for a group of Italian explorers lost in the polar ice with Umberto Nobile, was himself missing. She offered her ship, crew, and supplies to the government of Norway to take part in the rescue mission, along with other ships. Placed aboard with her were Captain Rieser Larsen, who had flown with Amundsen to Alaska; Captain Lutzow Holm, considered the best flier in Norway; Lieutenant Finn Lambrecht; and three petty officers who were mechanics for the two planes crowding the decks.

In spite of the grim mission in which they were enlisted, letters from Boyd speak of being supremely happy. For the first time, she was in the presence of "real" polar explorers, who seemed to accept her almost as an equal. She met the Swedish expedition and talked with survivors of the Nobile expedition. The *Hobby* traversed approximately ten thousand miles along the west coast of Spitsbergen as well as westward into the Greenland Sea and eastward to Franz Josef Land. Unsuccessful, the search was finally called off after four months.

Although Amundsen was not found, Boyd was honored for her part in the search by King Haakon of Norway, who presented her with the Chevalier Cross of the Order of St. Olav. She was the first woman not of Norway to be given the award. The French government gave her the Cross of the Legion of Honor. But the reward of most import to Louise was the companionship of fellow explorers. Their talk of polar expeditions in search of scientific data fired her enthusiasm for more than taking pictures and shooting bears.

Her plans for a third expedition, to be made in 1931, took a more serious bent. She felt an obligation to make her trips less recreational and more scientific. She would study as well as photograph the plant and animal life, and she would record geographical and geological data that might be of scientific value. The trip took her into hazardous waters with an exceptionally wide belt of ice between sea and land, giving access to a land of extraordinary grandeur and beauty.

She chartered the *Veslekari*, a 295-ton motorship, which was to be hers on each subsequent voyage. Gisbert was again director of the expedition. Several friends were invited, including a botanist, a writer, and a big-game hunter. Louise's maid went along, as on all her travels. At Scoresbysund they visited an Eskimo settlement. Louise described the Eskimos in the *Geographical Review* (vol. 22, pp. 529–61), and a series of articles by the writer, Winifred Menzies, about the settlement and the life of the Eskimos appeared in the *Christian Science Monitor* (Aug. 22–27, 1932). "No one can fail to admire and like these Greenlanders," wrote Louise, "with their quiet, charming manners, their direct eyes, and their faces that smile and radiate kindness" (*The Fiord Region*, p. 3).

Later, Louise learned that the land between the De Geer Glacier, which she had discovered, and the Jaette Glacier had been named "Miss Boyd Land." She explained that she was not guilty of giving her name to the area. "My first intimations that this land had been so designated came in a letter from Dr. Lauge Koch and on seeing the name on his published map'' (*The Fiord Region*, p. 23).

The 1931 trip was a turning point for Louise, for she spent much time with Dr. Isaiah Bowman, the director of the American Geographical Society in New York City. The society was a respected institution sponsoring original geographical research, and it became important to Louise in all her future plans. It sponsored her expeditions, published her three books and several articles, and in 1938 awarded her the Cullum Medal, given for the first time to a woman explorer. In 1960 she became the first woman member of its policy-making body, the council. In return, she represented the society at conferences, presented papers at its meetings, and donated to it almost all of her photographs and moving-picture films, which constituted a unique pictorial record of the topography of the Arctic. She initiated the Louise A. Boyd Publishing Fund for publication of studies resulting from field research.

The expedition that set off in the summer of 1933, under sponsorship of the society, had as its purpose the study of glacial marginal features, particularly in the Franz Josef and King Oscar fiord areas. It included a number of scientists: two surveyors, a physiographer, a botanist, and a geologist. The botanist left the expedition early because of appendicitis, and Louise collected plants.

The *Veslekari* left Norway at the end of June 1933 and first made tests with a sonic depth finder, the very latest development in ultrasonic depth-measuring techniques. After testing the equipment, they set off for Jan Moyen Island, between Norway and the east coast of Greenland. They carried to the Norwegians manning the lonely meteorological station on the island the first mail they had received in ten or eleven months. The tiny station became like home to the explorers; no matter what the weather, hot coffee and cakes were always available there. Boyd found in those she met in the far north ''greatness of spirit, sincerity, and strength of character'' (*The Fiord Region*, p. 8). She also appreciated Captain Johan Olsen and the crew of the ship, whose seamanship she admired and who entered into the work of the expedition with vigor and interest.

Her straightforward account of the expedition was published by the American Geographical Society as *The Fiord Region of East Greenland* in 1935. It was illustrated with many superb photographs. During two more trips, in 1937 and 1938, Louise studied the geology and botany of the region, made magnetic observations, took depth soundings, mapped the East Greenland fiord region, and took photographs. By this time, Boyd's expeditions were well known among scientists, and she was given or lent the very latest equipment. Although the team of scientists changed, almost all of the *Veslekari* crew remained with her.

A *New York Times* reporter, who interviewed Boyd before she set out in 1938, wrote that she shunned publicity. ''If the ship-news men discover her this time it will be the first occasion on which she has attracted their attention when going north'' (*New York Times*, May 1, 1938). Modest she may have been, but she was definitely the head of her expeditions: she planned them with great care, equipped them with the best of everything, got plenty of supplies for any contingency, and kept a tight rein on activities. She put in long, exhausting days mapping and photographing. She wore out two pairs of hobnailed hiking boots each summer walking over the gravel and ice. She carried a variety of photographic equipment and needed two men to do nothing but carry it. She took mainly black and white photos, but she always hoped to do more in color. "Until the beauty of the fiord walls is recorded on color film," she said, "their grandeur will not be completely realized except by those who have seen them" (*The Coast of Northeast Greenland*, p. 87).

She made notes on the wildlife: rookeries on the shores, white hares, musk ox, polar bears, seals, and blue foxes on Jan Moyen Island. She collected musk ox wool, which had been rubbed off on bushes and boulders, and had mufflers and sweaters made of it. The wool, its natural beige shading into brown, was spun and woven for her by Home Industries in Alesund, Norway.

Louise's books read more like scientific reports (as they were) than adventure tales, and she was inclined to downplay dangers and hardships. In 1937, the ship stayed just a bit too long, and coming out they were held up by ice. There was, indeed, danger that they would be unable to get out until the next season, or that the ship might be crushed by the heavy ice. The men used ice anchors to get leverage for pulling and shoving; they dynamited the ice; they attached the winch to an iceberg to pull clear. It took them fourteen days of battle with the ice to reach clear water. At other times, they interrupted their researches to go to the aid of other vessels caught in ice. Once they had a fire on the ship. Heavy seas put the sturdy vessel to the test and drenched all aboard.

The voyages could be made only in the summer months, for ice completely closed the passages during the winter. Between expeditions, Boyd had time for other activities. In August 1934, she gave a special lecture at the International Geographical Conference at Warsaw, where she represented the American Geographical Society, the National Academy of Sciences, and the Department of State. She was one of five official United States delegates to the International Photogrammetrical Congress in Paris in November 1934. In 1939 she was a member of the advisory committee of the Sixth Pacific Science Congress, and in that year she accepted honorary doctorates from Mills College and the University of California. From an amateur explorer with no college training, she had gone to the top of a respected profession.

It has been said that the seasons accommodated her three interests: gardening at Maple Lawn in the spring and fall, music in the winter, and travel in the summer. She was not only a member but a leader in many musical and charitable organizations in California. She was park commissioner of the city of San Rafael for many years, and in 1939 the city made her an honorary citizen.

Boyd's personality is difficult to assess. On her ship and while tramping over the ice she seems sturdy, almost tomboyish, enjoying the excitement and danger. Ashore, she displayed an entirely different character. Feminine, graceful, and gentle, with blue eyes and gray hair, Boyd was very much a lady, to the point of being somewhat intimidating. When in New York, she had a maid and a chauffeur and stayed at hotels like the Ritz Carlton. In San Francisco, she was the grande dame of Bay Area society, presiding over a showplace estate with numerous well-trained servants. She dressed expensively and fashionably. When inquiring reporters insisted on knowing how she dressed as an Arctic explorer, she explained, "I may have worn breeches and boots and even slept in them at times, but I have no use for masculine women. At sea, . . . I powdered my nose before going on deck no matter how rough the sea was. There is no reason why a woman can't rough it and still remain feminine" (Gray, "The Arctic Explorer," n.d.).

When she attended the Warsaw meeting in 1934, she seized the opportunity to visit the country of the Pinsk marshes in Poland. She described her visit to the marshes in the *Geographical Review*, and in 1937 her book, *Polish Countrysides*, was published. It is a unique photographic record of the prewar rural life of Poland, with emphasis on the more primitive eastern regions. Her studies of the marshlands folk and the remote forest communities untouched by industrial civilization are written in a style quite different from that of her other books. They show her interest in the people and the way in which the environment influenced their lives. "The marshes are commonly described as flat and monotonous in the extreme," she wrote, "but I did not find them so, possibly because my chief interest lay in the human element" (*Polish Countrysides*, p. 61).

The areas Boyd had visited in 1937 and 1938 became part of the war zone when Denmark and Norway were invaded. A book on the results of the expeditions was almost ready for publication in 1940, when the United States government advised her of the value of the reports and photographs, since all such documents in the invaded countries were unavailable. Even before the United States entered the war, it was carefully studying its defense areas. Boyd was selected to head an investigation of magnetic and radio phenomena in the Arctic waters. When she returned from this mission in 1941, she became a technical adviser to the War Department.

Her wartime activities were kept secret, but after the war they were recognized when in 1949 the Department of the Army awarded her a Certificate of Appreciation for "outstanding patriotic service to the Army as a contributor of geographic knowledge." Her *The Coast of Northeast Greenland* was published in 1948.

Boyd was now in her sixties and participated in no more polar explorations. But she had always wanted to fly over the northland, and in 1955, in spite of her dislike of airplanes, she chartered a plane and flew over the North Pole. General Finn Lambrecht, whom she had met on the Amundsen search, flew with her. It was the first privately financed flight over the pole, and the first such flight by a woman.

Boyd died on September 14, 1972, in a San Francisco nursing home, where she had resided for two years. She had used almost every penny of her estate doing what she most wanted to do. In an article written for *Parade Magazine*, on February 2, 1958, Boyd had given her view of the pleasure of exploration: "Aside from the contribution which every scientist makes to our nation's welfare, great personal rewards . . . also await him. The thrill of adventure as he probes an uncharted field—the sense of pride and gratification as he reaches an aimed-for goal—such things can be his meat and drink."

BIBLIOGRAPHY

Works by Louise Arner Boyd

"Fiords of East Greenland: A Photographic Reconnaissance throughout the Franz Josef and King Oscar Fiords." *Geographical Review* 22 (Oct. 1932): 529–61.
"Further Explorations in East Greenland, 1933." *Geographical Review* 24 (July 1934): 465–77.
The Fiord Region of East Greenland. New York: American Geographical Society, 1935.
"The Marshes of Pinsk." *Geographical Review* 26 (July 1936): 376–95.
Polish Countrysides. New York: American Geographical Society, 1937.
The Coast of Northeast Greenland. New York: American Geographical Society, 1948.
"The Louise A. Boyd Seven Arctic Expeditions." *Photogrammetric Engineering* (Dec. 1950).

Works about Louise Arner Boyd

Birmingham, Stephen. "San Francisco: The Grand Manner." *Holiday* 29 (Apr. 19, 1961): 98 + .
Current Biography. New York: H. W. Wilson, 1940–date, annual vols. 1960, 1972.
Donnelly, Florence. " 'The North Always Fascinated Me.' San Rafael's Louise A. Boyd Is World-renowned Arctic Explorer." *San Rafael Independent Journal*, Aug. 22, 1959.
Gray, Nancy. "The Arctic Explorer from San Rafael." *San Francisco Examiner, Pictorial Living*, undated clipping, Marin County Historical Society.
Menzies, Winifred. Articles on Eskimos met by the Boyd party in 1931, in *Christian Science Monitor*, Aug. 22–27, 1932.
National Cyclopedia of American Biography. New York: J. T. White, current vol. G (1946): 433.
Olds, Elizabeth Fagg. *Women of the Four Winds*. Boston: Houghton Mifflin, 1985, pp. 231–96. Olds interviewed many who knew Boyd and examined papers in private hands.
Owen, Russell. "A Woman Makes Her Mark in a Man's Domain." *New York Times Magazine*, May 1, 1938, pp. 6–7.
Rittenhouse, Mignon. *Seven Women Explorers*. Philadelphia: Lippincott, 1964, pp. 118–35.
Numerous volumes of the *Geographical Review* between 1931 and 1968 contain notes of Boyd's participation in the American Geographical Society. News articles and features on Boyd, in addition to those listed above, appeared in the New York, Washington, and San Francisco papers and in *Parade Magazine*, Feb. 2, 1958;

Christian Science Monitor, June 19, 1959; the *Oakland Tribune*, Feb. 18, 1968; and *New York Herald Tribune*, Mar. 19, 1949, and Feb. 8, 1960.
Obituaries appeared in the *New York Times*, on Sept. 17, 1972, and in the *Geographical Review* 63 (1973): 279–82.

Boyd papers, photographs, medals, and clippings are housed in the Marin County Historical Society in San Rafael, California. Some manuscript material is included in the collections of the American Geographical Society in New York and the Society of Woman Geographers in Washington, D.C. Boyd's large photographic collection and maps are located in the Golda Meir Library, University of Wisconsin-Milwaukee, transferred from the American Geographical Society in 1978. In 1984 the library exhibited Boyd's photographs of the Polish countryside, with a booklet on her work prepared by Susan Gibson Mikos.

MILDRED CABLE
1878–1952

EVANGELINE FRENCH
1869–1960

FRANCESCA FRENCH
1871–1960

Mildred Cable, Evangeline French, and Francesca French were English missionaries who between them spent almost a century in Central Asia, first with the China Inland Mission and then wandering, under the auspices of the mission, through the vast country beyond the Great Wall. They traveled through the Desert of Gobi and among its oases, coming to know the country and its people intimately. *The Gobi Desert*, written by Cable and Francesca French, is a rich distillation of their experiences during the 1920s and 1930s. Much more than a tale of adventure, it is a revelation of the deep spiritual treasures gained by the wayfarers over the years.

In 1942, the year the book was published, Cable was given the Lawrence Memorial Medal by the Royal Central Asian Society. The following year, the three women were jointly awarded the Livingstone Medal of the Royal Scottish Geographical Society. Their work was thus recognized not only as significant in the field of Christian missions but of value to geographers, archeologists, and philologists. Though they wrote a number of books about their lives in China, *The Gobi Desert* stands out for its literary and historical excellence.

Mildred Cable was born on February 21, 1878, in Guildford, Surrey, southern England. She chose her life work while a young woman and prepared herself for the mission field by studying chemistry and medicine. Accepted by the China Inland Mission, she went to China in 1902, where she met Evangeline (Eva) French, who had been with the mission since 1893.

Eva was born on May 27, 1869, in the Algerian foothills of the Atlas Mountains, of a French father and an Irish-English mother. The family moved about Europe, made friends among artists and intellectuals, and lived for some years in Geneva, where she attended the university. When the family moved to England, Eva, with her two languages, her university education, and her strong views of independence, was eager to use her life to some purpose. She decided on missionary work and was accepted for the China Inland Mission.

In 1900 the Boxer rebellion broke out, and the Empress Dowager gave orders to kill every foreigner. Many of the missionaries were massacred, and Eva had a narrow escape. For fifty days she and other women were conveyed as prisoners from city to city until they reached freedom in Shanghai, and Eva went home to England. Her father had died and her mother and sister Francesca had believed Eva to be among the victims of the Boxer terrorists.

When Mildred Cable arrived in China, Eva had just returned from England. The two missionaries were sent to Shansi province, where they found much to do to repair the destruction wrought by the Boxers. They started a school for girls in Hochow.

Eva's younger sister Francesca (born on December 12, 1871, in Bruges, Belgium) cared for their mother at home until her mother died. She then took a course in midwifery and went out to join her sister and Mildred in 1909. From that time on, the three women lived and worked together. They were known as Feng Precious Pearl, Kai All Brave, and Feng Polished Jade. Though they were different in temperament, they were alike in their dedication, hardihood, and love of China.

Early in the 1920s, they learned of the great unevangelized areas in the northwest regions and volunteered to go there. They had now lived in China so long that they considered themselves almost Chinese. They spoke the language, wore Chinese dress, and were thoroughly accustomed to the leisurely pace of Oriental life. They had learned to love the people. Nevertheless, it was with some foreboding that they faced the uncertainty of the vast desert known as the Gobi.

At the western end of the Great Wall was the fortress town of Kiayukwan (Barrier of the Pleasant Valley) with its imposing tower and its three gates. One of these gates was used daily by residents who carried water from springs outside the city. One gate was used by soldiers to bring supplies from the oasis of Suchow (Spring of Wine) to the governor and his ladies. The third gate, which opened to the northwest, was known as the travelers' gate. Through its arches wayfarers came from every part of China, arriving travel worn and weary to stay for a day or so, then leaving, bound for the remotest frontiers. Out of the third gate, also, went men who had broken the law or offended some official and who were banished into the desert to die or to live for the rest of their lives as exiles.

The soldiers and inhabitants of the fortress had a great dread of the desert. They told Cable that the Gobi was inhabited by demons who called out to travelers, but if one should answer the call he could be led farther away from the path and lose his way. The traveler could die there of thirst or freeze in the winter blizzards.

"Must you go?" they asked.

"Yes," Cable replied, "I must, for I seek the lost, and some of them are out there."

Her God, she said, would help her to find those she sought.

The next evening, as the sun was setting, the three Englishwomen, with their drivers and loaded carts, clattered through the gate into the forbidding desert. Two friendly soldiers came to see them off and told them it was the custom for each traveler to throw a stone at the wall. If the stone rebounds, they said, the traveler will come back safe. Each of the women picked up a stone and threw it. When the stones rebounded, the soldiers said, "Your journey will be prosperous."

Following a path known to the cart men and from which it would be death to deviate, they trudged the rough sandy wastes from one oasis to another. They saw deserted towns and waterless wells and were quite ready to share their guides' dread of these uninhabited spaces. But they also saw beauty in the rolling hills and enjoyed the solitude. They passed camel caravans bringing goods from far places. They were made welcome by the desert dwellers who were eager for news of the world within the wall. Everywhere they took a supply of Bibles and Christian writings and left them with the people.

Over the next fifteen years, with brief respites, they traversed the length of central China five times, from the border of Inner Mongolia to Russia, from the Spring of Wine to Chuguchak (Tahcheng).

Travel was slow. The average speed of a caravan, be it camel, horse, donkey, cart, or foot travel, was three miles an hour. Wells had been dug from twenty-five to thirty miles apart, and inns had been built at these stopping places; innkeepers were subsidized to keep the wells free from sand and to look after the travelers' needs. Most of the inns were mud huts, dirty and comfortless; the innkeepers and other oases dwellers were addicted to opium.

Once the missionaries were accepted on a footing of friendship, they were shown carefully guarded treasures, such as frescoed caves in remote hills and ancient stoneware, porcelain, and jade vessels, some of which had been hidden in caves or found buried in the desert sand, perhaps lost by an ill-fated caravan. They visited the Caves of the Thousand Buddhas where in 1908 Sir Aurel Stein had found great rolls of precious manuscripts, written in many different ancient languages, proving that Tunhwang was once a center of learning where men of varying paths met.

They talked to monks and lamas and other learned men about the history of the region and exchanged with them their differing views of religion. They were entertained at the shah's summer palace and at a Buddhist retreat. They sympathized with the women, who endured a life of degradation, and with the young girls whose feet were bound and who were wedded in childhood. They talked to the women, assuring them that they were all loved and valued by the Christian God, and sometimes on a second or third visit they saw a change in the woman's estimation of herself.

They visited many tribes—Kazakhs, Mongols, Turkis, Tibetans—and realized the inherent difficulty of governing peoples so vigorous, assertive, and diverse.

On returning from their last trip in 1931, they noted a disquieting mood. They set out for the fortress of the Great Wall, and as they went they became increasingly aware of a change in the bearing of the people. The camel drivers they passed whispered hints to the carters, warning them to keep on side roads and to avoid certain towns. They found that inn doors formerly kept wide open to travelers were now closed. Only when the innkeepers saw their faces was the door unbolted.

In one oasis the women and children had gone into hiding, taking the livestock and food supplies. "Communists are on the march," said the men. And when they reached the great fortress at Kiayukwan, they saw that the great tower was broken down, the houses were crumbling, and the place was deserted except for two families who were living in dugouts. They told a terrible story of battles and slaughter.

The Moslems had revolted against the new Chinese administration that came about when the last ruler of the Gobi, Khan Maksud Shah, died and the succession was not allowed to continue. His son, a descendant of Genghis Khan, was made a prisoner. In Kansu a young general, Ma Chung-ying, called General Thunderbolt, began a reign of terror.

For eight months, the Englishwomen lived under the general's rule in Tunhwang. The town people were robbed of everything in the nature of food, goods, and money. All the young men were conscripted for the army. Every day the women saw them being rounded up. "The ropes which they themselves had twisted from desert grass were used to tie their hands behind their backs, and to noose their necks in a running-knot" (*The Gobi Desert*, p. 239). The granary was emptied. Carts, horses, fuel, and fodder were all commandeered. Then typhus struck, adding its victims to those of murder and starvation.

The missionaries were ordered to the general's headquarters at Anhsi, where they were expected to cure his wounds. He treated them with civility and appeared to be interested in them, "probably owing to the fact that we were the only people who never flattered him and were obviously not afraid of him" (*The Gobi Desert*, p. 241). Official papers entitled the women to daily rations, but when they got to the food office most of the requested items were not available.

When the general's wounds were healed, the women received permission to return to Tunhwang. However, they were forbidden to leave that town. For months, during which time they were near starvation, they planned an escape to the west. They laid aside whatever food they could get, for unless they could save enough to take them over ten desert stages, escape would be impossible. Fortunately, they still had their mules, and one morning they drove out toward one of the loneliest of desert roads, known only to local men, and, after several frightening incidents, escaped to Turkestan.

In August 1932, they prepared to go home on furlough, but they were not alone. With them was Topsy, a deaf-mute child who had made a precarious living begging on the streets of Suchow before she had been taken into the missionaries' home. They had to get visas to travel through Russia, and Topsy, a Chinese child, required special permission from Moscow. The secretary of the consulate was a woman of uncompromising appearance, "the kind of material from which the fiercest Communist and the most uncompromising atheist is made" (*A Desert Journal*, p. 240). They feared for Topsy. When at last the news came that all visas, including Topsy's, were in order, the child's delight was beyond words. To the great surprise of the missionaries, the masterful secretary rose from her seat, took Topsy in her arms, and gave her a passionate kiss.

The three women were to remain at home in England for several years, appointed to other service. They lived in Willow Cottage, in Dorset, on a property the women had purchased sight unseen by telegram. They wrote about their travels and their Christian beliefs, and they were kept busy speaking, not only to mission societies but also to scientific societies and universities who regarded them as explorers. In 1935, when they revisited China, they were guided by Intourist and were not free to wander about; the changes they saw saddened them.

A journey to a different part of the world was made in 1946. The three women traveled from London to south of the African continent to Australia and New Zealand, then through India and Europe and back to London. In New Zealand they celebrated the centennial of the British and Foreign Bible Society. In India they took part in a conference of the Bible Society of India and Ceylon. A few years later, they visited South America. Shortly after their return from this trip, on April 30, 1952, Mildred Cable died at Willow Cottage. Eva died on July 8, 1960, and Francesca less than a month later, on August 2, 1960. Their estate went first to Topsy—now named Eileen Guy—and then to the Bible Society.

BIBLIOGRAPHY

Works by Mildred Cable

(With Francesca French) *Dispatches from North-west Kansu*. London: China Inland Mission, 1925.

———. *Through Jade Gate and Central Asia: An Account of Journeys in Kansu, Turkestan, and the Gobi Desert*. London: Constable, 1927; Boston: Houghton Mifflin, 1927. The first trip of 6,000 miles through Central China and home on furlough in 1923.

———. *The Story of Topsy, Little Lonely of Central Asia*. London: Hodder & Stoughton, 1932.

(With Evangeline and Francesca French) *Something Happened*. London: Hodder & Stoughton, 1933. Includes biographies of the three women.

"The Bazars of Tangut and the Trade-routes of Dzungaria." *Geographical Journal* 84 (July 1934): 17–32. A lecture delivered before the Royal Geographical Society, Mar. 19, 1934.

(With Evangeline and Francesca French) *A Desert Journal: Letters from Central Asia*. London: Hodder & Stoughton, 1934. Letters on their journeys from 1928 to 1932. Reviewed in *Geographical Journal* 85 (June 1935), 560–61.

"A New Era in the Gobi." *Geographical Journal* 100 (Nov.–Dec. 1942): 193–205. A
lecture delivered before the Royal Geographical Society, Oct. 26, 1942.
(With Francesca French) *The Gobi Desert*. London: Hodder & Stoughton, 1942; New
York: Macmillan, 1944. Reviewed in *Geographical Journal* 101 (May–June
1943): 266–68. Quotations in the text are from the 1944 edition.
————. *Journey with a Purpose*. London: Hodder & Stoughton, 1950. The trip to
Australia and New Zealand, India, Cairo, and home.
————. *Walls of Spears: The Gobi Desert*. London: Lutterworth, 1951.

The three women wrote a number of other books and pamphlets, not specifically about
their travels but on China, the work of missionaries, and Bible study.

Works about Mildred Cable, Evangeline French, and Francesca French

Allen, Alexandra. *Travelling Ladies*. London: Jupiter, 1980, pp. 190–224.
Dictionary of National Biography, 1951–1960. London: Oxford University Press, 1971
(under "Cable" and "French").
Europa Biographical Dictionary of British Women. Edited by Anne Crawford and others.
London: Europa, 1985 (under "Cable").
International Dictionary of Women's Biography. Edited by Jennifer S. Uglow and Frances
Hinton. New York: Continuum, 1982 (under "Cable").
Lindgren, Edith John. "In Memoriam: Miss Francesca Law French and Miss Evangeline
French." *Journal of the [Royal] Central Asian Society* 48 (1961): 4–5.
Martyred Missionaries of the China Inland Mission. Edited by Marshall Broomhall.
London: Morgan & Scott, 1901. Contains accounts of Eva's experiences during
the Boxer uprising.
Platt, William James. *Three Women; Mildred Cable, Francesca French, Evangeline
French: The Authorized Biography*. London: Hodder & Stoughton, 1964.
Scott, P. "Women of the Desert." *Christian Science Monitor*, June 15, 1938.
Thompson, Phyllis. *Desert Pilgrim: The Story of Mildred Cable's Venture for God in
Central Asia*. London: China Inland Mission, 1957. A fictionalized account.
Obituaries of Mildred Cable appeared in the *Geographical Journal* 118 (1952): 372–73,
and in the London *Times*, on May 2, 1952. An obituary of Francesca French
appeared in the London *Times*, on Aug. 3, 1960.

LUCY EVELYN CHEESMAN
1881–1969

Lucy Evelyn Cheesman's greatest pleasure was collecting insects, some of which she collected in the more remote and less frequently visited islands in the South Seas. Heat, humidity, torrential rains, and voracious mosquitoes, not to mention tribes still practising cannibalism, did not keep her from going wherever she thought a new insect or a new variation on an old one could be found. Discomfort and danger, she said, was part of being a scientist, "all reckoned in with the cost of the exceptional privilege of being among . . . superb, forested mountains, and actually in daily contact with . . . superb tropical life" (*The Two Roads of Papua*, p. 22).

She gave up a secure job in the London zoo to earn a precarious living from collecting and writing. Between 1923 and 1955, she made eight solo expeditions to the southwest Pacific islands. The last was to Aneityum, in the New Hebrides (now Vanuatu), when she was well over seventy. Her many books, although concerned primarily with insect life, are full of adventure, contributing delightfully to the literature of travel. They were not confined to scientific information and advice to other collectors; she added comments on the flora and fauna, the inhabitants of the islands, and the politics of the regions, as well. Though her trips were not meant to be geographical explorations, she went into many places where nobody had seen a white woman before, and she showed much initiative in going among isolated and primitive peoples.

Lucy Evelyn Cheesman (she rarely used the name "Lucy") was born in 1881 in Westwell, an English country village in Kent. She and her siblings, sons and daughters of Robert Cheesman, grew up in the comfortable, leisurely style of the privileged classes. They lived much out of doors and were allowed to bring their outdoor friends, including snails, cockchafers, and glowworms, into their nursery. More than one nursery maid was dismissed for throwing away both live treasures and cherished bits of moss and flowers. Cheesman's autobiography describes her childhood as "care-free happy days soaking in wildlife" (*Things Worth While*, p. 25).

Schooldays followed, and then the daughters seemed doomed by Victorian standards to lives of teaching or serving as governesses. At the age of twenty-nine, Evelyn was very ill. Her family doctor gently suggested that her poor health was due to "bottling it up"—in other words, ignoring her own innate bent toward natural history. She had set her heart on becoming a veterinarian, but the Veterinary College did not admit women. She began to educate herself by reading animal anatomy and then became a nurse in a canine hospital.

During World War I, Cheesman served as a temporary civil servant in the Admiralty. She then exchanged the use of a typewriter, on which to learn typing, for secretarial work at the Imperial College of Science. This led to a job at the Zoological Society's gardens in Regent's Park—not typing at all but taking care of the Insect House. She took a course on entomology and threw herself enthusiastically into making the exhibits a real drawing card for visitors to the zoo. She gave talks to children, broadcast stories in Children's Hour, and wrote several books for young people on insect life.

In 1923 she was given an opportunity to join a scientific research expedition to the Pacific islands. It seemed the fulfillment of a dream. For most people, she had said, one particular part of the globe holds special allure. For her, that part of the globe was the South Pacific. The expedition stopped at Madeira, Trinidad, Martinique, and the wildlife refuge on Barro Colorado Island in Panama, where Cheesman was able to do some collecting. They spent some time in the Galápagos Islands, then in the Marquesas islands, and the Tuamotu atolls, each of which presented different problems in collecting. The group did not stay long enough in any one place for her to go far inland, but she did a fair amount of exploring, going off by herself and relying on natives for advice on trails.

At Tahiti she was able to leave the expedition because her brother had sent her a hundred English pounds. As she had sailed across the globe with only ten pounds "by concentrating on my work and not looking for amusements at the ports" (*Things Worth While*, p. 125) she felt safe in remaining behind, keeping enough to buy her return passage on an ordinary steamer. She longed to be free to collect by herself, choosing the most desirable sites.

She met a Finn, the captain of the ship that had brought Robert Louis Stevenson to the Marquesas, who now lived in Tahiti. Through the captain's Tahitian wife, she was given a one-room hut on a coral reef. With her seaman's hammock, a table, a case of equipment, and a few borrowed pieces of camp furniture, she made herself comfortable. When the opportunity arose, she took passage to some of the other islands, including Bora Bora, "an enchanting island where I longed to buy a few acres and settle down for ever" (*Things Worth While*, p. 132).

Friends on one island introduced her to their acquaintances on others, so that she generally had help in finding places to stay. She ate native food and sometimes took nothing with her on day-long collecting trips, relying on meeting a native who would knock down and open a coconut for her. When she returned from her trips, she had a large audience to watch her sort the day's takings and pack those from the drying trays.

When she found no trail to take her where she wanted to go, she made one by cutting the vegetation. One time, she got lost, fell, negotiated streams and cascades, and gave up hope of ever finding her way back to her hut. She had to spend a night in the forest, and the whole village was alerted to search for her. "I still had a good deal to learn," she concluded (*Things Worth While*, p. 145).

After months of eventful travel, she returned home with a collection of about 500 specimens. She gave up her job at the zoo and transferred her loyalties to the British Museum of Natural History.

In 1928, having proved her competency by writing a taxonomic paper, she was given a grant by the museum to collect insects, and she went to the New Hebrides. She was warned that the natives were dangerous, especially the cannibalistic Big Nambas of Malekula. She did not know, until her return to England, that "the tribe was of special interest to anthropologists and had not been visited by white people, except by one or two with an armed escort" (*Things Worth While*, p. 163). She went with a Mr. Newton, the manager of a large plantation on Santo, to visit King Ringapat of the Big Nambas in his village, Tnmaru. The king had heard of Cheesman and was interested in her collecting equipment. They partook of a ceremonial meal. Each tribesman wore a wide girdle of bark and the tribal *nambas*, a large fiber tassel in front, and all were armed with spears. "When we took the narrow trail single file," she wrote, "with Newton and myself in the middle of these uncouth savages, an onlooker might have believed us to be cannibal victims being led away to slaughter" (*Things Worth While*, p. 167).

Ringapat had spent some time working for a Frenchman and knew a few words of French and some pidgin, which helped in their communication. He explained the tribe's ideas about ghosts and cannibalism; afterward, Cheesman felt comfortable enough with the tribe to remain behind, alone, after Newton left, so that she could do some collecting. Ringapat wished to send a message to the King of England that they no longer ate human meat and had substituted pig for human sacrifice. He also wished to send a gift to the king, which turned out to be a fourteen-foot spear, "rather a responsibility." Eventually, it was presented to her trustees and found a home in the British Museum. Cheesman was amused to find that her visit to the tribe was of widespread interest at home.

Evelyn spent two years in the northern and southern islands of the New Hebrides, camping alone, waited on by islanders from various tribes. She hoped to spend another six months at Aneityum, but she fell ill and had to leave for Australia.

New Guinea was her next objective, and in 1933 she set off for Papua. Her goal was to collect enough insects to "settle a few questions about the former connection of New Guinea with other islands and archipelagos of the Pacific" (*The Two Roads of Papua*, p. 60). Mere numbers were not the object. "As soon as I have a good series and am sure both sexes are taken, I leave that species alone" (*The Two Roads of Papua*, p. 62). At night, she set up a cloth screen to collect insects attracted by the light. "On the exceptionally good nights," she wrote, "there would not be an inch to spare anywhere on the screen, . . . new-comers would disturb several square inches of insects before they could get a footing. The noise made by hundreds of flops on the screen and little pattering feet was most remarkable" (*The Two Roads of Papua*, p. 77).

Although in her books for children she had made it plain that insects, birds, and animals cannot think and plan their actions as do man, Cheesman could not help describing ants, snakes, and bees in human terms: They were "cuddly" or "clever" and behaved in the most fascinating or outrageous ways.

Since the collecting of equipment, camping needs, trade goods, and food supplies filled many boxes and made moving about difficult, Cheesman's practice was to set up a more-or-less permanent camp and spend the days roaming about with her butterfly net and killing bottle. In Papua she was given a police escort when she traveled from place to place, and she felt perfectly safe. She made friends of the natives and took an interest in their beliefs and customs.

The Papuans believed that disease and injury were proof that the afflicted person was the victim of some antagonistic element. Cheesman reflected that the teaching of her own childhood that illness was sent by God as punishment "is surely as damnable as the natives' belief that it is the result of supernatural interference. How many promising lives must have been cut off in early Victorian days by the preaching of resignation to a state of ill-health" (*The Two Roads of Papua*, p. 138).

She went to the Cyclops Mountains of Dutch New Guinea, then spent a year roughing it in Waigeo and Japen islands and the Torricelli Mountains of the Mandated Territory. It was extremely strenuous, and, at the end, she felt like "a bit of frayed string" but thought it thoroughly worth while. On Japen she collected mammal skins for the museum: those of tree kangaroos, rock wallabies, and cus-cus.

In 1939 there were more than distant rumors of war with Japan, and Cheesman caught the last boat—a Dutch cargo boat—to leave for Europe. During the war, she returned to civil service, first as a censor, then as a plane spotter, and finally as an entertaining lecturer to the troops. She made a gazetteer of New Guinea. Her knowledge of the terrain in the South Pacific islands proved to be of military value. One of a series of contour maps she had made was photocopied for five different governments, for knowing the comparative heights of the mountains was important to airplane pilots.

Near the end of the war, she was injured in a railway accident, but her subsequent headaches and backaches were attributed to rheumatism, and she suffered greatly until an osteopath treated her. When she regained her ability to walk, she set off for New Caledonia, where she climbed mountains in a manner that astonished everyone. After returning from one climb, "I got an ovation," she wrote. "It is curious that people can hear about my previous expeditions without realising that... I can cope with local conditions that they consider insurmountable" (*Things Worth While*, p. 276).

On Lifu, one of the Loyalty islands, she stayed in a mission house, then with Polynesians who ceremoniously adopted her into their family. There was no strenuous climbing here, yet Cheesman felt that her arthritic hip would make it impossible to do much more collecting of the kind she had been attempting. Back in England, she sorted her takings, gave broadcast talks, and lectured; she resigned herself to remaining a semi-invalid.

In June 1953, after consulting a surgeon, she had an operation to replace part of the hip and, to her delight, was once again able to walk almost normally. The next year she revisited Aneityum. Planning to stay for a year, she had a hut built on a logging road near the coast. She was happy there alone, except that tiny biting flies called simuleum were a cause of continuous acute discomfort. "There is always much to endure at such camps," she wrote philosophically, "and that is why people—wise people—do not encamp in tropical forest" (*Things Worth While*, p. 314). This time, it was not the flies or poor health that ended her stay but a shutting down of the logging camp, the stopping of mail, and the falling price of copra, which meant that boats would no longer call with any regularity. The New Hebrides was cut off from the outer world. She radioed for a patrol boat to fetch her and her collection and left that part of the world forever.

Cheesman was a small woman, 5 feet 2 inches, and, by her own standards, prudish. She wore a modest "bush-suit" with shoes and stockings, yet she shocked the nuns in one isolated mission by not wearing a dress. Although she was often laid low by fevers and other illnesses, she never lost heart. At home, she lived on little in a London flat, for she had served the museum without pay as an honorary associate and she depended on earnings from her books and lectures. In 1953, her service to science was recognized by the Order of the British Empire, and her circumstances were eased by a civil list pension. She died on April 15, 1969, at the age of eighty-eight.

A lengthy obituary in the London *Times* the next day paid tribute to her gifts as a teacher:

> She was a kind and friendly person much loved by those who knew her, austere though she was with herself and single-minded in her devotion to natural history. Nor was she robust, but a frail little woman and full of courage, fearless in exposing pretence or tilting at authority. Her greatest gifts were as a teacher of the young. Her understanding of children and primitive peoples enabled her to befriend and live alone with even savage cannibal tribes such as the Big Nambas of the New Hebrides. Her tastes in food and comfort were simple in the extreme. Any money from her tiny income, beyond her humblest needs, was ploughed back in such form as a gift-book to a young naturalist or a microscope to a government department. (London *Times*, April 16, 1969)

BIBLIOGRAPHY

Works by Lucy Evelyn Cheesman

Islands near the Sun: Off the Beaten Track in the Far, Fair Society Islands. London: H. F. & G. Witherby, 1927. In Tahiti.

Hunting Insects in the South Seas. London: P. Allan, 1932; New York: R. O. Ballou, 1933.

Backwaters of the Savage South Seas. London: Jarrolds, 1933. New Hebrides.

The Two Roads of Papua. London: Jarrolds, 1935.

The Land of the Red Bird. London: H. Joseph, 1938. New Guinea.

Camping Adventures in New Guinea. London: Harrap, 1948.

Camping Adventures on Cannibal Islands. London: Harrap, 1948. New Hebrides.

Marooned in Du-bu Cove. London: Bell, 1949.

Six-Legged Snakes in New Guinea: A Collecting Expedition to Two Unexplored Islands. London: Harrap, 1949. Waigeo and Japen islands.

Things Worth While. London: Hutchinson, 1957. Autobiography. Reprinted. London: Readers Union, 1958. Quotations in the text are from the 1958 edition.

Time Well Spent. London: Hutchinson, 1960. Autobiography.

Who Stand Alone. London: G. Bles, 1965. New Hebrides and New Guinea.

Works about Lucy Evelyn Cheesman

Europa Biographical Dictionary of British Women. Edited by Anne Crawford and others. London: Europa, 1985.

An obituary appeared in the London *Times*, on Apr. 17, 1969.

VIOLET CRESSY-MARCKS
ca. 1890–1970

Violet Cressy-Marcks, a long-time Fellow of the Royal Geographical Society, had an impressive record of travel in many regions of the world. She studied archeological remains of ancient civilizations in the Arab and southern Asian countries. She made eight journeys around the world, the last in 1956. She hunted big game, took still and moving pictures, carried an array of scientific instruments, and lectured on her travels. As a news correspondent, she covered events in China from 1943 to 1945, the Nuremberg trials, and the Greek elections.

She published only two books of travel: one on a journey up the Amazon and over the Peruvian Andes; the other on a trip to China when she viewed Chinese communism, Japan's invasion, and the influence of Russia—she entered the country from Burma and went as far as the Koko Nor.

Often warned against the danger of entering strange countries, especially when they were embroiled in political battles, she answered that there was nothing brave about risking it, that leading a normal life in Europe exposed one to thieves, lunatics, and accidents, and that no man knew the hour of his death.

Violet Olivia Rutley, the only daughter of William Ernest Rutley, was born, presumably, in England. Her lengthy entry in *Who Was Who* fails to give the date or place of her birth. Nor are any other details of her life forthcoming, except for the bare facts of two marriages. The first, to Captain Cressy-Marcks, ended in divorce; the second was to Francis Fisher in 1932. She had one son by the first marriage, two by the second.

Her first important journey took her from Cairo to Capetown in 1925. In the winter of 1928–1929, she traveled by sled, drawn by reindeer, across Norway and Finland to Murmansk, above the Arctic Circle.

In 1930 she sailed for Brazil to see "a fresh country, and in many parts unmapped, fresh races, fresh scenes with all the feeling they arouse, solitude and time to think" (*Up the Amazon and over the Andes*, p. 65). Her plan was to go by river, the Amazon and the Ucayali, by motor launch and canoe as far as Puerto Opoca in Peru, thence by mule over the mountains to Huancayo, and finally by train to Lima.

In an appendix to her book describing the journey she listed the equipment recommended for travelers, including numerous scientific survey instruments, anthropological instruments, books (Aristotle, Plato, and the Bible, in addition to navigation tables and a textbook on topographical and geographical surveying), natural history requisites, firearms (two revolvers, two rifles, and a double-barrel shotgun), and four cameras with appropriate lenses, sun shades, and filters. The list of camp equipment included a tent she designed herself, made up in three bundles of fifty pounds each, furniture including a Rhoorkie chair and an Abyssinian table, a canvas bath and basin, cooking utensils, and a medicine chest.

A long list of clothing included three pairs of brogues, a pair of field boots, and two pairs of mosquito boots (one reaching above the thigh and fastened around the waist); six pairs of shorts, three of jodhpurs, two of riding breeches; and wool and rubber ponchos.

Whether she took all these items with her to South America is not stated; she did have a twelve-by-four-by-four-foot crate and a large amount of other luggage. At various stages of her journey, she got rid of a great deal. The crate was sent back to England from Iquitos, presumably unopened. From Massisea, she sent her dressing bag and all her valuable luggage by plane to Lima. At Atalya, she left all her camp furniture, except the bath and basin, the Rhoorkie chair, and all the tinned food. At Puerto Opoca she left the rest of her impedimenta to be brought to her when mules were available, for she could get only one mule, which was loaded with her hammock, medicine chest, and some food. She hung onto her cameras and took a large number of photographs, but unfortunately many were ruined by the damp, despite her attempts to keep them covered.

She had not counted on the terrible overcrowding of the Amazon launches, the fact that an Indian canoe held little besides passengers, and the difficulty of finding mule transport in the mountains. When the things left at Puerto Opoca finally reached her, she needed eight mules to pack them farther. Half of the baggage, she wrote, consisted of scientific instruments. Even so, she had to discard many more of her possessions before she reached Lima, including a number of frocks she gave to the Peruvian women.

An overabundance of baggage, however, was the least of Violet's problems. She had been used to rough and dangerous travel, but crossing the Andes by a route used only by Indians going from village to village was especially difficult. Mules were not easily nor everywhere available, and the ones she got were particularly independent and fractious. Guides and carriers were also scarce. There were scattered huts and small villages, but few places to get food or shelter. In one settlement, the people refused to sell her a mule or even woolen stockings. She could not understand their hard-heartedness. "They seemed to me to be devoid of anything in the way of fairness or kindness or common decency" (*Up the Amazon*, p. 225). Her guide drank, and the muledriver chewed coca.

She had the further misfortune to be bitten by a snake. It was not poisonous, but the wound, just below her kneee, became infected. Walking was painful, but riding mules were not to be had. It rained, and they slipped in the mud on the precipitous trail. She was ahead of the mules part of the way, alone, and at other times behind them, trying to catch up. She felt that if she stopped to rest, the men (guide and muleteer) would have left her behind callously and as a matter of course.

At one hut, a man gave her food and a woolen poncho to wear while she washed out her wet, muddy clothes. He allowed her to sit by his fire. She hung the clothes to dry but, during the night, the wind blew them into the fire. She awoke to find everything burned, only the shoes wearable. Fortunately, she had a silk frock bundled up with her hammock, but it left her arms and legs exposed.

She was almost at the end of her rope, seriously ill and numb with cold, when two men riding mules met her on the trail. When she told them she had come from Brazil, they were astounded. They put her on a mule and took her on the long, agonizing path to Runnatullo, 16,000 feet high, where it was snowing. The last part of the trip to Huancayo was made by a bus she chartered; there she found luxury at the International Hotel.

No matter how hard the journey, she could enjoy and record the beauty of the mountains. Here and there she met friendly and interesting people. One Spaniard, deep in the hills, asked her to marry him and remain there forever. She regretted that she did not know enough Spanish to let him down gently.

Once she reached Lima, she recovered quickly and went on to explore Cuzco, Machu Picchu, and Lake Titicaca before crossing the continent again to take ship for England. Her account of the journey, *Up the Amazon and over the Andes*, hastily and carelessly written, was published in 1932.

According to her entry in *Who Was Who*, she

> revisited Angkor (Indo-China); 1933, revisited Spain; 1934, flew from England to India, flew from Kabul over the Hindu Khush and Samarkand to Tashkent, journeyed through Turkistan and flew from Moscow to England; 1935, took the first motor transport from Addis Ababa to Nairobi; 1936, visited the Ethiopian and Eritrean War Fronts; 1937, Mandalay to Pekin overland; 1938, Turkey to Tibet by motor, yak and mule caravan. (*Who Was Who, 1961–1970*)

Dispatches from Nairobi to the *New York Times* in 1935 give some details of her visit to Haile Selassie in Addis Ababa. She considered the emperor "by far the cleverest man in the whole country" and felt sure that Ethiopia would win over the Italians (*New York Times*, Mar. 23, 1935). Haile Selassie had given her an armed guard of twenty-eight men to see her safely through his country to the border of Kenya.

The trip to China in 1938 was her sixth visit to that country. She wished to see what changes had taken place and to assess the influence of Russia on China, to visit the Communists and speak to the leader of the Eighth Route Army, and to study the Japanese war and the morale of the troops.

Violet had always traveled alone, except for guides and servants, but this time, she took with her Francis (Frank) Fisher, whom she had married in 1932. He had stipulated that he went only as a passenger and took no responsibility for the arrangements; also, that he was free to leave the expedition when it suited him. He insisted on eating European food, which necessitated taking along a cook and the necessary ingredients and then waiting for the meal. Violet preferred Chinese food ready to eat at the end of the day's journey. While she studied the political situation, he occupied himself in collecting information on Chinese agriculture. Violet thought him an excellent traveling companion except that he "refused to kill his own lice" (*Journey into China*, p. 1).

They used every form of transport—buses, lorries, airplanes, trains, automobiles, donkeys, and even a raft on the Yellow River. Of course, they met with difficulties with crowded transport and unpredictable schedules. They witnessed the Chinese building roads—men, women, and children carrying rocks, the mountains cut into by hand, and the earth removed in baskets. They admired Chiang Kai-shek's ability to mobilize the people to use what materials they had at hand and to make the best of everything.

They remained in Sian for some time while trying to arrange a visit to the Eighth Route Army, where Violet hoped to interview Mao Tse-tung. When permission was given, they went on to the Japanese war front. Their train was bombed; when a warning was sounded, all the passengers got out and fled to the fields, while the train was shunted back and forth to avoid the bombs. There were few casualties, and all helped repair whatever damage had been done. They witnessed trains coming in from the front filled with the wounded, some dying, others already dead. Violet visited hospitals and refugee camps. She had a five-hour interview with Mao Tse-tung.

Afterward, she went on alone to the Koko Nor; Fisher declined to go. At Ping-liang she was told she ought not to be traveling in the country, that the last travelers came through before the war, an Englishman and a Swiss lady. (They were, of course, Ella Maillart and Peter Fleming, although Cressy-Marcks knew nothing of their visit.)

During World War II, Violet served as a driver. From 1943 to 1945, she was headquartered in Chungking, where she served as a correspondent throughout the East for the War Office. Frank Fisher died in Nassau in 1956, on Violet's last round-the-world journey, and there is no record of further travel on her part.

In her constant moving about, Cressy-Marcks sought freedom and independence. "Complete freedom," she wrote, "can only be obtained by the greatest of efforts over a period of years, and in attaining it, mastery of self must have been gained" (*Journey into China*, pp. 59–60). She had little gift for transmitting the excitement and pleasure of travel, and the reader will lose nothing in skipping over the account of journeys in the "civilized" portions of the globe and her forays into history.

Violet Cressy-Marcks died on September 10, 1970. *Who Was Who* gives the date as September 12, but obituaries agree on the September 10 date. The obituary in the London *Times* noted that "no contemporary British woman equalled or indeed approached her record of adventurous journeys in unfamiliar lands" (London *Times*, September 16, 1970).

BIBLIOGRAPHY

Works by Violet Cressy-Marcks

Up the Amazon and over the Andes. London: Hodder & Stoughton, 1932.
Journey into China. London: Hodder & Stoughton, 1940; New York: Dutton, 1942.

Works about Violet Cressy-Marcks

News dispatches from Nairobi, *New York Times*, Mar. 20 1935, p. 14, and Mar. 23, 1935, p. 9.
Who Was Who, 1961–1970. London: A. & C. Black, vol. 6 (1972): 256.
Obituaries appeared in the London *Times*, on Sept. 16, 1970, and in the *Geographical Journal* 136 (Dec. 1970): 669–70.

ALEXANDRA DAVID-NEEL
1868–1969

Alexandra David-Neel prided herself on having been the first Western woman to penetrate Tibet as far as its "forbidden city," Lhasa. Her story of the journey through the mountains from China to Lhasa, made from 1923 to 1924, is one of the most thrilling travel books. Disguised as a beggar woman and accompanied by a young lama, she walked the rugged paths over mountain passes higher than 18,000 feet. Carrying everything they needed on their backs, the two walked through rainstorms and heavy snows, slept outdoors in freezing weather, went for days without food, and evaded robbers and officials who would certainly have stopped them had her identity become known.

David-Neel made this hazardous journey (at the age of fifty-five) partly because it was forbidden to foreigners and partly to test herself. She said she had no particular desire to visit Lhasa, only to be able to get there. She made light of the dangers and difficulties, dwelling on the wild beauty of the land and the many hours of solitude and peace the journey afforded her.

The absolute freedom of the pilgrim's life, with its joys and hardships, appealed to Alexandra. "I deem it to be the most blessed existence one can dream of," she wrote, "and I consider as the happiest in my life those days when, with a load upon my back, I wandered as one of the countless tribe of Thibetan beggar pilgrims" (*My Journey to Lhasa*, p. 18).

Preceding this epic journey, the French journalist, scholar, and traveler had studied Buddhist and Tibetan philosophy and had adopted Buddhism. She had lived in lamaseries at Gangtok in Sikkim, at Shigatse, and at Kumbum in China's Kansu province. She had even interviewed the Dalai Lama while he was in exile in Bhutan.

After her successful visit to Lhasa, where she remained undetected for two months, she wrote about her adventures. *My Journey to Lhasa* (written in English) was followed by many other books and articles, in English and French, about Tibetan life and religion. She was honored for her distinction in the field of Oriental studies as well as for exploration. The young lama, Yongden, who was her companion on the journey, became her adopted son after they returned to her native France.

Alexandra David was born in Saint Mandé, near Paris, France, on October 24, 1868, the only child of Louis Pierre and Alexandrine Borghmans David. They had been married for sixteen years before the child was born, and as Alexandra grew up she felt that she had not been wanted, especially by her mother. She escaped from a lonely childhood through reading, choosing books of adventure and travel. Several times she ran away from home, bent on exploring what she hoped would be wild and solitary landscapes. She spent part of her girlhood in England. In Paris her favorite spot was a reading room in the Musée Guimet, a museum devoted to Far East antiquities. There she spent hours reading books about Asia.

Except for a brief trip to India when she was in her twenties, Alexandra was for long unable to realize her dreams of Eastern travel. When she went abroad, to Hanoi and Haiphong, and to Greece and Tunis, it was as a singer with the Opéra-Comique touring company.

In Tunis she met Philippe-François Neel, chief engineer for a French railroad. They were married in 1904. It was a strangely unconventional marriage, one in which the couple rarely lived together but one in which each declared undying love for the other. Through her subsequent travels, Alexandra wrote long letters to Philippe, who saved every one. The letters he wrote were not saved. He supported her, stored her effects, shipped things around after her, made arrangements for publishing her manuscripts, and rarely complained. She planned to support herself and Philippe when she began to make money from her writing. It galled her that in order to buy a home she had to have his permission, which he gave willingly, and also to adopt Yongden, which Philippe was less willing to do. She established a separate home for herself and Yongden in the French Alps, where Philippe occasionally visited them.

During the first years after the marriage, Alexandra studied and traveled in Europe, writing for magazines under the name of David or using a pseudonym, Myrial, which she had used while in the opera company. Later, she used the hyphenated David-Neel. In preparation for a trip to India, she studied Sanskrit and attended lectures on Eastern studies. She herself lectured on comparative religions. In 1910 she was sent to India and Burma for Oriental research by the French Ministry of Education. She did not suspect that she was to spend most of the next fifteen years in regions where people rarely saw the face of a white person.

In India, Alexandra learned that the Dalai Lama, spiritual head of all Tibet, had fled from Lhasa when his country was invaded by the Chinese. He was living in Kalimpong, in British Bhutan, near the Indian frontier. There Alexandra went to interview him. He had up to that time obstinately refused to give an audience to foreign women, but she had such pressing letters of introduction from high Buddhist personages that "the desire of the Dalai lama to see me grew even stronger than mine to see him" (*My Journey to Lhasa*, p. x). The interview went well and ended with the Dalai Lama's advice to her to study

Tibetan. Later, in 1912, she went to see him depart for Lhasa; the Manchu dynasty had fallen and the holy city was again open to him.

Alexandra's first view of Tibet was fully as delightful as she had dreamed. Beyond the tropical vegetation and the forested hills,

> one suddenly discovers the immensity of the trans-Himalayan tableland of Thibet, with its distant horizon of peaks bathed in strange mauve and orange hues, and carrying queerly shaped caps of snow upon their mighty heads. . . . I was at last in the calm solitudes of which I had dreamed since my infancy. I felt as if I had come home after a tiring, cheerless pilgrimage. (*My Journey to Lhasa*, pp. x–xi)

She visited Sidkeong Tulka, crown prince of Sikkim, at his home in Gangtok. With him and his chaplain she had long discussions (in English, as he had been educated at Oxford) about the mysteries of Tibetan Buddhism. Through the kindness of Sidkeong, Alexandra was given an apartment at the monastery of Podang, where she studied Tibetan. She went on several trips to other remote monasteries, accompanied by an interpreter and porters. At Podang, she was given as a personal attendant a young Sikkimese boy, who was fifteen years old. He had entered a Red Hat monastery at the age of eight and had been initiated into Buddhist practices as a lama. So came into her life Yongden, her constant companion until his death in France forty years later.

Yongden was a perfect spiritual companion, a platonic friend. Alexandra respected his knowledge of Buddhism, and she became his teacher in other things. He respected her as an old and learned woman. Above all, both loved adventure and fun. They teased each other, protected each other, and never wearied of their life together.

Wishing to truly experience the contemplative life of Buddhist nuns, Alexandra established herself in a cave in Sikkim. The cave had a door and was divided into two rooms; otherwise, it was austere in the extreme. Yongden and several servants lived in a hut some distance away and brought her water and fuel. With an ample supply of provisions, she remained there at a height of some 13,000 feet, isolated by snow through the long winter of 1914–1915. A single meal was brought to her daily. She read the lives of Tibetan mystics and learned from another hermit to speak Tibetan with a Lhasan accent. She was many miles and psychologically worlds away from her European homeland, now torn by war.

Feeling no desire to return to a country at war, she sought further Tibetan experiences. She and Yongden went to the famous monastery of Tashilhumpo at Shigatse, the seat of the Tashi Lama, who was equal in spiritual rank to the Dalai Lama but who did not have the Dalai Lama's temporal power. There she was the guest of the Tashi Lama's mother, in a palace whose magnificence was a great contrast to her anchorite's cave.

On her return to Gangtok, Alexandra found herself ordered deported for having crossed the border from Sikkim to Tibet without a pass. This "absurd prohibition," she wrote, "decided me to go to Lhasa." No government would forbid her access to territory over which foreigners "could travel at will a few years ago, and where, in a still more ancient period, missionaries have even owned properties." In her view, "the earth is the inheritance of man, and . . . any honest traveller has the right to walk as he chooses, all over that globe which is his" (*My Journey to Lhasa*, pp. xii, xvii).

During the summers of 1915 and 1916, she made two short journeys into Tibet. In September 1916, she went to Burma and the next year to Japan and China. She reached the monastery of Kumbum in July 1918 and remained there two and half years, peacefully translating Tibetan books. The winter of 1922–1923 was spent wandering in the Gobi desert. She and Yongden once tried to enter Tibet as beggar pilgrims, but their disguise was penetrated and they were stopped. "I took a silent oath," she wrote, "to renew my attempt, if necessary, ten times" (*Asia*, May 1926).

The final approach was made from the extreme southeastern part of Tibet, at Li-chian, between the Mekong and the Salween rivers, where a path led around the sacred mountain of Ka Karpo and crossed the Dokar Pass. It was used by pilgrims from various Tibetan regions, each of whom spoke a different dialect. The women had a variety of dress and coiffures, so that Alexandra's peculiarities of accent, features, or clothes were less noticeable. To avoid suspicion, they announced that they were going on a short botanical expedition. They managed to get rid of the coolies and baggage with which they had started, then put what they needed in backpacks and took on the role of beggar pilgrims.

Alexandra donned a heavy, white woolen dress and darkened her face with a mixture of cocoa and crushed charcoal and her hair with black ink. She gave herself long braids of yak's hair. She posed as the mother of the young lama. Yongden, of course, could easily travel anywhere as a Tibetan priest. They carried neither blankets nor ground sheet, only a small tent. They had a kettle, and each carried a bowl and chopsticks. They had provisions enough for some time, for they wished to avoid people until well on their way. Hidden under their clothes, they carried revolvers and money.

At first, they traveled at night, avoided other pilgrims, and crept silently in the dark through inhabited places. They slept on the ground, not daring to put up the tent. When they reached the high country, they spread the tent over them, throwing a few leaves on top, hoping it would be mistaken for a patch of snow. They lived on the staple diet of the Tibetan traveler: buttered tea, barley flour, and soup made with the barley and a bit of bacon. As they reached more towns and met more travelers, they had to give up the night travel, which would have caused rather than allayed suspicion. They were then able to purchase and beg their food.

Yongden was often asked to foretell the future, cast spells, read the scriptures, and bless other pilgrims. Neither he nor Alexandra believed that he could foresee events, but the simple peasants had sublime faith in the lama's power. One man who had lost his cow asked whether he would find it. Yongden replied that the cow was alive but might soon die. The man went to look for the animal, found it in a dangerous spot, and rescued it, thus establishing Yongden's power as a mystic. In other cases, by being somewhat cryptic in his predictions, the lama appeared to succeed. Of course, he was rewarded for his divinations with food or gifts. Alexandra sometimes entered into the spirit of things and chanted *Aum mani padme hum*, but for the most part she made herself as inconspicuous as possible.

There were misadventures. They got lost. When Yongden sprained his ankle, Alexandra tried to carry him, then made him a crutch with which he hobbled painfully and slowly for some days. They met robbers and once had to use the revolver to frighten them away. They had anxious moments whenever an official appeared or they had to pass a guarded place, but quick wits and laughter helped them elude these dangers.

At one time, the flint and steel they used to start fires got wet. It was a serious matter, for the weather was extremely cold. Alexandra had once studied the mystics' strange art of increasing the internal heat of the body, the *thumo reskiang*. She put the steel and flint and a bit of moss under her clothes, sent Yongden to gather fuel, and concentrated on the rite. "Soon I saw flames arising around me; they grew higher and higher; they enveloped me, curling their tongues above my head. I felt deliciously comfortable" (*My Journey to Lhasa*, p. 133). She awoke and was able to get a spark from the flint and light a fire, much to the surprise of her companion.

They did not hasten their journey; they sometimes stopped to study the life and customs of the inhabitants. "Familiar talks allowed me to study their peculiar mentality, their views and beliefs. I heard witty stories and terrifying legends" (*My Journal to Lhasa*, p. 196). Also, Alexandra could not resist taking some side trips in order to study the terrain. She found the maps of the country anything but accurate. "It often happens that the line marked by the map-maker is traced, not from his actual knowledge, but according to information received from natives, and Thibetans are rather vague, if not quite fanciful, in describing the roads and the country which they cross" (*My Journey to Lhasa*, p. 118). Towns were invented; the names on the maps seldom corresponded to those used by the natives; "the rivers and mountain ranges are not really in the places they are shown to be, and a number of them are completely ignored, as are also the roads" (*My Journey to Lhasa*, p. 191). David-Neel regretted not being able to use scientific instruments to correct such geographical errors. She did discover a source of the Po, an important tributary of the Brahmaputra River.

They reached Lhasa on New Year's Day, 1924. A furious dust storm arose during which nobody could see them. "I interpreted it as a symbol promising me complete security, and the future justified my interpretation. For two months I was to wander freely in the lamaist Rome, with none to suspect that, for the first time in history, a foreign woman was beholding the Forbidden City" (*My Journey to Lhasa*, p. 257). Alexandra followed Yongden when he, in the role of a lama, guided other pilgrims through the mighty Potola, a cluster of habitations where the Dalai Lama was enthroned. They roamed the streets, saw the festivities of the New Year, and joined the crowds of Tibetans who were beaten back out of the way by police. A policeman hit Alexandra with his truncheon because she had trespassed in a place where only "quality" were allowed. She was delighted. "What a wonderful incognito is mine," she said to Yongden, "Now I am even beaten in the street!" (My Journey to Lhasa, p. 272).

Only to Philippe did she admit how dearly the victory had been bought. She was a tiny woman, and, at the end of her journey, she was nothing but skin and bones. An Englishman who saw her soon after she reached India reported that she was very frail. She rested at the Catholic Mission in Podang, from whence she wrote to Philippe. It had been two years since she had heard from him. She wanted him to let people know of her triumph. She began to receive letters from publishers who hoped to publish her story. In May 1925, she and Yongden were in France with the many Tibetan books and manuscripts she had collected.

My Journey to Lhasa appeared serially in Asia from March to June 1926. Its publication in book form the following year met with success. She could not have kept a journal or done any writing on the journey itself, yet she could recall its many incidents clearly and transmit to readers the excitement and pleasure of the trip.

She became the reigning authority on Tibet and Tibetan Buddhism, publishing, between 1931 and her death, a series of books on Oriental mysticism, books which have gained in popularity with the increase in interest in exploring psychic phenomena.

David-Neel explained to Westerners that Tibetans do not believe in supernatural happenings. They consider the extraordinary feats which astonish the world to be the work of natural energies which come into action in exceptional circumstances or through an individual who knowingly or unknowingly is able to release them. The idea that Buddhists believe in the reincarnation of the soul is also erroneous. The energy produced by the mental and physical activity of a being brings about the appearance of new mental and physical phenomena, once this being has been dissolved by death. The elite among Tibetan philosophers hold these views, but the masses accept the more simple explanation of an entity assuming various forms as it moves from one world to another.

Alexandra bought a house in Digne, in the south of France, named it Samten Dzong (Fortress of Meditation), and settled there with Yongden, now legally known as Arthur David-Neel. Philippe remained in Algeria. She and Yongden lived happily at Digne for ten years, surrounded by the treasures she had brought back with her from Asia. In 1936, however, the urge to travel impelled Alexandra to go once more to China.

The peaceable kingdom she had known there was disappearing under the onslaughts of the Japanese army. Foreigners were suspected as spies by the Chinese, and stories of brutality toward Westerners were rife. Alexandra and Yongden sought refuge in Tatsienlu (K'ang-ting), on the Tibetan frontier, where they lived for six years, right through World War II. She wrote books on

Buddhism and a stream of articles on events in China. She received news of Philippe's death in 1941. Without him to handle her affairs, she ran out of money and had to scrimp on fuel and food. At last, she was advised to join the many others who were fleeing China. She and Yongden put their baggage on mules and walked south until they found a French military mission and were flown out to India.

Back in Digne, Alexandra exchanged her royalties for exemption from city taxes. She was in her eighties, a small, white-haired woman, imperious and subject to furious tempers when things did not go her way. But she was famous, not only in the town but in all of France. The French geographical society awarded her a gold medal. In 1964 she was given her third promotion in the Legion d'honneur, to a Premier Commandeur. Yongden died in 1955. Alexandra lived on until September 8, 1969, when she died peacefully in her beloved home.

BIBLIOGRAPHY

Works by Alexandra David-Neel (in English)

My Journey to Lhasa: The Personal Story of the Only White Woman Who Succeeded in Entering the Forbidden City. New York and London: Harper, 1927. First published in five installments in *Asia* 26 (Mar.–July 1926) as "A Woman's Daring Journey into Tibet," pp. 195–201, 266–68; 320–28, 346–53; 429–35, 452–54; 512–16, 563–66; 624–33, 644–46.
Initiations and Initiates in Tibet. Translated by Fred Rothwell. London: J. Rider, 1931.
With Mystics and Magicians in Tibet. Translated from the French. London: Lane, 1931.
    Also published as *Magic and Mystery in Tibet*. New York: C. Kendall, 1932.
"Women of Tibet." *Asia* 34 (Mar. 1934): 176–81.
Tibetan Journey. London: Lane, 1936.
Buddhism, Its Doctrines and Its Methods. Translated by H. N. M. Hardy and Bernard Miall. London: Lane, 1939.
"Tibetan Border Intrigue." *Asia* 41 (May 1941): 219–22.
"Tibet Looks at the News." *Asia* 42 (Mar. 1942): 189–91.
"New Western Provinces of China." *Asia* 42 (May–June 1942): 286–89, 366–70.
"High Politics in Tibet." *Asia* 43 (Mar. 1943): 157–59.
"Mohammedans of the Chinese Far West." *Asia* 43 (Dec. 1943): 677–79.
"Edge of Tibet." *Asia* 44 (Jan. 1944): 26–29.
"Theater in China Now." *Asia* 44 (Dec. 1944): 559–60.
The Secret Oral Teachings in Tibetan Buddhist Sects. Translated by H. N. M. Hardy. Calcutta, India: Maha Bodhi Society of India, 1964.
(With Lama Yongden) *The Power of Nothingness*. Translated by J. van der Wettering. Boston: Houghton Mifflin, 1982.

Works about Alexandra David-Neel

Allen, Alexandra. *Travelling Ladies*. London: Jupiter, 1980, pp. 107–33.
Booz, Elisabeth B. "Alexandra David-Neel." In *Into the Unknown: The Story of Exploration*. Washington, D.C.: National Geographic Society, 1987, pp. 159–63.

Contemporary Authors. Detroit: Gale Research, 1922–date, 1st revision, vol. 25: 176.

Foster, Barbara, and Michael Foster. *Forbidden Journey: The Life of Alexandra David-Neel*. New York: Harper & Row, 1987.

Galland, China. *Women in the Wilderness*. New York: Harper & Row, 1980, pp. 46–54.

International Dictionary of Women's Biography. Edited by Jennifer S. Uglow and Frances Hinton. New York: Continuum, 1982.

Macdonald, David. *Twenty Years in Tibet*. Philadelphia: Lippincott, n.d., pp. 288–90.

Miller, Lurie. *On Top of the World: Five Women Explorers in Tibet*. London: Paddington, 1976, pp. 131–97.

Obituaries were published in the *New York Times*, on Sept. 9, 1929; the London *Times*, on Sept. 10, 1929; the *Washington Post*, on Sept. 11, 1929; the *Antiquarian Bookman*, on Sept. 20, 1929; and *Publishers Weekly*, on Oct. 6, 1929.

LADY FLORENCE DIXIE
1855–1905

Lady Florence Dixie was one of Victoria's subjects who rebelled against the restraints placed on women and who sought escape in travel. Her journeys took her to Patagonia in 1878 and to South Africa in 1881. She wrote travel narratives, novels, pamphlets, and articles expressing strong views on the rights of women, the Irish question, and the humanitarian treatment of animals and in defense of Cetewayo, the captured king of Zululand. She was instrumental in Cetewayo's release and return to power.

She began writing verse at the age of ten, and some of her childhood poems reveal a curiosity about problems which she was to tackle later in life: man's relationship with God and with his fellow men; war and its horrors; exploitation and poverty. Her feminism was expressed in a blank verse tragedy, *Isola; or, The Disinherited: A Revolt for Woman and All the Disinherited*, and in a number of pamphlets. "I wonder," she wrote,

> what the early thoughts of man would be if the position of the sexes were reversed, when he first realized the fact that secret contempt of sex was the reason for the disabilities imposed on him by woman. I know, speaking as a woman, that when I first opened my eyes as a girl on those disabilities, and realized that my sex was the barrier that hid from my yearning gaze the bright fields of activity, usefulness, and reform, the bitterness and pain that entered into my soul can never be obliterated in my lifetime. Child as I was, I resolved to defy those unnatural laws. [*Lady Florence Dixie in Glasgow* (Dundee: John Leng, 1891), p. 9, quoted in Stevenson, *Victorian Women Travel Writers in Africa*, p. 41]

Lady Florence was born in London on May 25, 1855, the youngest daughter of Archibald William Douglas, Marquess of Queensberry, and his wife, Caroline Margaret Clayton. She had a twin, James, and four older siblings. The date of Florence's birth has been given as May 24, 1857; however, *Burke's Peerage*, while it gives no date for Florence, states that James, her twin, was born on May 25, 1855.

When the twins were three, Lord Queensberry shot himself fatally while cleaning his gun. A few years later, Lady Douglas converted to Catholicism, and the younger children's guardians threatened to take them away from her. Having no legal rights over her own offspring, Lady Douglas fled to France with the twins. Much of Florence's early years were spent moving about the Continent, which undoubtedly gave her a taste for travel. Aside from a year in an English convent, she had no formal schooling. She grew up something of a tomboy, playing games with her brothers. She became an expert horsewoman and enjoyed vigorous health.

Florence married Sir Alexander Beaumont Churchill Dixie, a sportsman, in 1875. Within the next three years, they had two sons, George Douglas and Albert Edward (who was named for his godfather, the Prince of Wales). But their mother was not going to be trapped into the role of homebody. When the boys were mere infants, the Dixies and two of Florence's brothers organized an expedition to Patagonia to indulge their passion for travel and hunting.

"Patagonia!" cried their friends, "Who would ever think of going to such a place?" "Why, you will be eaten up by cannibals!" "What on earth makes you choose such an outlandish part of the world to go to?"

Florence answered that she chose this tip of South America precisely because it was so far away and so isolated. Later she expanded on her reasons:

> Palled for the moment with civilisation and its surroundings, I wanted to escape somewhere, where I might be as far removed from them as possible. Many of my readers have doubtless felt the dissatisfaction with oneself, and everybody else, that comes over one at times in the midst of the pleasures of life; when one wearies of the shallow artificiality of modern existence; when what was once excitement has become so no longer, and a longing grows up within one to taste a more vigorous emotion than that afforded by the monotonous round of society's so-called "pleasures." (*Across Patagonia*, pp. 1–2)

In the 100,000 square miles of the chosen country, she hoped to be able to gallop freely, to "penetrate into vast wilds, virgin as yet to the foot of man," to explore the "mysterious recesses" of the pampas.

The men were more interested in hunting. The party included two of Florence's brothers, John Sholto, Lord Queensberry (who formulated the famous "Queensberry rules" for boxing), and Lord James Douglas; her husband Beau; and a friend, Julius Beerbohm. It was Beerbohm, a naturalist, author of *Wanderings in Patagonia*, who sparked the idea of the journey.

On arrival in South America, they hired guides, bought hunting dogs, and selected some fifty horses. To keep their baggage down to such things as were absolutely indispensable, they packed two small tents, two hatchets, a pail, an iron pot for cooking, a frying pan, and a saucepan. Provisions included biscuits, coffee, tea, sugar, flour, oatmeal, preserved milk, butter (in tins), and two kegs of whiskey. On Beerbohm's advice, they took along a sack of yerba maté, which they grew so fond of as a brew that they used it instead of tea or coffee. They depended on hunting for meat and took a few items for trading in case they met Indians. The heaviest items of equipment were the guns and ammunition.

Four guides were chosen, three of whom proved to be highly satisfactory. One, L'Aria, was "a dried-up-looking being of over sixty," a beautiful rider, and wonderfully active and enduring. In town he was never sober, but once on the trail he became a total abstainer. Gregorio, an Argentine gaucho, had been an Indian trader and knew a little English. François, a French ostrich hunter, had once been a cook and was most useful in that capacity, as well as a cheery soul who entertained them with songs around the campfire or while riding. As for the fourth, Guillaume, another Frenchman, "all our party disliked him very much" (*Across Patagonia*, p. 39).

Shortly after they had started on the road, a party of horsemen galloped up. These proved to be not bloodthirsty mutineers but guests who had been invited for a day's shooting. Among them was H.I.H. Prince Henry of Prussia. They had provisioned themselves with such delicacies as *asperges en jus*, Alsatian patés, and German sausages, with which all of the party had a hearty camp supper, washed down with wine. In the morning, after an hour's hunt, Prince Henry cooked poached eggs for breakfast. Then the royal party left, as their steamer was waiting for them at Sandy Point.

A few days later, the group visited an encampment of Tehuelche Indians, a good-humored race, much interested in the strangers and their guns. Florence became popular when she passed out lumps of sugar, in exchange for which she obtained a small amount of meat. The Indians were as short of meat as was the hunting party, and Florence commented that the Indian men were too lazy to hunt until they were quite hungry. But the women were very industrious, making guanaco *capas*, weaving gay-colored garters and fillets for the hair, and working silver ornaments, all in addition to the usual women's work of collecting firewood and cooking. The Indian husband and wife showed great affection for one another and love of their offspring, who were petted and spoiled.

The hunters soon came within sight of game—guanaco and ostriches—and discovered a gourmet delight in *chorlitos*, birds "between a plover and a wood-cock," incredible numbers of which came to Patagonia to feed on cranberries. These birds, roasted on a spit over the fire, were "so seductively succulent, so exquisitely flavoured, so far beyond anything the gourmet might dream of" that "the sensation it produces on the palate when tasted for the first time may, without hyperbole, be described as rising to the dignity of an emotion" (*Across Patagonia*, p. 133).

After crossing the rather monotonous flatlands, the travelers were rewarded by the sight of the cordilleras of the Andes, described by Florence as

a mighty mountain chain, which lost itself westward in the gathering dusk of evening—standing like a mysterious barrier between the strange country we had just crossed and a possibly still stranger country beyond. . . . For a long time after complete darkness had fallen over everything, I stood alone, giving myself up to the influence of the emotions the scene described awoke in me, and endeavouring, though vainly, to analyse the feeling which the majestic loneliness of Patagonian

scenery always produced in my mind—a feeling which I can only compare—for
it would be impossible for me to seize on any definite feature of the many vague
sensations which compose it—to those called up by one of Beethoven's grand,
severe, yet mysteriously soft sonatas. (*Across Patagonia*, pp. 142–43)

As they sailed away from Patagonia, Florence remembered the days filled
with exciting chase, the evenings around a cheery campfire, and her pleasure in
the mountain scenery. The dangers and discomforts—an earthquake, a grass fire,
drenching rains, scorching sun, pitiless mosquitoes, and blasting winds—were
soon forgotten. "Taking it all in all, it was a very happy time, and a time on
whose like I would gladly look again" (*Across Patagonia*, p. 251).

Lady Dixie showed herself a hardy traveler, uncomplaining, never asking
special consideration as the lone woman of the party. She had enjoyed the chase,
but her sympathy with animals soon took precedence over hunting and she later
became a member of the Humanitarian League and even published a pamphlet
on *The Horrors of Sport* (1895). When she came back from Patagonia, she
brought with her a jaguar, Affums, which she led through the grounds on a
leash.

Across Patagonia was published in 1880. A lively and popular tale, it was
illustrated with sketches by Beerbohm and published in a number of editions.
The book was not yet off the press when Florence was planning another trip, to
still another wild and remote land. It was to take her across the ice-bound lands
of North America to a winter's sojourn in the Arctic. But politics changed her
plans.

In South Africa, the Boers had risen against the British, who had annexed the
Transvaal in 1877. For some reason, Florence, who had never been to Africa
and was not a newspaperwoman, was made a correspondent by the *Morning
Post* to cover the war. Her unsuitability for the position did not go unnoticed
by the rival press. *Figaro* commented that Society was considerably fluttered by
the appointment of a "real Baronet's wife" as a special correspondent and
predicted that other papers would send countesses and a "real dowager duchess"
to South Africa.

The Dixies arrived in Cape Town in March 1881 to learn that the British
troops had been cut to pieces at Majuba Mountain. Despite this discouraging
news, they spent the next day agreeably shopping and sight-seeing. Florence
had heard of the Zulu king Cetewayo, who was being detained in a farmhouse
just outside of town, and she went to visit him. He had refused a British ultimatum
to cease warfare against the Boers (before the Boers themselves rose against the
British) and had been captured at Ulundi in 1879. Florence found him a pleasing,
kindly, and noble warrior, not the ignorant and bloodthirsty despot he had been
depicted. He asked her to visit Zululand and bring him news of his people.

The Dixies sailed to Durban, then went by train to Pietermaritsburg, where
they bought horses. Then they visited battle sites and army posts and did a bit
of hunting. News came of the peace treaty with the Boers, which they felt was

a disgrace to England. English settlers they met also felt bitter about the treaty. Florence agreed with their bitterness and their dislike of the Boers, but she also felt uneasy about the British treatment of the Africans.

Since Zululand was disturbed by wars (the British had divided it among thirteen rival chiefs), Florence and Beau decided to fill in the time by a visit to the diamond mines at Kimberley. Much of the journey was rough and dangerous. Riding in wooden carts with careless drivers on precipitous mountain roads, they twice came close to disaster, once when the cart almost fell into a chasm and again when the cart turned over, falling on Florence, who mercifully was un-injured. The town that grew up around the mines was dirty and depressing. The hospital was a "den of misery" where injured men lay untended. They were glad to leave it.

The journey to Zululand was the high point of Florence's trip. She visited the sites of famous battles and thrilled at romantic thoughts of the mighty Zulu warriors. She interviewed, as best she could, the people of the country to find out their feelings about Cetewayo and determined that they wished to have him return. Again in Cape Town she visited the king and promised to do what she could to have him released and returned to power in his homeland.

They were back in England before the end of 1881. Florence had suffered from cold, rain, and poor food, but she had found something enchanting in the free Bohemianism of the life, and she had found a cause worth fighting for. Her articles on Zululand, published in *Vanity Fair* between December 10, 1881, and February 4, 1882, along with some of her dispatches on the subject to the *Morning Post*, were collected and printed as *A Defence of Zululand and Its King; Echoes from the Blue Books* (1882). The Blue Books were government documents from which Dixie had meticulously culled authentic data to back up her argument. Her story of the African travels appeared as *In the Land of Misfortune* (1882). Cetewayo visited England to plead his own cause, and he was restored to his country in 1883.

Florence had now cut her teeth in the arena of politics and by 1883 she was engaged in another cause—that of Irish Home Rule. She felt that the British policy in Ireland paralleled that in Africa; it was exploitation. She went to Ireland and raised money to help evicted tenants. She wrote pamphlets and letters to the papers and privately to William Gladstone against the Land League. She made enemies. She was threatened. She was attacked while walking her dog near Windsor by knife-wielding men dressed as women, and her St. Bernard ran them off. She felt that the men were Irish partisans but she had no proof, and no official action was taken.

Beau lost a large sum gambling on horses in 1883, and the couple was forced to move from their estate, Bosworth Park, to London. Along with their reduced circumstances, both Beau and Florence began to have medical problems that effectually put an end to thoughts of travel. Florence continued to write pamphlets on women's rights, the humanitarian treatment of animals, and dress reform. Her novels and verse were infused with ideas of a utopian society where women were equal to men. She attacked the exclusion of women from the workplace and the university. She spoke up for reforms in child custody, equitable property laws, and fairer inheritance laws. She felt that no nation could be free if its women were degraded by unjust laws. She wrote books for children depicting strong, independent women. She advocated the serious study of sexuality, sex education for children, and population control. She predicted that one day women would control their own biological processes.

Within her own circle, Florence knew tragedy and unpleasant notoriety. Her brother Francis had been killed in 1865 while attempting to climb the Matterhorn. James, her beloved twin, committed suicide in 1891. Her only sister died in 1893. In 1895 Lord Queensberry insulted Oscar Wilde, whose suit for criminal libel brought to light the writer's homosexual relationship with John's son, Lord Alfred Douglas, and resulted in the imprisonment and impoverishment of Wilde.

Lady Dixie did not contribute greatly to geographical knowledge, and she was not a particularly good observer of the countries through which she journeyed. Yet she had made a name for herself as a traveler, writer, and activist. She died suddenly on November 7, 1905, her dreams for the emancipation of women and justice for all peoples far from realized.

BIBLIOGRAPHY

Works by Lady Florence Dixie

Across Patagonia. London: Bentley, 1880; also published with subtitle, *Six Months' Wandering over Unexplored and Untrodden Ground*. New York: A L. Burt, 1880.
"Affums: A True Story." *Vanity Fair* 7 (Dec. 7, 1881): 4–6.
"Cetshwayo and Zululand." *Nineteenth Century* 12 (Aug. 1882): 303–12.
A Defence of Zululand and Its King: Echoes from the Blue Books. London: Chatto & Windus, 1882.
In the Land of Misfortune. London: Bentley, 1882.
"Memories of a Great Lone Land." *Westminster Review* 139 (March 1893): 247–56.

Works about Lady Florence Dixie

Burke's Genealogical and Heraldic History of the Peerage, Baronetage, and Knightage. Edited by Peter Townsend. London: Burke's Peerage, 1963 (under "Archibald William Douglas, 8th Marquess of Queensberry," p. 2005, and "Sir Alexander Beaumont Churchill Dixie, 11th Baronet," pp. 740–41).
Dictionary of National Biography. 2d supplement. London: Smith, Elder, 1912, p. 510.
Europa Biographical Dictionary of British Women. Edited by Anne Crawford and others. London: Europa, 1985.
Roberts, Brian. *Ladies in the Veld*. London: Murray, 1965, pp. 75–181.

Stevenson, Catherine Barnes. *Victorian Women Travel Writers in Africa*. Boston: Twayne, 1982, pp. 41–86, 167–69, 176–77. Includes a bibliography of primary sources.

Van Thal, Herbert. *Victoria's Subjects Travelled*. London: Barker, 1951, pp. 181–84.

An obituary appeared in the London *Times*, on Nov. 8, 1905.

CHRISTINA DODWELL
1951–

Christina Dodwell discovered an area that was in the 1980s still unexplored and largely unmapped, where natives used stone tools, made fires by friction, dressed in feathers and grass, and had never seen a white woman. Some were said, with good reason, to be cannibalistic. When she visited Papua New Guinea from 1980 to 1981, she had to reach the isolated tribes by foot, for there was only one road into the highlands and none to the native villages she chose to visit. She also traveled by horseback and canoe, paddling a native dugout down the Sepik River and its tributaries. She returned to the country later and joined an American crew on a raft trip down the Waghi River, through some of the wildest white water ever attempted. The Waghi is called "eater of men." The river trip, filmed by the British Broadcasting Company, was shown on its television series, "River Journeys."

She was well prepared for such a trip, for previously she had traveled nearly twenty thousand miles around Africa, taking a dugout canoe down the Congo River. After the New Guinea trip, she visited central China, where she paddled her inflatable canoe on lakes and rivers, some almost as rough as the Waghi. She has ridden on airplanes, busses, taxis, camels, and horses. She can shoe a horse, drive a donkey cart, speak a variety of languages, and make friends wherever she goes.

Christina Dodwell was born to English parents in Nigeria on February 1, 1951. She left there at the age of six, but returned a number of times to visit her parents after her father was reassigned to Nigeria and before the end of British rule in the country. She was educated in England and worked as a secretary and interior designer in London. She had never planned to be an explorer. Before she set out in 1975 for a vacation in Africa, she had lived a modern city life and was literally afraid of the dark.

Her introduction to wilderness travel came about almost by accident. She and three others left England intending to cross north Africa in a Land Rover. After they had crossed the Sahara Desert, the two boys in the party stole the jointly owned Land Rover and left Christina and a friend, Lesley Jamieson, stranded in northern Nigeria. Instead of flying back home, the two women decided to continue their journey, on foot if necessary. They recovered a small part of what the Land Rover had cost them and auctioned off almost all their possessions. Each took the bare necessities in a backpack, and they began to hike. They had no real intention of covering most of Africa or of taking three years to do so, but somehow the adventure became too compelling to give it up. They hitched rides, stayed with casual acquaintances, and made many friends, especially among the Europeans living or working in Africa. They wore long skirts, which they considerd more comfortable than pants and more acceptable. No driver, said Christina, would fail to help a girl in a flowing, long skirt. They also twisted their long hair into buns, which they thought made them look like schoolteachers, who naturally commanded respect.

They had no fixed itinerary and most of the time neither map nor compass; they went wherever they fancied. Christina had the advantage of knowing much about the ancient history of the country (it was by no means lacking in civilization), and she took her friend to see some of the old palaces and forts. They visited native villages and market places. They stayed with tribes who admitted to being cannibalistic but assured them they were in no danger. They acquired horses and rode gaily across country. Once they got lost in a desert and for almost a week went without food.

Finding themselves in Bangui, in the Central African Republic, they wondered how to get back to the coast. Against the advice of all, but with the wholehearted aid of a crew of Americans who were installing a telephone line, the women acquired a dugout canoe, patched it up, fitted it with a rudder, and set off down the Congo to Brazzaville. Neither had ever paddled a canoe. It took seven weeks to reach Brazzaville—weeks of riotous fun, excitement, and fear. The river had many whirlpools, which they learned to negotiate; floating water hyacinths, which clogged the rudder; hippos and crocodiles, which had to be avoided; and clouds of mosquitoes, which had to be endured. It also had villages with friendly people who gave them food and advice. When they did reach Brazzaville, they found they were famous. Indeed, they were amazed that the news of their presence in Africa had traveled faster than they had. People began to watch for them, entertain them, and help them along.

In Rhodesia, both took jobs—Christina worked in a kennel, Lesley worked as a nurse. Finally, Lesley flew home to be married, and Christina was alone. The two had become the closest of friends. Christina discovered, however, that she could survive on her own, and she went on traveling, sometimes on foot, later on a horse, wending her way in the general direction of northwest. Destination was irrelevant. "Pure travel is like dancing," she wrote, "It means moving in time with the land and the sky, being part of the music" (*Travels with Fortune*, p. 271).

Everywhere she acquired new skills. An old Afrikaner taught her how to pan for gold and how to find precious stones. A forester showed her which plants were edible. An African artisan taught her the lost-wax process of casting metal; another, how to work wood. Native women helped her to do traditional beadwork. She secretly watched Pygmy girls in a ritual dance. She saw rock paintings made by Bushmen, and she came upon a queer group of people who had descended from Hottentots and Dutch settlers.

All was not sheer joy. Christina had tick fever; she was bitten by a jackal and for fear of rabies had to take rabies injections; and for a week she was paralyzed by the bite of a huge spider. On that occasion, she managed to get to a Catholic mission infirmary, but the nurses ignored her cruelly. It was fortunate that it happened while Lesley was with her. Once Christina went to a witch doctor to be cured of bronchitis. Often she had to ignore her aches and pains and ride on, almost oblivious to her surroundings. When well, she rode or climbed joyously, swimming in rivers and the ocean, exploring caves, catching butterflies, and getting to know herself. When at last she went home, it was not because she was tired of Africa but because she had promised to be at her brother's wedding.

While recruiting her strength and writing *Travels with Fortune*, based on her diaries, she toured France and Greece, the United States, and Mexico, and looked in the world atlas for places that might be interesting to visit, places remote and wild. Finding that the eastern half of New Guinea was one of the last places on earth still much covered with jungle and inhabited by primitive tribes, she decided to explore it.

She had learned to travel with little. Her food supplies consisted of such items as beef jerky, nuts, raisins, and salt. She carried a hammock and a compass. Her wardrobe included raingear and long skirts. Her preparations seemed rather too casual; when she entered the jungle, she had forgotten boots, and she walked much of the way barefooted through the mud, crossing rain-flooded rivers on bridges of a single, slippery log. Although she lived off the country, eating whatever the natives ate and slinging her hammock in native houses, there were few times when she met with hostility or felt apprehensive. Her knowledge of pidgin—common among the many tribes, each with its own language—her self-possession, her friendly smile, and her lack of weapons ensured a welcome. She also felt that being a woman was a protection, for she offered no threat.

She did not find it easy to get to Papua New Guinea, partly due to government restrictions on travel by outsiders and close supervision of visa deadlines. After a long trip on a coastal steamer and then by an outrigger canoe powered by an outboard motor, she was dropped off at Vanimo, a small and remote settlement on the north coast. An American missionary family who lived there made her welcome. There was no place to buy a map, but she borrowed one and found that Vanimo was so isolated that no roads led to it or from it.

She spread out the map and let a pencil drop to touch it. It fell on a spot at the remotest part of the mountain cordillera. The nearest road shown on the map was a jeep track which ended at Lake Kopiaga. She found an airplane to take her as close to the chosen spot as possible. From there, she would walk to the lake. The plane left her at a small town, Oksapmin, and, as luck would have it, she found a young Englishman there. He advised her how to get to Lake Kopiaga, and he put out word that guides were needed. In due time, two guides appeared and were hired.

The Englishman thought Christina could not make it to the lake because a river she would have to cross was then in flood. She said she would swim it—and she did. It was a terrifying experience, but she emerged safe and sound, along with two Hewa tribesmen who provided her with a swimming raft of two logs tied together and then swam the river with her and guided her through the jungle.

She was heading into Duna territory, and she soon shared a meal with the inhabitants of a small hamlet. Two of the men wore tusks through their noses, and others wore shell necklaces. Using pidgin and gestures, she learned about their food, their legends, and their songs. She slept in one of the huts and hired a new guide for the next leg of her journey, which ended at Lake Kopiaga. There she sheltered with a Catholic missionary, "sleeping in a bed with crisp white sheets." She had also reached the road. It was the Highlands Highway, the most important road in the country, built in 1970 to aid in the economic development of the highlands. But it was a wretched road in wet weather. Dodwell got a lift in a jeep, but she and the driver spent much of the time hauling the jeep out of the mud and finally she had to abandon it. She went ahead on foot, preceded by word of her extraordinary feat of having walked all the way from Oksapmin.

The Sepiks believed that they were descended from crocodiles, and for initiation into manhood the young men were marked by cutting the skin in a series of slashes from the chest over their shoulders and down their backs in the likeness of a crocodile. After Christina watched a skin-cutting ceremony, she allowed them to mark a crocodile's star mark on her upper arm. The razor cuts were painful, but she knew she would bear the scar proudly and would always be welcome in Sepik homes.

By the end of the four-month journey, the last part spent paddling her dugout canoe down the Sepik River, Christina Dodwell was known. All along the river, the village people called out, "*Sepik meri*" (Sepik woman), and brought her fruit and gifts. She felt that she had become part of their lives. When she returned the following year, they greeted her fondly as a child who had been away. On the second trip, she joined the American rafters on the exciting and dangerous Waghi River.

She went next to China. She had a special interest in visiting that country, for her mother and grandparents had lived there. Her grandmother, Doris Beddow, was a special correspondent and a woman of lively curiosity who had visited as much of China as she could manage. Christina's grandfather, who had been in the country since 1919, was held in a Japanese prison for seven months before escaping by ship to Africa, where he stayed several years before returning to England. Her mother had been born in Hankow and was raised in Beijing (Peking). She had been sent out of war-torn China with her nanny in 1937, but she remembered the address of the Beijing house in which she had lived. Christina was able to find it, and although she could not get inside, it gave her "a glow of pleasure" just to stand outside.

Beijing was also the place of business of Dodwell International, an old established China trading company. Although not related, the company knew of her through her New Guinea river trip and bought her the plane ticket to Urumchi, where she started her Chinese journey. They entertained her handsomely in Beijing.

But she was not in China to visit cities. She had brought with her an inflatable canoe, and she hoped to find rivers and lakes where she could paddle about by herself. She had read the books of previous European travelers, including those of Mildred Cable and Ella Maillart, and she made a list of places she wanted to see. She was allowed only four months in the country and meant to make the most of them. In the preceding years, "foreign devils" had become "foreign friends," but Chinese officials sometimes seemed to delight in thwarting travelers' plans. Christina was careful not to go where she was not allowed to go, but since she tended to travel solo and to wander off the beaten track, she did see a few places not on the usual itinerary.

Her first goal was Kashgar. This fabled crossroads of Asia had recently been opened to travel. She went from Urumchi by bus, following the Silk Road through the desert, a four-day trip. To break the ice and get her fellow passengers to communicate with her, Christina tried a method she had used in Africa and New Guinea. She brought out photographs of her family and picture postcards of English scenes. The picture of her parents semed to introduce her not as a foreigner but as a person with a mother and father just like everyone else.

She got a special permit to spend some days in the Chinese Pamirs, which link China with Pakistan, and she hitched a ride in a truck, along with Peter, a young Dutchman. They stopped for the night at Tashkurghan, where Dodwell borrowed a horse and went for a ride. The people were shy, but she made friends with some of the women by showing them her photographs. On her way back to Kashgar, she stopped at Lake Karakul and went for a canoe trip, racing herself from one side to the other. Finding an exit stream, she followed it for several days until the river became rough. The canoe overturned in a rapid, drenching her in the icy river, but she continued downriver until she was near enough to the road to catch a truck ride back to town.

Later she visited Heaven Lake in the northern Gobi, paddled down the Yellow River, launched her canoe on the Tsing Hai (Koko Nor) at the foot of the Kunlun range, and canoed down the Yangtze. She encountered some pretty stiff rapids— all very exhilarating as well as exhausting.

The driver of the truck on which she had hitched a ride to Tsing Hai said he was going to Lhasa and invited her to go along. She had no permit to visit Lhasa, but she could not resist going part of the way into Tibet. Although she missed seeing a lamasery there, she managed to visit one at Taer'si. She saw the stone forest at Shilin and took the Burma Road to Dali, where she came down with fever. She did not trust the new practitioners of Westernized medicine and went to an herbal doctor, who gave her twigs, mushrooms, flowers, and bark with which to make tea. In a few days, she was well enough to get on with her travels, which included a visit to a sacred mountain, Ju Jie Shan. At the summit was a monastery inhabited by one old monk and a young novice.

With only a little time left on her travel permit, Dodwell put her canoe into the Lijiang River and spent two days making idyllic progress down the stream. She had arrived in China in the spring; now, it was autumn and harvesting had begun. It seemed to her an appropriate time to leave.

BIBLIOGRAPHY

Works by Christina Dodwell

Travels with Fortune: An African Adventure. London: W. H. Allen, 1979.
In Papua New Guinea. Sparkford, Yeovil, Somerset: Oxford Illustrated Press, 1983.
"The Sepik and the Waghi," in Russell Braddon and others, *River Journeys*. London: British Broadcasting Corporation, 1984, pp. 45–76.
An Explorer's Handbook: An Unconventional Guide for Travelers to Remote Regions. London: Hodder & Stoughton, 1984.
A Traveler in China. New York: Beaufort Books, 1985.

MARIKA HANBURY-TENISON
1938–1982

Marika Hanbury-Tenison was a Cornish writer and cookery expert, the wife of a phi-
losopher explorer, Robin Hanbury-Tenison. Together, they went to South America in
1971 and to Indonesia in 1973 to visit isolated tribes, each one with its distinctive culture,
each a cohesive group associated by race, language, and custom. Both husband and wife
wrote of their experiences.

Robin, founder of Survival International, wished to bring to the attention of the world
the plight of the tribes threatened by extinction or degradation through the spread of
modern technology and industrial exploitation. Marika wished to share the excitement of
discovery and her interest in the people, not far distant from the Stone Age, some hitherto
unvisited by Europeans. The message of both was that the future of such tribal people,
hurried into the twentieth century without time to adjust to change, is bleak unless present
policies change. The message has importance not only to Brazil and Indonesia but also
to the rest of the world, where obsession with progress, profits, and technological advance
threatens to override the preservation of cultural values and thus humanity itself.

Marika was born on September 9, 1938, in London, England, the daughter of
John and Alexander Hopkinson. She was educated in private schools and became
a journalist. When she married Robin in 1959, she was happy to move to his
farm on Bodmin Moor in Cornwall and stay there while he continued his travels
around the globe, for he was a traveler, as he said, from the age of six. Not
until 1971 did he propose that Marika accompany him on an expedition. It was
not an especially good time for her. She had recently had a premature son by
Caesarian section and was only just getting back her strength. She also had a
young daughter. She had begun a successful and interesting career as a cookbook
author and was cookery editor of the *Sunday Telegraph*. But she had longed to
travel with Robin and jumped at the chance to go to Brazil. Her account of the

trip, entitled *For Better, For Worse* by its English publisher, was called *Tagging Along* in America.

Marika made an important contribution to the three-month journey into the Brazilian interior. Her presence in itself was a help in visiting tribes who might have been hostile to men alone. Her charm and her sympathetic interest in people broke the ice when they met coldness, and her ability to communicate with the women, even without knowing their language, added a dimension that would otherwise have been absent. It was far from easy for her to keep pace with her energetic husband. Some of the food nauseated her. She was occasionally acutely miserable and frightened, but most of the time she was so thrilled and excited by all she saw that she thoroughly enjoyed herself, and, when she left South America, she was pleased only because she was going home to her two beloved children.

Robin's previous travels had taken him around the world, driving a jeep, climbing mountains, and riding country busses, bicycles, riverboats, and trains. He had been twice to South America, crossing the continent at its widest point and then journeying by boat from the Orinoco to the Plate. At first, he had traveled purely for the joy of exploration and adventure. Later, he had begun to feel concern for the primitive peoples endangered by land development and exploitation of the natural resources. For some countries, it was already too late; in Asia, Africa, and North America, colonization and political protectorates had robbed indigenous peoples of self-sufficiency and self-respect and had reduced them to a kind of slavery. Although the world was becoming quite aware of the danger of extinction faced by wild animals and plant life, there seemed little interest in the danger of destroying the wild tribes, with their store of knowledge and wisdom. Robin and others formed the Primitive Peoples Fund to help wild tribes throughout the world, to arouse public opinion, and to study methods of saving their lives and their culture. The name of the organization was later changed to Survival International.

Because of his leadership of this group and because of his previous travels in Brazil, Robin was invited by the Brazilian Foreign Ministry to visit the Amerindians there and to make a report on the situation. Marika was invited to go along and to write about the tour from a woman's point of view. They left England in January 1971.

Marika's story of the trip begins with a lighthearted description of the preparations. She had never traveled and had never roughed it. Relying on Robin's rather vague advice, she shopped for jungle boots and tropical clothes, both unobtainable in London's midwinter. Because of her many physical problems, her doctor fitted up a medicine chest with every remedy she might need. She tried to deal with the horror her friends expressed at her leaving a school-age daughter and an infant son. And, just before they left, she and Robin met with a solicitor who asked how long, in case they both disappeared in the jungle, he should wait before presuming them dead!

Although they had been invited by the Brazilian government, the official who was to make the travel arrangements made things as difficult as possible and assigned to them as a companion a young man who was quite out of sympathy with the whole purpose of their mission and who proved to be an unmitigated nuisance. Marika could understand the caution expressed by the official. The tribes they were to visit were known to be fierce. One of Robin's traveling companions on a previous trip had later been clubbed to death on the trail. Other Europeans had disappeared. These stories in the press gave Brazil a bad name. Brazilians themselves were afraid of the tribesmen and never went into the jungle if they could help it. Official concern was wholly with the development of the interior, road building, and resettlement of the dense coastal population. Official plans for dealing with the wild tribes were to take their children away, educate them, and then build government towns for them. The process had already begun.

Robin's persistence and imperturbability prevailed over the bureaucrats' reluctance to let them proceed more or less as planned. Their first visit was to the Xingu, a national park in the Mato Grosso run by two Brazilians, the Villas Boas brothers, whose work Robin knew and whom he was nominating for the Nobel Peace Prize. Amerindians displaced by settlers had been moved into the park and allowed to live in their tribal groups. Fifteen tribes lived there, separated from each other but with some communication and peaceful coexistence. They had been provided with such aids as steel axes and knives to replace stone implements, guns for hunting, and tackle for fishing. They were given medical aid. Above all, they were protected from settlers, mining prospectors, and the type of missionaries who did more harm than good.

The Hanbury-Tenisons were warmly welcomed at Xingu. They spent some time there, discussing the tribal question and visiting many of the tribes, who were indeed primitive: They wore almost nothing in the way of clothing, painted their bodies, and decorated themselves with feathers and necklaces. The men spent their time hunting and fishing, dancing and singing. Almost all, after some wariness, were friendly and helpful. Though the tribes were all different, basically their lives followed the same pattern. The men brought in meat and cleared the jungle; the women and children planted and harvested the crops. "Their lives are simple and ordered," wrote Marika. Although the jungle is frequently harsh, "the Indians of the Xingu have an aura of serenity and happiness which is enviable" (*For Better, For Worse*, p. 66). She herself began to relax and grow rested in the peaceful atmosphere, able to take in stride the sunburn, insect bites, and such dangers as crocodiles (one of which she shot) and man-eating piranha fish.

They left Xingu for the island of Bananal, the largest inland island in the world, once the home of a handful of settlers and a large tribe of Karaja Indians. Some eight thousand settlers had moved in and had built roads, towns, and a "luxury" hotel. The Indians had been pushed farther and farther back to the riverbanks and had finally settled in a compound. The so-called luxury hotel had no such luxuries as electricity, soap, towels, hot water, or a helpful staff. The Indian village was a shock: a mud compound surrounded by barbed wire, small and dirty huts built in rows, garbage and litter strewn around, and once-proud Indians living in depression and sadness.

Later, the couple saw one of the government development settlements of the interior, where, in an effort to clear the slums in the large cities, families had been given small plots of land and sent to begin a new life. The first year, the settlers cleared the scrub or jungle; the second year, they attempted to grow crops; by the third, many gave up the struggle and crept back to the towns they had left. Few were able to make a new life. They lacked the skills, the motivation, and the technical assistance that would have made all the difference.

The farther the Hanbury-Tenisons went, the less official help they were given. Notice was to have been sent to all the posts of the Fundacão Naçional do Indio in the places they wanted to visit, informing officials of their arrival and instructing them to arrange transportation. But few such notices were sent, and the party usually arrived unannounced and unexpected. Luckily, Robin had made some contacts beforehand and had been told of other people living among the tribes who could be helpful—anthropologists, American Peace Corps workers, medical teams, and missionaries. Many of them were in sympathy with the Hanbury-Tenisons' views and went out of their way to see that the visitors were able to find jeeps, boats, or planes to take them on their way.

They flew in small planes and once in a DC3 cargo plane. They traveled by river, by jeep, and on foot. Once, they resorted to a taxi, with a driver willing to take them in a battered, old automobile through extremely rough country for many miles over several days. Somehow, they managed to reach almost all the tribes Robin had wanted to see and to visit most of the people he had wished to talk to. Among them were missionaries. Some were compassionate, understanding, and truly helpful. Others had stripped from the Indians all remnants of pride, had forbidden them to continue the rituals that were part of their lives, and had reduced them to such misery that they had stopped having babies, through the use of an oral contraceptive made from roots.

The couple asked a sympathetic Roman Catholic priest how the people could be helped. His reply was that the Brazilians must stop treating the Indians like animals and regard them as people. The inevitable adjustment to new ways of life would be facilitated by giving the displaced tribes the tools and knowledge to change from hunting to farming.

Robin reported his findings in *A Question of Survival for the Indians of Brazil* (London: Angus & Robertson, 1973). Marika's book appeared some months earlier; both books had an impact on world opinion, though the results for the Brazilian Amerindians were disappointing. A road was soon built through the middle of the Xingu, cutting the tribes off from their hunting grounds, and the displacement process went on.

Robin wished to make a similar study of wild tribes in the Indonesian islands, and Marika went along again. Indonesia, the fifth largest country in the world, developed fast after the end of Dutch colonial rule. It was being exploited by lumbering and mining interests, and nobody was much concerned about the impact on the tribes isolated in the high mountains and on the several islands. If they were to be protected, it was essential that a survey of their situation and needs be made while policies were being developed.

Robin had collected the names of local people who might be helpful, but plans were necessarily vague until they reached the islands. They did not wish to wait for the long process of being made official representatives of Survival International (or to be saddled with an official guide), so they traveled simply as tourists, financed by a grant and out of their own pockets.

The government of Indonesia, wracked by two recent events, one sensational, one tragic, wished to confine visitors to areas around the larger towns. An American anthropologist, Wyn Sargent, had married the chief of a Stone Age tribe and had been hurried out of the country. Michael Rockefeller, visiting the Agat tribe, had disappeared, perhaps drowned, perhaps killed by animals. His body was not found, and there was a remote possibility that he had been captured by one of the wild tribes, some still of a cannibalistic bent. Visitors who wished to penetrate into little-known areas were closely questioned about their motives, and they were warned of dangers beyond the power of the government to avert.

Considering the political situation and the difficulties in transportation and even in communication between the islands, the Hanbury-Tenisons were lucky to be able to make contact with people who could give them information and help them reach the tribes. Among the tribes they visited were the Bataks, the Dyaks, the Mentawai, the Toraja, the Bajo, the Tana Towa, the Hua Ulu in Ceram Island, the Dani of the Baliem Valley in New Guinea, and the Agats— all in the space of three months. Much of that time was spent in getting about, so that visits to the individual tribes were short, but with the aid of interpreters they managed to get a good overall view of the tribes' habits and beliefs.

Almost all the tribes, after the first shock of seeing the strange white people, were friendly and hospitable. The tribes were surprisingly different in physique and appearance, and they ranged from extremely primitive to highly cultured. The groups in the interior, generally hostile to each other, lived in separate, self-contained communities. Each had buildings and agricultural practices peculiar to their own tribe, as well as distinctive dress and customs. All were patriarchal, governed by male councils and religious leaders. Women were the workers. All seemed to enjoy talking, singing, dancing, and just sitting around in beautiful surroundings. The homes of some tribes were clean and tidy, others filthy. The Dani were difficult to get close to because of their habit of smearing themselves with rancid pigs' grease. None had any idea of hygiene, and skin diseases were common. In some places, missionaries were able to provide a little medical care and education.

As in Brazil, the indigenous peoples who were relocated to the towns fared badly. The visitors were surprised to be asked questions by the natives about birth control; many of the tribes were so miserable that they wished to limit births and had only crude methods of abortion.

Marika found the trip no picnic. Although she was fascinated by all she heard and saw, she suffered stomach pains and headaches from the strange foods and was sore from wading through swamps, climbing rough jungle paths, and crossing rushing rivers. She returned home thin and weak, but after being assured that she had caught no strange jungle disease she settled down to write a lively travel book, *A Slice of Spice* (1974). Robin's more serious report was entitled *A Pattern of Peoples: A Journey among the Tribes of the Outer Indonesian Islands* (London: Angus & Robertson, 1975). Both books were illustrated with excellent photographs taken by the authors.

For the next few years, Marika wrote and lectured on food and cookery, charming audiences with her enthusiasm and good looks. She used her knowledge of the gastronomy of the people met on her travels to create interesting dishes. A conservationist, she believed in cutting down on meat, fish, and poultry and using more vegetables, cooked with imagination.

In 1979 she accompanied the Royal Geographical Society's expedition, led by Robin, to the forests of Mount Lulu in Malaysian Sarawak, taking her son and daughter with her. At the base camp in a native "long house," she cooked for the forty-five scientists for three months. She even turned her hand to cooking python.

On October 24, 1982, Marika died of cancer. When she found out that she had the disease, she courageously discussed her reactions on radio and on a television program called "Quest for a Unicorn."

BIBLIOGRAPHY

Works by Marika Hanbury-Tenison

For Better, For Worse: To the Brazilian Jungles and Back Again. London: Hutchinson, 1972. Also published as *Tagging Along*. New York: Coward, McCann & Geoghegan, 1972.
A Slice of Spice: Travels to the Indonesian Islands. London: Hutchinson, 1974. Reviewed in *Geographical Journal* 141 (July 1975).

Works about Marika Hanbury-Tenison

Contemporary Authors. Detroit: Gale Research, 1922–date, vol. 104, p. 194, vol. 108, pp. 203–4.
Hanbury-Tenison, Robin. *Worlds Apart: An Explorer's Life*. London: Granada, 1984.
An obituary was published in the London *Times*, on Oct. 26, 1982.

Marguerite Baker Harrison
1879–1967

Marguerite Baker Harrison was a newspaper woman, secret agent, traveler, writer, and film producer. At the end of World War I, she was a spy in Germany, then she spied in Russia. She was the first American woman to be imprisoned by the Bolsheviks. Of her eighteen months in Russia, ten were spent in prison. She traveled afterward in the Far East and wrote on the many changes occurring in Asia and Russia after the war. She coproduced, with two American photographers, a documentary film of the migration of a nomadic tribe in Persia. In 1925 she joined with three other women to form the Society of Woman Geographers.

She felt a special affinity for the peoples of the Middle East. She learned Russian, Turkish, and Persian with ease and adapted herself so comfortably to the customs, food, and manners of the Eastern people that she wondered whether she might not have had a previous Asiatic existence. One of her most unforgettable experiences was a barge trip down the Karun River in Persia with a group that included a native prince. The barge was a raft of inflated goatskins, covered with rich carpets and silken cushions, and shielded from the sun by a crimson satin canopy. Servants provided opium pipes for the guests, including Harrison. "It seemed the most natural thing in the world," she wrote, "that I should be riding on a barge of goatskins down a mountain river. Somewhere, some time, I knew that I had done it before" (*There's Always Tomorrow*, p. 606).

Her experiences reinforced a long-held belief that the world was one, and in her talks and writings she worked to counteract a narrow nationalism and racial antagonism.

There's Always Tomorrow, Harrison's autobiography, was, in its English edition, given the title *Born for Trouble*. As a matter of fact, her early life was singularly free from trouble. She was born in Baltimore, Maryland, in October 1879, the first daughter of Bernard Baker. Her father was a shipping magnate with social and business connections in England and Europe. The family traveled much abroad, meeting influential and interesting people on both sides of the Atlantic.

Marguerite learned to speak French and German, and she took an avid interest in international politics. She came out in Baltimore society and married one of its most eligible bachelors, Tom Harrison. They had a son, Tommy, and led a life of simple married happiness. She joined no women's clubs and had no interest in woman suffrage. Her only activity outside the small circle of her home and social life was the establishment of the Children's Hospital School. After fourteen years of a happy marriage, Marguerite's life was shattered with her husband's death from a brain tumor in 1915.

She was left with their home and debts of seventy thousand dollars, much of it accumulated during Tom's last tragic months. With a young son to educate, Marguerite needed an income. She got a job as assistant society editor for the Baltimore *Sun*, principally because she knew everybody in Baltimore. She had not been trained to earn a living, had never written anything, and could not type, but she succeeded beautifully. She went on to become a music critic and conducted interviews with visiting celebrities; she acquired the reporter's instinct for news.

In the summer of 1918, Marguerite was overtaken by a restless desire to see for herself the progress of the war in France and Germany. She could not believe that Germany, which she had known and loved, was quite the monster depicted by wartime propaganda. The only way to get into the country before the signing of the peace terms was to serve as a government agent. She applied to the Military Intelligence Division of the War Department for an opportunity to serve her country. The agent who interviewed her reported that she was a cultured woman, attractive and intelligent, an accomplished linguist. In addition, she was "fearless, fond of adventure," and discreet.

She was accepted, and even though the armistice was signed before she could leave, she was sent to Germany, ostensibly as a *Sun* reporter, instructed to supply information to American delegates at the Peace Conference. It was not easy to reach Berlin, for fighting was still going on between factions in the city, and it took all of Marguerite's ingenuity and daring to perform her duties. She was thrilled to be making a contribution to America's effort to "make the world safe for democracy." She kept her eyes open, talked to people, and made many friends, which enabled her to turn in excellent reports. After the Versailles treaty was signed, she returned home.

She went back to the newspaper and, with a legacy from her father, was able to clear up Tom's debts. But she was still restless. She foresaw that in the war's aftermath there would be tremendous changes and new social experiments. One of these was taking place in Russia, and Marguerite felt that she could do a service to America by going to see how the Bolshevik revolution operated. She approached the Military Intelligence Division again and got permission to collect information in Russia such as she had supplied about Germany. She was warned that it would be a far riskier operation, but she had no idea how risky!

Getting into the country took much time and effort. Marguerite found she might enter through a sector of Poland in which there was a tacit armistice keeping the border open to facilitate the repatriation of German prisoners of war and the exchange of hostages. The Polish authorities gave her a pass to cross through this no-man's-land but warned her that she might be shot if she did.

She and a companion, a Russian-born woman, set off for the border, carrying the minimum of baggage and hoping for the best. By sledge and cart and on foot, with warnings from everyone along the way, the two women entered Russia. Far from being shot, they were given a meal by a friendly young schoolteacher in the first small town and then entertained by the Russian officers at the post command, who were delighted to have visitors, especially an attractive American woman.

In Moscow, Marguerite was told that, although she had entered Russia illegally, she could stay for a short time as a reporter. Though scolded by the authorities, she was provided with a comfortable room in the official guesthouse. She interviewed officials and duly reported the news to her paper. She visited a variety of Soviet institutions—day nurseries, schools, and hospitals. All of them lacked proper equipment, even necessities, and she began to realize how low the standard of living had been among the masses in Imperial Russia.

Her initial permit to remain for a week was extended to a month. She attended the annual convention of the Russian Communist Party, as well as innumerable congresses and political meetings, concerts, and plays. She talked to people on the streets and formed a wide acquaintance. She felt very much at home, and she liked the Russians, Communists and reactionaries alike. "I loved their generosity, their Oriental sense of hospitality, their sensitiveness to beauty, their indifference to material discomfort, and above all, their delight in purely impersonal debates on every subject under the sun" (*There's Always Tomorrow*, p. 299).

Suddenly, she was arrested and taken to the dreaded Lubianka prison. At an interview presided over by a dark "black puma" member of the Cheka, Moghilievsky, she was told that all of her movements were known; a dispatch she had sent to the Military Intelligence Division had been intercepted. She admitted that she was an agent of the U.S. Government, but that she was in the country only as an observer. She had never obtained information illegally. Moghilievsky told her she would be given her freedom on condition that she become a counterspy and work for Russia, giving them information about the other foreigners in the guesthouse. Frightened and playing for time, she agreed. She hoped she could hold them off with partial or misleading information until she had accomplished her real mission of getting the mass of data she had collected back to the American authorities.

For the next few months, her life was outwardly much the same. She continued living in the guesthouse with other foreigners, but she had frequent meetings with Moghilievsky, during which she supplied harmless bits of information, and they had long conversations on conditions in America and England. She enjoyed the talks, finding her interrogator an intelligent man. "There gradually grew up between Moghilievsky and myself a curious sort of camaraderie," she wrote (*There's Always Tomorrow*, p. 316).

When she visited American and British nationals held in prison, she took them food and other necessities which she purchased out of her own funds. Among the prisoners was an American, Merian C. Cooper, who had fought with the Poles in Poland's war with Russia and had been captured. She had met him before, at a Red Cross dance in Poland. She was able to get word to his family that he was alive. He felt that he owed his survival to the medicines and food she brought him.

The strain of trying to satisfy the Russians without damaging her own country began to take its toll. For one thing, Marguerite had had no communication from home or from her son, whom she had left in school in Switzerland. At last, she got a message that Tommy was with his grandmother in Baltimore. She was able to get word to her family through friends. She felt that the time would come when Moghilievsky would realize that she was giving him no useful information, and she was almost relieved when she was at last arrested.

For the next ten months, she was Prisoner 2961. The first week was spent in solitary confinement; then she was moved into a room with a number of other women, with whom she became friendly. Her health suffered from confinement, and she became resigned to prison life. "I seldom thought of home or family or anything of the world outside. I was absorbed in the life that was bounded by the four walls of the prison" (*There's Always Tomorrow*, p. 416). She believed that she would remain there until she died. She became so ill that the authorities transferred her to Novinsky prison, a veritable paradise in comparison with Lubianka. She had no news from outside the prison walls and had no idea that her plight was well known to newspaper readers at home and that many efforts were being made to rescue her.

Russia was undergoing a severe economic depression. Her people were starving. Herbert Hoover, on behalf of the American Relief Administration, offered to send food supplies to Russia; in return, the Russians agreed to release unconditionally all Americans detained in the country. Marguerite was free. Her son was in London when she arrived there. In Baltimore, she was petted and pampered by her mother-in-law and offered her old job on the *Sun*. She went to Washington, D.C., where she gave the Military Intelligence Division a mass of information, and she had an interview with Hoover, then the secretary of commerce.

She was surprised to find that American officials, as well as most of the people she talked to, thought of the Soviet regime as merely temporary and were unalterably opposed to recognition of the Soviet government. She was shocked and disappointed at the trend of national politics, at the small-minded Harding administration, at the activities of the Ku Klux Klan, and at the indifference of the average American to foreign affairs.

After settling with her son in a small apartment in New York City, Harrison wrote *Marooned in Moscow: The Story of an American Woman Imprisoned in Russia*. She gave a series of lectures. Her manager wished her to continue to give talks on Russia, but she wanted new material. She could get it by going to the Far East, where there were stirrings among the yellow races. Eastern Siberia, where the Bolsheviks had not yet obtained a foothold, would bear watching. Relations between America and the governments of China and Japan, following the Nine-Power Pact, were still unsettled.

Marguerite left New York in May 1922, headed for Japan, with a commission from *Cosmopolitan* magazine to write a series of articles on the Far East. On shipboard she wrote for the magazine a series of vignettes of prison life, which were later published as *Unfinished Tales from a Russian Prison*.

In Japan, Korea, and Manchuria, she spent some months interviewing political figures, attending meetings, and gathering information. She traveled by varied means, including crowded trains, private cars, and wheeled carriages drawn by decrepit horses. She crossed the great Gobi desert to the Siberian border by the old caravan route. Hungry to update her information on Russia, she took a chance on returning westward through that country. She felt secure, for this time she had a valid visa.

Without warning, she found herself again in a Moscow prison, charged with espionage. At the time of her former arrest, she knew it was a consequence of her own actions, but this time she was innocent and bewildered. Her old enemy, Moghilievsky, had ordered her arrest. He gave her the choice of remaining in prison for the rest of her life or defecting to the Soviets and putting her talents as a spy at the disposal of the Russians. She refused indignantly.

She spent ten weeks in prison. Only a chance encounter with an official of the American Relief Administration, who recognized her in the corridor of the prison, led to her release. She was discharged and told to leave the country within a week.

Settled again in Manhattan, she wrote *Red Bear or Yellow Dragon* about the expansionist ambitions of Russia and Japan. In spite of the harsh treatment she had received in Russia, she felt that it would be to the advantage of the United States to recognize the Soviet government, but she could not convince others of this.

In New York she ran into Merian C. Cooper, whom she had last seen in a Russian prison. He had escaped while she was in Novinsky, and, at the time of her release, he had been ready with a plane to rescue her. He was now back from Abyssinia after making a film there with Ernest B. Schoedsack. He wanted to make travel films more imaginative than those currently being produced. She had recovered her health and her spirit of adventure and was only too ready to fall in with his enthusiastic ideas. They decided to film a nomadic tribe struggling for survival. They recruited Schoedsack, Marguerite got together ten thousand dollars, and the trio began work on what was to become an epic film.

The result, *Grass*, documents the movement of a Bakhtiari tribe, some fifty thousand men, women, and children, with all their livestock—cattle, goats, sheep, and horses—from their winter grazing grounds to summer grasslands in Persia. They went overland, crossing rivers and high mountains. Most of the tribesmen and women were on foot. When they reached the mountains, the men went ahead and chopped a trail through the snow and ice, over which the people walked barefoot, dressed in light cotton clothing. To cross the rivers, they inflated goatskins and tied them together in rafts. The animals swam the river. It took six days and nights to get the whole tribe and their animals across the swiftly moving Karun River.

Marguerite rode along with the tribe, while the photographers shot the film. She suffered from the heat, dust, flies, and the constant noise of the camp. She was moved by the great human drama of migration, which made the film unique and memorable, but she thought the people neither lovable nor interesting. They were "hard, treacherous, thieves and robbers, without any cultural background, living under a remorseless feudal system, crassly material, and devoid of sentiment or spirituality" (*There's Always Tomorrow*, p. 635). She became the physician for the people, dispensing what medicines she had and even attempting minor surgery. "My experiences as a doctor did much to disillusion me about any ideas I may have had as to the romance and glamour of tribal life" (*There's Always Tomorrow* p. 617).

She saw the film only once. It had been processed in Hollywood, and ridiculous titles and subtitles had been affixed to the sound film. "We had made an authentic record of a stupendous, natural drama," she wrote. The titles, "melodramatic, artificial, and of the theater," had taken away the naturalness of the picture (*There's Always Tomorrow*, p. 648). Critics agree with Marguerite about the titles, but the film remains a landmark of documentary film history.

Marguerite completed *Red Bear* just before making the film. Back home, she wrote a study of the new politics in the Far East, *Asia Reborn*. She wrote articles, lectured on her travels, and visited the Near East for a relief society. But she was becoming increasingly disillusioned: "I began to realize the futility of all ideals . . . in the face of the universal moral and political chaos which seemed to have engulfed the world" (*There's Always Tomorrow*, p. 647).

At the age of forty-seven, Harrison married Arthur Middleton Blake, an English actor, and gave up her life of wandering alone over the world. She did travel again, seeing parts of Africa and Australia; at seventy-eight, she went to South America via freight boat.

Blake died in 1949, and, for the eighteen years of her widowhood, Marguerite lived near her beloved son in Baltimore. After her death, on July 16, 1967, he scattered her ashes into the sea.

BIBLIOGRAPHY

Works by Marguerite Harrison

Marooned in Moscow: The Story of an American Woman Imprisoned in Russia. New York: Doran, 1921.

"Russia under the Bolsheviks." *Annals of the American Academy of Political and Social Sciences* 100 (Mar. 1922): 1–4.
"Cross Currents in Japan." *Atlantic Monthly* 132 (July 1923): 127–34.
"Bolos and the Arts." *Bookman* 58 (Dec. 1923): 384–94.
Unfinished Tales from a Russian Prison. New York: Doran, 1923.
"Whirling Dervishes." *Asia* 24 (July 1924): 541–43.
"Angora, Birthplace of the New Turkey." *Travel* 43 (Oct. 1924): 6–12.
Red Bear or Yellow Dragon. New York: Doran, 1924.
"Turkey Mistrusts the Western World." *New York Times Magazine*, Jan. 25, 1925, p. 5.
"I'm Not Afraid to Travel Alone." *Collier's* 75 (Feb. 21, 1925): 16–17.
"Women of the Orient." *New York Times Magazine*, Feb. 22, 1925, p. 10.
"Risky Motoring in Far Places." *New York Times Magazine*, Mar. 1, 1925, p. 10.
"Turbulent Kurds Stage Another Uprising." *New York Times Magazine*, Mar. 15, 1925, p. 8.
"Japan Guards Sakhalin, New Eldorado." *New York Times Magazine*, Mar. 29, 1925, p. 15.
"Islam Limits Caliph to Spiritual Duties." *New York Times Magazine*, July 5, 1925, p. 7.
"The Bitter Bread of Exile." *Century* 111 (Nov. 1925): 73–82.
"Reza Khan." *New York Times Magazine*, Dec. 6, 1925, p. 4.
"Gertrude Bell, a Desert Power." *New York Times Magazine*, July 18, 1926, p. 12.
"Uncrowned Queen of Mesopotamia." *Woman Citizen* n.s. 11 (Sept. 1926): 14–16.
"Black Magic on the Riviera." *Travel* 54 (Mar. 1930): 34–35.
"In Russian Prisons." In *All True! The Record of Actual Adventures That Have Happened to Ten Women of Today.* New York: Brewer, Warren, & Putnam, 1931.
There's Always Tomorrow: The Story of a Checkered Life. New York: Farrar & Rinehart, 1935. Also published (abridged) as *Born for Trouble.* London: Gollancz, 1936.
Asia Reborn. New York: Harper, 1938.

Works about Marguerite Harrison

"An American Newspaper Woman's Adventures in Soviet Russia." *Current Opinion* 72 (May 1922): 641–43.
"An Epic of Man's Fight with Nature." *Literary Digest* (Apr. 25, 1925). Review of the film, *Grass*.
Cooper, Merian C. "Barefoot Nation Migrates through Snow to Find Food: Three Americans, One a Woman, Take Part in Annual Trek of 30,000 Tribesmen." *New York Times Magazine*, Aug. 31, 1924, p. 14.
———. *Grass.* New York: Putnam, 1925.
———. "Grass, a Persian Epic of Migration." *Asia* 24 (Dec. 1924): 941–47; and *Asia* 25 (Jan. and Feb. 1925): 30–39, 118–127.
"A Modern Migration." *Outlook* 140 (May 6, 1925): 10. Review of the film *Grass.*
Olds, Elizabeth Fagg. *Women of the Four Winds.* Boston: Houghton Mifflin, 1985 pp. 155–230. Olds used many sources, including War Department records and news stories from the *Baltimore Sun* and the *New York Times* during the time of Harrison's imprisonments in Russia. They are listed on pp. 302–4.
"Persian Tribes Filmed on Brave Mountain Trudge." *New York Times Magazine*, Mar. 8, 1925, p. 5. Review of the film, *Grass.*

Ratcliffe, S. K. "La Belle Marguerite, Journalist and Spy." *The Observer* (Apr. 26, 1936).

Searl, H. H. "Marguerite Harrison, World Wanderer." *Woman Citizen* n.s. 11 (July 1926): 8–9. An interview.

Simons, F. H. "American Agent." *Saturday Review of Literature* 12 (Oct. 12, 1935): 5.

An obituary was published in the *Washington Post*, on July 18, 1967.

ELSPETH JOSCELINE HUXLEY
1907–

Elspeth Josceline Huxley has been closely connected with East Africa, beginning in the days of early white settlement in Kenya and through that country's achievement of independence from colonialism in 1963. At the age of six she left England with her parents to establish a plantation in what was then British East Africa, and she remained, except during World War I, until she was eighteen. After her marriage she continued to visit Kenya frequently, both to see her parents, who continued to operate the farm, and to visit different areas of the country collecting material for her books.

She began writing as a young girl, contributing articles to the Nairobi newspaper. Throughout her life, she has written novels, histories, journalistic and political works, and travel sketches. A great many of these deal with Africa.

She has observed that writing about Africa is like sketching a galloping horse, "out of sight before you have sharpened your pencil" (*With Forks and Hope*, author's note). Her descriptions of the people, places, and events are particularly valuable in analyzing and interpreting the changes that have taken place in the parts of Africa formerly under British government and protection. She is a perceptive observer, one who writes with style.

Elspeth Josceline Huxley wrote several autobiographical books, the first two of which, *The Flame Trees of Thika* (1959) and *The Mottled Lizard* (1962), were partly fictionalized. She admitted to "not always sticking exactly to factual details." These books tell the story of her childhood and youth in Thika, Kenya, from 1913 until she was sent back to England to continue her education. *The Flame Trees of Thika*, a delightful story of a young girl growing up in a remote and beautiful country, was dramatized by John Hawkesworth for television in 1982.

Elspeth's mother, who appears in the books as Tilly, was actually Eleanor (Nellie) Grosvenor Grant, and Elspeth's father, appearing as Robin, was Josceline (Jos) Grant. A more exact picture of the African farm and Elspeth's connection with it comes through in her edition of her mother's letters, published in 1980 as *Nellie: Letters from Africa*. Although Elspeth never made her home in Africa after adolescence, her father was there until his death in 1947, and Nellie remained until 1965.

Elspeth was born in London on July 23, 1907, almost exactly one year after her parents were married. She was their only child. Nellie was a niece of the first Duke of Westminster. Her father inherited the 10,000-acre ducal estate, Motcombe, in Dorset, where Nellie had grown up surrounded by great wealth. Her father, a peer with the title of Baron Stalbridge, later suffered financial misfortune, and the family was forced to economize. By the time Nellie was twenty, they had left Motcombe for a much more modest London home.

When Stalbridge died in 1912, he was unable to leave anything to his daughters because his great effort had been to keep free of debt the vast Motcombe estate. It went to the eldest son, who dissipated its vast resources over the years in horse racing and fox hunting. Nellie married Josceline Grant, a Scottish dreamer and adventurer, of impeccable lineage but almost as penniless as she was.

With a small inheritance from Nellie's godmother and an equal amount that Jos had salvaged from an ill-fated investment in a gold mine, the Grants decided to emigrate. Like many Europeans, they were attracted to East Africa by visions of great opportunity in a country rich in resources, with land almost free for the taking. They bought, unseen, a 500-acre plantation at Thika, some thirty miles north of Nairobi.

Leaving their child in England to follow them later, the couple arrived in Nairobi, loaded their goods onto a cart, and rode as far as a cart could go, then mounted ponies and hired porters to carry their possessions six miles farther to Thika. The land was quite undeveloped and seemingly inhabited only by zebra, hartebeeste, and leopards. The ground had never been cultivated, and nobody knew what kind of crops would grow or what methods of cultivation, planting, manuring, or irrigation would succeed. A bit of space was cleared, tents were set up, and housekeeping was begun with one Swahili cook.

It took some time to persuade the Kikuyu, who lived nearby on what was called the Reserve, to hire themselves out as laborers, for Jos proposed to plant coffee. The Kikuyu were shy, but Jos found that a safari lamp hung on the tent post attracted their attention. The tribe had never evolved any form of a lamp, and they were fascinated by the light. With a bit of Swahili and some gestures, Jos made them understand that he would give a lamp to each man who came and worked for him. Several families responded. They built themselves grass houses, then constructed similar shelters for the Grants, although the English strangers insisted on square rather than the traditional round huts.

Elspeth joined her parents as the task of making a home in the rough began. Nellie was the planner, organizer, and overseer of the plantation. Jos was often away on schemes of his own. Other European settlers began to arrive in the neighborhood, and a small circle of them tried to make a little England in Africa. They built stone houses and furnished them with a few treasured antiques, silver, and paintings. They had tea parties and hunting parties and later organized polo teams. There was much gossip and some scandal, as well as an exchange of information and assistance.

The Grants had hard going. There was either too much rain or not enough. Some plants thrived, others died. And just as things were going well, the war reached into East Africa. Jos went off to join the Royal Scots; Nellie and Elspeth returned to England to live with a friend. Jos was injured in France and on recovery was appointed military attaché in Madrid. Nellie did not enjoy Madrid and chose after a year to do war work in London.

After the war they all went back to Africa. Nellie undertook to educate her daughter. The education was unorthodox but Elspeth was bright. She attended the government European School in Nairobi for a time. When she left for England, she was able to enter Reading University, where she studied agriculture. She graduated in 1927, then spent a year at Cornell University in Ithaca, New York. Her third autobiographical volume, *Love among the Daughters* (1968), tells of her college years.

Nellie and Jos had found a much more desirable plantation in the Kenya highlands, Njoro, and sold the one at Thika. They believed they would eventually turn their Kenya property over to their daughter, but that never happened. Elspeth went to work in London for the Empire Marketing Board, where she met Gervas Huxley, of the noted Huxley family, and married him. At the beginning of the Depression the agency was to be eliminated, but Gervas was lucky enough to get a job with the Ceylon Tea Propaganda Board. Its object was to persuade people to drink more tea, thus moving great amounts of surplus tea into the market. It involved travel in many countries.

While Gervas was traveling, Elspeth undertook to write a biography of Lord Delamere, who was instrumental in bringing European settlers to Africa and whose life was woven into the history of East Africa from 1897 until his death in 1931. In Kenya she visited Nellie, but she spent most of her time in Nairobi, where Lord Delamere's widow gave Elspeth access to her husband's papers and where government archives and old settlers provided information. The biography, *White Man's Country*, was published in two volumes after Elspeth had returned to England.

In 1937, on another trip to Njoro, Elspeth camped in Kikuyuland with her mother while she gathered material for a novel based on Kikuyu life. The biography and the novel, *Red Strangers* (1939), made her name known in England. At the London School of Economics, where she took a course in anthropology, a fellow student was a Kikuyu Jomo Kenyatta, with whom she became friendly. Many years later, he served as the first prime minister of a free Kenya.

The Huxleys bought a farmhouse in Wiltshire, but World War II kept them in London for some time. Gervas worked for the Ministry of Information, Elspeth at the British Broadcasting Company until their son Charles was born in 1944.

In the same year, a volume of correspondence between Elspeth and Margery Perham, *Race and Politics in Kenya*, was published. The two women, with opposite views about British colonial policy, agreed to correspond with each other because both were too busy to meet and both wanted to try to resolve their differences and present a united view to the administration. When East Africa was first settled by Europeans the prevailing British perception was that the land was just waiting for stalwart farmers to cultivate it, making its resources available to the world and bringing civilization to nomadic savages. Years later an entirely opposite viewpoint made itself felt. The settlers were criticized as land grabbers exploiting the country and its people. As early as 1923, the British government proclaimed that Africa belonged to the Africans and that "the interest of the natives must be paramount."

Elspeth resented the criticism and pointed out how much the settlers had contributed to Africa by wiping out slavery and by controlling pests and diseases, human and animal. They had introduced modern methods of agriculture and had brought a modicum of peace between warring tribes. They had earned the right to participate in the government. "It is difficult to see how the country as a whole can make progress," she wrote, "unless the settlers are to some extent made partners in the enterprise" (Race and Politics in Kenya, pp. 16–17).

Perham believed, on the other hand, that the role of the Europeans should be to train Africans for eventual self-government instead of defending "a little island of privilege and Western way of life." She felt that British observers of imperial policy were justified in their fears for the future. They had seen "the gradual establishment in South Africa of a system by which a racial minority obtains absolute domination, political, economic and social, over the African majority," and by denying Africans a gradual advance in economic and political status, whites had achieved an uneasy and temporary success (Race and Politics in Kenya, p. 18).

At the end of the correspondence, which ran from March 10, 1942, to August 20, 1943, neither writer had changed her mind. Events would, in any case, take their course.

Elspeth kept up with these events through frequent visits to Africa and through Nellie's letters. She wrote The Sorcerer's Apprentice (1948), sketches of African life based on travels through parts of East Africa (Kenya, Tanganyika, and Uganda). In Four Guineas (1954), she drew pen pictures of West African countries (Gambia, Sierra Leone, the Gold Coast, and Nigeria), all of whom were reaching for democracy and complete self-government.

A New Earth (1960) depicts "Progress striding through a part of Africa, where he is on the move at breakneck speed" (p. 9). It deals with changes in regions where most of the Africans lived—not the deserts or the white highlands, nor the coast or the cities, but the part of Kenya where the African pursued a settled life, either as farmer or herdsman. It was country seldom visited by Europeans or written about by the traveler. The book details life under modern agricultural reform. Each tribal group jealously guarded its territory, and some refused to heed the advice or example of trained agriculturists. The signs of overgrazing, overpopulation, and threats of famine were beginning to appear.

With Forks and Hope (1964) was based on visits to parts of Tanganyika, Kenya, and Uganda in the first months of 1963, just before Kenya became independent and after the other two countries had done so. "Behind the dance of politics," Elspeth wrote, "the features of the ancient landscape, the birds and beasts . . . and the dilemmas of the people remain" (*With Forks and Hope*, author's note). She saw much that made her sad: the loss of wildlife, the degradation of the grassland and forests, and uncontrolled human and livestock population. The Masai were being pushed into the twentieth century. They wanted to preserve their own ways but at the same time to read and write and watch television, wear suits and shoes, and drive cars. They were being trained not to govern but to have wants.

Meanwhile, Elspeth's mother was running her farm by herself. She lived through the Mau Mau terror of 1952 to 1954. Her Kikuyu servants and labor, she knew, had probably taken the obscene Mau Mau oaths and might murder her at any time. Some of her friends and neighbors were brutally assassinated, their animals killed or stolen. Her letters to Elspeth, nevertheless, are of the garden shows and civic activities that occupied her, in addition to her many schemes for ways of adding to her income.

Kenya moved toward Uhuru under African leaders like Kenyatta. Many Europeans left, selling or abandoning their farms. Nellie sold bits of Njoro but stayed on until 1965. She wanted to retain enough so that her faithful Kikuyu families could hold onto their own garden plots and grazing land. She could not stand the cold and damp of England, so she settled in Portugal, where she died in 1977.

The Huxleys had sold their farm in 1970, and a year later Gervas died. Elspeth had served on the Advisory Council of the British Broadcasting Company from 1952 to 1959, and from 1959 to 1960 on the Monckton Commission, which advised the government on the future of the Central African Federation (which never materialized). In 1962 she was made a Commander of the British Empire. In 1967 she traveled in Australia and wrote about it in *Their Shining Eldorado*.

Out in the Midday Sun (1985) carries Elspeth's autobiography from 1933 to 1983. In its final chapter, she tells of meeting Major Esther Wambui Njomo in Nairobi. She was the daughter of Nellie's headman, was born on Nellie's farm, and was educated in the school Nellie started. She was one of the first women recruited for the Kenyan army in 1973. "It is almost as if a new species has appeared on earth, the young Kenyan woman who has put tribal ways behind her" (*Out in the Midday Sun*, p. 225). Yet, on the road within a mile of Nairobi, Elspeth saw women toiling under heavy loads as they had done for centuries, and she detected in the major a note of sadness in the loss of family closeness and security.

Elspeth has seen a swift and overwhelming change in Africa since she went there as an immigrant settler. She has observed and written about it perhaps better than any other person. She can view with qualified optimism the future of the country she knows and loves.

BIBLIOGRAPHY

Works by Elspeth Huxley

White Man's Country: Lord Delamere and the Making of Kenya. London: Macmillan, 1935.

"Camera Safari." *New York Times Magazine*, Feb. 11, 1940, pp. 10–11.

Race and Politics in Kenya: A Correspondence between Elspeth Huxley and Margery Perham. London: Faber, 1944.

Settlers of Kenya. London and New York: Longman, 1948.

The Sorcerer's Apprentice: A Journey through East Africa. London: Chatto & Windus, 1948.

"British Aims in Africa." *Foreign Affairs* 28 (Oct. 1949): 43–55.

"Tomorrow's Hope or Yesterday's Dream." *New York Times Magazine*, June 4, 1950, pp. 12–13.

"Cold War and the Colonies." *Nineteenth Century* 148 (July 1950): 1–9.

"Enigma of East Africa." *Yale Review* 41 (June 1592): 491–501.

"Area of Light in the Dark Continent." *New York Times Magazine*, Jan. 11, 1953, pp. 20–21.

"What Life Is Like for a Settler in Kenya." *New York Times Magazine*, June 6, 1954, p. 12+.

"Vast Challenge of Africa." *New York Times Magazine*, July 18, 1954, pp. 10–11.

Four Guineas: A Journey through West Africa. London: Chatto & Windus, 1954.

"Two Revolutions That Are Changing Africa." *New York Times Magazine*, May 19, 1957, p. 9+.

"African's Lions Go Out Like Lambs." *New York Times Magazine*, July 28, 1957, p. 11+. Same article, published as "Africa's Vanishing Big Game." *Science Digest* 43 (Jan. 1958): 1–5.

"Clouds over the Black Continent." *New York Times Magazine*, Sept. 1, 1957, p. 5+.

No Easy Way: A History of the Kenya Farmers' Association and Unga Limited. Nairobi: East African Standard, 1957.

"Africa's Testing Ground of Race Relations." *New York Times Magazine*, Apr. 27, 1958, pp. 14–15.

"Nationalist Tide Sweeps Africa." *New York Times Magazine*, Feb. 15, 1959, pp. 14–15.

"Science, Psychiatry, or Witchery?" *New York Times Magazine*, May 31, 1959, p. 17+.

"Wildlife, Another African Tragedy." *New York Times Magazine*, Oct, 11, 1959, pp. 22–23+.

"Drums of Change Beat for Africa's Tribes." *New York Times Magazine*, Nov. 29, 1959, pp. 24–28+.

The Flame Trees of Thika: Memories of an African Childhood. London: Chatto & Windus, 1959; New York: Morrow, 1959. Autobiography.

"Safari Business Is Booming." *New York Times Magazine*, June 19, 1960, p. 11+.

"Jungle Journal." *Saturday Review* 43 (July 9, 1960): 16.

"Grass Grows in a Desert." *Reporter* 23 (Sept. 15, 1960): 42–44.

"Africa's First Loyalty." *New York Times Magazine*, Sept. 18, 1960, p. 14+. Same article in *Reader's Digest* 77 (Dec. 1960): 124–27 (abridged).

A New Earth. New York: Morrow, 1960.

"Two Tribes Tell Africa's Story." *New York Times Magazine*, Apr. 30, 1961, pp. 14–15.

"Next to Last Act in Africa." *Foreign Affairs* 39 (July 1961): 655–69.

"Africa Struggles with Democracy." *New York Times Magazine*, Jan. 21, 1962, p. 10+.

The Mottled Lizard. London: Chatto & Windus, 1962. Also published as *On the Edge of the Rift: Memories of Kenya*. New York: Morrow, 1962. Autobiography.

"Kenya Tries to Put the Clock Ahead." *New York Times Magazine*, May 19, 1963, p. 18+.

"Dateline Africa." *National Review* 15 (Nov. 19, 1963): 437+.

"African Affairs." *National Review* 16–20 (Jan. 28, 1964–Nov. 5, 1968), passim.

"Rise and Fall of the Watusi." *New York Times Magazine*, Feb. 23, 1964, p. 10+.

"Witches Brew." *National Review* 16 (Mar. 10, 1964): 191–92.

"Clues to the African Personality." *New York Times Magazine*, May 31, 1964, p. 18+.

"Serengeti National Park." *National Parks Magazine* 38 (May 1964): 10–14.

"Bringing Home the Hippo." *New York Times Magazine*, Nov. 29, 1964, pp. 134–37.

Forks and Hope. London: Chatto & Windus, 1964. Also published as *With Forks and Hope: An African Notebook*. New York: Morrow, 1964. Quotations in the text are from the New York edition.

"Australia's Aborigines Step out of the Stone Age." *New York Times Magazine*, June 20, 1965, pp. 10–11.

"Bead on Roos." *New York Times Magazine*, Oct. 24, 1965, pp. 119–20.

"Letter from Africa." *National Review* 18–20 (Mar. 22, 1966–Jan. 16, 1968), passim.

"Blundering into Danger." *National Review* 19 (Nov. 28, 1967): 1339–40.

Their Shining Eldorado: A Journey through Australia. New York: Morrow, 1967.

"Letter from Rhodesia." *National Review* 20 (Apr. 9, 1968): 335–36.

Love among the Daughters: Memories of the Twenties in England and America. New York: Morrow, 1968. Autobiography.

"Letter from London." *National Review* 21 (Apr. 8, Dec. 16, 1969): 328–30, 1265–66.

The Challenge of Africa. London: Aldus, 1971.

"Search for African Detente." *National Review* 27 (Nov. 7, 1975): 1240+.

Memoir. In Grant, Nellie. *Nellie: Letters from Africa*. London: Weidenfeld & Nicolson, 1980. Also published as *Nellie's Story*. New York: Morrow, 1981.

(With Hugo von Lowick) *Last Days in Eden*. London: Harvill Press, 1984.

Out in the Midday Sun: My Kenya. London: Chatto & Windus, 1985. Autobiography.

Works about Elspeth Huxley

"Ahead for Africa: Dictators, Tribal Wars, Red Influence." *U.S. News* 49 (Sept. 12, 1960): 82–87. Interview.

"Authority on Africa Looks at the Road Ahead." *U.S. News* 50 (Mar. 6, 1961): 53–55. Interview.

Contemporary Authors. Detroit: Gale Research, 1922–date, 1st revision vol. 77: pp. 261–62.

The International Who's Who, 1987–88. London: Europa, 1987, p. 688.

"What a Top Authority Says about Africa's Future." Edited by J. Fromm. *U.S. News* 60 (Mar. 14, 1966): 56–57. Interview.

"Why Africa Is in Chaos." Edited by J. Fromm. *U.S. News* 56 (Feb. 17, 1964): 46–49. Interview.

OSA LEIGHTY JOHNSON
1894–1953

Osa Helen Leighty Johnson explored in two regions—the South Pacific islands and Africa. Her career began with her marriage to Martin Johnson in 1910; for twenty-seven years they worked together, photographing jungle tribes, hunting wild animals, and collecting live animals for zoos. They wrote, lectured, and produced motion pictures of wilderness adventure.

During the 1920s and 1930s they were the best-known American explorers. Youthful, handsome, daring, and happily married, they appealed to audiences who thrilled to their stories of wild tribes, exotic animals, and dangerous encounters. They used every device of modern technology to acquire, record, and spread their knowledge of wildlife, progressing from hand-cranked movie cameras to the latest (for that day) sound equipment, and traveling thousands of miles in their own amphibian airplanes. Their films, carefully constructed and provided with story lines, went far beyond ordinary wildlife documentaries and appealed to the public's sense of drama.

Martin was killed in the crash of a commercial flight in 1937, and Osa, though injured in the same accident, continued their scheduled lecture tour and went back to Africa to supervise the filming of a picture relating Henry M. Stanley's search for David Livingstone (released by Twentieth Century Fox in 1939). In 1940 her first book about her life of exploration with Martin, *I Married Adventure*, was a best seller. She followed it up with other books and many articles about their adventures, and she continued to produce films, serving as president of the Martin Johnson Film Company. She considered Africa her home, but from 1940 until her death in 1953, she spent most of her time in the United States. In Chanute, Kansas, her birthplace, the Martin and Osa Johnson Safari Museum, which stands as a memorial to the couple, houses an archive of their papers and photographs and a museum of the artifacts brought back from their travels.

Osa Leighty was born in Chanute, Kansas, on March 14, 1894, to Ruby and William Leighty. Leighty was a railroad engineer. Until she was sixteen, Osa lived a happy, uncomplicated life in the small town, with every expectation that she would marry, have a home of her own, and raise a family. But when she met Martin Johnson, a traveling photographer, she fell in love. The son of a jeweler in Independence, Kansas, he had already traveled to Europe and had just returned from a trip to the South Seas with the famous writer Jack London.

During their first years of marriage, Osa and Martin traveled about the midwest, where Martin displayed his photographs and told stories of adventure, while Osa sang and danced. In 1913 Martin's book, *Through the South Seas with Jack London*, was published. Earning a living in show business did not make them rich, but by 1917 they had saved a thousand dollars and with another three thousand borrowed from friends they were able to pursue Martin's dream of a return to the South Seas. He wanted to go to "the cannibal islands." Of course, his parents and Osa's objected strongly to such an expedition. The very thought of cannibals scared Osa, but she declared herself ready to go wherever he went—in fact, she insisted on it.

They went to the Solomon islands, then under British administration. Although the natives they saw and filmed on Malaita, Guadalcanal, Savo, and Tulagi seemed wild enough to Osa, Martin was disappointed. He wanted to find tribes untouched by civilization and to find out whether the stories of cannibalism were true. After cruising about and talking to people, he chose Malekula, an island in the New Hebrides group, as his goal. As it was then in dispute between the English and French, they thought they would meet less government interference. Parts of the island had never been explored, and the natives were said to be extremely wild and dangerous. If cannibals and headhunters existed, they would be found there. The captain of a small ship agreed to drop them off at Vao, a small island close to Malekula, but strongly advised Martin to go no farther, especially not to take Osa.

In Vao they stayed at a mission run by Father Prin, who had lived on the island for twenty-seven years. He added his cautions to those of others. Even in Vao, where there were only about four hundred savages, tales were told of cannibalism and cruelties. Malekula had about forty thousand natives, among them the "Big Numbers" (Nambas), whose chief, Nagapate, was strong, powerful, and unpredictable.

Martin was not to be dissuaded, and Osa refused to be left behind while he went to the island. They borrowed an unused whale boat, and Father Prin provided a crew of Vao natives. In this they cruised around the shores of Malekula and were able to take pictures of a few tribesmen. At last they met some of the Big Numbers and were guided up a long, slippery jungle trail toward their chief, Nagapate. They were suddenly surrounded by savages with bones through their noses who were carrying guns. Nagapate was "so frightful as to be magnificent" (*I Married Adventure*, p. 120). While Osa tried to give the chief calico and tobacco, Martin took pictures of him. But Nagapate was not interested in anything but the white woman. He examined her skin, tried to rub off the color, then pulled off her hat and peered closely at her hair and scalp.

Osa tried not to show her fear, which grew more intense as the chief pinched and prodded her. He grabbed her by the wrist and made it clear that he wanted her as a captive. When she realized that the natives had also seized Martin, Osa screamed in terror. Just then a British gunboat appeared in the bay below. Martin shouted that it was a man-of-war come to protect them. Their captors released them, and the Johnsons fled for their lives, followed by shouting savages. They reached the whale boat just a step ahead of their pursuers and pushed off.

Martin had managed to keep his cameras with him, and when they reached Australia they found they had excellent film, including some pictures of the scowling Nagapate. On their return to the United States, they produced *Among the Cannibal Isles of the South Seas*, the first of many adventure movies they were to make and distribute.

Their most interested audience, however, was in Malekula. On their next trip to the island, the Big Numbers and Nagapate greeted them, if not altogether cordially at least with some interest. This time the Johnsons had taken the precaution of going with three schooners and plenty of men for protection. They set up their projector and screen and showed the film to the natives, who were amazed and delighted to see themselves and their friends (some of whom had died since they were photographed). The white people had great magic.

The Martins went fearlessly into the interior to film other tribes. They met with some who were selling little girls. Their crew told them they were sold for meat! Horrified, Osa and Martin bought one of the girls and took her with them to a mission station on an offshore island. They witnessed savages drying human heads in a smudge fire. They visited a tribe of "long heads," who tied jungle vine around the heads of infants to elongate their skulls. They filmed a group of natives feasting by a fire and were certain they saw a human leg bone hanging on a spit. After the feasters ran away, Martin retrieved a human head and insisted on taking the horrid object along as proof of cannibalism.

Martin's objective at this time seems to have been to produce popular films emphasizing the sensational. The Johnsons went on to Borneo in search of the exotic, the colorful, and the strange. They returned with material for several films and short subjects—*Jungle Adventures*, *Head Hunters of the South Seas*, and *Cannibal-Land*—and a book, *Cannibal-Land*, published in 1922.

Martin was accepted into the Explorers' Club in 1921, where he met Carl Akeley, the African explorer. He visited the Johnsons many times and enjoyed the pet animals they had brought back from Borneo. A new element came into the Johnsons' travels when he advised them to focus on wildlife, to use their exploring instincts and splendid photography to further the knowledge of wild animals and their preservation. He suggested that they go to Africa. They took his advice and during the next years they built a reputation for serious African exploration.

They made one more trip to the South Seas, in 1935, when they visited North Borneo and explored the headwaters of the Kinabatangan River. They spent two years there, visiting the Rumanau and Tenggara tribes. Osa's manuscript account of this trip, found after her death, was published as *Last Adventure*.

Martin raised enough money to go to East Africa by forming a company and selling shares. Osa reluctantly disposed of their menagerie of pets, including Bessie, a titian-haired orangutan, who went to the Central Park Zoo. They could not part with their little gibbon ape, Kalowatt. Both of these frisky animals had been members of the household since their trip to Borneo, and their mischievousness had made the Johnsons virtual prisoners in their hotel. Kalowatt went to Africa with them.

Akeley had written to people in Kenya informing them of the Johnsons' plans to film animals, and when they took a house in Nairobi they found many friends willing to help them. Chief among them was Blaney Percival, who had spent twenty years in Africa as a game warden. He helped them make arrangements for their first safari to the Athi River, easily reached by automobile. He also told them of a crater lake far to the north that had been described by an early explorer but seemed to be unknown to anyone else. There they could undoubtedly find plenty of animals, far from the big-game hunters whom he considered to be the plague of Africa. The lake was to the north across a desert, somewhere near the Abyssinian border, and the Johnsons were determined to find it. They assembled tents, ammunition, photographic equipment, and supplies for a six-month trip. They had two safari Fords and four wagons, each drawn by twelve oxen, to carry the goods as far as Meru, where they were divided into loads for porters. The trip was long and exhausting, part of it over hills of volcanic slag that cut the feet of the barefoot carriers. They met Boculy, a wizened old black with sore eyes and a curiously lopsided jaw, who guided them across the hot desert and then helped them find the lake.

The lake, set in a volcanic crater with a beach of hard, washed lava, was surrounded by steep, wooded hills. Around it, the Johnsons saw more animals than they could count, standing knee-deep in the water, drinking. The woods were full of elephants. Osa named the beautiful spot Lake Paradise. There they pitched camp and remained for three months, becoming thoroughly familiar with the surrounding country. They went back to Nairobi with excellent films and with a plan to return to the lake for a four-year stay during which they would photograph the family life of all the wild animals that assembled there.

Such an ambitious project needed a good deal of money. Back in the United States, the couple went to see George Eastman, of the Kodak Company in Rochester, New York. He promised them ten thousand dollars toward expenses. Others contributed funds, and the Museum of Natural History in New York City sponsored their trip, which began in 1923. This time they had six Willys-Knights, four motor lorries, four ox carts, and a crew of 235 Africans, including porters and house servants. Since they planned to build a home and a laboratory at Lake Paradise, they took along such things as water tanks and a generator, as well as a supply of ammunition and loads of cameras and photographic equipment.

Osa had always dreamed of having a home of her own, and wherever they had stayed for any time at all she made their living quarters as comfortable and cheerful as possible. She planted vegetables in the jungle, and she always prepared excellent meals to keep Martin healthy. The Lake Paradise establishment was as close as possible to her dream home. The house had a large living room, a bedroom, and "a large pink stuccoed bathroom." "In no time at all," she wrote, "I had put frilled sash curtains at all the windows" (*I Married Adventure*, p. 278). She planted acres of vegetables and surrounded the house with flower gardens, all enclosed by a fence to keep out the wildlife—or, at least, part of it. She had a flock of chickens, which increased rapidly. She added to the produce of the garden by gathering delicacies in the forest—wild asparagus and spinach, cranberries, native coffee, mushrooms, and fruits.

Not that she settled down to domesticity. She helped Martin with the filming, she fished, and she hunted. She was by now a crack shot, but she hunted only to provide meat. They always carried guns for protection. They photographed hundreds of elephants but killed only one, which she dropped as it was pursuing Martin and was within fifteen feet of catching him. Working among big-game animals was full of danger and excitement.

After leaving Lake Paradise, they spent a year among the lions at Lake Tanganyika, and Osa again saved Martin's life by shooting an attacking lion within feet of her husand, who coolly kept on cranking the camera. The lion pictures made up the film, *Simba*, released in 1929.

The Belgian Congo was their next stop, where they filmed Pygmies and gorillas. Sound had now been added to motion pictures, and new equipment was needed. Their transportation equipment, too, was now much more sophisticated, with special camera cars and a truck that had been converted into living quarters. They found Pygmies in the Ituri Forest and managed to entice them out of the dark jungle into a clearing where they could be photographed. Osa found them to be biologically and psychologically much like the Pygmies they had seen on the island of Espiritu Santo in the New Hebrides. They lived a utopian existence, she concluded, "for they showed neither hate, greed, vanity, envy nor any other of the dominatingly unpleasant emotions" of civilization (*I Married Adventure*, p. 330). Somehow the Johnsons managed to keep the Pygmies, almost five hundred of them, at their camp for several months. Finally they paid them off with gifts, and the little people faded back into the woods.

They spent some time among the gorillas near Mt. Mikeno, where their friend Carl Akeley, who had died suddenly in 1926, was buried. Before they left, Osa planted hardy ferns and vines all about the grave. They moved on to the Alumbongo Mountains where they took good pictures of gorillas, an animal Osa did not learn to love. They captured two, who were sent to the San Diego Zoo.

Soon after their return to the United States in 1932, Martin and Osa learned to fly and bought two amphibian airplanes, which they christened "The Spirit of Africa" and "Osa's Ark." One was equipped with sleeping bunks, a washroom, and a stove. Osa added a typewriter desk, for she had been commissioned to write a book and some magazine articles. Their next trip to Africa was an airplane safari. Flying over jungle, without adequate maps, with few landing fields, and where the ground was often fogged over was quite different from flying in the United States. With skilled pilots and sometimes at the controls themselves, they logged thousands of miles over the African continent and later in Borneo.

The plane crash that killed Martin was a severe blow to Osa and a shock to the American public, who had come to know the Johnsons through their films, magazine articles, and books. How this energetic and busy couple ever found time to write is a mystery. Martin wrote seven books, most of them with Osa's help. He also contributed a steady stream of articles to *Asia* and other periodicals. Osa wrote children's books and numerous articles, including a series for *Good Housekeeping*. Her autobiographical *I Married Adventure* appeared in 1940; chosen by the Book-of-the-Month Club, it was condensed by the *Reader's Digest* and made into a motion picture. Osa followed it with several other books about their explorations.

From 1941 to 1949, Osa was married to her lecture manager, Clark H. Getts. She died in a New York hotel, on January 7, 1953, while she was making arrangements for a return to Africa.

Audiences who heard Osa lecture were amazed at her youth and beauty. One interviewer said of her that she had "the face and form of a movie star, the heart of a home-loving woman, and the courage of a lion" (quoted in *Current Biography*, 1940). She was once voted one of the twelve best-dressed women in America. She seems never to have lost the girlish figure or the eager, lively face of the young woman who appealed to the fearsome Nagapate on her first adventure with Martin in the South Seas.

BIBLIOGRAPHY

Works by Osa Johnson

(With Martin Johnson) *Cannibal Land: Adventures with a Camera in the New Hebrides.* Boston and New York: Houghton Mifflin, 1922.

———. *Camera-Trails in Africa.* New York and London: Century, 1924.

Twenty-four articles for *Good Housekeeping*, many for children, between 1924 and 1937.

"Mirrors of the Jungle." *Collier's* 80 (Dec. 10, 1927): 10–11.

(With Martin Johnson) *Safari: A Saga of the African Blue.* New York and London: Putnam, 1928.

———. *Lion: African Adventures with the King of Beasts.* New York and London: Putnam, 1929.

Jungle Babies. New York and London: Putnam, 1930. For children.

(With Martin Johnson) *Congorilla: Adventures with Pygmies and Gorillas in Africa.* New York: Harcourt, Brace, 1931.

Jungle Pets. New York and London: Putnam, 1932. For children.

(With Martin Johnson) *Over African Jungles: The Record of a Glorious Adventure over the Big Game Country of Africa, 6000 Miles by Airplane.* New York: Harcourt, Brace, 1935.

"Jungle Dinner." *Cosmopolitan* 102 (June 1937): 74–76, 79.

"Jungle." *American Magazine* 124 (July 1937): 146.

Osa Johnson's Jungle Friends. Philadelphia and New York: Lippincott, 1939. For children.

"Cannibals Roast a Man." *Life* 8 (Mar. 25, 1940): 12–14.

I Married Adventure: The Lives and Adventures of Martin and Osa Johnson. Philadelphia: Lippincott, 1940. Abridged in *Reader's Digest* 37 (Sept. 1940): 109–27. Excerpt in *Scholastic* 37 (Dec. 2, 1940): 19–20.

Four Years in Paradise. Philadelphia: Lippincott, 1941.

Pantaloons: Adventures of a Baby Elephant. New York: Random House, 1941. For children.

"Life in the Solomons." *Collier's* 110 (Sept. 26, 1942): 32–34.

Snowball: Adventures of a Young Gorilla. New York: Random House, 1942. For children.

Bride in the Solomons. New York: Houghton Mifflin, 1944.

Tarnish: The True Story of a Lion Cub. Chicago: Wilcox & Follett, 1944.

Last Adventure: The Martin Johnsons in Borneo. Edited by Pascal James Imperato. New York: Morrow, 1966.

Works about Osa Johnson

"Across the World with Mr. and Mrs. Martin Johnson." *Time* 15 (Feb. 3, 1930): 57–58.

Akeley, C. E. "Martin Johnson and His Expedition to Lake Paradise." *Natural History* 24 (May 1924): 284–88.

———. "Martin Johnson's African Photographs." *World's Work* 46 (July 1923): 184–92.

Armstrong, H. E. "The Martin Johnsons over Africa." *New York Times Book Review*, Oct. 20, 1935, p. 9.

"Coconut Pies for Boy Scout Lion Hunters." *Literary Digest* 99 (Nov. 1928): 36, 38, 40, 45–46.

Cooper, Alice C., and C. A. Palmer. "Martin Johnsons: Bringing Maps to Life." In *Twenty Modern Americans.* New York: Harcourt, Brace, 1942, pp. 23–39.

Cunningham, Elsie. "Daring African Explorer Is Daughter of a Santa Fe Engineer." *Santa Fe Magazine* 27 (Jan. 1933): 19–20.

Current Biography. New York: H. W. Wilson, 1940-date. Annual vols. 1940, 1953.

Dictionary of American Biography. New York: Scribner, 1927-date, supplement 5 (1977): 370–71.

Douglas, Robert D., Jr., and others. *Three Boy Scouts in Africa: On Safari with Martin Johnson.* New York: Putnam, 1928.

Eastman, George. *Chronicles of an African Trip.* Rochester, N.Y.: the author, 1927.

Green, Fitzhugh. "African Adventure: Three American Boys on Safari with Martin Johnson." *Delineator* 14 (Mar. 1929): 12.

Imperato, Pascal James. *Campsites of Martin and Osa Johnson in Africa.* New York: the author, 1964.

———. "The Martin Johnsons in Africa." *Africana* 2 (Sept. 1966): 18–20, 29–30.

Johnson, Martin. "Extracts from the Diary of Martin Johnson." *Natural History* 25 (Nov.–Dec. 1925): 571–78. With a portfolio of "Scenes about Lake Paradise."

———. "Picturing Africa." *Natural History* 27 (Nov.–Dec. 1927): 539–44, and "Land of Glorious Adventure" (photos), 545–60.

Liberty's Women. Edited by Robert McHenry. Springfield, Mass.: Merriam, 1980.

Mih, Mariam L. *Safari, a Short Travelogue of the Adventures of Martin and Osa Johnson.* Chanute, Kans.: the author, 1961.

National Cyclopedia of American Biography. New York: J. T. White, vol. 39, p. 39 (under "Osa Johnson") and vol. 28, p. 65 (under "Martin Johnson").

Preston, Douglas J. "Shooting in Paradise." *Natural History* 93 (Dec. 1984): 14–18.

Stott, Kenelm W., Jr. *Exploring with Martin and Osa Johnson.* Chanute, Kans.: Martin and Osa Johnson Safari Museum Press, 1978.

———. "In the Footsteps of Martin and Osa Johnson." *Zoonooz* 57 (July 1974): 4–11.

———. "Parrot Fever in the Solomons." *Zoonooz* 58 (Dec. 1975): 10–13.

Ward, Martha E., and D. A. Marquardt. *Authors of Books for Young People.* Metuchen, N.J.: Scarecrow, 1967.

Woods, Katherine. "The Adventurous Lives of the Martin Johnsons." *New York Times Magazine,* Apr. 21, 1940, p. 10.

News articles appeared also in the *Christian Science Monitor,* Feb. 16, and Mar. 23, 1940; the *Springfield Republican,* Feb. 18, 1940; and others.

Obituaries appeared in the *New York Times,* on Jan. 8, 1953; *Newsweek,* on Jan. 19, 1953; *Publishers Weekly,* Feb. 7, 1953; *Time,* Jan. 19, 1953; *Wilson Library Bulletin,* Mar. 1953; and in the *Britannica Book of the Year* 1954 and *American Annual* 1954.

Johnson manuscripts, clippings, and artifacts are located in the Safari Museum in Chanute, Kansas; manuscripts are located in the Pacific Geographical Collection at Stanford University, Stanford, California. Of the extensive list of books and articles by and about Martin Johnson, many contribute to a study of Osa's career.

MARY KINGSLEY
1862–1900

Mary Kingsley left her home in England for West Africa in 1893 to continue, as she said, an interest her father had pursued in primitive religion and law. Later in her life, she wrote that "dead tired and feeling no one had need of me any more, when my Mother and Father died within six weeks of each other in '92, and my Brother went off to the East, I went down to West Africa to die" (Gwynn, *The Life of Mary Kingsley*, p. 26). Opportunities for death existed in Africa, as she soon discovered: fevers, diseases, and parasites; crocodiles, leopards, and gorillas; cannibals; and sheer loneliness. None of these defeated her, however, and at the end of nine months of exploration she returned to England having found a place she loved. "I succumbed to the charm of the Coast . . . and I saw more than enough during that voyage to make me recognize that there was any amount of work for me worth doing down there" (Kingsley, *Travels in West Africa*, p. 11).

She went back to West Africa at the end of 1894 and stayed for eleven months, this time with two goals—to collect zoological specimens of fish and to understand fetish— by which she meant the underlying religious faith of the West African tribes untouched by Christianity or Mohammedanism. She made herself an authority on the native culture by traveling as a trader among the blacks of the coastal forests. She returned home a celebrity whose articles were eagerly read, a public speaker whose words had the ring of truth. She had firm views on England's proper role in African affairs, and she waged a lone campaign for change in its imperial policy and administration.

Mary Kingsley's career as an explorer and a public figure lasted a brief eight years, for she did indeed give her life for Africa. She caught enteric fever while nursing Boer prisoners of war in South Africa. She died there in 1900 and was buried at sea off Cape Point.

Mary Kingsley was born on October 13, 1862. She was the daughter of George Kingsley, a physician and traveler, and the niece of Charles and Henry Kingsley, both well-known writers. "The whole of my childhood and youth was spent at home, in the house and garden," she wrote (quoted in Gwynn, *The Life of Mary Kingsley*, p. 13). She had almost no social life outside of that home. George Kingsley, an inveterate wanderer, was present for only a few months at a time; his wife was an invalid and the domestic cares of the household fell on Mary, beginning when she was first big enough to hold a duster. While the family spent two thousand pounds on schooling for her brother, she received no paid education except a course in German so that she could help her father. "I cried bitterly at not being taught things," she said, but she found consolation in her father's library, reading "mostly old books on the West Indies, and old medical books, and old travel books and what not" (Gwynn, *The Life of Mary Kingsley*, pp. 13–14).

Mary was thirty when her parents died. She indulged herself with a trip to the Canary Islands. Then, finding herself with "five or six months which were not heavily forestalled" and liking travel, she decided to go to West Africa (*Travels in West Africa*, p. 1).

She traveled on a cargo boat, where she and a stewardess were the only women. There was much speculation among the seamen and fellow travelers as to her purpose; some believed her to be a missionary, others that she must represent the World's Women's Temperance Association. When she explained that she was a naturalist, collecting beetles, fish, and fetish, the Coasters accepted her and taught her a good deal about the country she was to visit as well as about navigation. She learned the coastal waters so well that she herself on several occasions piloted 2,000-ton vessels across the Forçados Bar. She grew to have great respect for the sailors and the traders.

There had been trading on the African coast for years, but little was known about the inland regions, except that there were populous areas and even large cities whose people traded across the desert to Tripoli. Near the shores whites were represented by missionaries, a few officials, and traders in ivory, palm oil, and rubber. The infamous slave trade had been put down. The Europeans—Portuguese, Belgians, French, Germans, Dutch, and British—were intent on obtaining territory with exclusive trading rights.

Of her first trip to Africa, Mary wrote little. After her second trip she published *Travels in West Africa*, a book crammed with observations on the people, a serious discussion of native culture, information on the flora and fauna, and tales of adventure. Mary was a born writer, a poet, and a keen observer. She wrote in a style all her own—the serious subject is lightened with a perpetual play of humor—and the book is a joy to read. It had a wide appeal when it was published in 1897, and it remains a classic in travel literature. It was followed by *West African Studies*, again a serious subject treated in a lighthearted style. A third book, *The Story of West Africa*, very different in bulk and stature, was published to be sold for one shilling and sixpence.

On the second trip Mary went alone to explore the Ogooué River between the Niger and the Congo, through a forest peopled by "a set of notoriously savage

Mary Kingsley in West Africa

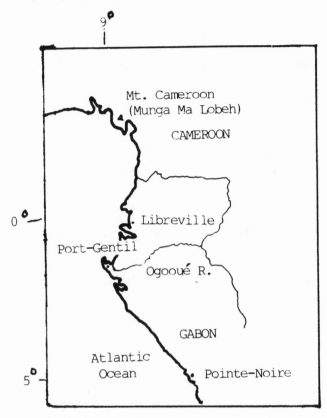

tribes chief among which are the Fans" (*Travels in West Africa*, p. 103). Though
they were cannibals and dangerous to a degree, Mary grew to respect the Fans
above other tribes, for they were "a bright, energetic sort of African" (*Travels
in West Africa*, p. 103). She loved the forest, which she described in glowing
colors.

  She traveled in a canoe with native crewmen. She dressed in her usual costume—shirtwaist, over stays, a long skirt, and small cap. She would have liked
to wear one of the native-made leather hats, with a brim to shield the eyes and
the neck, but she did not feel she "could face Piccadilly in one; and you have
no right to go about Africa in things you would be ashamed to be seen in at
home" (*Travels in West Africa*, p. 19). She had no tent. At each tribal village,
she was given a place to sleep, usually in the headman's own hut. She ate the
native food, but she observed one rule: Never drink unboiled water. In each
village, she hired guides who might possibly ensure a friendly welcome by the
next tribe. Approaching one of the first villages, she saw a scene she described
as "very picturesque":

The village was just a collection of palm mat-built huts very low and squalid. In its tiny street, an affair of some sixty feet long and twenty wide, were a succession of small fires. The villagers themselves, however, were the striking features in the picture. They were painted vermilion all over their nearly naked bodies, and were dancing enthusiastically to the good old rump-a-tump-tump-tump tune, played energetically by an old gentleman on a long, high-standing, white-and-black painted drum. (*Travels in West Africa*, p. 175)

Her first visit to a Fan village was more of a shock.

Never—even in a picture book—have I seen such a set of wild wicked-looking savages as those we faced this night, and with whom it was touch-and-go for twenty of the longest minutes I have ever lived, whether we fought—for our lives, I was going to say, but it would not have been even for that, but merely for the price of them. (*Travels in West Africa*, pp. 248–29)

When the two Fans known to her guides appeared, all was friendliness and noisy hospitality. As they entered the town, the noise swelled, for all the women, children, and dogs joined in. "Every child in the place as soon as it saw my white face let a howl out of it, . . . and fled into the nearest hut" (*Travels in West Africa*, p. 249).

Kingsley had decided to travel as a trader, paying her way partially by trading cloth and other goods for ivory and rubber. She described her methods:

I find I get on best by going among the unadulterated Africans in the guise of a trader; there is something reasonable about trade to all men, and you see the advantage of it is that, when you first appear among people who have never seen anything like you before, they naturally regard you as a devil; but when you want to buy or sell with them, they recognise there is something human and reasonable about you, and then, if you show yourself an intelligent trader who knows the price of things, they regard you with respect, but if you go in for trading knowing nothing about prices, etc., they, very properly, regard you as a fool. . . .

The trading method enables you to sit as an honoured guest at far-away inland village fires; it enables you to become the confidential friend of that ever-powerful factor in all human societies, the old ladies. It enables you to become an associate of the con-fraternity of Witch Doctors, things that being surrounded with an expedition of armed men must prevent your doing. (*Cheltenham Ladies' College Magazine*, No. 38, Autumn 1898, quoted in Gwynn, *The Life of Mary Kingsley*, p. 100)

She had many adventures, some pleasurable, some not. She got lost, almost drowned in a swamp, was covered with leeches, discovered in one hut a bag full of bits of human anatomy, got caught in the river rapids, and even fell into a pit dug to catch animals. On this occasion, and on another when she was attacked by geese, she was grateful for her long skirt. "'Grand things, good, old-fashioned, long skirts are for Africa!'" (*Travels in West Africa*, p. 145).

She did not speak any of the native languages, of which there were a great many. She depended on interpreters and on a knowledge of trade English, which all of them understood. Trade English, she explained, was by no means easy to pick up. "It is not a farrago of bad words and broken phrases, but is a definite structure, has a great peculiarity in its verb forms and employs no genders." She learned much of it, she joked, from listening to a second mate regulating the unloading or loading of cargo (*Travels in West Africa*, p. 432).

As for interpreters,

> to understand what an interpreter means who does not know your language, and whose own language you are not an adept in, and who is translating from a language regarding which you are both alike ignorant, is a process fraught with difficulty. I have tried it, so speak feelingly. It is true it is not an impossibility, as those unversed in African may hastily conjecture, because at least one-third of an African language consists in gesture, and this gesture part is fairly common to all tribes I have met, so that by means of it you can get on with daily life. (*West African Studies*, p. 201)

In spite of these difficulties, Kingsley was able to investigate many aspects of the culture: witchcraft, cannibalism, laws regarding property, the status of women, burial customs, and much more. She recognized the pantheism of the natives, much akin to her own beliefs, with the difference that, to the former, the god that created all had no further interest in what he had created. The African's gods are

> gods from whom he never expected pity, presided over by a god that does not care. All that he had to do with them was not to irritate them, to propitiate them, to buy their services when wanted, and, above all, to dodge and avoid them, while he fought it out and managed devils at large. (*West African Studies*, p. 106)

Mary faced danger herself with great courage. She had several encounters with leopards. In one, she saw what she thought was a fight between two dogs. She broke it up by hurling a native stool at the combatants, then discovered that one was a leopard, who was facing her. She pitched a water pot at its head and the animal "went for the bush one time" (*Travels in West Africa*, p. 546). Another encounter, not reported in her book, came about when she freed a leopard from a snare. Instead of running off, it came up to her and sniffed around her. "Go home, you fool," she cried—and it went (Gwynn, *The Life of Mary Kingsley*, p. 92). At one time she was marooned by the falling tide in a lagoon infested with crocodiles. One of them put his paws over the stern of the canoe, whereupon she fetched him "a clip on the snout with a paddle" and moved the canoe to the center of the lagoon until the tide came in and she could paddle away (*Travels in West Africa*, p. 88).

She knew that with the natives she walked "along a narrow line of security with gulfs of murder looming on each side," yet she knew as well that safety lay not in physical force but in getting hold of ideas in men's and women's minds. "It is not advisable to play with them, or to attempt to eradicate them, because you regard them as superstitious; and never, never shoot too soon." She advised travelers to keep a revolver, ready loaded, but she herself did not carry a gun. She did carry, concealed, a small dagger to be used on herself if things become too unpleasant. Self-respect, she said, is "the mainspring of your power in West Africa" (*Travels in West Africa*, pp. 329–30).

Her aim was always to understand the minds of the natives. "Unless you live alone among the natives, you never get to know them; if you do this you gradually get a light into the true state of their mind-forest" (*Travels in West Africa*, p. 103). The African was not to be looked upon as a child or a member of an inferior race. He was a different species, perhaps, but not a lesser one. In *The Story of West Africa* she wrote,

> The African is a strong type of humanity with virtues and vices arranged in his character in a different way to that of the European character. . . . These negroes are a great world race—a race not passing off the stage of human affairs, but one that has an immense amount of history before it. Whatever we do in Africa today, a thousand years hence there will be Africans to thrive or suffer for it. (Quoted in Gwynn, *The Life of Mary Kingsley*, pp. 231, 235)

Mary did not dispute England's right to seek power overseas or to trade with the Africans, but she did not think England had a duty to save other people's souls. She had little sympathy with the missionaries, although she loved and admired Mary Slessor, whom she met in Calabar, and she thought the Roman Catholics did well to offer the blacks industrial training. Above all, she pleaded with her fellow countrymen to study and treat the African as a brother human being with a culture of his own.

Her last adventure, the ascent of the great peak of the Cameroons, had nothing to do with fish or fetish. It was undertaken for the sheer pleasure of discovery, the need to pit herself against nature at its most difficult. The peak, called the Mungo Mah Lobeh, is 13,353 feet, one of the highest points in Africa. She claimed to be "the third Englishman to ascend the Peak, and the first to have ascended it from the south-east face" (*Travels in West Africa*, p. 550). The natives with her were fearful of the climb and tried to talk her out of it; then they tried to sabotage it by leaving the water behind. She sent them back for it and then continued her climb to the summit, alone, in a torrent of rain. She reached the top, but the heavy mists obscured the view. "Verily I am no mountaineer," she wrote, "for there is in me no exultation, but only a deep disgust because the weather has robbed me of my main object in coming here, namely to get a good view" (*Travels in West Africa*, p. 594).

When she returned to England, she took back specimens of fish—one new species named for her, six modifications of known forms, and many other specimens eagerly accepted by the Royal Botanical Gardens at Kew. She accepted invitations to lecture on her travels, wrote an astonishing number of articles as well as her books (including one on her father's travels), and was caught up in a number of causes—which did not include woman suffrage. But she said she had lost the power of enjoying life in England, that she "had caught the habit of thinking black," and she planned a third trip to her beloved West Africa (Gwynn, *The Life of Mary Kingsley*, p. 142). Instead, she answered the call for nursing help in South Africa. She died in Simonstown on June 3, 1900, a victim of enteric fever.

After her death, the merchants of Liverpool and Manchester, who considered her a trader like themselves, established in Liverpool the Mary Kingsley Hospital for the treatment of tropical diseases. The Mary Kingsley Society of West Africa (soon renamed the African Society) was established to study native customs and institutions.

BIBLIOGRAPHY

Works by Mary Kingsley

Letter in response to article, "The Negro Future." *Spectator*, Dec. 28, 1895.
"The Ascent of Cameroons Peak and Travels in French Congo." *Liverpool Geographical Society* (Mar. 1896).
"The Development of Dodos." *National Review* 27 (Mar. 1896): 66–79.
"Travels on the Western Coast of Equatorial Africa." *Scottish Geographical Magazine* 12 (Mar. 1896): 113–24.
"The Throne of Thunder." *National Review* 27 (May 1896): 357–74.
"Black Ghosts." *Cornhill* (July 1896): 79–92.
"Two African Days' Entertainment." *Cornhill* (Mar. 1897): 354–59.
"Fishing in West Africa." *National Review* 29 (May 1897): 213–27.
"The Native Populations of Africa." *Spectator*, May 15, 1897, pp. 695–96.
"The Fetish View of the Human Soul." *Folklore* 8 (June 1897): 138.
"African Religion and Law." *National Review* 29 (Sept. 1897): 122–39.
"A Parrot Story." *Cornhill* (Sept. 1897): 389–91.
Travels in West Africa. London: Macmillan, 1897. Reprinted, with an introduction by Elizabeth Claridge, London: Virago, 1982. Quotations in the text are from the 1982 edition.
"The Hut Tax in Africa." *Spectator*, Mar. 19, 1898, pp. 407–8.
"The Liquor Traffic with West Africa." *Fortnightly Review* 69 (Apr. 1898): 537–60.
"The Law and Nature of Property among the Peoples of the True Negro Stock." *Proceedings, British Association*, Sept. 1898.
"A Lecture on West Africa." *Cheltenham Ladies' College Magazine* 38 (Autumn 1898).
"Administration of our West African Colonies." *Monthly Record*, Manchester Chamber of Commerce, Mar. 30, 1899.
"The Forms of Apparitions in West Africa." *Journal of the Psychical Research Society* 14 (July 1899).
"The Transfer of the Niger Territories." *British Empire Review*, Aug. 1899, pp. 29–31.
"The Future of Negros." *Spectator*, Nov. 1899.

West African Studies. London: Macmillan, 1899. Reprinted, with an introduction by John
    E. Flint, London: Cass, 1964. Quotations in the text are from the 1964 edition.
"West Africa from an Ethnological Point of View." *Imperial Institute Journal*, Apr.
    1900.
"Efficiency and Empire." *Spectator*, June 1900.
The Story of West Africa. London: H. Marshall, 1900.

Works about Mary Kingsley

Blyden, Edward M. *The African Society and Miss Mary Kingsley*. London: J. Scott,
    1900. Articles reprinted from the *Sierra Leone Weekly*.
Borer, Mary Cathcart. *Women Who Made History*. New York: Warne, 1963, pp. 132–
    50.
Campbell, Olwen. *Mary Kingsley, a Victorian in the Jungle*. London: Methuen, 1957.
Clodd, Edward. *Memories*. London: Chapman & Hall, 1916. A chapter on Kingsley.
Dictionary of National Biography. London: Smith, Elder, 1st supplement (1901) vol. 3,
    pp. 67–69.
Europa Biographical Dictionary of British Women. Edited by Anne Crawford and others.
    London: Europa, 1985.
Flint, J. E. "Mary Kingsley: A Reassessment." *Journal of African History* 4 (1963):
    95–104.
Frank, Katherine. *A Voyager Out: The Life of Mary Kingsley*. Boston: Houghton Mifflin,
    1986.
Glynn, Rosemary. *Mary Kingsley in Africa*. London: Harrap, 1956.
Green, Alice S. "Mary Kingsley." *Journal of the African Society* 1 (Oct. 1901): 1–16.
Gwynn, Stephen. *The Life of Mary Kingsley*. London: Macmillan, 1933.
Hayford, Mark C. *Mary H. Kingsley from an African Standpoint*. London: Bear & Taylor,
    1901.
Holmes, Winifred. *Seven Adventurous Women*. London: Bell, 1953, pp. 136–54.
Howard, Cecil. *Mary Kingsley*. London: Hutchinson, 1957.
Hughes, Jean. *Invincible Miss: The Adventures of Mary Kingsley*. London: Macmillan,
    1968.
Kipling, Rudyard. *Mary Kingsley*. Garden City, N.Y.: Doubleday, 1932.
Ladies on the Loose: Women Travellers of the 18th and 19th Centuries. Edited by Leo
    Hamalian. New York: Dodd, Mead, 1981, pp. 229–49.
Mary Kingsley: A Memoir. British Commonwealth Leaflets, 1948.
Middleton, Dorothy. *Victorian Lady Travellers*. London: Routledge & Kegan Paul, 1965,
    pp. 149–76.
Morel, E. D. *Affairs of West Africa*. London: Heinemann, 1902. Foreword on Kingsley.
Mozans, H. J. *Woman in Science*. New York: Appleton, 1913, pp. 255–58.
Oliver, Caroline. "Mary Kingsley." *African Affairs* 70 (July 1971): 222–35.
———. *Western Women in Colonial Africa*. Westport, Conn.: Greenwood Press, 1982,
    pp. 76–94.
Stevenson, Catherine Barnes. *Victorian Women Travel Writers in Africa*. Boston: Twayne,
    1982, pp. 87–159. Contains an excellent bibliography.
Tabor, Margaret Emma. *Pioneer Women*. 3rd series. London: Sheldon, 1930, pp. 65–
    93.
Wallace, Kathleen. *This Is Your Home: A Portrait of Mary Kingsley*. London: Heinemann,
    1956.

AGNES SMITH LEWIS
1843–1926

MARGARET SMITH GIBSON
1843–1920

Agnes Smith Lewis and Margaret Smith Gibson, twin sisters, were Victorian scholar adventurers, pioneers in an esoteric field almost wholly a male province. On a journey to a remote Egyptian monastery in 1892, they discovered a priceless, ancient biblical manuscript. A venturesome independence led them to the site, and their linguistic skills and biblical knowledge enabled them to recognize the value of their find. When it became known, it excited as much interest as did the more recent unearthing of the Dead Sea Scrolls. The sisters won a measure of fame, academic honors, and respect from the world of scholarship.

Then they were forgotten.

No biographer had thought them to be of sufficient interest to delve into their past until 1985, when A. Whigham Price published *The Ladies of Castlebrae*. Their own accounts of their travels were published before the turn of the century but have not been read much since then. Yet the story is one of adventure, exploration in a new field, and the thrill of discovery. It is also a heartwarming revelation of women's achievement in a day when European women were generally denied the kind of opportunities the sisters enjoyed.

The manuscript, sometimes referred to in a footnote as *Syr Sin (Syriac Sinaiticus)*, is one of the earliest manuscripts in existence of the Christian Gospels in Syriac. The antiquity of the manuscript—the fourth or fifth century after Christ—and the fact that it is a translation from an original, lost Greek version make it of paramount value to scholars of the Judeo-Christian world. Syriac is the literary form of Aramaic, the language believed to be the closest to that used by Jesus and his disciples. Thus it might be expected to give a more authentic version of the Gospels than had hitherto been known.

The document—actually a palimpsest—had lain for centuries in a dusty cubbyhole in St. Catherine's Convent (which was not a nunnery but a Greek orthodox monastery), at the foot of Mt. Sinai in the Sinai peninsula. The convent had long been known to scholars as a repository of ancient manuscripts. It was there that the biblical scholar Lobegott von Tischendorf found, some years earlier, another valuable manuscript known as the *Codex Sinaiticus*.

Agnes and Margaret Smith were born in 1843 in the Scottish town of Irvine, on the Firth of Clyde. Their mother died shortly after they were born, and their father, John Smith, brought them up to the best of his ability. They were sent to schools in Irvine, Birkenhead, and London, and they traveled in Europe. By the time they made their first trips alone they were well-educated young women, able to speak French, German, and Italian. Later they studied ancient Greek and added some Arabic, Hebrew, and Syriac. John Smith died in 1866, after inheriting a sizable fortune, which he left to his daughters.

With no parents or close family, the sisters found themselves not only well off but also possessed of a freedom few women of their day had, and they made the most of it. Beginning in 1868, they traveled for almost two years in Hungary, Rumania, Greece, Turkey, and Egypt. For the sake of propriety, they included a slightly older woman friend in their otherwise unchaperoned journey. After publishing an account of their travels, they moved to London, where Agnes wrote two more travel books and several novels.

Both women married scholars, although not until they were in their forties. In 1883 Margaret married James Young Gibson, a Spanish translator, who died three years later. In 1887 Agnes married Samuel Savage Lewis, the librarian of Corpus Christi College in Cambridge; she, in turn, was widowed in 1891. The twins had rarely been separated, and marriage had made no difference, for Agnes shared the Gibsons' home and later Maggie lived with the Lewises.

The sisters had long cherished a desire to visit Mt. Sinai, "the scene of one of the most astonishing miracles recorded in Bible history . . . the passage of the Israelites through the desert of Arabia" (Gibson, *How the Codex Was Found*, p. 6). One of their Cambridge friends, James Rendel Harris, suggested that they might like to visit St. Catherine's Convent. He had been there in 1889 and had discovered a valuable manuscript. Maggie's husband had also visited the monastery before their marriage and had brought back reports of great treasures there. In preparation for the journey, the sisters studied modern Greek, and Agnes learned Syriac. Although they agreed to photograph a manuscript at the convent for Harris, they saw the site as interesting for its biblical associations; the search for papers would be a secondary benefit.

Their former travels had taught them something about organizing an expedition, for the convent was to be reached only after an eleven-day trek by camel across the desert. They had to carry everything needed for camping on the desert and provisions for a lengthy stay, including pens of live chickens and turkeys. They finally reached the convent, "a medley of buildings belonging to every epoch since its foundation by Justinian in the fifth century" (Gibson, *How the Codex Was Found*, p. 36). It was on the floor of a barren, dusty valley, between high mountains, one of which was Mt. Sinai, or Horeb. Here Moses received the Ten Commandments. The site of the burning bush was within the convent walls. Elijah and other prophets had lived in caves on the mountain. And it was here that the Israelites had lived on manna.

The monks lived in a walled oasis in the desert, with orchards, vegetable gardens, a beautiful church, and even a mosque. They welcomed their visitors and allowed them to pitch their tents in the gardens. Here in an atmosphere redolent of biblical associations, one might expect a miracle, but were these middle-aged, rather frumpy Scottish ladies the kind to invite miracles?

Before they had time to explore their surroundings, they were shown the monks' library and given access to its treasures. The papers were scattered, some in a little dark room that had to be seen with the light of candles. They had been stored in vaults where they were exposed to damp and then allowed to dry without care. But the kindly librarian, Father Galakteon, gave the visitors every facility for photographing the manuscripts they found, and he himself stood for hours holding the pages open for them. Dr. Harris had taught them how to photograph manuscripts, had designed a stand for large pages, and had given them specially printed sheets on which to collate the various texts, a refinement that astonished Galakteon.

By one of those odd quirks of fortune, the discovery of the famous palimpsest came about not through diligent search but because of the monks' casual way of serving the butter. It was not placed on a dish but on an old bit of vellum. Agnes saw with astonishment that it was a piece of manuscript written in Greek with some underwriting in Syriac. She read a little of the Syriac and suspected it was a part of the Gospels. She asked to be shown the rest of the document.

When she saw the pages, Lewis said, "they were covered with the dust of centuries, and were stained in parts with a greasy substance, so that the steam of the kettle had to be used . . . to separate some of them" (Lewis, Introduction to *The Four Gospels in Syriac*). The Greek version was a martyrology, a collection of lives of women saints, written by a monk named John the Recluse during the seventh or eighth century after Christ. Between the lines and on the margins other writing, in Syriac, could be discerned. The manuscript was a palimpsest, its vellum pages made up of sheets from old volumes which had been pulled to pieces; the original writing was scraped off, and the sheets used for the Greek text. If, as Lewis suspected, the Syriac was an early version of the Gospels, they must photograph the whole manuscript of 358 pages and try to decipher the underwriting.

The monks' library had no glass in the windows, and it was bitterly cold, as was the tent where the visitors slept. But the women managed to withstand the discomfort long enough to photograph the pages.

After a month of arduous labor, spiced with the excitement of discovery, the sisters came home with a thousand undeveloped photographs. It had been too dry and dusty in the desert to process the film. A friend suggested that they send some photographs to a professional to be developed to have a standard by which to judge their own work. When the films were returned, they were so faint that they could not be used for printing, and twenty-four pages of the palimpsest seemed lost. However, in taking the photos, Margaret had inadvertently missed her place in the volume and had exposed some thirty pages in duplicate—the exact pages that had seemed lost! This proved to the women that God had had a hand in the work.

In the midst of their labors, the sisters entertained several of their Cambridge friends at lunch, among them Mary Kingsley, soon to become famous as an African explorer, and Professor F. C. Burkitt of Trinity College and his wife. After all the guests had gone except these three, Agnes spread out her photographs on the piano for Burkitt to look at.

> She told him what the upper writing was, and that the under-writing was Syriac Gospels, which she hoped with his keen young eyes, he might be able to decipher. He became at once intensely interested, and asked if she would entrust some dozen of the photographs to him for a few days. (Gibson, *How the Codex Was Found*, p. 76)

Burkitt took the photos to an older scholar, Robert L. Bensly, and together the two men deciphered the under-writing; even from the small sample, Bensly recognized it as a companion to a Syriac manuscript known as the Cureton Text, discovered in 1842 and deposited in the British Museum. The Cureton was of the highest value to biblical scholars, and the discovery of a second text, supplementing the first and filling in its deficiencies, was indeed a find.

Bensly was understandably beside himself with excitement. He, at once, sent Lewis and Gibson a request to keep the matter secret until the palimpsest could be transcribed from the actual manuscript. Margaret wrote

> We did keep it a secret to some extent—at least to the extent of not publishing it, and of telling only a few friends whose advice we were in need of. Professor Bensly himself was so much excited that he forgot an engagement to dinner, and the very next day six of us had resolved to make the journey to Sinai six months later, and had communicated our resolution to each other. It seemed an instinct with us all to wish for the transcription of that manuscript. (Gibson, *How the Codex Was Found*, p. 79)

The party that set out for Sinai early in 1893 consisted of the twins; three Cambridge dons, Harris, Bensly, and Burkitt; and the wives of Bensly and Burkitt. At Cairo they called on the archbishop and obtained a letter to the monks at St. Catherine's asking that every facility be given to the party for examining the books and giving permission to Agnes to catalog the Arabic and Syriac manuscripts in the convent.

Gibson and Lewis found the desert road less monotonous than formerly, "for it was enlivened by philological discussions, by scraps of song, of wit, and of story." A year almost to the day after their first arrival, the two sisters found themselves back at the convent, welcomed "with a cordiality that was almost overpowering" by Father Galakteon, who was now the abbot (Gibson, *How the Codex Was Found*, p. 127).

Margaret got permission to take the palimpsest to their tents to be deciphered. Mrs. Bensly made a silk cover for the manuscript to protect it overnight, and the work of reading it was divided among the three scholars, Bensly, Harris, and Burkitt, each to have the manuscript for three hours a day, and each to be responsible for about one hundred pages. The men worked out of doors where the light was best, using a washstand as a desk. The twins began to work on the catalogs; ten or fifteen volumes were carried up at a time "from the various little closets, which are called libraries only by courtesy, and from old chests stored away in the queerest of corners." Mrs. Bensly was recruited to help in counting the pages, and the monks joined in. "The little draughty room, with its glassless windows, was sometimes filled with some half-dozen of the holy fathers, counting assiduously under their abbot's direction" (Gibson, *How the Codex Was Found*, pp. 132–34).

Agnes had asked Mr. Scott, the keeper of the manuscripts at the British Museum, how to revive faded writing without injuring the script or the vellum, and she had obtained hydrosulfide of ammonia, "a very ill-scented composition, from the fumes of which I hoped to be protected by a respirator specially designed for the purpose." After some days of hesitancy about using the concoction, she got Galakteon's permission to try it, and it immediately brought up the faded writing in brilliant color. Galakteon was so astonished that he wanted to paint up the whole volume and try it on other hoary documents. Bensly was not as impressed, but after a few days he asked for her brush to bring up faint words. It was thus that the final colophon came to light, telling that these were "the separated gospels" (Gibson, *How the Codex Was Found*, pp. 135–36, and Lewis, Introduction to *The Four Gospels*).

The sisters, Presbyterians themselves, were somewhat critical of the convent, which had existed for fifteen centuries, with prayers arising night and day, "but as far as being a center of light to the population around, it might as well never have existed" (Gibson, *How the Codex Was Found*, p. 54). Mrs. Bensly found, outside the gates, some Bedouin women, "two poor creatures who had never known the use of soap and water, who spent most of their time sitting with a couple of children outside the convent gate, and whose home was under a great rock." She tried to teach them to knit. "The stupid creatures refused to learn, but some men and boys took up the work so eagerly that their kind teacher could not supply them all with materials" (Gibson, *How the Codex Was Found*, p. 137).

The transcription of the Syriac text was published in 1894 by the Cambridge University Press under the name of Bensly, together with those of his fellow-transcribers, Harris and Burkitt, and with an introduction by Agnes Smith Lewis. Bensly had caught a chill in Rome on the return journey, and he died three days after reaching Cambridge. By the time the book appeared, Father Galakteon, too, had died. Lewis's English translation was published also in 1894. Meanwhile Gibson had published the account of the two visits to Mt. Sinai, and Mrs. Bensly wrote the story in Braille, for within a short period after her husband's death she became blind. She blamed the sisters for the loss of her husband, and her account, later published as *Our Journey to Sinai*, treats them as mere guides and interpreters, giving them no credit for their scholarship or their role as discoverers of the manuscript.

Between 1894 and 1897, the sisters made four other visits to the convent, where they discovered other valuable manuscripts. They went later to Coptic monasteries in Egypt and Beirut, one of which they had to enter by rope and windlass over the doorless walls (described and illustrated with a photograph in *Century Magazine*, Sept. 1904). They published, during the next few years, an impressive body of transcriptions of Syriac and Arabic texts. The two were given honorary degrees by several universities—Halle, St. Andrew's, Heidelberg, and Trinity College in Dublin, but not Cambridge. In 1915 Lewis was awarded the gold medal of the Royal Asiatic Society.

The women continued to live in Cambridge, in the large Gothic mansion, Castlebrae, built by Gibson at the time of his marriage. They entertained often and became well known in Cambridge, their eccentricities endearing them to their friends. In 1897 they helped to lay the cornerstone for Westminster College, a Presbyterian theological school, which was moved from London to Cambridge to occupy a site the twins bought for it.

Agnes Lewis died at Castlebrae on March 29, 1926. Margaret Gibson had passed away six years earlier, on January 11, 1920. Most of their estate went to the English Presbyterian Church, mainly to Westminster College. Portraits of the two women, in academic robes, hang in the Hall of Westminster, where undergraduates refer to them disrespectfully but fondly as "the Giblews." Castlebrae became a hostel for the undergraduates of Clare College. The famous palimpsest remains in the library of St. Catherine's, in a box Agnes designed for it. The library has been completely rebuilt and modernized, with the help of funds provided by Agnes and Margaret. The once-isolated convent is now an easily reached, popular tourist attraction.

BIBLIOGRAPHY

Works by Agnes Smith Lewis

As Agnes Smith

Eastern Pilgrims: The Travels of Three Ladies. London: Hurst & Blackett, 1870.
Glimpses of Greek Life and Scenery. London: Hurst & Blackett, 1884.
Through Cyprus. London: Hurst & Blackett, 1887.

As Agnes Smith Lewis

Two Unpublished Letters. Cambridge, England: privately printed, 1893. Pamphlet on the discovery of the palimpsest addressed to the London *Times* but evidently not printed by the paper.

Introduction to *The Four Gospels in Syriac, Transcribed from the Sinaitic Palimpsest* by R. L. Bensly, J. Rendel Harris, and F. C. Burkitt. Cambridge, England: Cambridge University Press, 1894.

A Translation of the Four Gospels from the Syriac of the Sinaitic Palimpsest. Cambridge, England: J. Palmer for Macmillan, London, 1894.

"What Language Did Christ Speak?" *Century* 53 (Dec. 1896): 307–311.

In the Shadow of Sinai: A Story of Travel and Research from 1895 to 1897. Cambridge, England: Macmillan & Bowes, 1898.

"Hidden Egypt: The First Visit by Women to the Coptic Monasteries of Egypt and Nitria, with an Account of the Conditions and Reasons for the Decadence of the Ancient Church." *Century* 68 (Sept. 1904): 745–58.

Work by Margaret Smith Gibson

How the Codex Was Found: A Narrative of Two Visits to Sinai, from Mrs. Lewis's Journals, 1892–1893. Cambridge, England: Macmillan & Bowes, 1893. Reprinted from the *Presbyterian Churchman.*

Works about Agnes Smith Lewis and Margaret Smith Gibson

Bensly, Agnes D. *Our Journey to Sinai: A Visit to the Convent of St. Caterina, with a Chapter on the Sinai Palimpsest.* London: Religious Tract Society, 1895.

Dictionary of National Biography, 1922–1930. London: Oxford University Press, 1937 (under "Lewis"). Biographies of James Young Gibson and Samuel Savage Lewis in the *Dictionary* give scant mention of their wives.

Europa Biographical Dictionary of British Women. Edited by Anne Crawford and others. London: Europa, 1985 (under "Gibson" and "Lewis").

Mozans, H. J. (pseud. of John A. Zahm). *Woman in Science.* London and New York: Appleton, 1913, pp. 327–32.

Price, A. Whigham. *The Ladies of Castlebrae: A Story of Nineteenth Century Travel and Research.* Gloucester, England: Alan Sutton, 1985. A bibliography includes the two women's many biblical works.

Lewis and Gibson papers, notebooks, photographs, and lantern slides are maintained by Westminster College, Cambridge, England.

ELLA MAILLART
1903–

Ella Maillart began, in February 1935, an epic 3,500-mile journey through central Asia. Japan, China, and Russia were struggling for supremacy there, and few foreign travelers were allowed to enter. Her account of the trek from Peking to Kashmir, *Forbidden Journey*, records a China existing as it had been for over two thousand years but will never be again. It is an absorbing story of the day-to-day experiences of a couple of European journalists who traveled for the love of it. Maillart, a Swiss, and Peter Fleming, an Englishman, walked and rode through deserts and mountains; they cooked over dung fires; they slept in inns, mud huts, tents, and lamaseries; they ate the food of the Asians and, when there was no food, they fasted.

Maillart's interest in the Far East was long lasting. Three years earlier, she had traveled as far as the eastern frontier of Russian Turkestan. There, from the heights of the Celestial Mountains, she could see the Takla Makan desert in Chinese Turkestan but was unable to get permission to go farther. Twenty years later, on one of her last journeys to that fascinating region, she visited Nepal.

> It is a strange fact that in order fully to understand my innermost European core, I had to live in the immensity of Asia, almost at the edge of time and space and far from our particular standards and our irrepressible dynamism. Asia, only yesterday still static and traditionalist, is so vast that man, aware of his own littleness, has given first place to the divine life, bestowing on it alone the glory of true reality. (*The Land of the Sherpas*, p. 13)

In her autobiographical *Cruises and Caravans*, Maillart says that in her childhood the thought of travel hardly crossed her mind. Born in Geneva on February 20, 1903, she was named Ella Katherine Maillart but became known as "Kini" to her friends. Her early years were devoted to sport and to photography. She spent summers on the shores of Lake Geneva, where she learned to swim, sail, and navigate. She was chosen to represent Switzerland at the boating events in the

Olympic games in Paris. She organized a women's field hockey team and then a Swiss ski racing team; she excelled in both sports.

When the time came for her to be independent, she could not settle on an occupation. She tried working on a yacht, teaching in an English girls' school, and excavating for six weeks, with two other women, a primitive Cretan village. She became an expert photographer and was much interested in making nature films, but she could not find anyone to finance her scripts.

Disillusioned after the "war to end war" by the "compromise, artificial ideals, and palavers that failed to establish a real peace," she decided to visit Russia, which seemed to have something new going on (*Cruises and Caravans*, pp. 28–29). Her announced reason for the visit was to study Russian films.

Life in Moscow, she said, "can be described in a word: it was a continual fight. . . . But when you are deeply interested material details—so important in a dull country—vanish into the background" (*Cruises and Caravans*, p. 34). She spent most of her time studying films, meeting cameramen "back from frozen Kamtchatka, scorched Turkestan, wind-swept Mongolia, or wooded Siberia" (*Cruises and Caravans*, p. 35). She joined a workers' athletic club, and, through a society that organized holidays for workers and students, she went with a group to the high valleys of the Caucasus.

Maillart found the Caucasus "a living museum of races, faiths, and languages" (*Cruises and Caravans*, p. 39). The upper Ingur valley, called Free Svanetia, cut off from the rest of the world except during the three summer months, was practically independent and blissfully ignorant of the Bolshevik revolution. Here, the travelers were welcomed by a Svane family, who offered them honey and almonds and flat wheat cakes cooked on a hot slab. The houses had no chimneys; the smoke rose through holes in the roof. The only vehicles were sledges dragged by oxen.

Kini, though hampered by her rudimentary knowledge of the Russian language as well as by lack of money and equipment, wanted very much to remain longer to study the customs of the people, but the party pushed on, finally reaching the Black Sea. "Traveling steerage among a dense crowd, sleeping next to crying babies, poultry baskets, and live sheep," was uncomfortable but Maillart was interested in the people, who came from many different parts of the country. "I felt attracted by that eastern world I was turning my back upon and I made a resolve to go there one day" (*Cruises and Caravans*, p. 46).

She returned to her home in Geneva, where she wrote an article on her Russian adventures, which was published as *Parmi la Jeunesse Russe*. The money the publisher gave her enabled her to start for Russian Turkestan in the spring of 1932. She traveled first with four Russians who were to spend their holidays in the Tien Shan.

They rode over the plains of Kirghiz, were entertained in a yurt (a round felt tent), and drank koumiss (fermented mare's milk). They watched the making of felt from camel wool and the construction of a yurt. In their honor, a lamb was slaughtered, and all shared in the banquet. The meal was followed by music on a "plaintive fiddle," and Maillart was enchanted. "I have really been initiated into the daily life of the Kirghiz as I longed to be in my dreams in far-away Paris" (*Cruises and Caravans*, p. 64).

From a mountain pass she viewed the Gobi desert, far below.

Here at my feet is one of the objectives I had set myself in coming so far: the Chinese mountains inhabited by Kirghiz, and Sin Kiang in the turmoil of opposing currents. And still remoter, still calling me, were Kucha, Basaklik with its temple-grottos containing the hundred thousand Buddhas, and Tokharian frescoes which bring to life again a whole Indo-European aristocracy whose amazing civilization flourished in the seventh century. . . . What joy it would be to go down there . . . intoxicated by the Unknown's thousand faces! (*Turkestan Solo*, pp. 114–15)

At Alma-Ata, Kini parted with her companions; they were to return to Moscow, but she was determined to remain in Turkestan until she had spent her last kopek. She would travel alone, living like the poor in a country short of food. She took only the necessities—clothing, films, medicines, bedding, and a cooking stove—and all the provisions she could buy. When she could not find a cart or porter, she had to carry everything herself. She learned to sleep anywhere.

She visited Tashkent, Samarkand, Bukhara, and Turktol. She interviewed administrators and refugees, trying to get a true picture of the effects of Sovietization on the people. Her many adventures included a barge ride on the Amu Darya and crossing the Kyzyl Kum desert in midwinter by two-wheeled cart and then by camel. Making her way toward Moscow, she passed pitiful refugees traveling in the opposite direction. The days were thrilling, but later she admitted that she would not like to live them again; they had been exhausting. She wrote of her journey in *Des Montes Celestes aux Sables Rouges* (translated and published as *Turkestan Solo*).

In 1934, still dreaming of crossing central Asia, she persuaded the editor of *Le Petit Parisien* to finance a trip to Manchukuo in return for reports on the state of affairs there.

Some months earlier, at a London cocktail party, she had met Peter Fleming, who shared her interest in travel. They had parted with a casual, "See you in China." They ran into each other in Harbin and went together on several short trips to northern China. They got on well. Kini spoke of Peter as "a great traveller. He had already crossed Brazil in the most singular circumstances and, two years before, he had been up and down Southern China in pursuit of Communists" (*Forbidden Journey*, pp. 7–8). When she told him of her plans to cross China to India, he said, "As a matter of fact, I'm going back to Europe by that route. You can come with me if you like."

"I beg your pardon," she replied, "It's my route and it's I who'll take you, if I can think of some way in which you might be useful to me" (*Forbidden Journey*, p. 8).

Indeed, it was doubtful that they could go at all, separately or together. The province of Sinkiang, toward which they wished to travel, had been closed to foreigners by a series of civil wars. Rumors had reached Peking that the entire province was now administered by Soviet Russia. The possibility of getting passports was highly doubtful. "Far more than the inherent difficulties of the journey, it is the politics of men that make these regions inaccessible," Kini wrote. "Nobody knew what had been happening in Sinkiang for four years past. Yet it is an immense province, which touches Tibet, India, Afghanistan and the U.S.S.R., a province in which the interests of these countries are engaged in secret and unending combat" (*Forbidden Journey*, pp. 4–5).

Kini happened to meet a White Russian couple, Stepan and Nina Smigunov, who had a home in the Tsaidam to which they wished to return. They agreed to serve as guides and interpreters if she could get the necessary papers to clear the way. That would help enormously to get her at least half of the way to India.

Fleming, who had formed a favorable opinion of Kini's intelligence and ability, now felt disposed to join forces with her. Kini appreciated Peter's "brilliant intelligence, his faculty of being able to eat anything and sleep anywhere . . . still more his horror of any distortion of facts and the native objectivity with which he recounted them" (*Forbidden Journey*, pp. 8–9). But could she stand his Oxford drawl, his everlasting pipe smoking, his passion for hunting? Could he stand her constant chatter and singing, her primitive cooking? Their friends pointed out that he had just published a book called *One's Company*, she, one called *Turkestan Solo*; surely joining forces would be inappropriate? A graver cause for hesitation about their plans was that Peter wanted to travel as fast as possible; Kini "wanted to dawdle in my usual fashion, as if I had the whole of eternity before me" (*Forbidden Journey*, p. 9). They decided to chance it. As Kini wrote, "the controversy still rages" (*Forbidden Journey*, p. 8).

Her Russian had improved greatly, and she was fluent in French, English and German; Peter had a smattering of Russian and Chinese. With the Smigunovs they would be able to talk to anyone they chanced to meet.

They secured passports, slightly irregular, and permits given by their legations and began hurried preparations. Doctors in Peking had prepared a vaccine against typhus, a disease carried by lice, which were abundant in that country. Peter and Kini were inoculated. They laid in provisions, such items as coffee, cocoa, marmalade, chocolate, curry, and tobacco, which were not available in the interior, and "half a dozen bottles of good brandy for very cold days and hours when morale fell low" (*Forbidden Journey*, p. 10). They bought presents for people on whose assistance their fate might depend. Each brought along a type writer, useful in case they had to spend time in jail. Peter got a couple of rifles an expert hunter, he was often to supply their food while on the march. They carried little money. Mexican dollars, the currency most commonly used, were heavy. They had been told that at some towns they might be able to cash checks. Kini carried a few English pounds, and they had a bar of gold, with a saw to cut off bits as needed. They had visiting cards engraved with their names in Chinese characters. His was Fu Lei-ming, the Learned Engraver on Stone; her was Ma Na-ya, the Horse of International Goodwill. The London *Times*, which he represented, was translated as the Newspaper for the Enlightened Apprehension of Scholars.

The first part of the journey was anything but pleasant, for they went by train, missed one and had to make do with an exceedingly slow one, then had to travel by lorries overloaded with bundles and passengers. At last they reached Lanchou where they were put up at the China Inland Mission with kind missionaries. Here their Peking passports were taken away and not returned for some days while officials decided their fate. The word, when it came, was devastating: "The Ma Ya Ngans may proceed, the Russians must return" (*Forbidden Journey*, p. 41). Without the Smigunovs as guides, the journey looked most formidable. Kini and Peter parted with Stepan and Nina sadly. (Many years later, they heard that the couple had fled through Mongolia and had reached Paraguay.)

The expedition of two, with one muleteer, set off rather lightheartedly, considering their prospects. Carrying out the journey alone, said Kini, "added some suggestion of bravura to our exploit" (*Forbidden Journey*, p. 43). She walked along with joy in her heart, the air ringing with her Alpine songs. She felt pity for the poor Kansu peasants, and especially for the women whose feet had been bound while young and for the little girls who were having their feet tied up with filthy bandages. At night, they stayed in inns, scoured the town for food, and spread their sleeping bags on *k'angs* (raised sleeping platforms, usually heated from below and inevitably buggy).

They settled naturally on a division of labor. Wherever they had to get official permission to proceed, arrange for guides, or hire animals, Peter was the negotiator. His charm and force of personality got them through many a sticky situation. Kini handled the commissary, did what washing and mending she could, and often served as doctor and nurse for the people who came to them with great faith in European medicine. At one point, they joined a caravan of some two hundred and fifty camels led by the Prince of Dzun. At other times, they traveled virtually alone. When they could no longer find animals for hire, they bought horses. Kini's was a small mare which she called Slalom and became very fond of. When they reached the mountains, the horse gave out; Kini and Peter literally pushed the animal over the mountain trail until they reached water and grass where they could leave her with some chance of her survival.

By June, they were well into Sinkiang. Far from being disturbed, they found the province relatively peaceful. Their chances of being turned back were now minimal, and they felt sure they would get through to India. Peter wrote to the *Times* that all was going well. "So far," he said cheerfully, "the journey has been uneventful . . . the regions traversed to reach Sinkiang are very little known. Nobody goes there and hardly anybody lives there, and I must say I don't blame them" (Hart-Davis, *Peter Fleming*, p. 177). The letter, however, did not reach London until after he himself was home; fears for the safety of the travelers had mounted as the months went by without word.

For the most part, they were healthy, in spite of long marches, shortages of food, the ever-present mosquitoes and flies, the heat of the desert, and the cold of the mountains. During part of the journey, Kini was smitten by rheumatism, and she suffered greatly on their ten- or twelve-hour stages. She remained cheerful, except that she berated Peter for his wanting to rush ahead instead of resting a few days wherever there was comfort.

Two days before they reached Kashgar, the donkey boy let their baggage fall into a river, and all their belongings got wet. They had to stop and dry out the camera, the typewriters, the medicine chest, and their papers. Peter had brought with him a tropical suit in order to make a decent appearance when they reached civilized Kashgar. It was now not only soaked but also streaked with green dye from a scarf. "I had now to decide," he wrote, "whether to enter Kashgar disguised as a lettuce, or looking like something that had escaped from Devil's Island" (Hart-Davis, *Peter Fleming*, p. 181). Kini, thinking about her pleated skirt, much the worse for having been rolled up into a ball in her suitcase, could not bring herself to feel too badly about the suit.

Next day, as the shabby, suntanned couple trotted along the road, they were met by a carriage, into which they transferred themselves for the last few miles into town. There they were met by the British vice-consul. They luxuriated in hot baths, clean sheets, good food, and good conversation—for once, Kini observed, everyone speaking the same language. Peter played squash, and they both played football with the Hunzas. The fact that Kini played for all she was worth gave credence to the rumor that she was a White Russian disguised as a woman.

They still had three mountain passes to conquer before they were at the end of their journey, but they felt that they had won. The 3,500 miles were covered in just six and a half months, at an estimated cost to each of a hundred and fifty pounds. "The success of our expedition will remain an unrivalled experience so far as I am concerned," exulted Kini. "Asia is unique, and I, who care most for old primitive countries, find none of the other continents comparable to it'" (*Forbidden Journey*, p. 250).

Whenever they had been hungry on the trail, the travelers had amused themselves by discussing what they would have for dinner to celebrate their arrival at Srinagar. When the time came, however, the reality did not come up to their expectations. They clinked their glasses of champagne almost without pleasure. They had become closer than brothers; yet, now that their common aim had been attained, there was nothing more to keep them together.

Peter left first and flew to London; Kini stayed a few more days, then flew to Paris by way of Lebanon. Fleming married soon afterward and settled into the life of a country squire. The two remained friends, meeting from time to time in London to reminisce and to catch up with each other's careers.

Both published books about the trip. Peter's was entitled *News from Tartary*, Kini's, *Oasis Interdites*, translated as *Forbidden Journey*. Both books were highly acclaimed, for they transformed seemingly mundane daily events into a tale of adventure, a romantic view of a secret and beautiful world. One cannot help guessing that had Kini been given a little more time to explore and make friends, she would have added depth to the human story. Though she studies the political scene as a journalist, her interest is not in politics but in people.

Maillart's quest for meaning in the world led her again to Asia. In 1939, with Europe once more in the shadow of war, she and a friend went from Paris to Afghanistan. This time, she traveled by automobile, but the trip was not the lighthearted adventure of her previous caravans. Her companion was unhealthy in body and spirit, a heavy cigarette smoker and a drug abuser. She was often unable to share Kini's pleasure in visiting Afghanistan's great monuments, and her unhappiness took the edge off Kini's joy. To Kini, her companion had chosen the ''cruel way'' of living, just the choice modern Europe was making.

Kini herself sought self-knowledge. ''My search for an Edenic mountain tribe was merely the excuse for breaking away from the helplessness prevalent in Europe'' (*The Cruel Way*, p. 27). After her companion returned home, Kini remained for some time in India and Tibet.

She was made a Fellow of the Royal Geographical Society and was given the Sir Percy Sykes Medal in 1955. She is an honorary member of the Alpine Club. She wrote in French and English, and several of her books have been translated into German, Spanish, Japanese, Swedish, and Dutch. None, however, has surpassed the account of her journey across China.

BIBLIOGRAPHY

Works by Ella Maillart

Turkestan Solo: One Woman's Expedition from the Tien Shan to the Kizul Kum. Translated by John Rodker. London and New York: Putnam, 1935.

Forbidden Journey. Translated by Thomas McGreevy. London: Heinemann, 1937. Reprinted, with an introduction by Dervla Murphy, London: Century, 1983. Quotations in the text are from the 1983 edition.

Cruises and Caravans. London: Dent, 1942.

Gypsy Afloat. London: Heinemann, 1942.

The Cruel Way. London: Heinemann, 1947.

''What Northern Tibet Meant to Me.'' In Richard Baker and others, *The Lasting Victories: Contributions by 44 Authors.* London: Lutterworth, 1948.

''My Philosophy of Travel.'' In *Traveller's Quest: Original Contributions toward a Philosophy of Travel.* Edited by M. A. Michael and William Hodge. London: W. Hodge, 1950.

'Ti-puss: A Travel Book. London: Heinemann, 1951.

The Land of the Sherpas. London: Hodder & Stoughton, 1955.

''Tibetan Jaunt.'' In *Explorers' and Travellers' Tales.* Edited by Odette Tchernine. London: Jarrolds, 1958.

Works about Ella Maillart

Fleming, Peter. *News from Tartary*. London: Cape, 1936.
Hart-Davis, Duff. *Peter Fleming: A Biography*. London: Cape, 1974.
The International Who's Who, 1987–88. London: Europa, 1987, p. 946.

ELIZABETH SARAH MAZUCHELLI
1832–1914

Elizabeth Sarah (Nina) Mazuchelli was the first European woman known to penetrate the interior of the Eastern Himalayas. Her trip is remarkable partly for its daring and partly for the contrast between the wild and unexplored country she visited and the physical and intellectual baggage with which she traveled. A Victorian cleric's wife, she went off to the mountain fastnesses attired in long white dresses, dainty boots, and beribboned hats. She was carried over precipitous trails in a *dandy* (a basketwork litter) or seated in a wicker chair roped to the back of a coolie.

The only woman in the expedition, she did none of the work but spent her spare time making sketches and watercolors of the party and the landscape and writing a humorous account of the tribulations and pleasures of herself and her companions. As the journey took a serious turn and they were lost in a trackless mountain wasteland, where it looked very much as though they might either freeze or starve to death, Nina's true character revealed itself. Her courage in the face of disaster and her concern for the disheartened porters helped to avert panic and possible mutiny. After her return home to England, she published, in 1876, *The Indian Alps and How We Crossed Them*, with her charming illustrations but without her name, simply as "By a Lady Pioneer."

Aside from a few hints given in her book, almost nothing is known about Nina Mazuchelli's life. She was evidently a child of well-to-do English parents. She mentions a governess who tried to teach her geography—which she hated—and she speaks of having traveled often in the European Alps. The dedication is "To my mother, these pages, the substance of letters sent home to her during almost the only time we were ever separated." A biographer used the India Office records to identify her as the wife of Francis Mazuchelli (born in 1820), an Anglican clergyman serving as a chaplain with the British army. In 1853 he married Elizabeth Sarah (last name not given) born in 1832 (Miller, *On Top of the World*). She was known as Nina.

Some five years after the marriage, Mazuchelli was sent to India. Presumably, Nina accompanied him. In 1869 he was posted for two years to Darjeeling, a delightful spot in the Himalayas where the British retreated from the heat of the Indian plains during the worst of the weather. To Nina, this was a heavenly relief, not only from the heat but also from the boredom of life as English civil servants. She made the most of it by riding through the hills, getting acquainted with the Lepchas (nomadic tribesmen from Sikkim), and sketching their homes. They called it "writing them" and much to her disappointment insisted on tidying up the homes and even themselves when they knew she would be coming with her paint box.

Never tired of gazing at the great snow-capped ranges in the distance, she longed for a nearer approach and finally suggested to Francis (always referred to as F—) that they explore the Himalayas. He pretended to be shocked at the very idea, but he agreed on a short excursion to the junction of the Teesta (Tista) and Rungheet (Rangit) rivers, then across the border into Bhutan. They sent six Lepchas ahead to build a shelter of boughs and to prepare their camp. They themselves mounted ponies and zigzagged cautiously down the steep mountain. They were distressed when they heard rumors that a great sahib with a train of servants was journeying to the very spot at the very same time, threatening to destroy the blessed solitude and to rob them of the thrill of discovery—until they realized that they themselves were the rumored great sahibs.

The trial run proving successful, Francis agreed to a real expedition. As his two years of service were ending, he took a three-month leave. A friend, designated only as C— but evidently a powerful English official who knew the country, offered to go along. They were to be his guests. He made arrangements for a headman, who procured servants and porters, and he agreed to see to the provisions for the expedition.

"We shall be travelling towards Mount Everest and Kinchinjunga [Kanchenjunga]—the two highest mountains in the world," wrote Nina:

> The perpetually snow-clad mountains of the great Kinchinjunga group, it must be understood, form an impassable barrier, incapable of being crossed; it is, therefore, our intention to cross the range of intervening Alps till we reach their base, and then explore the glaciers. . . . Many were the predictions that, even if F— returned alive, I, at any rate, should leave my bones to whiten on some mountaintop; and many were the warnings of anxious friends, who did their utmost to induce us to relinquish so rash an undertaking; but zest was only fostered by opposition, and we set about making preparations in real earnest. (*The Indian Alps*, p. 81)

The servants that were to go were not the submissive, trained Indians they were used to but the more colorful hill natives who worked well and willingly. They had an Indian cook, who could make delicious soups, curries, and stews over charcoal burning in a hole in the ground. They took along a cow, so that

Elizabeth Sarah (Nina) Mazuchelli in the Indian Alps

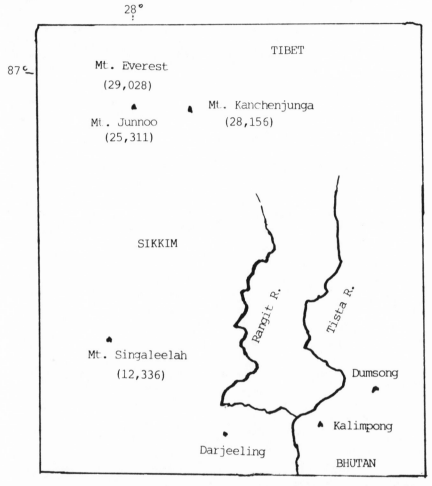

they could have milk, as well as live chickens and sheep to be slaughtered as needed. They had tents, a tent stove, lamps, furniture, tablecloths, cutlery, and dishes, all enabling them to camp in style. Nina had decided to get along without a maid, difficult as it might be, because she was unwilling to ask another woman to face the possible dangers.

When assembled, the expedition consisted of the headman, four servants, and an assortment of carriers and helpers, a total of almost eighty. Unable to get a full quota of Lepchas, they took a group of Bhootias (from Bhutan). Nina was provided with a Bareilly *dandy*, "a kind of reclining chair made of cane, and suspended by leather straps to a strong rim of wood—with a pole at each end," in which she could recline while porters carried her aloft. The two gentlemen were to ride ponies.

As I stood at the window [she wrote], watching the coolies one by one disappear beneath the hill with their loads, my pulse beat fast, and my heart throbbed; not, however, from the proud anticipation that we were about to travel amongst the most extensive and lofty mountains of the world, but—shall I confess it?—from misgivings lest, after all, the prophets of evil should be right, and I prove incapable of sustaining the fatigue of such a journey. Yonder lay the whole vast expanse of the Sub-Himalaya, Alp upon Alp, and wave upon wave of blue mountain, varying in height from eight to fourteen thousand feet, all of which we must cross before reaching even the *base* of the snowy range, fifty miles distant as a bird would fly, but nearly one hundred and fifty to us. (*The Indian Alps*, p. 183)

Several European men had penetrated into the interior along the river valleys, but few had traversed the crest of the Singaleelah chain, "And I was the first lady to explore the Eastern Himalaya by either way; so that it was no marvel, if I felt a few qualms, and a little trepidation, when our men had actually departed, and the irrevocable step was taken" (*The Indian Alps*, p. 183).

Nina commented with pleasure on the flowers, the trees, the many travelers they passed on the road, the life in camp, and the jolly Lepchas, to whom everything was a great joke. Accustomed to servile Indians, it took her some time to get used to the familiarity of the hill men and to their noisy behavior to each other. She thought they had bold, rugged natures and were incapable of meanness or cowardice. As she grew to know them, they became individuals, with names or nicknames and with definite personalities. Hatti, a Bhootia, was very big and strong, and when it was too precipitous to use the *dandy*, he was the one who carried her in a basket chair on his back.

The mice, bats, and rats that sometimes shared their abode and the mosquitoes and assorted insects that gathered about their lamp were all part of the fun. Some places she found scary. In a bamboo forest, "I take care to make my bearers keep well up with the gentlemen, for the gloom is painfully oppressive, and I would fain not be alone" (*The Indian Alps*, p. 129). At one time, she found herself alone and overtaken by a dense fog; unable to see the path, she schooled herself to stand still and wait, trembling, until the cloud lifted and she could make her way back to the camp.

Camp life was full of interest: "the smoke curling upwards, the red glow of the fire, the bright-robed figures sitting round it, some smoking, and some chatting, make a marvellously picturesque scene, and create a perfect festival of colour" (*The Indian Alps*, p. 212).

Unless we are fortunate enough to arrive after tents are pitched, the scene seems one of hopeless confusion. Some seventy men may be seen tearing about in all directions like maniacs—some hurrying off to fetch water; some cutting down wood for fires; others clearing the ground for the tents, the whole operation accompanied by a tremendous hubbub and confusion of tongues. There is a perfect chorus of shouts and yells; and as these nomad races, belonging to the southern class of the Turanian family, have each a separate language of their own, the Babel can be easily imagined. Neither do these Arabs "fold up their tents and silently steal away," for the breaking up of camp is an equally noisy process. But in an almost incredibly short space of time after reaching encampment, tents are not only pitched, but furnished; the little striped "dhurries," or carpets, are laid down, stoves lighted . . . kettles boiling over them, and everything wearing as snug an appearance as possible. (*The Indian Alps*, p. 215)

Another woman who appeared among the party, Fanchyng, the wife of one of the porters, became a companion and sometimes a maid to Nina. Later they were joined by Tendook, an agent of a lama, who brought with him a retinue of fifteen men. Nina noted that the camp now consisted of ninety souls, not counting Fanchyng, "who being a woman doesn't have a soul." But Buddhists, like Christians, she adds, allow women to have souls. Nina had the usual Victorian view about the place of women in society:

> I am by no means one of those strong-minded females who advocate what is mis-called "woman's rights;" on the contrary, I believe women have tenderer, sweeter, purer, if not nobler rights than such advocates wot of—rights best suited to the gentler nature of her sex, and hidden deep in the sweet and gentle life of home; but there are limits to the depreciation of womankind in the social scale, and in behalf of my Oriental sisters I object to the above order of ideas. (*The Indian Alps*, p. 332)

Life began to get serious as they penetrated more deeply into the mountains. C— had arranged with the soubah, a viceroy of the rajah of Sikkim, and the kajee, the rajah's minister of state, to send supplies of food for the coolies, who had each carried his own food but only for the first week. The food did not arrive, and messengers were sent to hurry it along. Not for some time did they suspect that the kajee had never had any intention of sending supplies.

It began to rain, and not a little rain of cats and dogs but a rain only a "little short of dragons and megatheria." Nina took refuge in a tent, where she sat on her travel basket under an umbrella. "I could have cried heartily had there been a clean, dry spot whereon to sit down and have it out comfortably" (*The Indian Alps*, p. 295). But even in such circumstances it had been possible to erect a dining tent, lay the table with a cloth, and set out a meal, and Nina was persuaded to partake of it. "Our host," C—, "conservative to a degree, was wont to regard irregular habits as demoralizing, if not altogether sinful" (*The Indian Alps*, p. 299).

The sappers—men who had gone ahead and broken trail—had disappeared, the cook became ill, the ponies were useless, the cow would not give milk. However, the soubah arrived, "the *prettiest* and most benevolent" old man, but without the needed provisions. He was able to give them a small supply of rice, and then he departed, leaving a "shifty-eyed" Nepalese as a guide. As they were now to climb the Singaleelah range, they sent the heavier baggage and the useless ponies to the monastery at Pemionchi (Pemayangtze) to await their arrival there. Nina donned moccasins—not the American Indian kind but knee-high cloth boots with heavy rope soles—so that she could walk on the rocky trail.

As they approached the Junnoo Mountains, they realized the danger of their situation. It was clear that the soubah and the kajee had deceived them. None of the messengers C— had sent ahead had returned. The party was in the snow, where there was no longer a track, no sign of habitation, no game, and no firewood. They began to suffer from mountain sickness. Their sun glasses had disappeared. Their faces became blistered and swollen, their lips cracked. Some of the men were blinded by the glare of the ice.

In spite of warnings from the Lepchas, they had followed the guide, who, at last, admitted he was hopelessly lost. F— and C— conferred. The hungry coolies urged a return to Darjeeling; while they hesitated, on the verge of panic, Nina cried out, "Let us return at once; don't hesitate for a moment," stamping her foot in her vehemence, "It is the only way to save us" (The Indian Alps, p. 421).

They agreed to backtrack to Mount Singaleelah, but the men were too demoralized to lift their loads. Nina walked among them, encouraging them, helping to lift their bundles, arousing others from lethargy, and formed them into a train. C— led them, Nina took up a position in the middle of the ranks, and F— brought up the rear. "There are now but two sheep and a few handfuls of Indian corn," wrote Nina, "standing between our camp and absolute starvation" (The Indian Alps, p. 428). They gave the men portions of rum, except for the Nepalese, whose religion forbids the use of alcohol. Later, when persuaded that it was medicine, they accepted a tot. Garments were torn up to use for bandages for men whose feet were in bad shape. When the rum was gone, Nina used a bit of wine she found in her dressing case to revive a fainting lad.

C— took a few coolies and went on ahead in search of provisions. Just as all were ready to give up, he returned, followed by the kajee's men with rice and Indian corn. "Hurrah," cried one of the men, "no more dying, food has come!" All dropped their bundles, including the porters who were carrying Nina on her litter and "allowed me to follow the law of gravitation unaided, and find my own level on the ground" (The Indian Alps, pp. 477–78).

Fed and heartened, they continued the journey, and as they approached Pemionchi they passed through numerous villages, where they were greeted with astonishment and some fear. The kajee, "the old ruffian," welcomed them.

The expedition was once more enjoyable. They attended a service at the Tibetan Buddhist temple, where Nina was impressed with the earnestness and simplicity of their worship. "One cannot help feeling an interest, and something akin to reverence, too, for a sytem of religion which numbers amongst its votaries more than half the world" (The Indian Alps, p. 537).

> Strange as were the surroundings of these Pagans, and grim as were their symbols, how can I find language to express the majesty and grandeur of their worship, which impressed me more deeply than anything I have ever seen or heard, and in which I realised faintly a sort of abstract idea of what the worship of the All-

Supreme by poor feeble human lips should be? It filled me with wonder and admiration; and the chanting of their Service is a thing never to be forgotten while memory lasts. (*The Indian Alps*, p. 532)

They left the hospitable monks with regret, but since arrangements had been made to have ponies sent from Darjeeling to Sikkim to meet them, they had to keep to their schedule. In spite of the dangers they had faced, Nina, F—, and C— were sorry to see the expedition end. Nina thought it would feel odd to return to civilization, and she knew life would never be the same after her Himalayan adventures.

The Mazuchellis went home to England, where Francis served in several English parishes. Nina outlived her husband by thirteen years, and died in Wales in 1914. Another book has been attributed to her, said to be "by a Fellow of the Carpathian Society, author of 'The Indian Alps.' " Entitled "*Magyarland,*" it was published in 1881 in London. But it seems such a dull, run-of-the-mill travel book that it is hard to believe it was from the pen of the irrepressible and adventurous Nina Mazuchelli.

BIBLIOGRAPHY

Work by Elizabeth Sarah Mazuchelli

The Indian Alps and How We Crossed Them: Being a Narrative of Two Years' Residence in the Eastern Himalaya and Two Months' Tour into the Interior. By a Lady Pioneer. New York and London: Dodd, Mead, 1876.

Work about Elizabeth Sarah Mazuchelli

Miller, Luree. *On Top of the World: Five Women Explorers in Tibet.* London: Paddington, 1976, pp. 23–45.

YNES MEXIA
1870–1938

In the last thirteen years of her life, Ynes Mexia traveled throughout Mexico and South America. For the most part, she traveled alone or with a native guide, collecting plant specimens in a variety of environments—along rivers, on mountain ranges, and in arid plains. One trip took her to a source of the Amazon, where she lived with a tribe of headhunters. She became one of the most respected workers in the field of botanical collecting. Herbariums in the great institutions of America and foreign countries obtained specimens from her. She discovered three new genera and over five hundred new species, some of which were named for her.

Although she kept exact notes on her collecting and wrote long letters reporting on her travels, she had little time to publish anything other than a few articles in specialized journals. Thanks to friends and a devoted assistant in Berkeley, California, her papers, letters, and photographs were carefully preserved and presented to the Bancroft Library at the University of California. These will provide the materials for some future biography of an unusual woman and the story of her years of exploration.

Ynes Mexica was born on May 24, 1870, in Washington, D.C. Her father, Enrique Antonio Mexia, was serving in Washington as a representative of the Mexican government. Her mother, Sarah Wilmer Mexia, was related to Samuel Eccleston, the Roman Catholic archbishop of Baltimore. The child was christened Ynes Julia Henrietta (translated to Enriquetta Julietta) Mexia. She spent the first nine years of her life in Mexia, Texas, a town named for her grandfather, General José Antonio Mexia, who was a leader in Mexico's Federalist party. Her parents separated when she was of school age, and she moved with her mother and older sister to Philadelphia, Pennsylvania. She was educated there and in Toronto, Ontario, and Emmitsburg, Maryland. In her teens she was sent to Mexico City to live with her father, an official of the Diaz government of Mexico. She supervised his household until his death in 1896.

Ynes married Herman Laue in 1898. They lived in Tacubaya, near Mexico City, on a ranch she had inherited. Laue died in 1904. In 1908 Ynes married a kind and loving man, Augustin de Reygadas, but she was unhappy in the marriage. She suffered a mental and physical breakdown so serious that her physician advised her to leave Mexico. He referred her to Philip King Brown, a noted physician of San Francisco and Berkeley.

With Brown's help, Ynes gradually gained some interest in life. She never returned to her Mexican home. She divorced Augustin, sold the ranch, became an American citizen, and took back the family name. But she was never able to sustain a close relationship of any kind. That very fact may have made her an ideal explorer in lonely spots.

In the 1920s she began to go on field trips with the Sierra Club, and in 1921 was admitted as a special student to the University of California, at Berkeley, where she studied natural history. She went on an expedition with the university curator of paleontology and was introduced to botanical collecting. In 1925, after taking a course in flowering plants at the Hopkins Marine Station in Pacific Grove, she agreed to accompany Roxana Stinchfield Ferris on a field trip to Sinaloa, where they were to collect specimens for the Dudley Herbarium of Stanford University.

Shortly after her arrival in Mazatlan in September, Ynes decided that working with Mrs. Ferris, whose husband had come along, was not productive. She wanted to collect in her own way and she was unhappy in their company. She wrote for her own equipment, planning to go off into the hills and down the coast by herself. She confessed to feeling lonely and discouraged at the obstacles and expense, but she felt that collecting at her own pace would produce more satisfactory results. In Mazatlan, she met a fellow botanist who was of great help in advising her of places where no collecting had yet been done and helping her to get her supplies through customs.

The pattern of abandonment, or at least of separation from other members of the expedition, which happened first in Mexico, was to be repeated a number of times during Mexia's career, as though she were living out a life script of self-induced loneliness. After her death, Thomas Harper Goodspeed, with whom she had collected in the Andes, wrote of her, "She was the true explorer type and happiest when independent and far from civilization" (*Plant Hunters in the Andes*, p. 12). It is probably true only in a limited sense that she was happiest when she was alone. She often had to fight against depression, and several times she wrote of her sense of isolation when far from friends and people with whom she could talk. She took refuge in her work, and she worked hard. Not only did she collect plant specimens, press them, sort and label them, but she also took voluminous field notes. She photographed wherever she went and kept careful records of the negatives.

Necessary equipment for collecting, camping, photographing, and record keeping meant that she did not travel lightly. On one trip her baggage consisted of four canvas trunks, a dunnage bag, a steamer trunk, two suitcases, a carton of books, and a carton of labels. On another she took 60,000 sheets of paper for the presses. This meant an enormous amount of packing, and it involved much red tape in getting her material through customs and onto steamers, railway cars, and pack animals.

Although connection with a university or institution helped her to go through customs and to get railway passes, Ynes was not always able to obtain commissions of this sort. She was contemptuous of field collectors who stayed in hotels and went out only by day to the surrounding country. Her idea was to range as far as necesary to find materials, camping out as she went. She despised the dirty little country hotels and preferred to set up her cot under a banana tree or in a pine forest rather than sleep in a crowded flea-infested native hut.

She was fortunate to find fellow scientists who were interested in her work. Some took her into their homes, made her comfortable, and eased her way. Her Mexican heritage and her knowledge of Spanish were of great benefit. At one time she was away in the mountains for a long stretch, and her friends consulted the American consul about instituting a search for her. It had not occurred to her that anyone would bother about her. "I was touched," she wrote, "to think anybody cared enough for me to hunt me up if I did not turn up" (Nov. 20, 1926, Mexia Papers, Bancroft Library).

This perception of friendlessness and her inability to form close relationships with others was the result of a lifetime of loneliness and broken ties. Her school years were never happy. She did not feel close to her mother and sister. When she was sent to live in Mexico, not knowing a word of Spanish, she was expected to supervise a house full of Mexican servants. She disapproved of her father's succession of mistresses. Her own marriages were not fulfilling. She was devoted to Dr. Brown, to whom she had confided her story of a desperate search for peace of mind.

Mexia spent 1926 and 1927 collecting botanical specimens in the western states of Mexico, under the auspices of the Department of Botany of the University of California. She went to Mazatlan, Mexcaltitlan, and Puerto Vallarta. When she was ready to leave, she found that the northbound steamer did not stop at Puerto Vallarta, so she packed over the mountains to San Sebastian, high in the Sierras, with two men and a mule train. The trail was steep, "over ridges, then down into canyons, across the streams and up the other side, but always climbing higher" (Jan. 10, 1927, Mexia Papers, Bancroft Library). Her guide was a garrulous old fellow who had carried the mail for years in President Diaz's time and who regaled her with stories of misfortunes suffered along the trail.

From San Sebastian she went to El Real Alto, where she was "beyond electric lights, beyond kerosene lamps, beyond candles, beyond even dips, and writing by the light of a fat pine torch!" (Jan. 31, 1927, Mexia Papers, Bancroft Library). The village of seven houses was nestled just below the pinnacle of the Bufa, the highest peak of the Sierra Madre in this range. She collected on the slopes, where oaks and herbaceous plants had obtained a precarious footing and where the cattle had not been able to graze. Twice while collecting with her guide

Ynes became so fascinated with the wealth of specimens that she let the time slip by, and they had to find their way home by the faintest of trails in the dark.

She came home from Mexico with nearly 1,600 numbers of plants, consisting of lichens, mosses, ferns, grasses, herbs, shrubs, and trees. One new genus was found, as well as some fifty new species. Two years later, *Madroño*, a botanical journal, published her article describing the trip, with much detail on the flora encountered and a full itinerary.

She spent part of 1928 surveying the plants in Mt. McKinley National Park in Alaska. A woman companion withdrew at the last moment, and Ynes was left alone in a tiny cabin, far from any other human being. The park rangers who were to look out for her never came, although occasionally she had visits from hunters and once from a party of tourists. At last an Alaskan resident rescued her by dogsled. Far from being frightened, she had thoroughly enjoyed the solitude and the beauty of the mountain.

While traveling, Ynes kept up a steady correspondence with Dr. Brown, whom she addressed often as "Dear Mentor," signing most of her letters "Your child, Ynes," or the "Wilful Wanderer" or "Madame"—names given her by the Brown family. Brown became her business manager as well as her physician and surrogate father.

Aside from the Browns, Ynes' closest California friend was Nina Floy Bracelin. The two met through a mutual interest in natural history, and in 1929 Ynes arranged for "Bracie" to work as her assistant. She received the field specimens and notes, had them identified (mainly by the Gray Herbarium at Harvard), sorted them into sets, and sent them to the various subscribing institutions. She corresponded with the herbariums of the major American universities, the Smithsonian Institution, the Field Museum, and the California Academy of Sciences, as well as with an impressive number of foreign institutions from Copenhagen to Zurich.

In 1929 Mexia went to Brazil. She had learned the special collecting interests of many botanists, and she looked for particular plant specimens to send to them. After months of collecting, an opportunity opened for her to follow her dream of traveling up the Amazon. One of its sources, starting high in the Andes about one hundred and fifty miles from Lima, Peru, is the Marañon River. The stretch where it breaks through the last great range of the Andes, where the whole flow of the river piles into a narrow gorge, is called the Pongo de Manseriche. The only way to get there was by private launch, something beyond Mexia's purse. However, she learned that a party of geologists and surveyors from the Standard Oil Company were willing to take her in the company's launch from their base camp to the Pongo.

To reach their camp she traveled part of the way in a dugout canoe manned by four strong paddlers. For twelve days she sat on a box in the canoe, under an umbrella when it rained and wearing a sun helmet when the sun shone, until she persuaded the men to build a palm-leaf shelter over her box. "And so the days flow on like the river."

I watch the scenery, and then I wash my clothes (there is water without a meter). I write my travel notes, I take notes on the birds, I mend my stockings, occasionally I fall asleep, but am too upright to do more than doze, or I study up in my Botanical note book or the few books I have with me. It is a little odd that as active a person as I am should not fret at the confinement of one small seat from 7 in the morning until 5 in the afternoon, but as long as we keep moving I do not tire. (Nov. 7, 1931, Mexia Papers, Bancroft Library)

Sometimes she felt homesick. Letters from home were held up for weeks and months. She had been away from home for more than two years. "On analyzing my sudden and severe attack of nostalgia," she wrote, "the cause of it seems to be the lack of letters."

The letters tie me to familiar things, to what I know and to which I am bred and they give me a foundation . . . from which I can securely observe and enjoy the novel surroundings in which I find myself. Without these periodical reinforcements of my morale I feel lost in a vast world inhabited only with strangers, never to return to my own. (Nov. 18, 1931, Mexia Papers, Bancroft Library)

At last, they met some of the Indians, the Aguarunas, who lived near the Pongo. The Indians were relieved to find that the newcomers had not come to kill, enslave, or rob them, for blood feuds existed among all the separate tribes. Ynes traded fishhooks and needles for food. When the men of the geological expedition came into view, Ynes introduced herself to them, astonishing and delighting them by digging out a large package of their mail with which she had been entrusted. They told her there was a good camping place above the Pongo, with three good shelters built by surveyors. They also offered to tow her canoe through the gorge with their outboard motor.

The river was low, so the passage through its rapids and whirlpools was comparatively safe. Still it was exciting, though it lasted only about half an hour.

Mexia and the two Brazilian boys established themselves at the surveyors' camp. José Schunke, her assistant, came in another canoe, arriving several days later. Ynes took one of the *tambos*, or palm-leaf shelters. Another served as the kitchen. A third was used as a sleeping room for the men and also as the workroom, where the plant specimens were sorted and put into presses.

Indian visitors came, and soon they were surrounded by men, women, children, and their dogs, all fascinated by the white people and their possessions. The Indians were scrupulously honest, and, although they touched everything, nothing was taken. They were also friendly and quite willing to trade labor and food for such things as needles, fishhooks, and cloth. They knew nothing of money. What they most desired were guns and ammunition, for they were hunters, but, since they also hunted other Indians, Mexia was not willing to let them have guns.

The Aguarunas had no idea that sickness and death had natural causes, so when an Indian became ill or died, the witch doctor was called in. He saw in a vision the wizard, or the person who had caused the ill. Relatives of the defunct one undertook to kill the supposed wizard, who had no idea that he had done any harm, so the feuds never ended, and no Indian man was ever sure of his life. The killers preserved, dried, and shrank the heads of their victims, which they proudly displayed.

After almost two months in the jungle, Ynes had a collection of botanical specimens—though not as good as she had hoped for—and the rains began, signaling that it was time to leave. The Indians brought great balsa logs and constructed a large and sturdy raft on which the small expedition was to go out through the Pongo.

They bade farewell to their Aguaruna friends and launched the raft into the river. It was a trip full of excitement.

> The water boiled and churned, tossing our raft as though made of straws. There was no visible down current, though the rate at which we were whirled along showed the pressure, but everywhere the waters swelled up from below into domes, broke, writhing and tossing, while just below the famous whirlpools formed, racing around at greater and greater speed until a tremendous funnel forms deeper and deeper and into which the water rushes forming almost a cascade. All the laws of hydrostatics are at naught in the Pongo, for everywhere there are great shelves and inequalities of the tumbling, maddened waters. (Jan. 5, 1932, Mexia Papers, Bancroft Library)

After getting through safely, they continued down the stream, doing their best to keep the raft from catching on snags and to get it to shore for each night's camping. Mexia was delighted with rafting. She had enjoyed going up river by canoe, "but going down on a raft is marvelous" (Jan. 6, 1932, Mexia Papers, Bancroft Library).

She flew out to the end of the Central Peruvian Railroad, which took her over the Andes to Lima, then took a coast steamer homeward. An account of her Amazon trip was published in the *Sierra Club Bulletin* in February 1933.

Mexia covered many miles in South America between 1934 and 1936, and almost two years were spent collecting in Mexico. In her letters to Dr. Brown she reported from time to time on various ailments and physical problems not unusual for a traveler or for a woman reaching retirement age. She had amoebic dysentery, which made travel impossible for a time. She had trouble with her eyes. She broke her hand, sprained an ankle, fell on a shoulder, and had a horse roll on her, but, despite accidents, discomforts, and temporary incapacities, she continued to collect her specimens.

Early in 1938 she confessed to Bracie that she was not expecting to make many more expeditions.

> I am not as young as I was, nor is my health as sturdy, and I have no wish to come back a wreck as many explorers do. I have had my fling and pretty nearly

a good measure of it. Besides I have to get that degree. (MS, Mexia Papers, Bancroft Library)

She was sixty-eight years old and still a semester short of the degree she had been working for at Berkeley.

To Dr. Brown, she wrote that she was having pains in her chest and experiencing shortness of breath. The physician in Mexico City advised her to return at once to California for treatment. She arrived home on May 29, 1938, "feeling bum" but unaware that she had cancer of the lung, too far advanced for anything to be done for her. Dr. Brown did everything he could to make her less miserable, and Bracie sadly gave herself to watching over her ailing friend. Ynes Mexia died on July 12.

The always independent, self-effacing traveler, who never really had a home of her own, seldom bought herself clothes, owned no car or luxury of any kind, left a considerable estate. Her collection of pottery, textiles, and artifacts brought back from South America and Mexico was donated to the University of California. She provided a monthly income for Bracie and gave the Academy of Sciences three thousand dollars. The Sierra Club and the Save-the-Redwoods League were also recipients of bequests. The former set up a publications fund to finance books on the mountain regions of California. The latter established the Ynes Mexia Memorial Grove, forty acres of redwoods in Montgomery Woods State Reserve, Mendocino County, California—a fitting memorial to the spirited and adventurous woman who always considered herself an amateur naturalist.

BIBLIOGRAPHY

Works by Ynes Mexia

"Bird Study for Beginners." *Bird Lore* 27 (Jan.–Feb. and Mar.–Apr. 1925): 68–72, 137–41.
"Experiences in Hospitable Mexico." *Better Health* (Oct. 1927).
"Botanical Trails in Old Mexico—the Lure of the Unknown." *Madroño* 1 (Sept. 27, 1929): 227–38.
"Birds of Brazil." *The Gull* 12 (July and Aug. 1930).
"Three Thousand Miles up the Amazon." *Sierra Club Bulletin* 18 (Feb. 1933): 88–96.
"Ramphastidae." *The Gull* 15 (July 1933).
"Vignettes of Birds Long Since Flown." *The Gull* 17 (June 1935).
"Camping on the Equator." *Sierra Club Bulletin* 22 (Feb. 1937): 85–91.

Works about Ynes Mexia

Bartram, Edwin B. "Mosses of Western Mexico Collected by Mrs. Ynes Mexia." *Journal of the Washington Academy of Science* 18 (1928): 577–82.
Bracelin, Nina F. "Itinerary of Ynes Mexia in South America." *Madroño* 3 (1935): 174–76.

Cook, O. F. "A New Commercial Oil Palm in Ecuador." *National Horticultural Magazine* (Apr. 1942): 70–85.

Copeland, E. B. "Brazilian Ferns Collected by Ynes Mexia. In *University of California Publications in Botany* 17. Berkeley: University of California Press, 1932, pp. 23–51.

Franklin, Nancy Dillard. "The History of Mexia, Texas." Master's thesis, Southern Methodist University, 1966. Notes on Mexia family.

Goodspeed, Thomas H. *Plant Hunters in the Andes*. Berkeley: University of California Press, 1961. Brief mention of Mexia.

Goodspeed, Thomas H., and H. E. Stark. Notes on Mexia. In *University of California Publications in Botany* 28. Berkeley: University of California Press, 1955, pp. 79–142.

Leaflets in Western Botany. San Francisco, 1932–1966 (Jan. 1957): 95–96.

Notable American Women, 1607–1950. Edited by Edward T. James and others. Cambridge, Mass.: Harvard University Press, 1971.

Spencer, Marjorie. "The Botanical Quests of a Woman in Latin America." *Pan American Magazine* 42 (Apr. 1930): 389–91.

"U.C. Scientist Back from Trip into South America for Plants."*San Francisco News*, Mar. 6, 1937.

"Woman Braves Amazon Wilds for Specimens." *San Francisco Chronicle*, Mar. 22, 1932, p. 22.

Obituaries appeared in the *San Francisco Chronicle*, on July 13, 1938; the *New York Times*, on July 14, 1938; *Madroño* 4 (1938): 273–75; *Science* 88 (Dec. 23, 1938): 586; and the *Sierra Club Bulletin* (June 1939).

The chief source of information about Ynes Mexia is a large collection of the Mexia family papers and the Ynes Mexia papers located in the Bancroft Library at the University of California, Berkeley. Papers of Nina Floy Bracelin are also maintained in the Bancroft. Some Mexia letters are located in the California Academy of Sciences in San Francisco, the Missouri Botanical Garden in St. Louis, and the New York Botanical Garden.

DERVLA MURPHY
1931–

Dervla Murphy was an incipient traveler and travel writer at the age of ten, when she was given an atlas full of maps and descriptions of the fascinating places of the world. She was also given her first bicycle and was thus able to begin her wandering on the small scale of her home in southern Ireland. Except for a few brief cycling holidays in Europe, however, her dream of traveling to India was deferred until 1963, when she was freed from heavy family responsibilities. Since then she has been on the go, first alone and later with her daughter, who was "blooded" as a world traveler at the age of five. Murphy has seen and written about Europe, Persia, Afghanistan, Pakistan, India, Nepal, Ethiopia, the Andes, and Madagascar.

Her entertaining and enlightening books are based on diaries kept on the road. The entries were written almost nightly, often after strenuous bicycling, hiking, or climbing, by the light of oil lamps, candles, or blazing juniper branches. They have the intimacy of letters to a friend, the immediacy of experience. The reader shares not only the traveler's thoughts but her emotions—and Murphy is not finicky about revealing herself. Beneath all the adventures is a serious message—perhaps too often reiterated—to the effect that isolated peoples are best left to their own devices, without the intrusion of Western technology, materialism, and the more tacky manifestations of the modern world.

Dervla Murphy was born in Lismore, county Waterford, Ireland, on November 28, 1931, the only child of Fergus Joseph and Kathleen Dowling Murphy. Fergus was the county librarian. Kathleen was stricken with crippling arthritis at the age of twenty-six and was soon bedridden. Dervla had to leave her convent school at the age of fourteen to care for her mother and to keep house for her father. Housebound much of the time for the next sixteen years, she educated herself by reading great literature. She began to write adventure stories, all rejected by the editors she sent them to. Through correspondence with a Sikh girl in Kuala Lumpur, she learned much about the Sikh religion and acquired more than a passing interest in India.

Though she chafed at the restrictions and the loss of a normal girlhood, she felt afterward no resentment. She had been forced to confront her own weaknesses and to develop her own strengths.

> What had so often seemed wasted years, in my many moods of bitterness, now seemed otherwise. . . . At thirty, I could ignore neither my own flaws nor the endless variety of causes that can lie behind the flaws of others. The school was hard, but the knowledge was priceless. (*Wheels within Wheels*, p. 230)

Her chief recreation, when she could get a holiday, was bicycling. Sometimes her father could arrange other care for her mother, and Dervla could escape, to ride sixty or seventy miles a day. She managed a three-week tour through Wales and southern England, and she sold articles on her impressions of Stratford, London, and Oxford. She made a five-week tour of Belgium and went twice to Spain. She began her habit of keeping a diary and afterward selling travel stories.

In 1962, Kathleen Murphy died. Dervla had lost her father a short time earlier, and she was now free to plan the bicycle trip to India about which she had dreamed so long. "I thought then, as I still do, that if someone enjoys cycling and wishes to go to India, the obvious thing is to cycle there" (*Wheels within Wheels*, p. 230). She soon realized that others looked upon the idea as foolish, and she became a trifle inhibited about discussing her plans.

Her bicycle, a sturdy man's bicycle, was named Rozinante—for Don Quixote's steed—and nicknamed Roz. In its panniers she packed twenty-eight pounds of kit, including toilet articles, medicines, clothes, books, and spare parts for the bike. She took no sleeping bag or tent because she planned to stay in tourist hostels. She got visas, inoculations, travelers' checks; she bought a .25 caliber pistol and learned to use it; she pored over maps; she sent spare tires ahead to several British embassies or consulates.

When she left Dunkirk in January 1963, she did not know that it would be the coldest winter Europe had experienced in eighty years. She crossed the breadth of Europe and the Middle East, arriving in Delhi after six months of a grueling, sometimes frightening, but glorious trip. She rode the train over the Alps; in Bulgaria icy roads forced her to ride trucks. Near Belgrade she had an encounter with wolves, which had been driven into the city by the cold weather, and she shot two of them dead; a third ran away. She was to use the gun twice more, not on wolves but to warn off threatening men.

In Persia, she found the weather fine, the scenery glorious, the terrain wild and almost deserted. She was warned that a woman alone could not travel in Persia or in Afghanistan. But in Tehran she met Colonel Jahan Zeb and two other Pakistani officers on a military mission to Persia, who assured her that she was not likely to be murdered in Afghanistan. Word went out to watch for "Dervla with the bicycle," and she found that the Persian gendarmerie existed to protect travelers. She was able to sleep in army barracks, and a number of times she was aware of watchful army patrols on the roads. She had been told to look as much like a man as possible; with her sturdy build, short hair, and a contour-obliterating army shirt, she was often taken for a boy and once or twice slept in the barracks with unsuspecting gendarmes.

It was true that many of the Persians were less than friendly, but in the end she was sorry to leave the country.

> Beneath all the physical dirt and moral corruption there is an elegance and dignity about life here which you can't appreciate at first. . . . The graciousness with which peasants greet each other and the effortless art with which a few beautiful rags and pieces of silver are made to furnish and decorate a whole house—in these and many other details Persia can still teach the West. (*Full Tilt*, p. 41)

The authorities in Afghanistan tried to keep her from traveling alone, but she was determined to try. She managed to wangle from the embassy of a "friendly power" an impressive-looking document, which had little real authority but served her purpose, since most of the officials were illiterate. In spite of a sense of tension induced by the warnings, she found that friendliness was met with friendliness and that courtesy was the rule of travel.

She explored the great carved Buddhas and caves at Bamian, once the center of the Buddhist religion, and one of the highlights of the journey was her trip through the Hindu Kush, where she was seriously tempted to consider settling. "Nothing is false there, for humans and animals and earth, intimately interdependent, partake together in the rhythmic cycle of nature" (*Full Tilt*, pp. 94–95).

If she was sorry to leave Persia, it almost broke her heart to leave Afghanistan. Her admiration for the fine, handsome, and honest men was unbounded. She felt sorry for the women, of whom she saw very few. Almost none appeared on the streets; those who did were heavily veiled in a *burkah*, a tentlike garment with a piece of lace over the eyes. Once, while she was riding a bus because the road had been closed to other traffic, she saw two women traveling on the roof of the bus amid everybody's goods and chattels, where they were exposed to the hot sun and the cold night air. "I simply can't imagine what torture it must have been for them . . . and my horror was multiplied by ten when I discovered that these two were going to Kabul hospital because they were very *ill*" (*Full Tilt*, p. 52).

Her Pakistani friends in Tehran had advised her which were the best parts of Pakistan to see and had provided her with a list of their friends and relatives along the way who would be glad to have her visit. When she got to Saidu Shariff in Swat (a princely state in Pakistan), she asked for Colonel Zeb's brother's house and, to her astonishment, was directed to a palace. Aureng Zeb was a prince, the son of the Wali of Swat. His wife, the Begum Naseem, was an educated and charming woman, the daughter of President Ayub. In Rawalpindi, Murphy stayed with another of Colonel Zeb's brothers.

In West Pakistan, Dervla was presented with the calling card of "Raja Jan Alam, Punial Mountain State, Gilgit Agency, West Pakistan, Where Heaven and Earth Meets [*sic*]" (*Full Tilt*, p. 166), and she was invited to visit. She found the rajah's home a good imitation of the Garden of Eden and the rajah "an absolute darling who reminds me of something out of a fairy tale" (*Full Tilt*, p. 174). She stayed several days luxuriating in the beauty of the spot, watching a spirited polo match (the national game), and imbibing the local drink, Punial water. She translated some of the rajah's English mail and wrote answers to the letters, since he could speak English but could not read or write any language. He offered her a farm in the area where she could settle down for life, but she explained that she could not be happy permanently exiled from Ireland any more than he could be happy if exiled from Punial.

All was not wine and roses, however. Once, on a crowded bus, a riot broke out over fares, and Dervla was accidentally struck with a rifle butt, which broke three ribs. She was stung by a scorpion. In the mountains, she had frostbite; in India, heatstroke. In spite of being careful about drinking untreated water, she got dysentery. She was smart enough to treat herself and to get medical attention as soon as possible.

Her worst experience came when she crossed the Babusar Pass out of Gilgit. Much of the time she could not ride but had to push or carry the bicycle over stony paths or across slipping glaciers. No one was about, although she was following the tracks of a pony caravan. At last, she came in sight of the pony men, shouted to them, pushed Roz down over a glacier, and followed it by sliding down herself. "When I arrived at their feet, in a bruised and breathless ball, I was greeted with joyful acclamation" (*Full Tilt*, p. 198). "For a combination of beauty, danger, excitement and hardship (of the enjoyable variety), today wins at a canter," reads the diary for that day (*Full Tilt*, p. 191).

She abandoned her plans to cycle about India during the hot weather, and she looked around for some volunteer work she could do until it became cooler. She found it working with Tibetan refugee children.

When she began, she knew no more about Tibet and its people than the average newspaper reader. She knew that China had annexed the country and that the Dalai Lama had fled to India in 1956. Many Tibetans had been brutally massacred, and thousands had fled its borders. Some of the adults were working in India on road construction, living in road camps; most of the children were taken into homes and refugee camps. The plight of the children had touched the hearts of people of India and other countries, and generous relief in the form of funds, supplies, and workers had been sent.

Murphy went to a camp in Dharamsala, in the Himalayan foothills, where His Holiness the Dalai Lama had a palace. She found the children there in very poor condition. They were in rags, poorly fed, in inadequate shelters. Most were afflicted with scabies and had ear and eye infections. To care for over a thousand young children there were one doctor, a nurse, a cook, several volunteers, and a few Indian ayahs. Murphy was frustrated by the bureaucratic and poorly coordinatated administration of the program, but she fell in love with the Tibetan children, the "Tiblets."

She was there for four months, then she visited a number of road camps where the adults worked. As the weather cooled, she was able to have some trips into the mountains on Roz. In her last diary entry for 1963, she wrote:

> It's strange to think that when I left Ireland I was seeking only the satisfaction of adventure and discovery—but now, after spending the first half-year "traveling hopefully," I have realized that it is far better "to arrive"....I am determined to return to the Tibetans in 1965. (*Tibetan Foothold*, p. 182)

A garbled account of her journey, "Miraculous Overland Cycle by Lone Irishwoman," had appeared in an Indian paper, and it brought her inquiries from several London publishers who wanted to see her story. She had been advised to send her manuscript to Jock Murray. To Dervla, that her first book might be accepted by the prestigious house of John Murray, which had published the lives and works of great English writers, was too much to hope for. However, she sent the manuscript to Murray, and when it was accepted she knew that she had arrived "at the predestined end to a much longer journey than my cycle to India" (*Wheels within Wheels*, p. 235).

A less jolly result of her trip was a round of press conferences and radio and television interviews planned by the Save the Children Fund, under whose auspices she had worked in Tibet. She hated posing as a heroine, but she had seen too much suffering in the refugee camps to refuse her help in raising funds.

When she returned to the Tibetans in 1965, she went to a recently formed refugee camp in Nepal. She became a resident of Pardi, a hamlet in the Pokhara Valley, and she grew to love the Nepalese and their philosophy of life. During her seven months' visit she not only worked in the refugee camp but she also had an opportunity to travel into the Langtang area north of Katmandu accompanied by a Sherpa guide.

For years she had read romantic tales connected with Abyssinia (Ethiopia), and for her next journey she chose the highlands of that country. Her reading of travelers' accounts had built up "a picture of some improbable land of violence and piety, courtesy and treachery, barrenness and fertility" (*In Ethiopia with a Mule*, p. 1).

Since she planned to cover mountainous country, she left Roz at home and outfitted herself for hiking. There was no good map of the country, but those she got "were inaccurate enough to give me, at times, the gratifying illusion of being an explorer in trackless wastes—yet accurate enough to tell me that Addis Ababa is due south of Massawah" (*In Ethiopia with a Mule*, p. 8).

She found that the transformation from cyclist to hiker was painful. She was more weary after eighteen miles on foot than she would have been after a hundred and eighteen on her bike. Since she was carrying a large number of books, her pack weighed fifty pounds. A foot traveler, also, is more sensitive to the local attitude and less secure than a cyclist.

Foot blisters almost incapacitated her before she reached Asmara. The British consul there, John Bromley, and his wife invited her to stay at the consulate while her feet healed. They suggested that she find a mule to carry her heavy pack, especially as it would be necessary to carry provisions and plenty of water. She accompanied Bromley to Mekele, where she met Her Highness Leilt (Princess) Aida Desta, the eldest grandchild of Emperor Haile Selassie. The princess not only helped find a mule but was Murphy's guardian angel throughout her trip, keeping in touch with authorities along the route so that they watched for her and gave her assistance.

The mule, Jock, proved to be an excellent carrier, invaluable in crossing the Simyens, but eventually he collapsed from the shortage of food and water and had to be exchanged for a donkey named Satan. Even Satan finally went lame and had to be abandoned. At the end of three months, Dervla counted the miles on her pocket pedometer; she had walked over a thousand miles. She had had some difficult and potentially tragic experiences but had also developed a great affection for the Ethiopian highlanders and their country.

Some years passed before Murphy's next travels, which were made with her daughter Rachel, an extraordinarily robust and self-possessed five-year-old. While considering a destination, Dervla talked to a friend who had just returned from India and ''as we talked a most delightful feeling took possession of me . . . a delicious restlessness, a stirring of the imagination, a longing of the heart, a thirst of the spirit.'' She had not really liked India on her previous visit, yet now it seemed not only a personal challenge but a challenge posed by trying to fuse the roles of mother and traveler. India would be ''Rachel's apprenticeship to serious travelling'' (*On a Shoestring to Coorg*, pp. 2–3).

They traveled by bus and train or on foot; they stayed with friends, friends of friends, and strangers who opened their homes to them. After seeing some of the poverty, filth, and beauty of India, they settled in Coorg, an unspoiled valley in southern India. The journey was so successful that they returned the following year to visit Baltistan and to spend the winter months in the Karakorams.

People she met in India sometimes asked Murphy why Christians were fighting each other in Ireland, and she realized that she had no answer. She had been in Northern Ireland only once, to give a talk, and had returned home immediately. She knew little of the dissensions tearing Ireland apart. In 1976 she decided to tour it by bicycle as she would a foreign country. She talked to people of all political persuasions and concluded that Ireland's problems would take long to solve.

Her book on Ireland, *A Place Apart*, won for her the Ewart-Biggs Memorial Prize in 1978. She had already been accepted as a member of the Royal Geographical Society, the Royal Asiatic Society, and the Tibet Society, and she had won, in 1975, the Literary Award from the American-Irish Association.

A trip to Peru came next. She and Rachel—now almost ten—went from

Cajamarca in northern Peru to Cuzco, with a pack mule. They followed much of the conquistadors' route. Murphy relates the history of the Inca and their Spanish conquerors throughout her book, *Eight Feet in the Andes*. She traveled light, as always, but now possessed a Himalayan flea-bag weighing but one and a quarter pounds, high-altitude clothing, space blankets, and a tent.

She postponed publication of her book on Peru for a more pressing project. She happened to be visiting friends in Pennsylvania when the nuclear accident occurred at Three Mile Island. She began to study nuclear power and nuclear weapons. Her strong statement on the danger facing all of mankind was published in 1981 as *Race to the Finish?*

Murphy next visited the island of Madagascar and reported on her trip in *Muddling through Madagascar*. With each book, her skill in communicating the thrill of travel grows.

BIBLIOGRAPHY

Works by Dervla Murphy

Full Tilt: Ireland to India with a Bicycle. London: Murray, 1965.
Tibetan Foothold. London: Murray, 1966.
The Waiting Land: A Spell in Nepal. London: Murray, 1967.
In Ethiopia with a Mule. London: Murray, 1968.
On a Shoestring to Coorg: An Experience of South India. London: Murray, 1976.
Where the Indus Is Young: A Winter in Baltistan. London: Murray, 1977.
Wheels within Wheels: Autobiography. London: Murray, 1979.
Eight Feet in the Andes. London: Murray, 1983.
Muddling through Madagascar. London: Murray, 1985.
Murphy's *Race to the Finish?* was published in the United States as *Nuclear Stakes. A Place Apart* (1978) describes Ireland; and a history, *Ireland*, appeared in 1985.

Works about Dervla Murphy

Contemporary Authors. Detroit: Gale Research, 1922–date, new revision, 21: 322–23.

BLAIR NILES
1880–1959

Blair Niles became a traveler and explorer through marriage—not once, but twice. Her first husband, Charles William Beebe, was a naturalist who, when they were married in 1902, was the curator of ornithology at the New York Zoological Society. For ten years she shared his bird-hunting expeditions into remote areas of Mexico, South America, and the Far East. Beebe's special interest was the pheasants of the world, spectacular and elusive birds whose habitats ranged from the jungles of Malay to the slopes of northern India. They included the peacock, the ring-necked pheasant, the ocellated argus, and many more. Mary Blair Beebe co-authored with her husband one book and several articles about their adventures.

When their marriage came to an end, she chose another husband with a taste for exploration—Robert Lyman Niles, an architect and city planner whose avocations were photography and travel. With him she returned several times to South America, her favorite continent, and later they visited Haiti. As Blair Niles she wrote novels, articles, stories, and biographies but became best known as a travel writer.

The most exciting trip she and Robert made was to the island penal colonies in French Guiana. Blair, the first white woman to visit Devil's Island, and Robert, the first person to photograph the colony, became famous when they published their story, first in a series of articles in the *New York Times* in the summer of 1927 and then in a novel entitled *Condemned to Devil's Island*. Though fictionalized, the book focused attention on the wretched and brutally treated men who had been condemned to long terms on a jungle island from which escape was almost impossible. Shortly after their visit, the French took the first steps toward abolishing the colonies.

Mary Blair Beebe and Blair Niles seem to be two different persons. As Mrs. William Beebe, she was a cherished companion and wife who followed her husband into adventure. The books and articles she wrote were full of romance and poetry. When she became Blair Niles, she led her own expeditions, accompanied by her husband, and her books were less romantic, the places visited less exotic, the adventures less exciting. Although the writer remained a perceptive and understanding traveler, her pace was slower and her tone was more sentimental than those of her earlier self. Her reputation as a travel writer was based almost wholly on the later books. Although they won her honor and recognition in her time, they are seldom read today. She wrote no autobiography, and her personal story comes through only in the bits of information contained in her works.

Blair Niles was born in Coles Ferry, Virginia, on June 15, 1880, and christened Mary Blair Rice. Her father, Henry Crenshaw Rice, owned a plantation near the James River, some twenty miles from the nearest railroad. He claimed descent from the earliest English settlers in Virginia. Her mother was Gordon Pryor Rice, daughter of Roger Atkinson Pryor, congressman, Civil War general, and judge of the Supreme Court in New York City. Blair's grandmother, Sara Agnes Pryor, was an author.

Mary Blair attended school in New England and the Pratt Institute in Brooklyn. On August 6, 1902, she married Charles William Beebe, who was of New England ancestry. It was the first step toward a lifetime of travel and exploration for the young Southerner.

She and William (he early dropped the Charles) spent part of their first year in Florida, where they reveled among the angel fish, corals, and sponges of the Keys. At he end of 1903 they began an ornithological expedition to southern Mexico. For four months they traveled and studied around Guadalajara, on the slopes of the volcano of Colima, and on the western coast near Manzanillo, crossing the country from Vera Cruz to the Pacific and back again. They lived an almost idyllic life, and for Mary it must have been not only a blissful honeymoon but also a revealing education in natural history. Beebe's interests in nature were wide, and although he went to study birds, he knew a good deal about every aspect of life in the wild.

Near Guadalajara, the maize fields were divided not by fences but by deep ditches fringed by tall cactus. One day William fell into one and stayed there, not because he could not climb out but because he found it so delightful. Cool and shady, it was teeming with interesting birds, insects, butterflies, and small furry creatures. For days the couple explored together this wonderland of ditches.

Beebe's *Two Bird-Lovers in Mexico* (1905) tells the story of their journey. It was dedicated "To my wife, the *other* bird-lover, whose sympathy and help in the field and in the study have made this book possible." Mary Blair contributed a final chapter to the book, entitled "How We Did It." "If one's husband is a naturalist," she writes, "one necessarily travels with much that is heavy— photographic plates, bottles of formalin, guns, ammunition, etc. I always say that our trunks contain everything except clothing" (*Two Bird-Lovers in Mexico*, p. 365). Since part of the travel was by train, their baggage was limited to 110 pounds per person. She lists the supplies and clothing they had chosen. She advises the use of Mexican saddles: "no one should attempt to ride side-saddle over these steep mountain trails." Women might need veils to keep their hair out of their faces, but

I hope my camping woman will not mar her pleasure by wearing her veil *over* her face. A wild gallop over the plains on horseback loses much of its charm if there is anything between one's face and the pure invigorating mountain breezes. And after all, a little honest tan is a good thing! (*Two Bird-Lovers in Mexico*, p. 368)

The reader is surprised to learn that before Mary went to Mexico she had never ridden a horse. "I simply got on and rode off. . . . The rule for a good dancer applies equally to a good rider—do not be rigid, let yourself go" (*Two Bird-Lovers in Mexico*, p. 374). The *señorita* must be prepared to create a sensation among the Mexican country people by her riding costume—a divided skirt—and the revolver at her belt.

She cautions camping wives to insist on a good cook. "Have it distinctly understood that she is camping for *pleasure*," and not to spend her evenings cooking over a smoky campfire and washing dishes by candlelight (*Two Bird-Lovers in Mexico*, p. 372). Her chapter ends:

Though I were to write a volume I could not adequately picture the great charm of our wild free life in camp! One lives so near the heart of Nature, and in this simple natural life learns many a great truth. The pure joy of life itself is ever present. Every possible trouble or perplexity seems a thing of the past—almost left in another world. What matters anything in this great wild country—the day nor the hour nor the year are of any account. What a glorious thing is a cold plunge in early morning in the swift-flowing river near the tent, where the night before the deer drank, and along which all the furtive wild creatures of the night stealthily made their way in the moonlight. Here one feels how good a thing it is to be alive, to be hungry and to eat, to be weary and to sleep. (*Two Bird-Lovers in Mexico*, pp. 374–75)

In 1908 the Beebes began a series of bird-hunting expeditions in the northern coastal regions of South America. They went up the Orinoco River where they explored the country near La Brea, a pitch lake in Venezuela. A year later they made trips from Georgetown, British Guiana (now Guyana), into the wilderness and another on the Little Hoorie River, in the northwest, and again to the savannah region farther south. Together they wrote a book describing their travels, *Our Search for a Wilderness* (1910). The "search" was for an untouched wilderness, where guns were unknown, trees had not been felled or grasslands burned, where wild creatures had not learned to fear man. They found much unspoiled beauty and new and surprising flora and fauna. They wrote of it in terms to be appreciated by naturalist and layman alike. The book was dedicated to Mary's grandparents, the Pryors. Mary also wrote several periodical articles on their South American journey. Later she would say that this was the continent she most enjoyed and felt most at home in.

The last trip ended suddenly and prematurely when Mary fell and broke her wrist, and the Beebes left at once for home. But, wrote William, "we know in our hearts that someday we shall return. . . . The supreme joy of learning, of discovering, of adding our tiny facts to the foundation of the everlasting *why* of the universe; all this makes life for us—Milady and me—one never-ending delight" (*Our Search for a Wilderness*, p. 387).

The most ambitious and fateful of the Beebes' expeditions began late in 1909 and extended until early 1911. William had begun, during this time, his study of pheasants, a study that would result in his magnum opus, a four-volume *Monograph of the Pheasants* (1918–1922). The couple visited twenty countries and traveled about 52,000 miles. William, whose term as curator of ornithology was served mostly in absentia, got a five-year leave of absence from the Zoological Society and found a wealthy sponsor, for the cost of travel, outfitting large expeditions, and research at home was tremendous.

Both of the Beebes wrote of their adventures in the search for pheasants. Mary's three articles were published in *Harper's* magazine in 1911 and 1912. The journeys were a good deal harder than any they had undertaken before. At times William went off by himself, leaving Mary behind in a small village or in a travelers' hut. Upper Burma was "a wilderness of lonely mountains, sparsely peopled with wild hill folk" (Mary Beebe, "Wild Burma," *Harper*, April 1912). The wild folk were the Kachins, a tribe who used bows and poisoned arrows and who rolled rocks down the hillsides at intruders.

The most vivid account Mary wrote is of their visit to the Dyaks of Sarawak, a tribe who collected the heads of slain enemies, which were then shrunk and displayed as trophies. The Beebes visited a Dyak house, where they were surrounded by tribesmen, "beautiful bronze figures like shining, polished statues, great and small." They managed to converse with their hosts through a Eurasian taxidermist traveling with them, who spoke English and Hindustani, and an Indian sepoy, one of their crew, who spoke Hindustani and Dyak. The Dyaks entertained them with a long, frenzied, and hypnotic dance and then helped them back to their canoe. In all of their contacts with the tribe, reported Mary, they "received universal courtesy and hospitality, which could not be excelled in any land" (Mary Beebe, "With the Dyaks of Borneo," *Harper*, January 1912).

William accompanied his *Monograph* with stories of the search for the pheasants. Later, in his *Pheasant Jungles* (1927), he tells the same stories, but his accounts never mention Mary, his companion and helpmeet. His readers get the impression that he traveled virtually alone except for his crew. Something had happened during those seventeen months of hard and dangerous travel, some malaise of the body and spirit, and at last a serious tarnishment of the bright companionship the couple had previously enjoyed.

Early in 1913 Mary left William. She went home to her parents and then to Reno to obtain a quick divorce. Since no-fault divorce was then unknown, she had to charge William with cruel and abusive treatment. She told of threats of suicide, of frightening episodes, of domestic discord. The divorce, which was granted in August 1913, created headlines in New York, where the Beebes were well known.

Within a short time Mary Blair Beebe became Blair Niles, the bride of Robert Lyman Niles. She never again used any other name, and in her biographical notes she forgot to mention that she had ever been Mrs. William Beebe. William, who later became famous for his pioneering underseas explorations, chose also to forget his connection with Mary Blair Rice. His biographer, Robert Welker, could not forgive Beebe for his treatment of Mary; however, the facts are that she remarried at once, and he remained single until 1935.

Blair Niles did not give up travel. It was now in her blood. She and Robert went to Ecuador, Colombia, Haiti, Guatemala, French Guiana, and Peru. They lingered long enough in each place to become acquainted with the people, and, as the only tourists to visit some towns, they were of great interest to the inhabitants. Robert took the photographs to illustrate her books, and they added much, for he took excellent pictures of the wild scenery and the people who lived in the plains and mountains.

Blair studied the history and literature of each country. She writes of the connection between reading and travel:

> It is only in travel, I think, that history comes . . . alive, that it appears with the reality of personal memory. You set forth with your mind stored with history and with contemporary opinion. But from the first moment of entering the harbor the history begins to appear as memory, its characters as ancestors, and contemporary opinion as gossip, while the country itself becomes a living personality. (*Black Haiti*, p. 199)

In 1925 Niles was one of four women who met to form the Society of Woman Geographers. In 1938 her *A Journey in Time: Peruvian Pageant* won her a gold medal from the city of Lima, Peru, on the occasion of its 117th anniversary of independence. In 1941 the Women's National Book Association and the Bookseller's League gave her the Constance Lindsay Skinner Medal of Achievement. In 1944 the Society of Woman Geographers awarded her a gold medal for "original achievement of outstanding merit."

In addition to her travel writing, Blair Niles wrote novels, stories, and biographies. She wrote *The James* (1939), one of a series on the rivers of America, and *Journeys in Time*, an anthology of travel pieces. Her last book, a biography of George Washington, was published in 1951.

Blair Niles died in her home on Park Avenue, New York City, on April 13, 1959. Her husband and two brothers survived her.

BIBLIOGRAPHY

Works by Blair Niles

As Mary Blair Beebe

"How We Did It." In Beebe, C. William. *Two Bird-Lovers in Mexico*. Boston and New York: Houghton Mifflin Co., 1905, pp. 363–75.

(With C. William Beebe) "A Naturalist in the Tropics." *Harper* 118 (Mar. 1909): 590–600.

———. "In the Venezuelan Wilderness." *Harper* 118 (May 1909): 838–48.

———. *Our Search for a Wilderness: An Account of Two Ornithological Expeditions to Venezuela and to British Guiana*. New York: Holt, 1910.

"A Quest in the Himalayas." *Harper* 122 (Mar. 1911): 489–501.

"With the Dyaks of Borneo." *Harper* 124 (Jan. 1912): 264–78.

"Wild Burma!" *Harper* 124 (Apr. 1912): 759–71.

As Blair Niles

Casual Wanderings in Ecuador. New York: Century, 1923.

"Clanging Bells of Quito." *Century* 105 (Apr. 1923): 823–32.

"By Air to the Heart of the Andes." *Harper* 148 (Feb. 1924): 289–302.

"In the Banana Country." *Century* 108 (Sept. 1924): 703–8.

"In Streets of Rose and Blue." *Century* 108 (Oct. 1924): 757–65.

Colombia, Land of Miracles. New York: Century, 1924.

"Over the World and Back." *Woman Citizen* n.s. 11 (Dec. 1926): 25–27.

Black Haiti: A Biography of Africa's Eldest Daughter. New York: Putnam, 1926.

Feature articles on Devil's Island and other penal colonies in French Guiana. *New York Times Magazine*, July 3, 1927, p. 1; July 10, 1927, p. 1; July 24, 1927, pp. 3–4; Aug. 7, 1927, pp. 4–5.

"Devil's Island." *Forum* 78 (Dec. 1927): 836–47.

A Journey in Time: Peruvian Pageant. Indianapolis: Bobbs-Merrill, 1937.

Journeys in Time, from the Halls of Montezuma to Patagonia's Plains: A Treasury Gathered from Four Centuries of Writers (1519–1924). With comments, profiles, and personal experiences. New York: Coward-McCann, 1946.

Works about Blair Niles

Henderson, R. "Feminine Ulysses." *Independent Woman* 13 (Mar. 1934): 13–73.

Mabie, J. "Philosophy for Exploration: Blair Niles Finds a Purpose in Her Adventuring." *Christian Science Monitor*, Sept. 4, 1935, p. 3+.

National Cyclopedia of American Biography. New York: J. T. White, 1888–date, vol. 45 (1962): pp. 118–19.

Twentieth Century Authors. Edited by Stanley Kunitz and Howard Haycraft. New York: H. W. Wilson, 1942, p. 1027.

Warfel, Harry R. *American Novelists of Today*. New York: American Book, 1951, pp. 320–21.

Welker, Robert Henry. *Natural Man: The Life of William Beebe*. Bloomington: Indiana University Press, 1975.

Obituaries appeared in the *New York Times*, on Apr. 15, 1959; *Publishers Weekly*, on May 4, 1959; and *Wilson Library Bulletin* (June 1959).

MARIANNE NORTH
1830–1890

Marianne North had a unique way of communicating the pleasure and excitement of global travel. She sought out the plants native to many parts of the world and painted them in all their color and brilliance. She gave her paintings to the Royal Botanic Garden at Kew, England, complete with a gallery in which to show them. Visitors to the North Gallery there can see her paintings, from the redwood trees of California to the orchids of South Africa, botanically true to life and with authentic backgrounds.

North was almost obsessive in her constant movement from one part of the world to another. As a young woman she traveled a good deal with her family through Europe. After her mother died and her sister Catherine married, Marianne and her father made many trips to Turkey, Syria, and Egypt. When her father died in 1869, she was devastated. She picked herself up and went to visit Madeira. For the rest of her life she traveled and painted constantly. In her sister's words,

> She seemed to bear a charmed life. She could apparently sit all day painting in a mangrove swamp, and not catch fever. She could live without food, without sleep, and still come home, after a year or two, a little thinner, with a more careworn look in the tired eyes, but ready to enjoy to the full the flattering reception which London is always ready to give to any one who has earned its respect by being interesting in any way. (*Some Further Recollections of a Happy Life*, p. 316)

Marianne North was born in Hastings, England, on October 24, 1830, of a distinguished ancestry and into a family of means and culture. Her father was a member of parliament. Marianne had little formal education, but like other young women of her class she seems to have absorbed knowledge through reading and observation. Her parents numbered among their friends some of the most productive and interesting people of the time, including the president of the Royal Society and the director of Kew. She was interested in botany and spent much of her time at the botanic gardens of Chiswick and Kew. She never felt the lack of schooling. "A really distinguished woman," she later wrote, "needs no colleges or 'higher education' lectures" (*Recollections of a Happy Life*, I, 91).

During the family's rambles about Europe Marianne studied music. With one singing teacher she studied "all Mozart's operas and masses, singing and transposing all the solos and duets; and between singing and playing I often passed eight hours a day at the piano. I learnt many of Beethoven's sonatas by heart" (*Recollections*, I, 19). In Dresden "the chief singer of the king's chapel found out my voice was contralto instead of soprano, so I tried no more high tunes. I learnt with him to know the grand old sacred music of Italy" (*Recollections*, I, 21–22). Again, "the Prince's Kapelmeister introduced me for the first time to the music of Handel," a thrill to Marianne but not to her father, to whom all music was "a horrid noise" (*Recollections*, I, 25). In Brussels she studied with a pupil of Mendelssohn and heard many concerts. But her voice failed, and she gave up music for art.

She took lessons in flower-painting from a Dutch lady, "from whom I got the few ideas I possess of arrangement of colour and of grouping" (*Recollections*, I, 26). She began to carry sketching materials with her and to look at everything from a purely pictorial point of view. In 1868 a visitor at Hastings taught her oil painting, and she changed from watercolors to oils. She developed her own distinctive style, which changed little over the years.

Marianne spoke of her father as "from first to last the one idol and friend of my life, and apart from him I had little pleasure and no secrets" (*Recollections*, I, 5). He became ill while they were in Germany; she managed to get him home, where he died

> and left me indeed alone. I wished to be so; I could not bear to talk of him or of anything else, and resolved to keep out of the way of all friends and relations till I had schooled myself into that cheerfulness which makes life pleasant to those around us. I left the house at Hastings for ever. (*Recollections*, I, 38)

She was then forty. She never married, and the opportunity to do so seems not to have occurred. From that time until a few years before her death North found happiness in visiting new places, enjoying new scenes, and painting what she saw.

Many of the places she visited were then part of the British Empire. She needed no passport and the only bureaucracies she encountered were postal clerks and bankers. She carried with her letters of introduction to government officials, friends, and friends of her circle. Although she often stayed in hotels or inns, she was entertained almost everywhere by governors, rajahs, and ordinary, hospitable people who sought her company. She never missed visiting a botanical garden and learning from the keepers the names and characteristics of the plants therein.

In 1871 she accepted an invitation to accompany a friend to the United States.

"I had long had the dream of going to some tropical country to paint its peculiar vegetation on the spot in natural abundant luxuriance," she wrote, and "I thought this might easily be made into a first step for carrying out my plan" (*Recollections*, I, 39). She spent some time in Massachusetts, where she lunched with Henry Wadsworth Longfellow, a luncheon "worthy of a poet—nothing but cakes and fruit, and cold tea with lumps of ice in it" (*Recollections*, I, 50). She visited the Adams family in Quincy and she met Annie Fields, "a pretty poetess who went into floods of tears at the mere mention of Charles Dickens" (*Recollections*, I, 48). She talked with Elizabeth Agassiz, who told her of the wonders and delights of her famous Amazon expedition and offered her letters to people there if she went.

She was thrilled with Niagara Falls; she called on Dr. Emily Blackwell in New York; she was somewhat puzzled to be invited to dinner at the White House by President and Mrs. Ulysses S. Grant. Afterward she learned that Mrs. Grant had believed her to be the daughter of "Lord North, the ex-Prime Minister of England." This made her feel very antique, inasmuch as Lord North had died in 1792.

After six months North went to Jamaica. She had found it difficult to carry out her plan to paint because everyone wanted to lionize her, so she was glad to find a deserted house on a hill near Kingston, "half hidden amongst the glorious foliage of the long-deserted botanical gardens of the first settlers," which she could rent for a small sum (*Recollections*, I, 81). She furnished one or two rooms of the twenty and stayed there, with two servants to look after her, for weeks.

I was in a state of ecstasy, and hardly knew what to paint first. . . . There was a small valley at the back of the house which was a marvel of loveliness, bananas, daturas, and . . . giant fern-fronds as high as myself, and quantities of smaller ferns with young pink and copper-coloured leaves, as well as the gold and silver varieties. I painted all day, going out at daylight and not returning until noon, after which I worked at flowers in the house. (*Recollections*, I, 83)

During the several months she spent in Jamaica, she traveled all over the island, escorted by kind friends, and then visited Haiti before she returned to England. She was home less than two months before she set off for Brazil. She continued her pattern of painting all day and every day and returning to her hotel too tired to pay evening visits. For eight months she stayed with a family in Minas Geraes, who took her on many trips through the country, some of them very difficult but all rewarding in the beauty and luxuriance of plant life. Before leaving Brazil she met the emperor and empress.

During her visit home in the winter of 1875, she learned to etch on copper. She soon began to feel the cold and sought a warmer climate in Tenerife. Not long afterward she joined a couple who were going to Japan. Crossing the United States she stopped in Utah where she shook hands with Brigham Young, a "horrid old wretch" (*Recollections*, I, 201), then traveled on to California, where she saw the Mariposa Grove of redwoods in Yosemite Valley, San Francisco, Lake Tahoe, and the Calaveras Grove of big trees.

Her pleasure in Japan was marred by rheumatism brought on by sketching in the cold weather. She moved on to Singapore but the rheumatism followed her. Nevertheless she visited the botanical garden there and a jungle where she "screamed with delight" at finding real pitcher plants growing wild. In Sarawak she saw much of the rajah and rani and had a tailor make her a silk dress; her others had become quite shabby. She was taken to visit a limestone cave, but "I stuck to my old rule of not going willingly anywhere where I could not see my feet" (*Recollections*, I, 251).

Marianne was not interested in politics or in social problems. Her enthusiasm was for beautiful landscapes, fine monuments, colorful scenes, and, of course, the vegetation. She rejoiced also in watching birds, butterflies, monkeys, and even caterpillars. In Tasmania she bought a family of tiny marsupial mice and carried them home with her. "Those little beasts were a great delight to my fellow travellers, and helped to make me a popular character" (*Recollections*, II, 172). On the way across the United States, her Pullman porter took a great interest in the animals. Returning from an hour's absence, she was informed by the porter that "my mice had just waked up and inquired where I was" (*Recollections*, II, 207).

Readers today will be surprised by the wealth of plants North found in most unlikely places. On Staten Island she was taken on walks in the woods and gloried in the "cypripediums, magnolias, azaleas, kalmias, andromedas, and other nice things" (*Recollections*, II, 208). She was only too aware that in many places the march of progress was encroaching on the plant life and that many of the species she immortalized in her sketches would inevitably disappear forever.

By 1882 North had visited almost every continent and numerous islands in the Pacific and the Atlantic, but there were still gaps in her collection, so her last visits were made in search of elusive plants in South Africa, the Seychelles, and Chile. In South Africa, she was well rewarded:

> We came to a marshy hollow, and saw the *Sparaxis pendula* for the first time. Its almost invisible stalks stood four or five feet high, waving in the wind. These were weighed down by strings of lovely pink bells, with yellow calyx, and buds; they followed the winding marsh, and looked like a pink snake in the distance, making me scream with joy when I first saw them. "I was sure you would do that," said my guide contentedly. As we rounded the mountain he showed me a blue-green patch on the top of it, . . . and said it was a mass of agapanthus! It was a day of days! (*Recollections*, II, 244)

She went to the Seychelles in search of the *coco de mer*. At Praslin she saw a great grove of them, "the huge straight stems and golden shiny stars of the giant palm'' (*Recollections*, II, 289), but she had time only to sketch them and never had a chance to return. She found a new capucin tree, later named for her, *Northea seychellana*. She could not leave the island without going through quarantine, for there had been a number of deaths from smallpox. Here she had a disturbing experience.

> Some of the inmates took to playing tricks on me, and I thought they would rob and even murder me. . . . For two days and nights I tied up my door, barricaded my window, and was in fear of my life, hearing things said behind the low divisions, which they tell me never had been said. (*Recollections*, II, 309)

Doctors said her nerves had broken down. The paranoia continued until after she had been at home among friends for some time. It seems to have been due to her increasing deafness and a continual noise in her head that tortured her last years. But she could not be content until she had seen the forest growth of South America's mountains. She had read descriptions of the great *auricaria imbricata*, known as the monkey puzzle tree, and she found it, as well as other fascinating plants, in Chile. On her way back she ended her journeying by a stop in Jamaica to visit old friends.

Her home in England, whenever she was at home, was a flat on Victoria Street in London where she and her father had lived. Her sister said it was crowded with things Marianne had brought back from her wonderful journeys—glass cases containing stuffed birds and tropical butterflies, musical instruments, a big stuffed albatross, a tiny Australian bear and stately lyrebird, a platypus, shells, crystals, and oriental bronzes. Now that she felt her traveling days were over, Marianne began to look for a house in the country where she could grow her own plants. She found it at Alderley, in Gloucestershire. "No life is so charming as a country one in England," she wrote, "and no flowers are sweeter or more lovely than the primroses, cowslips, bluebells, and violets which grow in abundance all round me here" (*Recollections*, II, 330). She died at Alderley on August 30, 1890, leaving as her monuments the North Gallery at Kew, a number of plants that had been given her name, and three volumes of memoirs.

As early as 1879 she had conceived the idea of giving her paintings to the Royal Botanic Gardens at Kew, and she had written to Sir Joseph Hooker proposing the gift, along with a gallery in which to show them. He accepted gladly, and from then on every time she was at home she worked with the architect to plan the building; she kept track of its progress; and finally she arranged the pictures themselves. They remain as she placed them, covering every inch of the walls. She provided descriptions of the plants, and a botanist prepared a guide. A dado near the floor is made up of samples of woods from many countries of the world. The gallery was opened to the public in 1882. It brought Marianne a letter from the Queen of England regretting that no honor equivalent to a knighthood was available for a woman.

During her last years at Alderley, North prepared her memoirs from her notes, diaries, and letters. After her death, her sister, Mrs. John Addington Symonds, edited and published *Recollections of a Happy Life* (1892) and then *Further Recollections of a Happy Life* (1893); the latter book includes the early journeys with her father, which had been omitted from the former book. As travel books, they are almost too generous of detail. They show a Marianne North who reveled in every colorful event and to whom no hardship was too hard if it resulted in a grand view or the discovery of an exotic plant.

For those unable to see the North Gallery, a beautifully illustrated book, with color reproductions of many of the paintings, was produced in 1980. Entitled *A Vision of Eden*, its text is an abridgement of North's own memoirs. It naturally emphasizes the botanical aspects of her autobiography rather than its humorous and insightful commentary on the places and people she saw in her way around the world.

BIBLIOGRAPHY

Works by Marianne North

Recollections of a Happy Life: Being the Autobiography of Marianne North. Edited by Mrs. John Addington Symonds. London and New York: Macmillan, 1892.
Some Further Recollections of a Happy Life. Selected from the journals of Marianne North chiefly between the years 1859 and 1869. Edited by Mrs. John Addington Symonds. London and New York: Macmillan, 1893.

Works about Marianne North

Allen, Alexandra. *Travelling Ladies*. London: Jupiter, 1980, pp. 134–55.
Dickins, M. "Marianne North." *Cornhill* 172 (Spring 1962): 319–29.
Dictionary of National Biography. London: Smith, Elder, 1885–1900, vol. 41: 168–69.
Europa Biographical Dictionary of British Women. Edited by Anne Crawford and others. London: Europa, 1985.
Hemsley, W. B. *The Gallery of Marianne North's Paintings of Plants and Their Homes, Royal Gardens, Kew*. 4th ed. London: Kew Gardens, 1886. Descriptive catalogue.
International Dictionary of Women's Biography. Edited by Jennifer S. Uglow and Frances Hinton. New York: Continuum, 1982.
Middleton, Dorothy. *Victorian Lady Travellers*. London: Routledge & Kegan Paul, 1965, pp. 54–71.
A Vision of Eden: The Life and Work of Marianne North. Abridged from *Recollections of a Happy Life* by Graham Bateman. Exeter, England: Webb & Bower, 1980; New York: Holt, Rinehart and Winston, 1980.
Obituaries appeared in the *Athenaeum* (Sept. 6, 1890); *Critic* (Sept. 27, 1890); and *Scientific American* (Oct. 8, 1890).

ANNIE SMITH PECK
1850–1935

Annie Smith Peck was one of the first American women to win fame for mountaineering. In 1895 she climbed the Matterhorn, fittingly dressed in knickerbockers. It is a question whether her success as a climber on that occasion brought her as much notoriety as her audacity in doing so without long skirts. She followed that exploit with more climbing in Europe, then in California and Mexico. In 1903 she went to South America, determined to climb the Andes. There, after several attempts, she won in 1908 the distinction of having climbed to a greater height than anyone else residing in the United States.

Peck's interest in South America led her to study its economic and industrial possibilities, in particular its railroads and its mines. She wrote a descriptive guidebook and a statistical handbook on the continent. An aviation enthusiast, she flew from 1929 to 1930 around South America's coast, using all the companies engaged in regular air service in the various republics, except Bolivia and Venezuela.

Peck was honored by the government of Peru for her climb to the top of Huascarán, the highest mountain in Peru. One of its peaks was later named "Cumbre Aña Peck." She was a founder of the American Alpine Club, a Fellow of the Royal Geographical Society, and a member of the Society of Woman Geographers. In addition to her works on South American economy, she wrote two travel books, one on her mountain climbing experiences and another on her trips by air. She wrote extensively for American periodicals and lectured on platforms across the United States, promoting peaceful and mutually beneficial relations between North and South America.

On one of Annie Peck's voyages, a fellow passenger asked her where her home was. "Where my trunk is," she replied. "No," he said, "Where is your real home?" "Where my trunk is," she reiterated (*A Search for the Apex of South America*, p. 202). He could not understand anyone having no home. To Annie the situation was not unusual. She was a traveler, and between trips she lived in hotels. A flyer advertising her lectures included the information that "Miss Peck may be addressed at Hotel Albert, New York."

Her family home was in Providence, Rhode Island, where she was born on October 19, 1850. Her father, George Bacheler Peck, was a lawyer and a dealer in coal. Both he and Annie's mother, Ann Power Smith, were descended from very early New England families. Although they were well to do and sent Annie to the best schools, they were embarrassed rather than proud of her later achievements, and, except for one brother, they seem not to have contributed anything to her support or expeditions. She attended normal school, taught, graduated from the University of Michigan, taught again, and in 1885 became the first woman student to be admitted to the American School of Classical Studies in Athens.

On her way to Athens she glimpsed the "majestic, awe-inspiring peak" of the Matterhorn and vowed to return one day and climb it. Ten years later she did just that—she was the third woman to make the ascent in the nineteenth century. She gave up teaching and made her living by lecturing on Greek archeology, but this subject did not draw large audiences. She thought that mountain climbing might be a more popular theme. If she told the story of her adventures, she could conscientiously spend her time in climbing. Thus satisfying her New England conscience, she went on to climb other European mountains, Mt. Shasta in California, and Orizaba (Citlaltépetl) in Mexico. After her ascent of Orizaba, the highest peak in Mexico (18,700 feet) and the highest point that had yet been reached in North America, her ambition was "to conquer a virgin peak, to attain some height where no *man* had previously stood" (*A Search for the Apex of America*, Foreword).

To find such a peak, she went in 1903 to Mt. Sorata (also called Illampu), in Bolivia, then thought to be the loftiest mountain in the Western Hemisphere. To get together enough money for the expedition, she had applied to newspapers and magazines, advertisers, and personal friends. She found that those who were sympathetic were mostly impecunious. Those who had money considered the scheme foolish and unprofitable. They advised her to stay home, to which she replied saucily, "I would if I had one."

When she felt she had enough to mount an expedition, she cabled to Switzerland for two professional guides to meet her in New York, where she would also meet a professor of geology who was to accompany her. She regarded the presence of a white male gentleman necessary for protection and company, and when the young officer who had planned to go with her had to withdraw, she chose the professor, who had been recommended to her but with whom she had had no more than an hour's conversation. He was to provide scientific data and take photographs.

In La Paz Peck presented letters of introduction—without which no one thought of traveling abroad—and met many of the local dignitaries. The professor at once proved difficult, for he not only left all the work of preparation to Annie but informed her that he had to leave by August 20 to be home for duties there.

Annie Smith Peck in South America

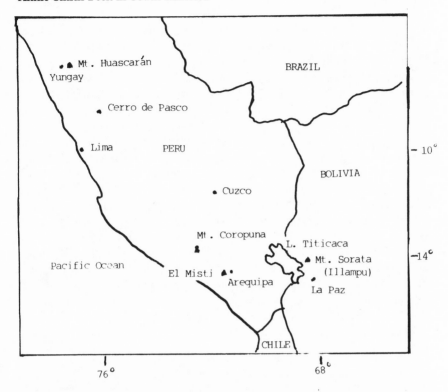

This left less than a month to travel to the base of Illampu, climb it, and return. In spite of anxious forebodings, Annie, "in knickerbockers riding astride," led her caravan to Sorata.

The climb was a fiasco. One of the guides, Maquignaz, was a skilled climber and had been on Illampu before, with an English climber. They had been stoned by Indians and he feared similar attacks. The mule driver was drunk, the professor was sick, and the Indians refused to go into the snow (for which, indeed, they were ill clothed). Maquignaz "manifested no moral force or energy," wrote Annie, "but was limp as a rag." The Indians assumed that the professor was the head of the expedition, and when he no longer seemed to be interested, they decided he had given up the ascent. "To manage three men," wrote Annie, "seemed beyond my power. Perhaps some of my more experienced married sisters would have done better" (*A Search for the Apex of America*, p. 51). She consoled herself with the thought that they had reached an elevation of 15,350 feet, higher than any mountain in the Alps except Mont Blanc.

Peck was glad to see the last of the professor and the guides. Hoping somehow to salvage the trip, she went to Arequipa, in Peru, and ascended volcanic El Misti. Although it was 19,031 feet high, it was reachable by horseback. She descended into the volcanic crater, and peered into a new crater, still emitting yellow vapors.

Back in the United States, Annie suffered an attack of shingles, which she was certain had been brought on by the ignominy of returning defeated. After she recovered her health and spirits, she began to collect funds for another expedition. "I had heard of other mountains," she wrote, "more lofty than Sorata: a volcano, Sajama, . . . and Mt. Huascarán in Peru, the latter said to have an altitude of 25,000 feet" (*A Search for the Apex of America*, p. 123). She took ship on June 21, 1904, "a perfect wreck," having had no time for exercise or rest, and was soon back in La Paz for a second attempt at Illampu.

This time her gentleman companion was Victor Sintich, an Austrian who had offered his services. She brought with her equipment similar to that of the preceding year, which included an Eskimo suit that had been used by Admiral Robert E. Peary and was loaned to her by the American Museum of Natural History. Sintich's climbing irons and her ice axe were duplicated for the other climbers. Mittens of vicuña wool and vicuña fur were made for her, and she made herself a pair of bed shoes of the same fur. To the food supplies she added three bags of coca leaves and four quarts of alcohol, three for the Indians to drink. A small draught night and morning kept them in good humor. Another innovation was a wooden cross to be planted on the summit of the mountain, to overcome the superstitious fears of the Indians.

On the earlier trip she had noted that

> Without coca the indians would decline arduous labour; a strong stimulant and sedative as well, it is excellent to use in emergency, but injurious as a custom; undoubtedly stupefying to the intellect. Chewing coca leaves . . . the indians can defy hunger, thirst, sleep, and fatigue; travelling continuously for several days, if need be, with little food or drink. (*A Search for the Apex of America*, p. 33)

She herself found chewing the leaves helpful in stress, and, when fatigued, a drink of hot water and cognac put her to rights.

They had not yet reached the base of the mountain when she decided that Sintich, in common with many of his sex, did not take kindly to suggestions. Several times he declared he would go no farther. It was too cold, the loads were too heavy, and snow was falling. Annie cajoled her companion and the Indians to go above 18,000 feet, when she wisely decided she could not continue without their willing help. She gave up and went to Peru to assess the difficulty of climbing Mt. Huascarán.

She reached Yungay, near the foot of Huascarán, with an introduction to the Vinateas, a well-to-do family of several households, and there she was welcomed most hospitably. She met other townspeople, all of whom were impressed with her plans and eager to help her find assistants for the climb. She had already chosen for her male companion a strong young miner, Peter, whom she had picked out at the hotel in Lima. Other young men from Yungay decided to go along for a lark.

The mountain had two peaks, with a saddle between them, and seemed to be well covered with glaciers. Annie and Peter disagreed about the best place to make the ascent; he went off in one direction, she in another, accompanied by Don Arturo Alba and his major domo, Aurelio. Don Arturo's account of the expedition was quoted by Peck:

> To the right and left were impassable walls of snow. We began, therefore, to scale the perpendicular rocks in front. . . . The courageous American woman, notwithstanding that below her feet was a precipice reaching down to the glacier, took the cross which Aurelio was carrying and resolutely traversed this dangerous place where at every step she was liable to go down to certain death. Peter had ascended a chimney and both together went on up the cliff to a small ledge at the edge of the ice above; from there to the summit was still 5,000 feet. . . . We saw Miss Annie erect the cross at a height of 19,000 feet and then descend rapidly. (*A Search for the Apex of America*, p. 189)

All retreated to the tent just as an avalanche descended, fortunately missing them. Peck reached Yungay tired and disappointed in not having gone higher, but rejoicing that she had had "the privilege of beholding scenery more magnificent than any which had previously come within my vision" (*A Search for the Apex of America*, p. 191).

She was not beaten yet. She decided to try again on the west side of the mountain. She dismissed Peter, "who had proved of no real service," and planned to make the ascent with Indians alone, two who had been with her before and two new ones. She provided them with footwear, climbing irons, and ice axes, and she urged them to wear warm clothes. After spending hours trying to pick their way up the mountain side in a labyrinth of crevasses, the Indians pleaded to go home. Peck reluctantly decided that she could not subject them to the bitter cold and gave up.

Defeated, her funds gone, Annie went back to the United States and tried to raise funds for still another expedition. In 1906 *Harper's* magazine gave her $700 to write an article, and she set off for Peru, with less than enough money, no guides, and no companion. She learned that E—, who lived near Yungay, wished to go along. Her friends admitted that although he was *loco*, he would be an excellent companion, for he was intelligent, gentlemanly, energetic, and courageous.

It did not turn out so. E— was impossible, and after various disasters this climb and another (also, incredibly, with E—) had to be abandoned. She was therefore surprised when she arrived home to find that the account of her efforts had already been published in *Harper's*; the editors welcomed her with open arms and an offer of support for her next try.

Even with the magazine's backing, it took Peck over a year to get enough money for another expedition, for this time she felt it was essential to have Swiss guides. At the eleventh hour, the money came, and she wired for the guides to meet her.

The two guides, Rudolf and Gabriel, performed better than the former two, but nevertheless the last ascents of Huascarán were fraught with great difficulty and, for Rudolf, with tragedy. They lost valuable possessions, including the Eskimo suit loaned by the Museum of Natural History, their stove, one of Annie's fur mittens, and both of Rudolf's mittens. The cold was intense; the ice was so slippery that Annie, roped between the guides, frequently had to be pulled to her feet. They gave up the first ascent, but the second was successful. Near the peak, she and Gabriel stopped to try to measure the altitude—an impossible task because of the wind. Meanwhile Rudolf had gone on and had reached the peak before her—a breach of mountaineering etiquette that enraged Annie. She saved her wrath until they should be on the ground again, and, by that time, it was evident that Rudolf was in trouble; his hands and feet were badly frozen. He eventually lost most of one hand, a finger of the other hand, and half of a foot.

To Peck, the arrival at the peak left something to be desired. "There was no pleasure here, hardly a feeling of triumph" (*A Search for the Apex of America*, p. 345). The descent she remembered only as a horrible nightmare. The cold and fatigue, the constant slipping and sliding, the darkness, and the hunger seemed never to end. When they reached the homeward road she wanted to shake her fist at the mountain. She had beaten it at last and planned never to go up there again.

When the news of her successful assault on the mountain came out, still another disappointment awaited. Unable to measure the height of the peak, she had estimated it to be between 23,000 and 24,000 feet. If 24,000 feet, she had make a world record for men as well as for women. A fellow American, Fanny Bullock Workman, immediately challenged this. Workman herself had reached the height of 23,300 feet in the Himalayas, and, in defense of her record, she went so far as to send engineers to measure Huascarán's peak. The engineers determined the lower peak, which Peck had climbed, to be 21,812 feet. Annie could claim only the record for the Western Hemisphere. Incidentally, neither woman was youthful: Annie was fifty-eight at the time of her triumph; Workman made her record ascent in her late forties.

From the outset, Peck had many strikes against her. She could not get adequate support for her expeditions, and she was never well equipped or supplied. As a woman alone, she felt the need of a male companion, but she chose men on slight acquaintance and was singularly unfortunate in her choices. She did not take the best care of herself, she never exercised between trips, she once allowed herself to get badly sunburned, and she drove herself mercilessly. She did not try to know her Indian helpers and did not trust them. In fact, she never seemed really in charge of her expeditions—sometimes giving in meekly to others' decisions, sometimes alienating others by insisting on her own way. Her mountain climbing achievements were made in spite of such handicaps.

Annie's climbing days by no means ended with the ascent of Huascarán. She conquered Mt. Coropuna in Peru in 1911, carrying a "Votes for Women" pennant to the top. Her further visits to South America resulted in a guidebook,

The South American Tour (1913), and *Industrial and Commercial South America* (1922).

Her trips around the country by air she reported in *Flying over South America* (1932). Leaving from Barranquilla, Colombia, she flew by different lines around almost the entire coast of the continent, ending in Miami, Florida. She spent plenty of time in ground travel and took excellent photographs everywhere. Getting up early in the mornings to catch a plane, flying in small planes at low altitudes, and landing often in empty fields would have been too much for most eighty-year-old women, but Peck loved every bit of it.

Later she went on a cruise to the West Indies, then visited Newfoundland. In January 1935 she started a seventy-five-day world tour, but she turned back in Athens, tired out from climbing the road to the Acropolis. She died on July 18, 1935, a few months short of her eighty-fifth birthday.

A moving tribute to Peck appeared in the *New York Times*:

> Probably no one could present a better picture of the earth at its beautiful best—at any rate of the Western Hemisphere—than she who climbed its highest heights and surveyed the landscape o'er, from the "White Hills" of New England and the slopes of Mount Shasta to the peaks of Peru. No American, man or woman, has on foot reached a greater height on this continent than had she. That record she held for twenty-six years and died possessed of the distinction. It is of special interest that the last "climb" which she made (in February, 1935) was up the steep ascent of the Acropolis in Athens, where fifty years ago she had been a student in the American School of Classical Studies. (*New York Times*, July 20, 1935)

BIBLIOGRAPHY

Works by Annie Smith Peck

"Practical Mountain Climbing." *Outing* 38 (Sept. 1901): 695–700.
"Mountaineering Feats." *Outing* 42 (Aug. 1903): 623–24.
"A Woman in the Andes." *Harper* 114 (Dec. 1906): 3–4. Same article in *Harper's Weekly* 52 (Aug. 8, 1908): 11–12.
"The First Ascent of Mount Huascarán." *Harper* 118 (Jan. 1909): 173–87.
"How I Prepared to Climb Mt. Huascarán." *Collier's* 42 (Mar. 13, 1909): 18.
"The Conquest of Huascarán." American Geographical Society *Bulletin* 1 (June 1909): 355–56.
"Most Dramatic Event in My Life." *Delineator* 74 (July 1909): 43.
"Miss Peck Replies to Mrs. Workman." *Scientific American* 102 (Feb. 26, 1910): 183. Workman's letter challenging Peck's claim re Mt. Huascarán appeared in the Feb. 10 issue, p. 143; one by Dr. Workman appeared in the Apr. 16 issue, p. 319.
"My Home in Peru." *Harper's Bazaar* 45 (May 1911): 218.
A Search for the Apex of America: High Mountain Climbing in Peru and Bolivia, including the Conquest of Huascarán, with Some Observations on the Country and People

Below. New York: Dodd, Mead, 1911. Also published as *High Mountain Climbing in Peru and Bolivia*. London: Unwin, 1912.

The South American Tour. New York: Doran, 1913. A descriptive guide.

"Scenic Wonders of South America." *Mentor* 7 (Jan. 1, 1920): 1–11.

Industrial and Commercial South America. New York: Dutton, 1922.

"International Exposition of Brazil." *Current History* (*New York Times*) 17 (Mar. 1923): 1043–49.

"Wings over South America." *Scientific American* 141 (July 1929): 46–49.

Flying over South America: Twenty Thousand Miles by Air. Boston and New York: Houghton Mifflin, 1932.

Works about Annie Smith Peck

International Dictionary of Women's Biography. Edited by Jennifer S. Uglow and Frances Hinton. New York: Continuum, 1982.

Liberty Women. Edited by Robert McHenry. Springfield, Mass: Merriam, 1980.

National Cyclopedia of American Biography. New York: J. T. White, 1888-date, vol. 15 (1916): 152.

Notable American Women, 1607–1950. Edited by Edward T. James and others. Cambridge, Mass.: Harvard University Press, 1971.

Olds, Elizabeth Fagg. *Women of the Four Winds*. Boston: Houghton Mifflin, 1985, pp. 5–70. Olds used many sources, including interviews with members of the Society of Woman Geographers, making her study the most complete and accurate biography of Peck.

Peavey, Linda, and Ursula Smith. *Women Who Changed Things*. New York: Scribner, 1984.

Willard, Frances, and Mary A. Livermore. *A Woman of the Century: Leading American Women in All Walks of Life*. Buffalo, N.Y.: C. W. Moulton, 1893.

"Woman's Conquest of the Andes." *Review of Reviews* 38 (Oct. 1908): 488–89.

Obituary notices appeared in the *New York Times*, on July 19 and 20, 1935; and *Publishers Weekly* 128 (Aug. 3, 1935): 293.

Peck's papers are located in the Society of Woman Geographers collections, in the National Archives (letters to and from Robert E. Peary), and at the American Alpine Club.

Dame Margery Freda Perham

1895–1982

Dame Margery Freda Perham was an authority on Africa and a writer on British policy in the African colonies. Her long and close acquaintance with Africa began in 1922 soon after she left Oxford University and went to visit her sister in British Somaliland. The first white women to live on the border of Somalia and Ethiopia, they were there when the country was considered both wild and dangerous. She became deeply interested in the Africans, and that interest was never extinguished.

She returned to Africa next in 1929. Most of the continent was then under the administration of one or another European country; many were British protectorates. Study of the problems faced by British administrators in shielding Africans from exploitation and preparing them for eventual self-government occupied Perham's energies from that time on.

Between 1929 and 1932, she visited various parts of Africa, talking to officials and tribal leaders, agriculturists and farmers, educators and students, missionaries and witch doctors. In England, she produced books, articles, letters, and lectures on colonial administration. She was the biographer of Lord Lugard, the first governor general of Nigeria and a dominant figure in colonial affairs. She also edited four volumes of his diaries. She was one of a group of Africanists who gathered around Lugard in his English home and exerted influence on the government on behalf of the Africans.

Perham's own diary-letters, written from the field for a small group of friends, are travel literature of a special kind. All remained unpublished until several decades after they were written. Full of fresh impressions of new experiences in a strange and alluring country, the diaries are eminently readable and informative. Although Perham attained her reputation chiefly for her political writings, it is as a traveler and observer of the African scene that we consider her here; her contribution to understanding Africa came from actual experience.

No continent has gone through more radical change in the last part of the twentieth century than has Africa. The speed with which native rule has supplanted colonial administration has focused world attention on the new republics. Public sympathy and political action are aroused by news of widespread famine in many parts of Africa, of the distasteful apartheid system of South Africa, and of unresolved conflicts throughout the continent. Africans and others of the Third World lay the blame for some of the continent's ills on European misrule. Perham's observations throw light on the roles played by Europe and Great Britain in African history.

Margery Perham gave a talk for the British Broadcasting Company on January 11, 1972, in a series entitled "The Time of My Life." As a child, she said, she read Rudyard Kipling and Rider Haggard and early declared that when she grew up she would like to be a big-game hunter in Africa. At the turn of the century, of course, a British female had very little hope of achieving such an ambition. It was therefore a delight when she was unexpectedly able to spend 1922 in what was then British Somaliland. It was a turning point in her life.

She was born in Lancashire on September 6, 1895, the youngest in a family of seven children. Her father was a prosperous wine merchant. Margery was brought up in Harrowgate, Yorkshire. Her mother, of French descent, often went abroad in the winter, sending Margery to a series of boarding schools, but for the greater part of the child's early years she was unhampered by formal schooling. Much of her time was spent roving about the Yorkshire moors with her brothers, for whom twenty miles was a normal walk. Her first consistent education was at St. Anne's, Abbots Bromley. From there, she went to St. Hugh's College, Oxford University, on a hard-won scholarship.

She was at Oxford during World War I, where she had a good record, and she was appointed to a lectureship in history at Sheffield University. The first woman ever appointed to Sheffield's academic staff, she was made to feel unwelcome. Alone in a strange and grimy city, trying to live on a half-time salary of a hundred pounds a year, and teaching a group of poorly prepared and restless ex-servicemen, Margery was miserable. She broke down from overwork. The university gave her a year's leave of absence, which her mother thought she should use convalescing in a luxury hotel in the Lake District. But Margery chose another destination.

Her sister Ethel, eight years Margery's senior and the only other girl in the family, was married to Henry Rayne, a New Zealander who went to Africa during the Boer War. He remained in Africa and became one of the first settlers near the Juba River, on the border between the British and Italian territories of Somaliland. It was to this country, inhabited by tribal Somalis, surrounded by bush full of lions and on a river full of crocodiles, that Ethel Rayne was brought as a bride in 1911. Rayne was made district commissioner for the Somalian frontier district of Hargeysa, where Ethel and Margery went to join him.

While the sisters were waiting for a ship to take them across the Gulf of Aden to Africa, Margery experienced a nightmarish spasm of revulsion against committing herself to living on a far frontier, utterly cut off from her own race. She supposed it was racial fear. The feeling passed, and never again did she have any similar sense of danger in Africa.

All was not peaceful in Hargeysa. Some of the Somali tribes were fighting each other. Major Rayne liked the Somalis and had faith in them as soldiers, even though they had tried to murder him and had killed one of his colleagues. The home he had established was close to an encampment of the Camel Corps, consisting of two Somali companies and some British officers. It was in dry, stony country, not at all the beautiful and dramatic Africa of Margery's dreams. Yet she loved it. She admired the people, who were slim and upright, with fine-cut features and a proud carriage.

Perham had her first experience of bush life when she was allowed to go with Rayne to "beat the bounds" of his district up to the frontier of Ethiopia. They traveled by horseback, with a string of camels, ponies, and mules, accompanied by Somali police and a few cooks and orderlies. They rode during the cool early morning, rested during the midday heat, and slept in the open, with large fires on each side to scare away lions, hyenas, and leopards. One night a lion killed a Somali camped next to them, and Rayne said they must go after the lions. After tracking them all day, they finally came close to them. Margery became separated from her brother-in-law—they had dismounted—just as a lion stepped out of the bush in front of her. Her gunbearer had silently stolen away. Fortunately Rayne had heard the lion growl; he shot into the air, and the lion ran off. It was the climax of Perham's adventurous trip through a country still marked on the map, "Unexplored."

When she returned to Africa in 1929, it was as a Rhodes Traveling Fellow. The fellowship had been given her to study native problems, and it had taken her around the world: to America to study blacks and native Indians; to Hawaii, Fiji, Samoa, New Zealand, and Australia to study indigenous peoples; and finally to Africa. The years between 1923 and 1929 she had spent teaching and lecturing, first at Sheffield, then at her old college, St. Hugh's. She wrote a novel, *Major Dane's Garden*, pouring into it the problems and adventure of Somaliland. She continued to study Africa and colonialism, and she returned to the continent full of questions about how the British administered the colonies there and how the world was changing for the Africans themselves.

She began her study in South Africa. Her first port, after two weeks at sea from New Zealand, was Durban, where the wharf was lined with Africans of many different tribes. Her fellow passengers had the typical white attitude toward the blacks: They thought them picturesque and threw coins on the wharf to see the men scramble for them. Margery's heart sank. The prospect of trying to understand this huge country, with its oppressions and cruelties, its primitive people, its senseless political divisions, seemed overwhelming.

In her short time in the port she drove about the town and its suburbs. It was a European community built on a foundation of black servants, none of whom was allowed to remain in town unless he was on European premises or in the native compound. Perham got permission to visit the compound, where she walked through the kitchens and the sick wards. It was not bad, she thought, but why should it exist at all?

For a fortnight she stayed in Cape Town, most of the time as a guest of friends she had met at Oxford. The house was luxurious and living was enjoyable, including trips to a race meeting, visits to the former Rhodes estate, lunches and dinners with British residents, and walks on the campus of Capetown University. Margery was impressed by the beauty of the country, but she was disappointed that she could not get an interview with the prime minister of the Boer government, General Hertzog. He was doing his best, she wrote, to "swing policy in a pro-Boer and anti-African direction" and to destroy the last limited voting rights of Africans in Cape Province (*African Apprenticeship*, p. 37).

She went to Lovedale, a famous missionary school for Africans, and to Fort Hare's black University College. At the college she met Africans who were studying to be medical doctors, ministers, agriculturists, and leaders of their tribes. A few were women, one of whom had already taken a degree. Some would go on to England, Scotland, or America for further training. At Lovedale she saw students who were learning carpentry, metal work, wagon making, and printing. The color bar prevented their being given any work at skilled labor in South Africa. Some of them had been to the Belgian Congo, where they were astonished to find natives allowed to do any work of which they were capable.

In Basutoland (now Lesotho), the mountain state surrounded by South Africa, Perham was given a taste of life in the interior. She was invited to accompany the assistant commissioner on a two-week trek into his district. There were no roads. They took pack animals and rode horseback through the country. Her companion, always referred to as the A.C., introduced her to the natives as his sister. Margery, who had, she said, not been "in training," found riding on the terrific heights very difficult. They traveled long hours, sometimes in pelting rain or hail, but they camped in dry tents magically erected by the men. At one stop, they were entertained by Basuto dancers, "a striking example of the Africans' use of the dance to express their feelings and preserve their history" (*African Apprenticeship*, p. 99). They visited little schools in the bush, talked to headmen, bathed in a mountain stream, and, in the evenings, carried on long discussions about poetry, history, and life in general.

Feeling decidedly ill after one of the native cook's meals, Margery took charge of the camp kitchen. She made a speech, through an interpreter, on cleanliness, then she had every pot and pan, rag and teacloth boiled. She made a stew, "allowing none of the dirty Basuto to put a finger into it" (*African Apprenticeship*, p. 103). They came to a little village high in the mountains, where the inhabitants were "a very farouche looking lot, without much civility to spare" (*African Apprenticeship*, p. 108). They visited cliffs on which Bushmen had painted delightful frescoes of elands and hartebeests, deer and cranes, and figures of men jumping or drawing arrows.

They stopped for several days in a small village where there was a store. Margery found that the store threw light on the contact of black and white, for it contained things the Africans needed and those they had produced. The English, she observed, did not study the market, for most of the goods bought by the natives came from France, Germany, Japan, Czechoslovakia, and America. The products the Africans would soon want—cheap ploughs and agricultural implements, sewing machines, and gramophones—were not available at all.

Later, after a visit to a market in Ashigashiya, a British outpost in Nigeria, she wrote of the economic impact of Europeanization. The natives who had lived naked, free, and independent were forced to pay taxes. In order to do so, they had to produce surplus food. To sell it, they had to leave the hills and come to the market place. In this manner, they were lured into "the outermost rim of the world's economy" and brought to serve the European gods of production and exchange and to "keep the peace which these gods demand" (*West African Passage*, p. 149).

When she left Basutoland, she hoped that the small state could be "saved from the threatened grip of the Afrikaner government. . . . The Basuto are not angels but . . . they have a spirit of freedom long crushed out of many of the tribes within South Africa" (*African Apprenticeship*, p. 129). She was sorry to leave the assistant commissioner, who had become a friend. Perham had a talent for making friends, sometimes with those who at first sight did not attract her.

Before the year was up she had visited many parts of South Africa—the Rand, the Transvaal, and Zululand—then Bechuanaland, the Belgian Congo, and Northern and Southern Rhodesia. For the most part, her itinerary and the routine of her days were determined by her self-imposed task of "trying to see it all at levels from the lowest bush-station to Government House and the Colonial Office" (*African Apprenticeship*, p. 27). She spent long, active hours seeing as much as possible and still longer hours poring over documents made available to her by administrators, who were, on the whole, helpful and informative.

She left South Africa determined to devote herself entirely to a study of the government of native races, especially in the parts of Africa under British dominion. The situation, she wrote

is among the most complex the world has ever had to face and some political machinery has got to be invented that will enable the twentieth-century European to live with "primitive" man without the latter swamping the former or the former exploiting the latter. (*African Apprenticeship*, p. 263)

East African Journey is the account of her visits to Kenya and Tanganyika from 1929 to 1930, which were made possible by an extension of her Rhodes fellowship. As a result of her observations there she took part, on her return to England, in public discussion of "closer union" for East Africa. By economizing on her Rhodes grant she was able to stretch it through a visit to West Africa from 1931 to 1932. She followed her previous routine of talking to natives and officials in Chad, Nigeria, and the British and French Cameroons, where she compared French and British methods of government.

The greater part of her time in West Africa was spent in Nigeria, the largest of Britain's dependent African territories, except for the Sudan. Wherever she went, whether escorted by officials or alone, she met no antagonism but much friendliness, as well as curiosity, on the part of the Africans.

She could still find in northeastern Nigeria and around Lake Chad an Africa not much change since her Somaliland adventures.

> I saw the still-naked pagans who had been driven to live on their terraced rocks to escape the centuries' old slave-raiding of their Muslim neighbours: they either fled at my approach or flung themselves at my feet pouring earth on their heads. Over the remoter parts of this tropical Africa of the early thirties European rule had still done little more than stop slave-raiding and inter-tribal war; it had checked ritual murder or the killing of witches and twins, and alleviated famine, sleeping sickness, rinderpest and other dramatic scourges. (*Colonial Sequence, 1930–1949*, p. xv)

Perham was connected with Oxford University until she reached the statutory retirement age of sixty-seven. She was the first director of Oxford's Institute of Colonial Studies. She received many academic honors, and in 1948 she was named a Commander of the British Empire. In 1965 she was made a D.C.M.G.— not in the conventional Order of the British Empire but in the predominantly colonial service Order of St. Michael and St. George. She died on February 19, 1982, in Oxford.

Perham commented on the sudden end of colonialism in Africa:

> I went through all the colonialist's attitudes—the belief that we had almost un-limited time in which to develop our administrative methods—the growing reali-zation of the need to prepare our wards—not *too* urgently—for *eventual* self-government—then helter-skelter rush over the edge and into independence when our African friends and pupils became ministers, top secretaries and even Heads of State overnight. But this abrupt conclusion has not changed my unfashionable view that, by any balanced historical judgement of the history of imperialism and the character of the Africa we annexed, our colonial rule was, on balance, an immense and essential service to Africa. (*Colonial Sequence, 1930–1949*, pp. 27–28)

BIBLIOGRAPHY

Works by Margery Perham

Race and Politics in Kenya: A Correspondence between Elspeth Huxley and Margery Perham. London: Faber, 1944.

Colonial Sequence, 1930–1949. London: Methuen, 1967. The Introduction, pp. x–xxi, contains autobiographical details.

African Apprenticeship: An Autobiographical Journey in Southern Africa, 1929. London: Faber, 1974; New York: Africana, 1974.

East African Journey: Kenya and Tanganyika, 1929–30. London: Faber, 1976.

West African Passage: A Journey through Nigeria, Chad, and the Cameroons, 1931–32. London and Boston: Peter Owen, 1983. A. H. M. Kirk-Greene's introduction summarizes Perham's life and her achievements.

Perham wrote many other books on colonial policy. Those listed are travel books.

Works about Margery Perham

Brittain, Vera. *The Women at Oxford: A Fragment of History.* London: Harrap, 1960, pp. 145, 176, 191, 223, 245.

Contemporary Authors. Detroit: Gale Research, 1922-date, new version. Vol. 1, p. 502, and 1st version, vol. 106, p. 393.

Obituaries appeared in the London *Times*, on Feb. 22, 1982; and the *Chicago Tribune*, on Feb. 24, 1982.

IDA REYER PFEIFFER
1797–1858

Ida Reyer Pfeiffer was a celebrated European traveler and travel writer in the mid-nineteenth century. Between 1842 and 1857, this Viennese housewife went around the world twice and visited many corners of the globe. Her books of travel, although not literary gems, are full of drama and excitement. She was middle-aged when she began her travel career, and during the final years of her life she was making plans for further ventures. She collected insects, shells, and botanical specimens, which were duly sent to museums, but the collecting was secondary to her need to go everywhere, especially to places she was warned against, and her curiosity to see everything, no matter how distressing the sight might be. She was never in a hurry. Her first round-the-world trip took nineteen months; her second, more than four years.

The naturalist Alexander von Humboldt thought highly of Madame Pfeiffer's energy and perseverance, and through his efforts she was made an honorary member of the Geographical Society of Berlin. The King of Prussia awarded her a gold medal for distinction in the field of arts and sciences. Her books, translated into several languages, sold well enough to help finance her journeys.

Ida Reyer, the only girl in a family of six children, was born in Vienna on October 14, 1797. Her father was a wealthy merchant who had strict ideas on the education of children. Ida was allowed to dress like a boy, and she was taught, along with her brothers, to be courageous, fearless, and independent. They were fed with Spartan simplicity, though their elders, at the same table, enjoyed hearty meals. Reyer died when Ida was nine, and it took several years for her mother to institute her own methods of education. But her daughter could not be persuaded to exchange trousers for petticoats until she was thirteen. Ida submitted unwillingly to piano practice (and years later found herself playing before the queen of Madagascar). At seventeen she fell in love with her tutor, who also loved her, but Madame Reyer would not consider the match. Disappointed and subdued, Ida agreed when she was twenty-two to a loveless marriage. The groom was Dr. Pfeiffer, a distinguished lawyer from Lemberg, who was much older than Ida.

Not long after the marriage, Dr. Pfeiffer exposed to the authorities the peculations of several dishonest government officials, some of whom were found to be guilty and removed from office. Pfeiffer was made to suffer for his honesty. Considered a troublemaker, he was forced to resign his appointment as a councilor, and he was never afterward able to obtain suitable employment in Lemberg, in Vienna, or even in Switzerland, his native country. The family, used to living in luxury, was faced with poverty. Ida's paternal inheritance vanished. She gave lessons in drawing and music but finally had to bear the humiliation of applying to her brothers for help in feeding her two sons. In 1831 Madame Reyer died and left a small inheritance, enough to enable Ida to live comfortably and to educate the boys. She returned to Vienna, while Dr. Pfeiffer, now in advanced age, remained in Lemberg to be near his son by a first marriage.

In 1842, when her sons were both established in homes of their own, Ida's childhood dreams of travel were revived. She had little money, but, she wrote, "I was determined to practice the most rigid economy. Privation and discomfort had no terrors for me" ("A Biography of Ida Pfeiffer" in *The Last Travels of Ida Pfeiffer*, p. xxiv). To the objection that it was unwise for a woman to travel alone, she replied that she trusted to her years (she was forty-five) and to her habits of self-reliance that had been acquired in the hard school of life. She announced that she was going to visit Jerusalem. She did not tell her friends and relatives that she planned to remain in the Middle East for nine months, to see Egypt, and to cross the desert from Cairo to the Isthmus of Suez. After her return, she read to her friends about her experiences from a diary she had kept on the trip, and, although she had not planned originally to publish the account, it appeared in 1843. It was reprinted several times in German and in an English translation as *Visit to the Holy Land, Egypt and Italy*.

With a little money from the copyright, Ida went to Iceland for six months. With royalties from *A Visit to Iceland* and the sale of geological and botanical specimens, Ida felt able to plan a more extensive journey—nothing less ambitious than a voyage around the world.

She went first to Brazil, traveling on a Danish brig. She found little to admire in Rio de Janeiro, where "there is nothing to offer compensation for the disagreeable and repulsive sights that meet your eyes at every turn" (*A Lady's Voyage Round the World*, p. 6). At Petrópolis, a new town colonized by German immigrants, she and a male traveling companion had an ugly experience when a Negro attacked them with a knife while they were walking along a forest path. Fortunately, they were rescued before they were seriously wounded, and Ida did not allow the misadventure to deter her from seeing more of the interior. Armed with a pair of good doubled-barreled pistols, she went into the forest with a guide, in search of the Indians, the original inhabitants.

The trees, orchids, ferns, and vines delighted her, as did the birds that inhabited the enchanted groves. "It seemed to me," she wrote, "that I was taking a ride in fairy-land. . . . I was over happy, and felt every exertion I had made most richly rewarded" (*A Lady's Voyage*, p. 20). She reached a tribe of Puri Indians. She thought their huts, open on three sides and roofed with palm leaves, the worst habitations she had ever seen. The Indians were "still uglier than negroes" with "a peculiar expression of stupidity"; their only clothing consisted of a few rags. Her guide "trumpeted forth my praises as a woman of astonishing learning," and many of the Indians asked for medical advice. Since Ida never carried any medicines, either for herself or others, she advised the use of soap and water or medicinal plants (*A Lady's Voyage*, pp. 25–26).

She accompanied some of the Indians on a monkey hunt and admired their skill with bows and arrows. They offered her shelter for the night, and she gladly spread her cloak on the ground, took a clump of wood for a pillow, and looked forward to a night's rest. Her hosts served a meal of roast monkey, tuberous roots, and Indian corn, then they performed a dance, accompanied by unpleasant music and wild yelling. She slept uneasily, thinking of the wild animals at large in the forest, until she consoled herself with the thought that, if it were dangerous, the savages would not sleep so composedly in their open huts.

On her way to China, she stopped for a couple of weeks in Tahiti, where she was shocked at the uninhibited behavior of the women. Though generally open-minded, Ida had strict ideas of propriety. She visited Hong Kong, and she took a Chinese junk to Canton. Europeans were not at all popular there, but, in spite of some unpleasant experiences, she insisted on walking about the city and its environs; on one occasion, she dressed herself in male attire to walk outside the city walls.

She knew that it was almost impossible for a foreigner to give accurate information about Chinese habits and customs, "but I saw all I possibly could, never missed an opportunity of mingling with the people, and carefully noted down all I saw" (*A Lady's Voyage*, p. 49). She remarked on the terrible punishments meted out to criminals, on the foot binding of young girls, on the poverty of the Chinese boat dwellers; and she concluded that "a baser, falser, crueller people than the Chinese I never met with" (*A Lady's Voyage*, p. 53).

For the next months, Pfeiffer thoroughly explored India. She visited nutmeg groves, a sago factory, and a sugar factory; she went on a tiger hunt; she attended a funeral and a Feast of Lanterns; and she rambled about alone, collecting plants and insects. She traveled very simply, relying on the kindness of those she met for her meals and for shelter.

My best meals were of rice boiled in milk, or eggs, but usually I had only rice, with water and salt. A leathern bottle for water, a small pan for cooking, a handful of salt, and some bread and rice, constituted my whole preparation for wants of this kind. (*A Lady's Voyage*, p. 148)

Much of the time, she carried not even a blanket, and she was so modest that for many days she did not bathe or change her clothes because she was always surrounded by people.

From India she went to Persia, traveling up the Tigris River to Baghdad, where she joined a caravan for the three-hundred-mile desert trip to Mosul, then to Tabriz in Kurdistan. Before leaving Mosul, she took the precaution of sending home all her papers, "in order that if I should be robbed or killed my journal at least might reach the hands of my sons" (*A Lady's Voyage*, p. 203). She adhered to her rule of living off the country.

> Wherever human creatures are to be found, I carry with me no eatables; what they can live on, I can, and if I do not like their food, it must be because I am not really hungry, and the remedy for that is to fast till I like any thing. (*A Lady's Voyage*, p. 183)

She came to expect people to shelter and feed her and was quite indignant when they failed to do so.

In Tabriz she caused great astonishment when the English consul learned that she had made her way there alone, with no knowledge of the country or the language of the people.

Tabriz, the residence of the heir to the throne of Persia, was a large town, with good houses and clean streets, a welcome relief to the traveler. Ida, however, looked forward to entering Russia, a Christian country, governed by a civilized European, a monarch who believed in law and order. To her dismay, she found quite the contrary to be the case. As she walked near her caravan, armed Cossacks in a Russian car seized her and carried her off, holding her fast and clapping a hand over her mouth so that her cries could not be heard. She calmed herself with the thought that she had been mistaken for a dangerous spy and that as soon as she had cleared herself they would release her. They held her overnight until her portmanteau had been recovered from the caravan and her passport had revealed her identity. She was released, but no apology for the rude treatment was made.

"Oh you good Arabs, Turks, Persians, Hindoos!" she wrote, "How safely did I pass through your heathen and infidel countries; and here, in Christian Russia, how much have I had to suffer in this short space" (*A Lady's Voyage*, p. 243).

She met with endless bureaucratic red tape, long delays, uncomfortable travel, and rude treatment until she left Russia and proceeded, by way of Turkey, Greece, and Italy, to Vienna. On November 4, 1848, she was reunited with her family. She had traveled 2,800 miles by land, 35,000 by sea.

In 1851 Ida went to London, where she had intended to take a ship for Australia, but the gold discoveries there had caused a rush of immigration and had raised the cost of living. Even with a grant from the Austrian government,

Ida could not afford to go there. She decided to go, instead, to the Dutch East Indies.

The publication of her first round-the-world journey had made her famous, and as a result she was given free passage on many ships and entertained wherever Europeans were to be found. She left London on May 24, 1851, bound for the Cape of Good Hope. After four weeks in Cape Town, she found that another plan, to travel into the interior of Africa, was impossible; the expense was beyond her purse. She decided again on Australia, by way of Singapore. There she changed her plans again and determined to visit Sarawak, an independent territory on the island of Borneo under the government of the English rajah, James Brooke.

She was in Borneo for six months. Her greatest adventure was a visit to the Dyaks, a tribe known to be headhunters. To reach them, she had to walk many miles on jungle paths so slippery that she had to go barefooted. The Dyaks lived in long huts, which served also for feasts and

> for the preservation of war-trophies, which consist of the heads of their slain enemies. I could not look without horror at a row of no less than six-and-thirty of these agreeable memorials hung up in ornamental style like a garland of flowers, and with the sockets of the eyes filled with white oval shells. . . . I shuddered, but could not help asking myself whether, after all, we Europeans are not really just as bad or worse than these despised savages? Is not every page of our history filled with horrid deeds of treachery and murder? What shall we say to the religious wars of Germany and France—to the conquest of America—to the deeds of violence and blood in the Middle Ages—to the Spanish Inquisition? . . . I do not think we Europeans can venture to say much about the cruelty of these ignorant savages, who kill their enemies (as we do), but do not torture them, and, for what they do, may plead the excuse that they are without the light of religion or of intellectual culture. Can we with a very clear conscience preach to them upon the subject of mildness, mercy, and aversion to bloodshed? (*A Lady's Second Journey*, pp. 51, 60–61)

Against the advice of her friends, Ida determined to go farther into the interior among the free Dyaks, planning to go by boat up the Rajang River, to cross the mountains on foot, and to return to Pontianak on the coast by the Kapuas River. She dressed herself for the formidable journey in ''a simple and appropriate costume,'' consisting of trousers, a petticoat not reaching below the ankle, a jacket, and a magnificent bamboo hat. She was prepared to pull her petticoat up around her waist and to go barefoot when necessary. After toilsome marches she reached a river which flowed into the Kapuas.

> I must own I should have liked to have passed a longer time among the free Dyaks, as I found them, without exception, honest, good-natured, and modest in their behavior. I should be inclined to place them, in these respects, above any of the races I have ever known. (*A Lady's Second Journey*, p. 76)

In her later travels, Ida often compared so-called savages with the Dyaks, and none ever measured up to these tribes in "their quiet domestic mode of life, their moral conduct, the love they evidently bear their children, and the respect they show their old people" (*A Lady's Second Journey*, pp. 76–77).

In Sumatra she visited other primitive people, the Bataks, about whom terrible stories were told. Pfeiffer was, of course, warned against going among them, but she was determined. She bade farewell to the last Europeans she might ever see; she took letters to the rajahs of the different tribes—for each chief bore that title—and she left papers to be sent to her family in the event she failed to come back.

She was passed from one rajah to another, having to ask permission each time to pass into the new district. In most places she was accepted; in others, she was threatened. She took part in a number of tribal ceremonies and watched dances. Once, at her insistence, the Bataks performed the dance at which a man is to be killed and eaten, using a mock victim. "Play as it was, though, I could not witness it without some shuddering, especially when I considered that I was entirely in the power of these wild cannibals" (*A Lady's Second Journey*, p. 172).

At one touchy point, she found herself surrounded by men who made it plain with gestures that they wished to kill and eat her. She had the presence of mind to remember a little speech, partly in Malay and partly in their language, that she had prepared for just such an emergency. "I knew if I could say any thing that would amuse them, and perhaps make them laugh, I should have a great advantage over them, for savages are quite like children, and the merest trifle will often make them friends" (*A Lady's Second Journey*, p. 176). She told them that she was very old and tough, not very good eating, which, indeed, made them laugh! She was not, however, out of danger, and some time later she was forced to give up her plan of reaching a village supposed to be under the rule of a woman. She was made to return to the coast, though not by the same route and not immediately; she was sent from one place to another until she thought she would never be allowed to leave the Batak country.

The terrors and hardships of that journey did not deter her, when she reached Ceram, from going to visit the wild Alforas, "more enthusiastic collectors of human heads, I understood, than even the Dyaks" (*A Lady's Second Journey*, p. 221). Twenty men were given her as escort. The Alforas, however, turned out to be so shy and fearful of human approach they they hid in their houses, and it was some time before she saw any of them. When she did, she found them to be inoffensive, even friendly.

On July 6, 1852, Pfeiffer left in a sailing ship bound for San Francisco. She was understandably weary, suffering intermittently from "Sumatra fever," and a bit peevish. She went to see American Indians in California—a letdown after the Indonesian wild men—and she visited South America before returning for a tour of the United States. Her second journey around the world ended in London on June 14, 1855.

Pfeiffer's last journey, in 1857, was to Madagascar, an island almost unvisited by Europeans. It was under the rule of Queen Ranavola, a bloodthirsty tyrant who demanded unlimited labor from her subjects for which they were never paid. Ida was unwittingly caught up in a conspiracy with the six other Europeans on the island to depose Ranavola in favor of Prince Rakoto, who promised a more humane rule. All visited the queen at Tananariva, the capital, high in the coastal mountains. The proposed coup d'etat was discovered, and the Europeans were exiled, ordered to leave the city within the hour, and escorted to the harbor by armed guards.

The Europeans had witnessed so much of the queen's terrible anger, particularly that directed against Christians, that they never expected to be able to leave the island at all. It took them nearly fifty days of rough travel to reach the coast, a journey that should have taken less than two weeks. They were kept imprisoned for days at a time in miserable huts along the way and were rudely treated. Ida and one of the others suffered greatly from fever, but they were given no medical help or even rest. When they were at last able to escape by ship, Ida was very ill indeed. "Nevertheless," she wrote, "I do not regret having undertaken the journey" (*The Last Travels of Ida Pfeiffer*, p. 275).

Friends in Mauritius took her in and nursed her, but it was some weeks before she was able to move about again. She went back to Europe, still hoping to see more of the world. At last she was brought home to Vienna and cared for by relatives. She died in the night of October 27–28, 1858.

Ida Pfeiffer's story invites comparison with that of another globe trotter, Isabella Bird Bishop. Both explored places much off the beaten track, and both seemed tireless in their pursuit of novel experiences. Unlike Bishop, Pfeiffer seems to have made little effort to understand any of the people she met. She thought most non-Europeans ugly and stupid. She never liked any of her guides, even though they stuck with her when she insisted on walking into danger. Both women were daring, even foolhardy, a trait to which we owe some of the most thrilling adventure stories in print.

BIBLIOGRAPHY

Works by Ida Pfeiffer

Numerous English translations of Pfeiffer's books have been published, with varying titles. The first published English editions are listed below.

A Lady's Voyage Round the World. A selected translation by Mrs. Percy Sinnett. London: Longman, 1852. Vol. 13 in *The Traveller's Library*. London: Longman, 1856. Quotations in the text are from the 1856 edition.
Visit to Iceland and the Scandinavian North. London: Ingram, Cooke, 1852.
Visit to the Holy Land, Egypt and Italy. Translated by H. W. Dulcken. London: Ingram, Cooke, 1852.
A Lady's Second Journey round the World, from London to the Cape of Good Hope, Borneo, Java, Sumatra, Celebes, Ceram, the Moluccas, etc., California, Panama,

Peru, Ecuador, and the United States. New York: Harper, 1856. Part was also published as *A Lady's Visit to California*. Oakland, Calif.: Biobooks, 1950.

The Last Travels of Ida Pfeiffer, Inclusive of a Visit to Madagascar, with an Autobiographical Memoir of the Author. Translated by H. W. Dulcken. New York: Harper, 1861.

Works about Ida Pfeiffer

"A Biography of Ida Pfeiffer," in Pfeiffer, *The Last Travels*, pp. ix–xxxvii. Based on Pfeiffer's own notes, this is the main biographical source. Ida failed to give the first names of her parents and her husband. The biography and the story of the last journey were published posthumously by her son, Oscar Pfeiffer.

International Dictionary of Women's Biography. Edited by Jennifer S. Uglow and Frances Hinton. New York: Continuum, 1982.

Ladies on the Loose: Women Travellers of the 18th and 19th Centuries. Edited by Leo Hamalian. New York: Dodd, Mead, 1981, pp. 149–68.

Mozans, H. J. (pseud. of John A. Zahm). *Woman in Science*. London and New York: Appleton, 1913, pp. 255–56.

The Story of Ida Pfeiffer and Her Travels in Many Lands. London: Nelson, 1884. The unnamed author of this volume includes a biography, based on the above mentioned "Biography," and summaries of the journey to Iceland, the first round-the-world trip, and the visit to Madagascar.

SUSIE CARSON RIJNHART
1868–1908

Susie Carson Rijnhart spent the years from 1894 to 1898 in southwest China and returned later for the few years before her death. She was the second white woman to enter Tibet with the hope of reaching the forbidden city of Lhasa. Like Annie Royle Taylor, who had made a similar attempt six years earlier, Susie was a Christian missionary, inspired by a desire to take the gospel teachings to a country as yet untouched by evangelism. Also like Taylor, she failed to reach Lhasa. Both traveled the same route; both were turned back at Nagchuka (Nagqu). Both were set upon by robbers and deserted by their guides, and both suffered extreme hardships of travel in wild and difficult terrain. Both overcame many obstacles and retained their boundless faith in the Christian God.

Taylor was British, a single woman, who had been attached to the China Inland Mission for many years before her journey into Tibet. She traveled there with a faithful servant, Pontso. Rijnhart was a medical doctor from Canada traveling with her husband, Petrus Rijnhart. Of the two women, Rijnhart was the better educated; she became more deeply involved with the people of China and Tibet; she took a more informed interest in the Buddhist philosophy; and she showed greater tolerance for and understanding of the natives.

Susie Carson was born in 1868, the daughter of J. S. Carson of Strathroy, Ontario, Canada. An eager Methodist, she early decided to be a medical missionary. Her parents encouraged her and sent her to the Woman's Medical College in Toronto, where she completed the medical course in 1888. Six years later she married Petrus Rijnhart, a Dutch explorer recently returned from China, who had been lecturing in Holland, the United States, and Canada. They planned a lifetime of service as missionaries, and, although they were not under any church sponsorship, they set off at once for central Asia.

Their first objective was the great lamasery of Kumbum on the Chino-Tibetan frontier. It was a great center of Buddhist learning and worship, second only to

Lhasa. Petrus had visited it two years earlier and had found no difficulty in entering Tibet from the Chinese side. No official had ever asked for his passport or questioned his intentions as he traveled about. Few of those he met there had ever seen a European or heard the name of Christ. It seemed to be a field crying out for evangelization, and the Rijnharts planned to begin their work by establishing a medical mission near the lamasery.

Entering China by way of Shanghai, they traveled up the Yangtze by British steamer, then continued their journey by houseboat, cart, and mule. They brought with them a large amount of stores, including household utensils, medicines, dental and surgical instruments, firearms, a box of Bibles in Tibetan, a sewing machine, and a bicycle. In Shanghai they donned Chinese garments. "After adjusting the unwieldy garments to my own satisfaction," wrote Susie, "I attended a service in the Union Church, where, to my consternation, I discovered I had appeared in public with one of the under garments outside" (*With The Tibetans in Tent and Temple*, p. 13).

Susie gradually adjusted to new experiences: the rough mode of travel, the primitive inns, the use of chopsticks, and Chinese food. (She thought Chinese cooks vied with even the French in preparing delicious meals.) She began to learn Chinese, which Petrus spoke well.

In Sining, not far from their goal, they stopped with missionaries from the China Inland Mission before going on to Lusar. Lusar, a small town of about a thousand inhabitants, was the trading center for Kumbum and was visited by merchants from China, Mongolia, and Tibet. The religious festivals held at the lamasery attracted large crowds. The lamasery itself was home to about four thousand lamas. Life there was full of color and interest.

The Rijnharts' house, where they would spend the next two years, had two guest rooms, one for men and one for women, who might come for medical treatment or "to inquire about spiritual matters." The walls were hung with colored Bible pictures, which made openings for the discussion of such matters. They engaged a young lama, Ishinima, to teach them Tibetan, and they in turn taught him the use of soap and water. In common with other foreign visitors, the Rijnharts were appalled to find that the Tibetans never washed their bodies or their clothes and coexisted happily with vermin.

At first the foreigners were regarded with reserve, if not suspicion, but as soon as the people found out the white doctor could treat their ailments, they came freely, even the priests. The couple were soon adopted into the life of the town. The sewing machine, which they called "the iron tailor," was a thing of wonder. The bicycle was of little use in the hilly country, but the "one-man cart" was a source of much amusement. Men and boys watched Petrus ride it, but not one could be induced to try it.

Ishinima invited them to visit his home in the lamasery. "Several red-robed lamas with bare heads and smiling faces gave us a Mongol welcome, holding out toward us both hands with the palms turned upward." The visitors were given tea and held "a very pleasant conversation about the great monastery with its revered lamas and sacred traditions, about Lhasa, the home of Buddhist learning, and of the great Dalai Lama,'' as well as about Christianity and the Western world, of which the lamas knew almost nothing (*With the Tibetans*, pp. 38–39).

Not long after their arrival in Lusar a terrible rebellion broke out among the Mohammedans of western Kansu. The Rijnharts were urged to go to well-fortified Sining or to leave for home, but they decided to remain where they were needed, for the crowding together of refugees led to outbreaks of diphtheria and smallpox. They prepared for a siege by storing their goods in a cave. Then, to their surprise, they received an invitation to take up residence in the lamasery.

They lived in the lamasery for six months. The neighborhood was a center of violent and savage warfare between the Mohammedans and the Chinese. Thousands were killed, and many were left homeless by the burning of the towns. The lamasery became a hospital, and the doctors worked day and night caring for the wounded. Twice they went to the battlefield to help those who fell. They even treated the Mohammedan wounded, which utterly amazed the Chinese and Tibetans. They did not understand ''the law of Christian kindness impelling love and mercy even for one's enemies'' (*With the Tibetans*, p. 101).

After the war ended, the Rijnharts continued their friendly relations with the abbot, Mina Fuyeh. He was about the same age as they were and far above the average lama in intellect. He was an accomplished linguist and knew the Tibetan, Chinese, and Mongolian languages. He studied the Christian Gospels written in Tibetan characters which they gave him, and he was able to converse with them about the life of Christ, but he saw no reason to choose one religion over another. He was woefully ignorant of the outer world and was astounded when Petrus demonstrated to him that the world was round.

On the one day of the year when women were allowed to enter the great temple, Susie went in and watched the Buddhist ceremonies. She found something pathetic in the spectacle of idol worship, yet ''it is not,'' she said, ''the part of the Christian missionary to assume an air of ridicule and contempt for the religious ideas and practices of peoples less enlightened than his own'' (*With the Tibetans*, p. 111). Every religious service, she felt, acknowledged the existence of one great God; the work of Christian missions was only hindered by dogmatic assertion of doctrines and failure to recognize the great underlying truths of all religions.

After two years in Lusar, the Rijnharts moved to Tankar, another town on the trade route between China and Tibet, about twenty-four miles from Kumbum. They had been happy in Lusar, and they were sad when the time came to say goodbye. They had lived through dark days with the people of the town and formed tender ties. But they felt that their mission was to reach out to others, ''looking out new fields and preparing the way for other laborers'' (*With the Tibetans*, p. 138).

One day they were visited by an English traveler, Captain M. S. Wellby, who had come from India through Ladakh and northern Tibet. He had tried to enter

Lhasa but had been turned back. Forced to take a roundabout route, his provisions had given out, his mules had died, and most of his men had deserted him. He stayed at Tankar but one day, then left for Kumbum, accompanied by Petrus. Not long afterward, Petrus went with Wellby to Peking, acting as an interpreter.

During his absence, Susie, who was expecting a child, was looked after by the Tankar people, especially the women, who seemed to feel that they had her under their protection. "During those memorable weeks," she said, "I learned to understand and sympathize with the heathen women as never before" (With the Tibetans, p. 155).

Susie entertained still another foreigner, the Swedish explorer Sven Hedin. Hedin's Through Asia mentions his visit, remarking that "it was quite a pleasure to talk to somebody whose interests ranged beyond grass and pastures, dangerous passes, wild yaks, cattle and sheep" (quoted by Rijnhart, With the Tibetans, p. 160).

On June 30, 1897, little Charles Carson Rijnhart was born. The women were astonished at the preparations made for his coming, and when Susie undressed him for his daily bath they considered it an act of insanity. Tibetan babies were "pasted with butter and put out to bask in the sun" (With the Tibetans, p. 165). The household had been augmented by Rahim, a native of Ladakh, who had been with Wellby and now offered himself as a servant to the Rijnharts. Rahim delighted in the child and carried him about singing weird Hindustani and Ladakhi airs. The people were further amazed when Susie, Petrus, and the baby set out on horseback for a journey to the Koko Nor when Charlie was only forty-two days old.

The Koko Nor, or Blue Lake, was a sacred lake. The Rijnharts had attempted to reach it once before but had been frightened out of completing the journey by robber bands. They now felt secure enough in their knowledge of the Tibetan language and the people to try again. The Tanguts, nomads who lived in the area, had visited them in Tankar and had given them information about the nature of the country. "Although we knew most of them were robbers," Susie admitted, "we lost all fear of them" (With the Tibetans, p. 170). They camped near the nomads' tents, and though the people were filthy, the visitors ate the food and drank the tea offered them. "There is no more genuine hospitality than that to be found among these nomadic people and not to accept it with the grace with which it is proffered, at once raises a barrier between you and them" (With the Tibetans, p. 184).

Their success in reaching so many Tibetans with their gospel message encouraged the Rijnharts to attempt a journey farther into the interior, perhaps as far as Lhasa itself, to gain the confidence of the people and to take note of places where missions could be established. "Let it be clearly understood," explained Susie, "that the purpose of our journey was purely missionary; it was not a mere adventure or expedition prompted by curiosity or desire for discovery. . . . From a human standpoint there was absolutely nothing inviting in such an undertaking" (With the Tibetans, p. 195). They had heard about the robber districts, the high mountain passes, and the dangerous river crossings, but their apprehensions had faded. They had talked to many, including women, who had safely made the journey from Lhasa numerous times, and they were told they would have no trouble getting near Lhasa so long as they did not attempt to enter the city itself.

Rahim was a great help in making the arrangements. He was eager to return to his home in Ladakh, and he was pleased to go along with them. They took supplies for two years, but they planned a small caravan: two other men, five riding animals, and twelve pack animals. About the middle of May 1898, they joined a caravan of traders leaving for the mountains. Their departure from Tankar was almost as sad as the leaving of their first home in Lusar, for they had formed great friendships there.

The caravan soon left the Rijnhart party behind. One of their guides deserted them; later, two more abandoned them. They met another large caravan going toward Tankar, and, when it left, five of the Rijnharts' best animals were gone. Also their happy little boy was fretful, which they attributed to his teething. Susie records sadly, "In the most deserted region through which we had yet passed we found ourselves without guides, lost five of our ponies and saw the hand of affliction laid upon our little child" (*With the Tibetans*, p. 244).

As they went on, things seemed to brighten—Charlie soon had eight teeth; they were approaching the Lhasa district and hoping to find a place where they could remain and establish a mission; they talked happily of their future and the future of their son. They planned, when their stay in the interior was over, to go to the Indian border, then home to America and Holland for a visit before returning to Tibet again.

Suddenly, the world darkened. The baby, who seemed to be sleeping peacefully, quietly died. "We clasped in our arms only the casket which had held our precious jewel; the jewel itself had been taken for a brighter setting in a brighter world" (*With the Tibetans*, p. 248). The sorrowing parents and the wailing Rahim buried the little body on a mountainside, covering the grave with a boulder. Charlie had lived but one year, one month, and twenty-two days.

The journey had lost its savor. From time to time they saw Tibetans, but not all were friendly. One of their horses died, leaving Rahim and Petrus to ride and walk alternately. At Nagchuka they were politely told they could go no farther, nor could Rahim proceed to his home in Ladakh. After many days of negotiating, they were given fresh horses, some food, and three guides and were sent on the return journey. They were told that they were to take a different road from that by which they had approached Nagchuka, one through Jyekundo to Tatsienlu. As the Rijnharts planned to winter somewhere on the way, it made no difference to them which road they took. Rahim went part of the way with them and then took a road toward his home in Ladakh, well supplied with a horse, food, ammunition, and money. The parting was sad, for they had grown very fond of the young man. How different might have been the story had he remained with them!

Although the Rijnharts had difficulties crossing swollen rivers and suffered from snow and rain, they met some friendly groups, who warned them of robbers. Susie and Petrus celebrated their fourth wedding anniversary by resting for a day and preparing a feast of rice pudding. The guides seemed to be pleasant and reliable, although they had never been over the road before. As they were approaching the lamasery at Tashi Gomba, where they hoped to be able to spend the winter, the guides left the well-traveled road and took a footpath along the river. Suddenly they were attacked by armed robbers, who wounded one of the guides, killed several of the horses, and stole the others. The guides, who still had their ponies, quickly saddled up and rode off, saying they were going to the lamasery to get help. They never returned.

Petrus and Susie were left alone with one horse and seven loads of baggage. They were lost and were, perhaps, under surveillance by the robbers. They buried some of their goods, left the saddles and tents under a cliff, and set off, carrying the barest necessities. Coming within sight of an encampment on the opposite side of the river, Petrus decided to swim across the river for help. As Susie watched, he entered the water, then turned, shouted something she could not understand, and walked upstream on her side of the river, around some rocks and out of sight. She never saw him again.

After waiting several terrifying days in hope of his return, Susie went on alone, trying to get help from people reluctant to do anything for her. Traveling as a woman alone was a frightful experience. Susie was never allowed to enter a tent, simply because she was a woman. She spent one night in the snow, wrapped in rugs and surrounded by savage Tibetan dogs. She spent four nights in a cowshed. Almost all her possessions were taken from her or given as pay for guides. One made crude suggestions to her. Others, she was certain, were capable of abandoning her or even killing her. She let them know she had a revolver and was capable of shooting it. She realized more than ever the low status of Tibetan women, for she was now sharing it.

She met a few friendly people and managed to get a passport from the abbot of Tashi Gomba which entitled her to official escort and transport. At the end she was reduced to walking, in thin-soled Tibetan boots, over rocky ground. She walked thirty miles one day, twenty another. Just two months after Petrus disappeared she reached Tatsienlu. She walked into the China Inland Mission house, where she was met by two missionaries, Mr. Amundsen and Mr. Moyes. Fully as dirty as any Tibetan woman and indistinguishable from one, she confounded them by announcing, "I am Dr. Rijnhart."

She remained at the hospitable mission house for six months, recuperating and making inquiries into the fate of her husband. It was finally determined that he had been murdered by robbers. Among those who investigated the case was her old lama teacher, Ishinima. The murderer was never found.

Though stricken by her tragic losses and suffering physically from her long trek, Susie went home still believing in the need and rightness of her mission. In Canada she lectured, wrote *With the Tibetans in Tent and Temple*, and tried to induce others to choose a missionary life. She returned to China in 1902 and began to work in Tatsienlu. Three years later she married the missionary, Mr. Moyes. In 1907, when she became ill, her husband took her back to Canada, where she died on February 7, 1908, leaving a three-week-old son.

One cannot help admiring the Canadian doctor for her courage, her knack of making friends, her willingness to tolerate the beliefs of others, and her strong faith in the goodness of her own particular God.

BIBLIOGRAPHY

Work by Susie Rijnhart

With the Tibetans in Tent and Temple: Narrative of Four Years' Residence on the Tibetan Border, and of a Journey into the Far Interior. Chicago: Revell, 1901; Edinburgh: Oliphant, 1901. Quotations in the text are from the 4th edition (Oliphant, 1904).

Works about Susie Rijnhart

Hacker, Carlotta. *The Indomitable Lady Doctors.* Toronto: Clarke, Irwin, 1974, pp. 97–123. The author cites student records and church archives among her sources.
Robson, Isabel S. *Two Lady Missionaries in Tibet.* London: Partridge, 1909, pp. 113–160. The two missionaries were Susie Rijnhart Moyes and Annie Royle Taylor.

ANNE NEWPORT ROYALL
1769–1854

Anne Newport Royall spent the years between 1817 and 1831 traveling about the United States, from the eastern seaboard to the Mississippi. She wrote twelve volumes of detailed description of the towns and cities she visited, spiced with pen pictures of almost every man and woman of note in the country. Her first biographer compiled an index of 229 places to which her journeys took her, located in twenty-four states, Canada, and the District of Columbia. At the age of sixty-two she settled in Washington, D.C., and began publishing newspapers, which she continued until her death at the age of eighty-five.

With a flair for investigation, a sharp pen, and a fearless disregard of political dangers, Mrs. Royall became a gadfly on Capitol Hill, a crusader for civil rights and freemasonry, among other causes. When she died, she was famous as the first successful newspaper woman in America, yet her body was buried in an unmarked grave, her books were allowed to crumble to dust, and for half a century she was vaguely remembered only as an eccentric troublemaker. Popular writers dwelled on one fictional anecdote and one notorious event in her life. The fiction is that she was so eager to get an interview with President John Quincy Adams that she caught him when swimming and sat on his clothes until he agreed to talk. The notorious event occurred in 1829, when she was the only American woman ever to be convicted of being a "common scold."

Since 1909, when Sarah Harvey Porter published a brief biography of Royall, much has been written about the nineteenth-century traveler, writer, and newswoman. Her ideas, many much more acceptable today than in her own time, have been weighed and judged sound. Her grave has been located and suitably marked. Still, the value of her early descriptions of cities, towns, colleges, and public figures has not been fully assessed. Royall as eccentric newswoman and political commentator has overshadowed Royall as traveler and writer of travel books.

In one of her books, Anne Royall refers to her mother's providing scores of *little histories* for me to read. . . . I knew they were stories, that is, falsehoods; and . . . it was long before I could believe that history was a narrative of facts; and had I not fortunately fell in with a person of learning, I should always have delved at *little histories*. (*Letters from Alabama*, pp. 178–79)

The person of learning was William Royall, a wealthy and cultivated man for whom Anne's illiterate mother worked as a housemaid. He it was who recognized in Anne, then eighteen, a bright mind, eager to learn. He gave her unlimited access to his library and talked to her about Thomas Paine, Voltaire, and the world of ideas. They fell in love and were married when she was twenty-eight and he was in his mid-fifties. Thus the uneducated backwoods girl was transformed into a woman capable of assessing the social and political trends of her day and writing about them in a spirited fashion.

Anne was born in Baltimore, Maryland, on June 11, 1769, the daughter of William and Mary Newport. At the age of three, she moved, with her parents and a younger sister, to western Pennsylvania. There the family lived an isolated frontier life in a cabin furnished with the minimum of necessities, in constant fear of Indians. When her father died, or disappeared (no record has been found), Mary Newport married a man named Butler. When he, too, died, the widow did housekeeping chores for others. Thus Anne and her mother came to Sweet Springs (now in West Virginia), and Mary Butler took a servant's position for William Royall, a gentleman farmer.

The Royall marriage seemed a happy one. The couple read together, entertained and were entertained, and were comfortable with each other. When Royall died in 1813, his will left most of his estate to Anne. His relatives sued, on the grounds that he had made the will under duress, and, after a long court battle, they won. At the age of fifty-four, Mrs. Royall was left with no property and no children. Since Royall was a veteran of the Revolutionary War, she sought a widow's pension.

During the years in which her property was in litigation, Anne lived and traveled in the South. She wrote lengthy letters to a young protegé and kept copies, with a vague idea of putting them together into a book. When the suit was decided in favor of Royall's relatives and her petition for a pension was being shuffled about in Washington, Anne began to travel, to write, and to sell her books as a way of making a living.

She went from city to city, taking subscriptions for her travel sketches. The funds were never sufficient, and she often had to beg, borrow, and sell bits of her clothing to pay her way. She found that Masons could almost always be counted on to give her a helping hand. Landlords often gave her free lodgings, and free passes were sometimes forthcoming for the steamer or coach. In other cases, she was brutally refused help; often she suffered from cold, hunger, weariness, and even physical attacks.

Disappointment haunted her. She first prepared a book on her southern trip, to be entitled "Letters from Alabama." It was turned down by the first publisher to whom she submitted it. She continued to advertise it as "a miscellaneous production embracing strictures on Manners, Customs, Dialects, Religion, Education, Literature, and Females, of the United States, with Biographical sketches of the most distinguished men of Alabama and Tennessee." Her "Sketches by a Traveller" was announced as comprising "physical and moral remarks on the Eastern and Western parts of the United States, including the history of the principal cities and towns from their origin." The price of the "Letters" was to be one dollar; of the "Sketches," a dollar and a half.

The advertisement, as published in an Albany, New York, paper, continued with a description of the writer:

> The author is a female of respectability . . . the widow of . . . an officer of the revolution. This Lady, by one of those unforseen misfortunes common in the human family, has fallen into distress, and appeals to the humane and benevolent citizens of this great and patriotic city for their patronage. These Works, we find, are patronized by the most distinguished men of the United States. (Albany *Daily Advertiser*, Feb. 12, 1825, quoted in James, *Anne Royall's U.S.A.*, pp. 138–39)

With a publisher willing to give her credit, Anne's *Sketches of History, Life and Manners in the United States, by a Traveller*, was published in 1826. The response to her book was not universally favorable. One paper noted that the printer had left her name off the title page, "unwilling probably to share in the disgrace which would fall harmlessly upon the head of a poor, crazy vagrant." It suggested that the wandering author should be committed to a Home of Correction (*Hampden Journal*, July 12, 1826, quoted in *Anne Royall's U.S.A.*, p. 162). Readers noted that she had attacked with a vitriolic pen those who had refused her help and had praised those who had been kind, an inducement to be generous when next she asked for assistance.

Everywhere she went, Anne visited notables. She paid a call on Emma Willard at her female seminary in Troy, New York, and she described the famous educator as being of "masculine size." In Hartford she visited the Asylum for the Deaf and Dumb and spent an evening with its founder, Thomas Hopkins Gallaudet, and his wife, a former student. She met Mrs. Lydia Sigourney, the Sweet Singer of Hartford.

In Boston she was surprised to find the Unitarians and Universalists "humane and benevolent." One of her main targets all through her writing was the established churches, whose members she called "blueskins." She saw the almshouse, the state prison, the Navy Yard, the Old South Meeting House, and Faneuil Hall, "sacred cradle of American Liberty." She met Dorothy Quincy Scott, widow of John Hancock, and complained that it was a reproach to the state to allow the widow of such a man to live so poorly.

In the town of Quincy she visited ex-president John Adams, then eighty-nine, toothless, dim of sight, and weak in the legs, but much interested in hearing

Anne's description of Alabama and of her friendship with his son, President John Quincy Adams. Another Adams—not related—was Hannah, a famous historian who had wormed her way into the Athenaeum, a Boston library and a masculine preserve. Lafayette happened to be in Boston at the time of Royall's visit to help lay the cornerstone of the Bunker Hill Monument. Anne called on the great man and was presented with a rose.

Royall described the people she met in graphic terms. A man who told her to "go back where she came from" was "tall and stout and wears powder in his hair. His eye has the color and fierceness of a rattlesnake; his complexion is a dirty yellow" (*Anne Royall's U.S.A.*, p. 153). Of Noah Webster, whose learning she had admired, she wrote "He eyed me with ineffable scorn and scarcely deigned to speak at all. I am sorry...I ever saw the man" (*Anne Royall's U.S.A.*, p. 154). But the geographer Jedediah Morse was "sociable and condescending." The country was growing so fast, she remarked, that "the old gentleman hardly gets one geography out before it is out of date, and he has to commence anew" (*Anne Royall's U.S.A.*, p. 154).

With copies of the books in a market basket, she set off for New York, after arranging to have some shipped to other towns. She would deliver them personally to all subscribers. Even though her friends in New York—James Gordon Bennett and Mordecai Noah—gave her good publicity, sales were few. She accused the ladies of New York of looking only at books "if they have any red on the outside" (*The Black Book*, I, p. 102). She returned to Boston, where sales were so good that the binders could not keep up with the demand. Criticism only increased the sales.

Anne had announced that *The Black Book* would deal with the "black deeds of evil doers." Her main targets were the blueskins and the anti-freemasons. A wave of intolerance against the Masons, with their elitist membership and secret rituals, was ascribed to churchgoers, who accused the brotherhood of conspiring against the government. Anne had received much help from Masons and defended them fiercely. This brought down on her head denunciations from the godly.

She went to Saratoga Springs, New York, a resort which she criticized for its high-priced hotels with bad cooking, society without charm, and indolence. She went on through New York state, a hotbed of anti-Masonry, and found herself characterized in newspapers as a bore and a mischief maker. She retaliated by describing Buffalo as "a flourishing village, with many fine brick buildings and two thousand inhabitants" who could not read (*The Black Book*, I, pp. 46–47).

She campaigned against the "missionary scheme"—foreign missions, home missions, Bible societies, and Sunday School societies, all pretending to spread the Gospel. She charged that the Reverend Ezra Stiles Ely, of Philadelphia, headed a Christian party which would support no candidate for office who did not acknowledge the Lord Jesus Christ for his Lord. She believed that the missionaries were planning the adoption of a national religion—a religion of bigotry, fanaticism, and hypocrisy. The revival of a church and state party, she claimed, was treason. As she traveled, she gathered up religious tracts and threw them away.

She was becoming famous and in some circles extremely unpopular. In Burlington, Vermont, while seeking subscriptions, she called on a Mr. Hecock, who received her rudely, pushed her out of the door, down a flight of steps, and into the snowy street. She lay there until passersby delivered her on a sled to a tavern and called a doctor. Her leg was broken. It took a long time to heal and interrupted her travels. Her second volume of *The Black Book* gave Hecock full credit for the accident, and his attorney staved off a suit for damages by giving Anne an unknown sum.

A group of religious leaders met and decided that Anne should be silenced. Since they were unable to find any crime to charge her with, except an old statute that had not been used for years, they indicted her as a "common scold," for which the penalty was to be ducked in water. The Navy Yard actually constructed a ducking stool. The trial was a farce, but the jury convicted her and fined her ten dollars. Anne addressed the jury. As reported by a newspaper, she said "This prosecution was but one branch of the general conspiracy of the blue and black-hearted Presbyterians, the priests and missionaries, against the freedom of speech and of the press." Secretary of State Eaton and two others offered to pay her fine, but two newspapermen got there first and paid it "for the honor of the press" (*Anne Royall's U.S.A.*, p. 261).

She settled, for a time, in Washington, D.C., where she lived with Sally Stack, her friend, assistant, and economic lifesaver, in a small house on the spot now occupied by the Library of Congress. It was known as the Bank House. She became a frequent visitor at the Capitol, welcomed by some lawmakers and shunned by others. All had profited from reading *The Black Book*'s characterizations of friends and enemies.

She shook up the residents of the capital city. She visited the several government departments: State, Treasury, Navy, and War. "The whole of these departments," she wrote, "wants overhauling" (*Anne Royall's U.S.A.*, p. 222). She complained that the trees in Capitol Square needed watering and manuring. She criticized the workers living in the city who drank their earnings, the politicians who did nothing to relieve distress, and the godly who spent their money on newspapers and churches instead of helping the poor. The congressional library was full of religious tracts and Sunday School books. The Capitol Hill neighborhood was full of "black coats."

Learning that the second volume of *The Black Book* did not sell well in Pennsylvania because there was nothing in it about the state, Royall devoted her next book to Pennsylvania. Then she went South again. The postal stage owners agreed to frank her through the lines, so she rode free. In New Orleans her benefactors included the Grand Master of the Masons and the manager of the St. Charles Theater. She visited the battle scenes of the American Revolution and the Battle of New Orleans. In St. Louis she found the Bible Belt residents hostile, and she actually feared for her life. She was snubbed by William Clark, hero of the Lewis and Clark expedition, then superintendent of Indian Affairs. He was "only the shadow of a man, reduced to a skeleton, feeble, superannuated, and fit for no business in the world" (*Mrs. Royall's Southern Tour*, III, 154–55).

She found a new danger to the republic, the renewal of the charter for the Second Bank of the United States. She referred to the bank as "the monster"; she thought it "a dangerous engine of oppression and corruption," the cause of an economic depression beginning to be noticeable in the country, especially in the west and southwest.

In 1830 the *Letters from Alabama* was published. The last and best of her books, though actually the first to be written, it covered her travels through Virginia, Kentucky, and Tennessee, as well as a lengthy stay in Huntsville, Alabama. The book consists of twelve letters, dated between November 1817 and June 1822, to "Matt," who is believed to be Matthew Duncan, a young lawyer. As a well-to-do widow, she had traveled in her own carriage and with a servant, staying, for the most part, in comfortable taverns or boarding houses. She described the countryside, recounted tales, many in dialect, that she thought would amuse her correspondent, and gave her opinions on civil rights, education, politics, and evangelism. Her remarks were more temperate than they were in her later writing, although she was always strong in her opinions.

She saw villages recently abandoned by Cherokees, who had been displaced by white settlers, and felt great sympathy for the Indians. "Why, these Indians have been like us!—could not be savage—cornfields—apple trees, and peach-trees. Fences like ours. . . . There could not exist a greater evidence of unbounded avarice and ambition which distinguished the Christian world" (*Letters from Alabama*, pp. 131–32).

She was disturbed by the general ignorance of the people. "If education was better attended to," she wrote, "it would greatly alleviate the evils of fraud and oppression." Ignorance "is to be our downfall. It strikes at the vitals of our liberty. It affects morally and politically, and the *few* are soon to rule the *many*, instead of the many ruling the few" (*Letters from Alabama*, p. 236).

About the same time that the *Letters from Alabama* was published, Anne began to fear physical attacks, and she was no longer vigorous enough to defend herself. Besides, she was weary of the constant travel. She decided to settle in Washington, D.C., and start a newspaper. *Paul Pry* began publication on December 3, 1831. She declared that "we shall expose all and every species of political evil, and religious fraud. . . . We shall advocate the liberty of the press, the liberty of speech, and the liberty of conscience." As publisher and reporter, she became a familiar sight in the Capitol—a poorly dressed old woman, bustling from office to office in search of news and gossip. In 1836 she dropped *Paul Pry* and started a new paper, *The Huntress*, which she continued until her death.

The papers did not make money. Anne was always in need. Her petition for a widow's pension was finally granted in 1848. The greedy heirs who had taken all of William Royall's money now took half of Anne's lump-sum payment of

$2400. When Anne died on October 1, 1854, she had thirty-one cents to her name and owed rent on Bank House. A funeral was held in Grace Episcopal Church—some of her old friends served as pallbearers—and she was buried in the Congressional Cemetery.

In 1914, after Mrs. Porter's biography of Anne Royall had aroused a spark of interest in the long-forgotten writer, a group of reporters placed a monument on her grave. The stone reads: "Anne Royall, Pioneer Woman Publicist, 1769–1854. 'I pray that the Union of these states may be eternal.' "

BIBLIOGRAPHY

Works by Anne Royall

Sketches of History, Life and Manners in the United States, by a Traveller. New Haven, Conn.: the author, 1826.

The Black Book: or, A Continuation of Travels in the United States. 3 vols. Washington, D.C.: the author, 1828–1829.

Mrs. Royall's Pennsylvania: or, Travels Continued in the United States. 2 vols. Washington, D.C.: the author, 1829.

Mrs. Royall's Southern Tour: or, Second Series of Black Book. 3 vols. Washington, D.C.: the author, 1830–1831.

Letters from Alabama on Various Subjects: To Which Is Added, an Appendix Containing Remarks on Sundry Members of the 20th and 21st Congress. Washington, D.C.: the author, 1830. A new edition, which omits the appendix, has been edited with a biographical introduction by Lucille Griffith. University, Ala.: University of Alabama Press, 1969. Quotations in the text are from the 1969 edition.

Works about Anne Royall

Blankenhorn, Heber. "The Grandma of the Muckrakers." *American Mercury* 12 (Sept. 1927): 87–93.

Dexter, Elizabeth. *Career Women of America, 1776–1840.* Francetown, N.H.: M. Jones, 1950, pp. 110–15.

Dictionary of American Biography. New York: Scribner, 1927–date, vol. 16 (1935): 204–5.

Douglas, Emily. *Remember the Ladies.* New York: Putnam, 1966, pp. 53–57.

Helfer, Harold. "Potomac Newshen," *American Mercury* 90 (Apr. 1960): 139–43.

Jackson, George S. *Uncommon Scold: The Story of Anne Royall.* Boston: B. Humphries, 1937.

James, Bessie Rowland. *Anne Royall's U.S.A.* New Brunswick, N.J.: Rutgers University, 1972.

Liberty's Women. Edited by Robert McHenry. Springfield, Mass.: Merriam, 1980.

Notable American Women, 1607–1950. Edited by Edward T. James and others. Cambridge, Mass.: Harvard University Press, 1971.

Porter, Sarah Harvey. *The Life and Times of Anne Royall.* Cedar Rapids, Iowa: Torch Press Book Shop, 1909.

Ross, Ishbell. *Ladies of the Press*. New York: Harper, 1936, pp. 27–30.

Somerlott, Robert. "Anne Royall: 'Common Scold.' " *MS Magazine* 2 (Mar. 1974): 14, 16, 18.

Wallace, Irving. *The Square Pegs*. New York: Knopf, 1957, pp. 243–66.

Whitton, Mary. *These Were the Women, U.S.A. 1776–1860*. New York: Hastings, 1954, pp. 60–64, 66.

Woodward, Helen Beal. *The Bold Women*. New York: Farrar, Straus & Young, 1953, pp. 8–23.

Wright, Richardson. *Forgotten Ladies*. Philadelphia: Lippincott, 1928, pp. 156–86.

An obituary appeared in the Washington *Evening Star*, on Oct. 2, 1854.

GRACE GALLATIN
THOMPSON SETON
1872–1959

Grace Gallatin Thompson Seton began foreign travel in the 1920s, visiting many countries of the Orient to study the status of women in different cultures. She accompanied the Field Museum Expedition to Brazil in 1926 and afterward went alone into the interior of Paraguay, Bolivia, and Peru, studying the Incan and pre-Columbian civilizations. She lectured on her travels and produced a number of prize-winning books. She was a charter member of the Society of Woman Geographers.

Before she became a lone traveler, she worked for over twenty-five years with her husband, the naturalist Ernest Thompson Seton. She had studied book design, and she was responsible for the makeup, design, and proofreading of his books. With him, she founded, in 1910, the Girl Pioneers, soon renamed the Camp Fire Girls. Her first books of travel were two charming accounts of their camping trips in the American West and Norway.

Grace was a leader of the woman suffrage movement in the United States. She was active in the National Council of Women and in the National League of American Pen Women. Between 1928 and 1937, she attended four Pacific conferences for women. She gave her services to her country during both world wars and was decorated for relief work in France. She was honored by numerous organizations in the fields of conservation, public service, writing, and geography. In addition, she was a photographer, song writer, and chemical researcher.

As chair of Letters and Archives of the National Council of Women, Grace assembled a collection of books by women, representing thirty-seven countries in five continents. The remarkable collection, known as Biblioteca Femina, was presented to the library of Northwestern University. Seton, known and respected for wide interests and diverse accomplishments, is remembered also as a traveler interested in the advancement of women all over the world.

Grace Gallatin was born in Sacramento, California, on January 28, 1872. Her father, Albert Gallatin, was a pioneer in the development of hydroelectric power.

Five years after Grace's birth, she moved with her father, her mother, Clemenzie ("Nemie") Rhodes Gallatin, and two older siblings into a newly built Victorian residence in Sacramento. The house, later home to Lincoln Steffens, was purchased by the State of California in 1903 as its governor's residence. Used as such until 1967, it is now a California State Landmark.

Grace and her mother left the mansion in 1881, when divorce separated her parents. She was the only one of the Gallatin children whose custody Nemie gained. They went to New York, where Grace attended Packer Collegiate Institute. She began writing newspaper stories when she was sixteen, from Paris, France. It was here that she met Ernest Thompson Seton (originally Ernest Seton Thompson), to whom she was married in 1896. The two were of quite different backgrounds and interests. His autobiography speaks of her as in her element "among receptions and pink teas . . . hobnobbing with artists and writers" in New York. "The girl had very strong views on woman's rights; and yet showed plainly her French ancestry; for dress, society, and city life were most attractive to her" (E. T. Seton, *Trail of an Artist-Naturalist*, pp. 343–44, 349). Seton, a lover of the outdoors, soon introduced his bride to camping. "As a camper," he wrote, "she was a great success, never grumbled at hardship . . . a dead shot . . . met all kinds of danger with unflinching nerve; was always calm and clear-headed" (*Trail of an Artist-Naturalist*, p. 349).

Her humorous accounts of the camping trips were published as *A Woman Tenderfoot* (1900) and *Nimrod's Wife* (1907). In the latter, she appealed to city dwellers to "throw off your fetters for awhile, your prejudice, your narrow-mindedness, all the petty things that make your daily trappings and . . . come with me back to the woods, pry open your blind eyes and grow as the flowers grow" (*Nimrod's Wife*, pp. 16–17). During her years with Seton, she herself grew in self-confidence and independence. During World War I, she raised money to buy, equip, and operate six Ford trucks for transport service between Paris and the front, and for two years she directed the Women's Motor Unit of La Bienêtre du Blessé. For this she was decorated by the French government. She and Ernest saw little of each other, and after the war she began the foreign travels that set them even farther apart. Their only daughter, Ann, was a binding link, but after she grew up and was married, Grace and Ernest were divorced.

Grace went to Egypt in 1921. She had been there once before, but this time she wanted to see the country less as a traveler and more as an observer "to know people." The New Woman had reached Egypt as early as 1911 when a woman's group organized La Femme Nouvelle. In 1919 women who had suffered in the struggle to win their country's independence from England formed a "Ladies' Delegation for the Independence of Egypt," usually called the "Ladies' Wafd." The movement began with the upper, or pasha, class and spread to the bourgeoisie and even to the *fellaheen*, or peasants. The leaders were the wives, daughters, and sweethearts of militants who had been banished by the British as agitators. One was Madame Zaghlul Pasha, wife of Saad Zaghlul Pasha. Grace spent much of her time with the women and applauded their efforts to throw off the yoke of foreign rule. She also went caravaning into the desert, traveling with a friend called only "the poet" and having adventures and mystical experiences. Her account, *A Woman Tenderfoot in Egypt*, was published in 1923. It was later selected by the Century of Progress exposition in Chicago as one of the best one hundred books by American women in the preceding century.

Grace went next to China with a similar purpose: "to throw a little light on what is happening there, especially upon the 'dark places' of the 'woman's quarters' of New China, where the white light of publicity has not yet beaten" (*Chinese Lanterns*, p. ix). As a foreign writer, she managed to get interviews with political leaders and to speak to many progressive women. She speaks of the "gracious hospitality, . . . sympathetic and co-operative kindliness and courtesy extended to me, a woman travelling alone" (*Chinese Lanterns*, p. ix). Her next trip was to India, about which she wrote in *"Yes, Lady Saheb": A Woman's Adventurings with Mysterious India*. Here she "thrilled to the marvelous work of the British Raj" while she "burned with rebellion at some of its results" (*"Yes, Lady Saheb,"* p. xvii). She appreciated the high resolve of both British and Indian leaders in working out the many problems of that troubled country, but she eschewed political comment to write of the "continuous scroll of interest and delight" in the land and its people.

Again, she was particularly interested in the life of the women.

> The marriage customs of the East being as they are—arranged for by the parents, consummated at a very early age, the *purdah* and illiteracy of the wife, mean that each lives a life apart from the other. The man holds his home sacred and expects to be master of it. . . . The active part of his life is passed among men, business associates, friends. To the friends he looks for his stimulation and amusements.
>
> The woman's circle of existence is very limited. The rigid grip of custom holds her as in a vise. The walls of her home and, if she be rich, her gardens, are her horizon. Her mind is not fed by books, nor do enlarging thoughts from others send her intellect soaring. (*"Yes, Lady Saheb,"* p. 22)

The upper-class Indian man, she observed, was very highly educated, "while the vast majority of the mothers of the race still live in subjection, seclusion, and ignorance" (*"Yes, Lady Saheb,"* p. 35).

Grace did not spend all of her time in India studying the position of women or the political situation, for she was intent on doing some big-game hunting. She had hunted deer, bear, and moose in the American Rockies, and she was a good shot. She went to the Sivoke Forest, at the foot of the Himalayas, on a tiger hunt, which was unsuccessful. She visited monuments, ancient palaces, and jungles. Before she left, she saw some encouraging signs of progress among the women: a Women's Indian Association, started in Madras in 1917; a well-edited women's magazine, published partly in English and partly Tamil and Telugu; women slowly coming into the professions of teaching, medicine, and law; a woman member of the Senate Council, representing Madras University;

and the first woman publisher, educated at Cambridge University, who published a literary magazine.

"Yes, Lady Saheb," which completed her trilogy of travel in Oriental countries, was selected in 1926 by the League of American Pen Women as the best book of the year.

Seton was next offered an opportunity to join a scientific expedition to South America. The scientists included a herpetologist, a mammalogist, an ornithologist, and a geologist. Grace was to be the historian of the journey. One other woman went along; dubbed by Grace "Editha Rockerford," she financed the expedition for the Field Museum. In their six weeks spent in Rio de Janeiro, Saõ Paulo, and Mato Grosso, they took 350 birds, representing 150 species, and over a thousand specimens of reptiles, fish, and mammals. Seton catalogued, labelled, and chronicled the specimens. The expedition took approximately three thousand feet of motion picture film and many still photographs.

"In addition to these cold, hard facts," wrote Grace, "six persons were living a brilliant pattern of emotional reactions" (*Magic Waters*, p. 131). She did not get along with "Editha Rockerford" at all, and there was tension among the other members of the party. At Corumbá, Brazil, by prearrangement, Seton left the rest of the expedition to cross to the west coast alone, for to be in South America and not visit the land of the Inca was to her unthinkable. She went by herself down the Paraguay and Paraná rivers, into the Andes, to Bolivia and Peru. She stopped to hunt tigers in the jungle, and though she does not claim to have shot a tiger, she did return with a beautiful orange-spotted jaguar skin for her cottage on Long Island Sound.

In Santiago she attended the First International Congress of Women in Chile. "There I found the real women with the hoe of progress in Chile. Their sturdy weeding of obsolete conventions and planting of new ideas is evidenced in the formation of a Woman's Suffrage Party" (*Magic Waters*, p. 211). She met Gabriela Mistral, one of the best-known writers of South America. She visited the fabled city of Cuzco with its Incan remains. The entire South American trip was one of contrasts. One day, she might be entertained in the luxurious home of an official; the next, riding a train with few comforts and little food. But "in spite of tropical fever, garrapatas, siroche and hurricane, it was doubly, trebly worth while" (*Magic Waters*, p. 281).

Her next trip was again to the Orient. Wanting a guide to Angkor, she was told about a French gentleman, a baron, who was reliable except that he was an opium addict! Nevertheless, she hired him, and they journeyed together through Vietnam and Cambodia with some exciting adventures, and they parted friends. She wished to visit the Moi tribe, who used poison arrows, ate raw flesh, and had a matriarchal society. To cut red tape, she announced that her purpose was to hunt tigers, but to the baron she told her real reason. She wanted to see, firsthand, women who held the purse strings under the survival of a matriarchal system as old as primitive civilization. Primogeniture followed the eldest daughter instead of the eldest son. She hoped to find women enjoying a social status which "for all our votes for women, the American and European does not have" (*Poison Arrows*, p. 41).

But her preconceived idea of women under a matriarchal system had to be modified. "Although the women own the property and the children and are custodians of the tribal authority, they do not 'wear the pants' " (*Poison Arrows*, p. 67). The system was primarily communal; both sexes shared in the life and obligations of the household and the village. Men provided food, shelter, and protection from enemies. The authority of the Moi woman, indeed, seemed less than that of the Chinese Mother of the Household. But at least there was no enslaving control of one class over another.

Poison Arrows, published in 1938, was Grace Seton's last travel book. She later published two books of songs. She had long had an interest in mysticism and Eastern religions, an interest which grew stronger in her later years. She lived with her only daughter, the novelist Anya Seton, in Connecticut and Florida. She died on March 19, 1959, in Palm Beach, Florida.

BIBLIOGRAPHY

Works by Grace Seton

A Woman Tenderfoot. New York: Doubleday, 1900; Toronto: Marong, 1900.
Nimrod's Wife. New York: Doubleday, 1907; London: Constable, 1907.
"Women Leaders of Modern Egypt." *Review of Reviews* 66 (Oct. 1922): 380–86.
"New Woman in Egypt." *Century* 105 (Jan. 1923): 402–9.
"Other Woman in Egypt." *Century* 105 (Feb. 1923): 621–28.
"Overlord of Four Hundred Millions." *Outlook* 134 (June 6, 1923): 128–32.
"Great Leader of China As Seen through the Eyes of Mrs. Sun Yat-sen." *Review of Reviews* 67 (June 1923): 600–34.
"Caravaning in the Libyan Desert." *Travel* 41 (Aug. 1923): 26–30.
A Woman Tenderfoot in Egypt. New York: Dodd, Mead, 1923; London: Lane, 1923.
Chinese Lanterns. New York: Dodd, Mead, 1924; London: Lane, 1924.
"Modern Plum Blossom." *Woman Citizen* n.s. 9 (Feb. 7, 1925): 15.
"Gandhi, the Great Man of India Today." *Review of Reviews* 71 (Feb. 1925): 171–76.
"Yes, Lady Saheb": A Woman's Adventurings with Mysterious India. New York: Harper, 1925; London: Hodder & Stoughton, 1925.
Log of the "Look See": A Half-Year in the Wilds of Matto Grosso and the Paraguayan Forest; over the Andes to Peru. London: Hurst & Blackett, 1932. Also published as *Magic Waters: Through the Wilds of the Matto Grosso and Beyond; Autobiographical Log of the "Look-See."* New York: Dutton, 1933. Quotations in the text are from the 1933 edition.
Poison Arrows: Strange Journey with an Opium Dreamer; Annam, Cambodia, Siam, and the Lotos Isle of Bali. London: J. Gifford, 1938; New York: House of Field, 1940.

Works about Grace Seton

Cameron, Mabel Ward. *Biographical Cyclopaedia of American Women*. New York: Halvord, 1924.

Dictionary of American Biography. New York: Scribner, 1927-date, supplement 6 (1980): 575–76.

National Cyclopedia of American Biography. New York: J. T. White, 1888-date, vol. 47: 80–81, and current vol. E (1938): 340–41.

Notable American Women: The Modern Period. Edited by Barbara Sicherman and others. Cambridge, Mass.: Harvard University Press, 1980.

Seton, Ernest Thompson. *Trail of an Artist-Naturalist: The Autobiography of Ernest Thompson Seton.* New York: Scribner, 1940.

Obituaries appeared in the *New York Times* and the *Sacramento Bee*, on Mar. 20, 1959.

Manuscript materials on Seton's life and work are located in the Sophia Smith Collection at Smith College, Northhampton, Mass.; the Schlesinger Library at Radcliffe College, Cambridge, Mass.; and in the possession of her daughter, Anya Seton Chase.

MAY FRENCH SHELDON
1847–1936

May French Sheldon was an American who led an expedition into East Africa in 1891. Accompanied by native porters, guides, and servants, she traveled from Mombasa to Kilimanjaro. She won the devotion of her men, who called her Bébé Bwana (Swahili for Lady Boss), and she made friends among the tribes she met along the way. She was dissuaded from entering the territory of the dreaded Masai only by the fears of her porters.

A few other Europeans had preceded her into the country; the British and Germans had just divided Mombasa territory into two regions and were squabbling over the borders of what are now Kenya and Tanzania. The Europeans planned to induce white settlers to establish plantations there. The natives were to be "subdued" and their lands taken over. Sheldon was not so enlightened as to object to the idea in general, but she did feel that military expeditions against the tribesmen and the harsh methods generally employed by would-be colonizers were "unnecessary, atrocious, and beyond the pale of humanity" (*Sultan to Sultan*, Foreword). Her visit to Africa was undertaken to prove that Europeans who approached the Africans in a friendly way would meet with acceptance.

When she returned home, she wrote about her expedition in *Sultan to Sultan*, and lectured about it in England and America. She visited the Belgian Congo in 1903 and defended the Belgians' treatment of the Africans. She was one of the first group of women to be admitted as fellows of the Royal Geographical Society in 1892.

She was a woman of deep conviction and enormous self-confidence. Although some of her travel arrangements might seem lavish and eccentric, her purpose was sincerely humane, and she came close to giving her life to it.

May French was born in Beaver, a community near Pittsburgh, Pennsylvania, on May 10, 1847. Her father, Colonel Joseph French, was an engineer, and her mother, Elizabeth Poorman French, a physician. May (christened Mary) married Eli Lemon Sheldon in 1876. He was an American banker and publisher in London, where May herself owned a publishing house, Saxon & Company. In

1890 Henry Morton Stanley, whom she knew well, had returned to England after his years of African exploration. His accounts were stirring the imaginations of Londoners. Sheldon was among his most enthusiastic admirers and when she, herself, was inspired to explore Africa, she sought his advice, though she did not follow it. He warned her not to go beyond the Free Methodist station near Mombasa.

From the time she decided to mount an expedition, she met with opposition. Friends, relatives, and advisors tried everything to dissuade her from such a foolish venture—all, that is, except her husband. Perhaps he had been her husband long enough to know that she could not be dissuaded once she had set her heart on anything and that she was eminently capable of carrying out any plan.

At Mombasa the British authorities scoffed at her intention to enter East Africa; they refused to assist her in any way and told her that no porters were to be had. The Imperial British East Africa Company, a newly formed concession to develop trade in the interior, said that the jungle was no place for a lady. No doubt the company would also have discouraged men attempting to explore the area, for there were real dangers and hardships, and the few British and German posts established in the region were unable to cope with small expeditions. Africans did not welcome outsiders. There were dangerous snakes and pests, wild animals, rough trails, poisoned traps set for game, and always the chance of illness or injury far from medical aid. Porters might steal stores, mutiny, or desert, leaving the expedition stranded and defenseless.

Cooly ignoring the warnings, Sheldon returned to Zanzibar in search of porters, but her reputation of being a madwoman had preceded her, and she found it impossible to recruit any porters until she appealed directly to the Sultan of Zanzibar. He not only got her porters but gave her a letter commanding all she met to receive her "with absolute regard and attention."

With 103 Zanzibari porters, headmen, guides, and personal servants, she returned to Mombasa to unpack her many boxes and crates of equipment and to repack loads for the porters. After the first week, it would be a foot safari, over narrow jungle trails, and everything needed for a migratory community had to be carried. Food for herself and for the native men and women for the first eight days was to be taken; later, they expected to barter for provisions. Camping equipment, goods for barter and gifts, weapons, medical supplies, utensils, water, photographic apparatus, tools, and livestock were loaded into wagons drawn by Indian bullocks and made into packs for the carriers.

Among her many effects was a palanquin, especially built to her specifications: a wickerwork basket, large enough to sleep in, its roof circling overhead, with handles at the sides for lifting and carrying. In this, she slept at night and rode when weary, but for the most part she walked, dressed in a neatly tailored suit and wearing a variety of shade hats. She carried an alpine staff and waved a banner inscribed *Noli me tangere*. The Africans did not understand Latin, but they acknowledged the staff as a badge of authority.

Sheldon had brought with her an elaborate court dress made of silk tissue, with a train and encrusted with stage jewels, to wear when she had an audience with a chief. One of her aims was "to meet the men of tribal importance in their own sultanates, as a woman of breeding should meet the highest officials in any land, under any circumstances, and be civil and polite for favors granted" ("An African Expedition," p. 132).

Among her supplies were several thousand finger rings, her name engraved on each one, to be given as presents. They served as calling cards and proved to be much sought after. She had toys for children—paint boxes, tops, balls, kites, dolls, picture books, and fireworks—and a variety of notions, trinkets, and tools to be used for barter and to purchase the right of way from tribes as needed.

Seeing that the mad American was bound to attempt her journey, the East Africa Company withdrew its opposition, and one of the officers drew up a plan for defense, covering such points as the choice of campsites, posting of sentries, protection of stores, organization of the column, and provision of simple medical supplies. He added a comment Sheldon must have especially appreciated: "You as a woman possess many points that no man would have in dealing with Africans. You therefore should find an *entree* easy anywhere" (*Sultan to Sultan*, p. 171). As she knew some Swahili, he advised her to conduct any palaver herself, without trusting overmuch to interpreters.

Her crew assembled, the Lady Boss had a moment of doubt. "I looked with amazement over all these strange black and every shade of brown faces, with much brutality imprinted thereupon, and marvelled if I should always be able to control them and make them subservient to my commands" (*Sultan to Sultan*, p. 105). But she did not falter for long. Several of the men, she found, had been with great explorers and big-game hunters in the area she intended to pass through. To the headman, Nepara Hamidi Bin Ali, she communicated every morning what she wished to accomplish that day, and it was up to him to see that it was done.

The Lady Boss marched at the head of the caravan; Hamidi brought up the rear. Fleet runners carried messages back and forth. At one point a crisis occurred when Hamidi was far in the rear, and the men, thinking that Bébé Bwana did not know the way, sat down and refused to go farther. "Then or never I realized," she wrote, "I must demonstrate to these mutinous, half-savage men that I would be obeyed, and that discipline should be enforced at any cost" (*Sultan to Sultan*, p. 173). Aiming at a flying vulture, she brought it down, demonstrating that she was a sure shot, and then she offered to shoot any man who refused to take up his load.

The porters went barefoot or wore sandals, were half clothed, carried only a stretch of cloth for shelter at night (worn as a turban during the day), and existed on little more than a cup of rice a day. Each carried on his head from fifty-six to sixty pounds. Several women porters were in the group. Added to the caravan but not in her employ, Sheldon was surprised to find a number of slaves of her porters, who were themselves slaves hired out by their masters.

In the beginning Bébé Bwana had the idea that porters could be governed by kindness and moral suasion, but actual experience modified her views. Some she found reckless creatures, with ungovernable passions, at times endangering the whole caravan by their actions, and she had to order them disciplined. In time they accepted her authority and before the trip was over they were to a man devoted. Though she felt it necessary to be stern, she was good to the men, treated them fairly, and cared for them. She had been trained in medicine, and she vaccinated each man and woman against smallpox. She gave them carbolized grease for sore feet. Any who fell ill were carried in hammocks. Most expeditions, she learned, simply abandoned those who fell sick along the trail; one ill and starving man left behind by a previous traveler was found on the road and taken to a place of refuge.

The Lady Boss took excellent care of herself, too. She found that walking conduced to her well-being. All the water she drank was first boiled and filtered. She took daily hot baths and had one of the women massage her. Somewhere along the trail she got a thorn in her eye, which became exceedingly inflamed and painful and had to be bandaged. It was thus when she first saw Kilimanjaro, the magnificent ice-capped peak. "With one eye I saw more than I can ever hope to recount of the grandeur of Kilimanjaro" (*Sultan to Sultan*, p. 189).

There was much to enjoy along the way. It was early spring, bright with sunshine between showers. Bébé Bwana recognized many familiar plants— clematis, poppies, magnolia, rhododendrons, narcissus, buttercups, asters, gladiolus, geraniums, heliotrope, and maidenhair ferns. Beautifully colored butterflies and flocks of tiny yellow birds delighted her. Of course there were annoyances—mosquitoes and stinging flies, jiggers, grass ticks; thorns, nettles, and sharp grasses; sticky clay soil; and destructive white ants. It was hot in the daytime, cold at night. She saw, or heard, or was told about lions, jackals, hyenas, warthogs, rhinos, and buffalo. One of the men, straying off the path, was killed by a lion; it was the only fatality of the expedition. One night while she was sleeping a fifteen-foot python coiled itself around her palanquin. "I am not ashamed to confess it was the supreme fear of my life, and almost paralyzed me" (*Sultan to Sultan*, p. 311).

The caravan visited thirty-five different tribes. Those near the coast were wanderers; living on barter, they were dirty and degraded. The Wa-Duruma she thought wretched and ill favored; they suffered so much from famine that they often sold themselves into bondage; and, once enslaved, they refused to be liberated. At Taveta Bébé Bwana found that the gates, formed by trees trained to enclose the area, were too small to admit the palanquin, but her fame as a white queen had preceded her, and the tribe was persuaded to open a way for them. Here they found a flourishing community, including an English trading post and great plantations of bananas, corn, sugar cane, and tobacco. Honey and other foods were brewed and fermented, and Sheldon noted that men and women "are during harvest times in a perpetual state of jollification" (*Sultan to Sultan*, p. 220).

A Taveta woman introduced her to many ceremonies never before seen by whites, such as a moon dance of the men and a funeral ceremony. On her part, the white queen entertained the children. Some of the toys were successful; others were not. She found little difficulty communicating with the natives because of their very significant gestures. A pantomimist, she felt, would be able to get along with them famously. Remembering a childhood trick, she cut an orange skin into points to imitate teeth, and she put it into her mouth. This delighted the tribesmen, and, when she gave the orange to a chief, he plucked out one of his own teeth and presented it to her, indicating in sign language that if she wore it around her neck she would never be hungry.

In spite of some odd habits—a fondness for rotten eggs, a custom of spitting instead of kissing, and the use of rancid butter, or ghee—Bébé Bwana found the natives friendly and happy. "They live to enjoy, and enjoy to live, and are as idyllic in their native ways as any people I ever encountered" (*Sultan to Sultan*, p. 259).

Leaving most of her party at Taveta, Sheldon went to visit Lake Chala, an almost circular lake located in the crater of an old volcano, accompanied by the resident English officer and a few porters. The descent to the surface of the lake was so precipitous that it had rarely been attempted. Two sections of an old copper pontoon left behind by a previous visitor were the only things floatable to be found, and they served as a boat. She made the trip down to the water by hanging to branches and crawling through tangled vines. Porters managed to carry the pontoon down, but none would venture on the makeshift craft. Finally, the Englishman, the interpreter, Sheldon, and one other perched themselves on an old door laid across the pontoon and pushed off, with guns and cameras.

She made several voyages on the lake, flying an American flag and putting up markers with her name and the date at various points along the shore. In her own quaint style, she wrote:

Everything was most eldritch and immense. . . . The hours spent upon this lake at different times held me in a thraldom of wonder. There was little said, very much thought, and imagination thrilled my brain with the ineffable pleasure which I had craved and sought for years, of being the first to visit a place undefiled by the presence of man before. (*Sultan to Sultan*, p. 270)

Though the Rombos were said to be ferocious, Bébé Bwana went to their village; she found the people to be "most civil," though in an absolute state of nudity. "They were clothed with *toga virilis*, a robe of manhood unfashioned by any mode of civilization, but inborn" (*Sultan to Sultan*, p. 278).

Less than six weeks after Sheldon left Africa, she records, Dr. Carl Peters, the German explorer, in order to pass through this territory, "felt obliged to turn his guns on these Rombos, . . . and kill a hundred and twenty of them before breakfast one morning" (*Sultan to Sultan*, p. 282).

The caravan visited Kimangelia, 4,700 feet high on the slope of Kilimanjaro, the frontier of Masailand, with a guide from Taveta. (Sheldon found it useful to recruit guides from the various tribes, with a shrewd intent to make hostages of them in case any tribe attacked the caravan. By the end of the safari, the force had increased by forty.) She found the sultan of Kimangelia paralyzed, "a victim to his own debaucheries," but he placed at her disposal his palaver ground. Here natives came from the mountain villages to see the white lady and invite her to visit them, in spite of the fact that there were no roads.

At Marunga the expedition was met by two or three thousand tribesmen and women and Sultan Mireali:

> . . . tall and distinguished, who appeared a perfect guy, tricked out in a pair of German military trousers, with side stripes, a white knitted shirt with a brilliant pin on the bosom, a celluloid high collar, a cravat of the most flaming color, a striped woollen Scotch shooting-coat, a flamboyant pocket-handkerchief, and a pair of Russia-leather shoes, exposing blue silk clocked socks. His fine head was disfigured by wearing a black silk pot hat, which was canted backwards, bonnet fashion, by the long porcupine quill ear ornaments thrust through the rims of his ears. He carried an English walking-stick with a huge silver knob, and held in his hands a pair of kid gloves. This clown then was Mireali, conceded to be the handsomest native man in East Africa, the most noble and most majestic sultan if not the most powerful. (*Sultan to Sultan*, pp. 356–57)

The closer the party came to her objective, the Masai territory, the greater grew the anxiety of her crew. The Masai warriors were the terror of every tribe, "the heavy tragedians of Africa, full of theatrical display in manner and personal get up." Early in the journey, they had met a small group of Masai, trading ghee and calabashes. Sheldon's description of the encounter was dramatic:

> A warrior, hideously bedecked in his war paint and war toggery . . . came rushing up to me brandishing his spear violently, then uplifted it as though he aimed to cleave me in two, planted it into the ground before me, yelled in a deafening tone as he bounded high in the air, "Wow! wow! wow!" Quick as a flash, I reached behind me and seized my gun, rushed forward with it, pointing the muzzle towards him and in turn yelled, "wow! wow! wow!" discharging it in the air. (*Sultan to Sultan*, pp. 330–31)

The warrior quickly vanished and Sheldon plucked his spear from the ground as a memento. But the reaction of her porters to these seemingly "fine, fearless children" made her wonder about the wisdom of visiting Masailand. Hamidi at first refused to cross the Masai frontiers, then said he would go although it meant certain death. Faced with the wholesale threat of mutiny among the carriers and guides and touched by Hamidi's offer to sacrifice himself, she reluctantly gave up the idea. The next thrown spear might really "cleave her in two."

Everywhere, Sheldon was interested in the Africans' decorations, food, clothing, medical practices, customs, and religion. In Chaga land she admired the skill of the craftsmen in metal work and acquired some specimens to take home with her. She collected bracelets, rings, bits of clothing, weapons, and other artifacts in exchange for the gifts she had brought with her. The large stage jewels covering her court gown and her own bracelets, necklets, rings, and shoe buckles were one by one bestowed upon the natives.

Disaster struck on the homeward journey when the expedition was near Pangani. Bébé Bwana was riding in her palanquin when the porters, crossing a bridge of poles, slipped; men, palanquin, and rider dropped to the stream twenty feet below. Other frightened men scrambled down the steep banks, extricated her from the tangled pillows and awnings, and carried her up the rocky incline, only to drop her again, causing injury to her spine. Paralyzed and delirious, she was carefully laid in a hammock and carried along the trail. By the time the party had reached the next post, a German one, she was more or less rational. Wishing to get out to a ship and home as soon as possible, she let it be thought that she was merely feverish; she refused medical help and ordered the caravan to proceed by the shortest route. Her bearers proved "faithful, uncomplaining, chivalrous, and marvels of patience, endurance, and consistent marching day after day" ("An African Expedition," p. 132).

At Mombasa, she paid off the porters and boarded a ship for home, where she subsequently recovered. In spite of her sufferings, she felt repaid tenfold by the friendship of the Africans.

Her book, *Sultan to Sultan*, published in London and in Boston in 1892, was illustrated with her photographs and the charming drawings of a friend. The book was reviewed at some length by the *New York Times* on December 12, 1892; the reviewer called her journey "one of the most remarkable performances in recent travel and exploration." Drawing somewhat on imagination, he described the court dress, with jeweled sword and dagger at the belt: "Who but an American woman would have conceived the idea of making a Worth gown help her win her way into the interior of Africa?" The reviewer added that Sheldon had financed the expedition at a cost of fifty thousand dollars and remarked that she was fortunately the wife of a banker.

Eli Lemon Sheldon died while his wife was writing *Sultan to Sultan*. She dedicated the book to him:

> to whom I owe all I have accomplished. My inspiration, my critic, my advocate, my refuge, my anchor, my sympathizer, my friend, my comrade, my husband. Honorable, gifted, noble, unselfish, gentle man, beloved by all, whose sudden demise has laid upon me a tragic burden of sorrow during the completion of this volume.

She was in America on a lecture tour when she learned of his death. In 1893 she appeared in Chicago to speak to the Congress of Women at the World's Columbian Exposition. Her lecture, "An African Expedition," was published in the edited papers of the congress, and she was awarded two medals, one for her exhibits of African artifacts and another for her palanquin and camping equipment.

At the outbreak of World War I, she gave lectures to raise funds for the Belgian Red Cross. For her fund-raising on behalf of the Red Cross and for her work in the Congo she was given in 1921 the honor of the Chevalier de l'Ordre de la Couronne of Belgium. During the postwar years she traveled and lectured. She was in San Francisco in 1924, where she lectured many times, surprising her audience with her youthfulness. The *San Francisco Chronicle* on February 20, 1924, marveled that at age seventy-eight she was "spry, straight as a young sapling, gay, entertaining, the personification of youth." A portrait shows her as round faced, with deep-set eyes.

In 1936, approaching the age of ninety, Sheldon died in London. She was the last of her family; her only sister, Belle French Patterson Lathrop, a Boston physician, had died in 1922.

One of the first European observers to describe Africans and African culture in a sympathetic and understanding way, May Sheldon agreed with the Victorian view that the wild tribes must be Christianized, civilized, and brought into the world of trade and progress. She advised colonizers of Africa to establish manual training stations and medical posts. "Africa is no place," she said, "for impractical zealots of any kind" ("An African Expedition," p. 134).

BIBLIOGRAPHY

Works by May French Sheldon

Sultan to Sultan: Adventures among the Masai and Other Tribes of East Africa. By M. French-Sheldon, Bebe Bwana. London: Saxon, 1892; Boston: Arena, 1892. Also published as *Adventures in East Africa; or, Sultan to Sultan: The Narrative of a Woman's Adventures among the Masai and Other Tribes of East Africa.* Boston: D. Estes, n.d.

"An African Expedition." In *The Congress of Women, Held in the Woman's Building, World's Columbian Exposition, Chicago, U.S.A., 1893.* Edited by Mary Cavanaugh Eagle. Denver, Colo: C. Westley, 1894, pp. 131–34.

Works about May French Sheldon

Allen, Alexandra. *Travelling Ladies.* London: Jupiter, 1980, pp. 21–42.

International Dictionary of Women's Biography. Edited by Jennifer S. Uglow and Frances Hinton. New York: Continuum, 1982.

Middleton, Dorothy. *Victorian Lady Travellers.* London: Routledge & Kegan Paul, 1965, pp. 90–103. A shortened version appeared in the *Geographical Magazine* 35 (June 1962): 83–87.

———. "Some Victorian Lady Travellers." *Geographical Journal* 139 (Feb. 1973): 73–74.

Mighels, Ella. *Life and Letters of a Forty-Niner's Daughter.* San Francisco: Harr Wagner, 1929, pp. 271–72.

Royle, Alice. Articles in *Womanhood*, Nov. 1901, *The Lady's Gazette*, Jan. 1902, and *The Temple Magazine*, Sept. 1901.

Western Pennsylvania Historical Society Publications 9 (1926), pp. 96 and 186, and the 1850 Census for Allegheny, Pennsylvania, have information on the French family.

Willard, Frances, and Mary A. Livermore. *A Woman of the Century: Leading American Women in All Walks of Life*. Buffalo, N.Y.: C. W. Moulton, 1893.

Newspaper articles include "What She Saw in Africa," a report of a lecture, in the *New York Times*, on Mar. 22, 1892; a review of *Sultan to Sultan* in the *New York Times*, on Dec. 11, 1892; news notes in the *New York Times*, on Mar. 21, July 3, and Dec. 19, 1892; news notes in the *San Francisco Chronicle*, on Feb. 20, 21, 28, and Apr. 7, 9, 1924; and in the *San Francisco Examiner*, on Apr. 9, 1924.

An obituary appeared in *Geographical Journal* 87 (1936): 288.

The Mary [*Sic*] French Sheldon Papers in the Library of Congress, Manuscript Division, include published and unpublished writings, correspondence, scrapbooks, photographs, and Sheldon's passport.

DAME FREYA MADELINE STARK
1893–

Dame Freya Madeline Stark is known and respected on three continents. An English-woman, she lives in Italy, and her life has been for many years close to the Middle East. England has made her a Dame of the British Empire, equivalent to knighthood. Geographical societies have given her their highest honors, and universities have acknowledged her scholarship with honorary doctorates. She has produced a long list of books, including four volumes of an autobiography and eight volumes of letters, all literature of the first class. Most of the books tell of her explorations and travel in the Middle East, where she first went in 1927 and where she has journeyed many times throughout her life.

She did not travel for honor, wealth, or fame, but simply because she has the soul of an explorer. She herself thought and wrote about what it means to be an explorer and concluded that "the lure of exploration still continues to be one of the strongest lodestars of the human spirit, and will be so while there is the rim of an unknown horizon in this world or the next" (*The Zodiac Arch*, p. 46).

Freya Stark had done a good deal of traveling before she was old enough to know that moving from place to place was not the usual thing for little children. She explained her father's theory that a child goes through various stages in the history of mankind and therefore "children should travel, at the time when in their epitome of history they are nomads by nature" (*Perseus in the Wind*, 1984 edition, pp. 144–45). His theory may have been right; at least one of his daughters remained a nomad.

Born in Paris in 1893, while her peripatetic parents were studying art, Freya was carried over the Dolomites in a basket before she could walk. Her parents moved about the Continent freely, and her earliest memories include railway stations and glimpses of the European countryside from train windows. By the time she was eight years old she had acquired a taste for moving about and seeing new worlds.

Her childhood was spent partly in England, at the home of her father, Robert Stark, and partly in Italy, where her mother, Flora, who was Robert's cousin, had grown up. It was a household of affluence, culture, and, at the first, love. When Freya was ten, the family went to Dronero in the Italian Piedmont to spend the summer; they stayed for sixteen years, until after World War I. Her mother became involved in a carpet factory, first as an advisor, then as a part-time worker, then as a partner with Count Mario di Roascio. Freya came to hate Mario for his control over her mother and his domination of her younger sister, Vera, who eventually married him. She blamed him, also, for forcing her parents apart, although she realized that they had never been truly compatible.

Her father spent most of his time in the hills near Dronero, where he rented a small hut. He eventually bought property in British Columbia and went there to live, after giving both of his daughters a sum of money. Freya spent part of hers on college. She entered Bedford College in London, but World War I came before she got her degree. It was the first formal education she had ever received.

During the war years Freya served as a nurse in Italy. Afterward she persuaded her father to buy a house near the Italian Riviera for her and her mother. She tried to support them by raising grapes and fruit. She longed to travel and had decided that, when she had accumulated enough to guarantee an income of a hundred pounds, she would start. Meanwhile she studied Arabic, first at home with an old missionary friar, and then in England with an Egyptian teacher and at the School of Oriental Studies.

By 1927 she had come to the conclusion that she needed not a degree in Arabic but the living language, and the best way to acquire that was to go where it was spoken. She spent the winter in Syria studying Arabic. In May she was joined by a friend with whom she ventured into the Druse borderlands, which were under French control. The women managed to visit a few families before they were stopped by the police, who wanted to keep them from traveling about the country.

Freya cunningly pretended that they were guests of the officers instead of prisoners, thanked them effusively for their hospitality, advised them to have the guide book corrected to show that there was a motor road, which would bring lots of tourists, and then asked to be taken for a ride through their beautiful country. The travelers were taken about the town of Shahba, with a bodyguard of six soldiers, but they were held for two days before they were allowed to go on with their journey. Freya wrote that she did not believe that the French ever had any intention of letting the people govern themselves. She was outraged at their treatment of the natives.

She wrote an article on the Druses which appeared in the *Cornhill Magazine* sometime after she returned to England; it brought her the friendship of Miss Doughty, a cousin of C. M. Doughty, the Arabian explorer, and Freya realized that one of the pleasures of authorship is "to imagine into how many places one's words may wander, unknown to oneself, to become friends'' (*Beyond Euphrates*, p. 30).

In 1929, after reading much of the history and literature of Arabia and continuing her study of the language, she went to Baghdad, which she reached with ten pounds ''and all the East before me.'' She was entranced with Baghdad, which enlarged her world to include an East independent of the Mediterranean, a land ''roughly separated from the Mediterranean world by a curtain of wastelands, of which the Syrian-Iraqi desert is the easiest to cross'' (*Beyond Euphrates*, p. 83).

Too poor to live in the more respectable hotels and unwilling to live in the British Club, where Arabs were excluded, she took lodgings with a shoemaker's family. She was considered a rebel—either a dangerous eccentric or a spy, but in time she made her own friends. In addition to studying Arabic, she began to study Persian; she had her heart set on visiting the Alamut valley.

She went to Lorestan and spent two weeks ''in that part of the country where one is less frequently murdered'' and saw the Lurs dressed in medieval garb. Since the Persian government was trying to make the natives change to Western clothing, she felt it worthwhile to picture them ''before too much tidiness spoils them.'' She persuaded some of the tribesmen to dig for archeological treasures. She concluded that the Lurs were treacherous and cruel, that stealing was the national art, and that all women were there regarded as insignificant. Yet she was sorry to leave the tribesmen and their mountains. She found it pleasant to visit people who ''are not so taken up with the means of living that no thought and time is left over for the enjoyment of life itself'' (*The Valleys of the Assassins*, pp. 13, 57–58).

She had another adventure in search of hidden treasure, described to her as cases of gold ornaments, daggers, coins, and idols buried in a cave in the mountains, in a country unsurveyed. Freya agreed to search for it, telling herself that there just might be such treasure and that finding it before others smuggled it out of the country would be a benefit to historians and antiquarians. Her informant gave her a map and promised to meet her at the cave. She managed to cross the frontier and, after many adventures, she reached the vicinity of the rumored treasure. But she never could free herself from police surveillance long enough to discover the cave, and she had to give up. The informant never met her. She was entertained by tribesmen, saw much of the country, and escaped from numerous uncomfortable situations. She came back with an ancient skull, taken from a Larti grave, which was placed in the Baghdad Museum.

In Mazandaran, just south of the Caspian Sea, she explored old fortresses. She had studied the rudiments of surveying and was able to add a few names to the maps of the area and to correct some of their inaccuracies. At the Castle of Nevisar Shah, in a deserted place three thousand feet above the nearest habitation, she found a piece of thirteenth-century pottery and felt it was proof that Marco Polo had once been there. Near another castle, the Throne of Solomon, she fell ill and spent nearly a week lying in the open, cared for tenderly if inexpertly by a woman whose language Freya could not understand. She recovered and felt well enough to ride on, only to fall ill again in a village she had visited before, where she was among friends. A Persian doctor who happened to be near was sent for, and he cured her malaria with doses of quinine which seemed to her excessive. It was not the last time she found herself ill and near death while far from medical attention, but such experiences did not dim her need to travel the wild places.

She worked on the *Baghdad Times* while she was planning other excursions, and in the 1930s she spent some time exploring the Hadhramaut (Yemen) in southern Arabia. Her knowledge of the Quoran and the ancient literature of the country made her acceptable in the Moslem world, even at a time when Arabia was rife with intertribal warfare and the sheiks were inclined to look upon European visitors with suspicion. Her enemy, again, was illness. In Du'an she caught the measles, and in the Wadi Hadhramaut she suffered a heart attack. On that occasion she was rescued and carried out by a Royal Air Force plane. Her second visit to Yemen was marred by the presence of two women scientists she had agreed to shepherd about the country when she took a dislike to one of them. The visit ended with another illness, dengue fever.

Freya was by this time becoming known as a traveler. Although her books on Persia and Arabia were still being written in 1933, the Royal Geographical Society that year awarded her the Back Grant for her travels in Lorestan. She spoke to the society, as well as to the Royal Central Asian Society and the Royal Asiatic Society, which presented her with the Burton medal—she was the first woman to receive it. She signed an agreement with John Murray, the publisher of famous explorers, for *The Valleys of the Assassins*. It was the first of several books on her Eastern adventures to appear between 1934 and 1940, and its publication began a lifelong friendship with the Murray family.

Although she had many friends in England and spent much time there, she made her home in Italy, where she lived with her mother and close to her godfather and a dear friend, Herbert Young, who lived in Asolo. She never enjoyed robust health, and she spent much time in hospitals and nursing homes. At the age of thirteen she had suffered a serious accident when she visited Mario's mill and got her long hair caught in the machinery. It had taken four months for her to recover from that accident, and she continued throughout her life to feel the effects.

Late in the 1930s Freya became acutely aware of the political dangers posed by Mussolini. She could see the war coming, and although her mother and Young elected to remain in Italy, Freya decided to move to England. She waited for a warning from a friend, who telegraphed to her on September 26, 1938, that "Olga is dying." Olga was Peace.

Stark offered her services to the British government. She went first to Aden as an assistant information officer to the Ministry of Information, then to Cairo, and later to Baghdad, where she engaged in propaganda designed to persuade the Middle East to join the Allies. In Baghdad she helped burn the files when the British embassy was besieged by the Iraqi. In 1943 she was sent to the United States to counteract Zionist propaganda, which was fomenting anti-British feeling. On her way to America on a troopship, Freya suffered a ruptured appendix and was saved from death only by good medical care in Halifax.

She traveled about the United States speaking to colleges and women's clubs and being interviewed by newspaper reporters. She visited India at the time when British rule was ending. Then, back in Italy, she tried to put her home in order after the war's devastation. Her father had died in Canada, and her mother in California. (Flora had been imprisoned by the Italians, rescued by friends, and sent to other friends in the United States.) Herbert Young, too, had died during the war, leaving Freya his Asolo home.

In 1952 she began to travel about the western coasts of Asia Minor and the southern coast of Turkey, visiting ancient sites connected with the life and travels of Alexander the Great and with the beginnings of civilization. She went to see what Alexander saw, for "in Turkey particularly, and in all the Levant and the Aegean, a journey without history is like a portrait of an old face without its wrinkles" (*The Lycian Shore*, p. 4). Three books, all illustrated with outstanding photographs by the author, resulted from these journeys. The ancient cities she visited have almost all now changed their names (for example, Smyrna is Izmir, Erythrae is Ildir, Pergamum is Bergama, and Ephesus is Seljuk), but the ruins remain much the same, and for the reader the books are guidebooks in time as well as place.

Stark was in her seventies when she visited a part of Turkey inhabited by Kurds, and several times during the trip she vowed never again to venture into such wild places. "I will give Jock [John Murray] my hat and parasol to keep in his archives as the record of a past age," she said, "and will sit in my garden and write" (*Riding to the Tigris*, p. 34). For several years afterward she did stay at home, writing the scholarly *Rome on the Euphrates*, collecting some of her shorter writings for books of essays, and gathering together for publication what she could find of her voluminous correspondence. She burned her love letters; she had been in love often, and for a few years, beginning in 1947, she was married to Stewart Perowne, with whom she had worked in Aden.

Her last straight travel book is *The Minaret of Djam* (1970), which is an account of a visit to Afghanistan. The minaret, a beautifully preserved tower dating from before the days of Genghis Khan and his Mongols, was unknown to the outside world until 1958, when news came of its discovery by an airman from Herat who had wandered off his course. When Freya heard about it, she was determined to see it, if possible. She arrived in Kabul only to learn that it was a longer ride than she had time for and that to hire a Land Rover and a driver would be too expensive. With her usual luck, she met an English couple who were driving a Land Rover and invited her to go with them to the minaret. To see it in its secluded spot, they had to leave the road and travel by a mere track over rocky ground, but every bit of the trip was a joy to Freya. She describes their first sight of the tower, "soaring into the sky with the impetus of its design still active upon it—a volume seemed shut there in a language no human key could open, a joyous strangeness whose natural laws we shared but could not understand.'' It filled her with delight (*The Minaret of Djam*, pp. 66–67).

The Minaret of Djam is itself a gem, one which embodies all the humor, charm, and mature philosophy of this great travel writer.

BIBLIOGRAPHY

Works by Freya Stark

"Women and the Service of the Empire." *Contemporary Review* 141 (Jan. 1933): 56–61.
The Valleys of the Assassins and Other Persian Travels. London: Murray, 1934. Reprinted Los Angeles: Tarcher, 1983. Quotations in the text are from the 1983 edition.
"Visit to a Sultan." *Asia* 36 (June 1936): 394–98.
The Southern Gates of Arabia: A Journey in the Hadhramaut. London: Murray, 1936.
Baghdad Sketches. London: Murray, 1937; New York: Dutton, 1938. An edition was published in Baghdad by the *Baghdad Times* in 1933; an enlarged version, London: Murray, 1946.
"People of the Hadhramaut." *Living Age* 355 (Jan. 1939): 456–59.
A Winter in Arabia. London: Murray, 1940.
"Iraq." *Nineteenth Century* 132 (Sept. 1942): 110–17.
Letters from Syria. London: Murray, 1942.
East Is West. London: Murray, 1945. Also published as *The Arab Island: The Middle East, 1939–1943*. New York: Knopf, 1945.
"Yemen Chose to Be Poor." *Asia* 46 (Feb. 1946): 78–80.
Beyond Euphrates. London: Murray, 1950. Autobiography.
Traveller's Prelude. London: Murray, 1950. Autobiography.
The Coast of Incense. London: Murray, 1953. Autobiography.
The Freya Stark Story. New York: Coward-McCann, 1953. Combines *Traveller's Prelude*, *Beyond Euphrates*, and *The Coast of Incense*.
Ionia: A Quest. London: Murray, 1954.
The Lycian Shore. London: Murray, 1956.
Alexander's Path, from Caria to Cilicia. London: Murray, 1958; New York: Harcourt, Brace, 1958.
Riding to the Tigris. London: Murray, 1959; New York: Harcourt, Brace, 1959.
Dust in the Lion's Paw. London: Murray, 1961; New York: Harcourt, Brace, 1961. The fourth volume of autobiography.
"Saying What One Means." *Atlantic* 212 (Oct. 1963): 102–3.
"Excitement of Travelling with a Civilized Companion." *Vogue* 143 (June 1964): 948–49.
"On Traveling with a Notebook." *Atlantic* 214 (Dec. 1964): 95–96.
"On Silence." *Holiday* 38 (Dec. 1965): 12 + .
"On Smuggling." *Holiday* 40 (Oct. 1966): 8 + .
The Zodiac Arch. London: Murray, 1968; New York: Harcourt, Brace & World, 1969.
The Minaret of Djam: An Excursion in Afghanistan. London: Murray, 1970.
The Furnace and the Cup, 1893–1930. Edited by Lucy Moorehead (who also edited

volumes 2–6 of the Letters, below). Salisbury, Wilts: Compton Russell, 1974. Letters, vol. 1.

The Open Door, 1930–35. Tilsbury, Wilts: Compton Russell, 1975. Letters, vol. 2.

The Growth of Danger, 1935–39. Tilsbury, Wilts: Compton Russell, 1976. Letters, vol. 3.

Bridge of the Levant, 1940–43. London: Michael Russell, 1977. Letters, vol. 4.

New Worlds for Old, 1943–46. London: Michael Russell, 1978. Letters, vol. 5.

The Broken Road, 1947–52. London: Michael Russell, 1981. Letters, vol. 6.

Some Talk of Alexander, 1952–59. Edited by Caroline Moorehead. London: Michael Russell, 1982. Letters, vol. 7.

Traveller's Epilogue, 1960–80. Edited by Caroline Moorehead. London: Michael Russell, 1982. Letters, vol. 8.

Other works by Stark include volumes of essays—*Perseus in the Wind*, 1948; *The Journey's Echo*, 1963; *A Peak in Darien*, 1976—and historical books—*Rome on the Euphrates*, 1966; *Turkey*, 1971 (American edition, *Gateways and Caravans*). Three volumes of her photographs were published: *Seen in the Hadhramaut* (1938); *Space, Time and Movement in Landscape* (1969); and *Traveller through Time: A Photographic Journey with Freya Stark*, by Malise Ruthven (1986).

Works about Freya Stark

"British Agent: Helped to Hold the Arab World to the Allied Cause." *Newsweek* 23 (Jan. 17, 1944): 51.

Europa Biographical Dictionary of British Women. Edited by Anne Crawford and others. London: Europa, 1985.

"Freya Stark of Arabia." *Newsweek* 42 (Nov. 2, 1953): 92–93.

Glauber, R. H. "Evocation." *Christian Century* 73 (June 27, 1956): 773.

———. "Lyric Travel." *Christian Century* 73 (Dec. 5, 1956): 1430.

International Dictionary of Women's Biography. Edited by Jennifer S. Uglow and Frances Hinton. New York: Continuum, 1982.

The International Who's Who, 1987–88. London: Europa, 1987, p. 1414.

Maitland, Alexander. *Tower in a Wall*. Edinburgh: Blackwood, 1982. The focus is on Stark.

Moorehead, Caroline. *Freya Stark*. London: Viking, 1985.

Porter, A. "Mission for Miss Stark." *Collier's* 113 (Apr. 8, 1944): 113–14.

Wells, L. "Female Explorers in the Near East." *Saturday Review of Literature* 23 (Nov. 30, 1940): 14.

Woodward, H. B. "Englishwoman in the Sands." *Saturday Review of Literature* 37 (Jan. 23, 1954): 21.

CARRIE ADELL STRAHORN
1854–1925

Carrie Adell Strahorn wrote a single book of travel, a classic description of stagecoach days in the American West during the late 1870s and the 1880s. Her *Fifteen Thousand Miles by Stage*, subtitled "A Woman's Unique Experience during Thirty Years of Path Finding and Pioneering from the Missouri to the Pacific and from Alaska to Mexico," was illustrated by the great western artist Charles M. Russell and published in 1911.

Carrie and her husband, Robert Edmund Strahorn, traveled together by stage, steamboat, horseback, and train. Robert's job was to entice settlers to the West; his employer was a railroad. His accounts of the fertility and beauty of the Pacific northwest did not always square with Carrie's unvarnished truth about the mud, dust, execrable lodgings, and poor food they encountered. But she balanced her tale with lyric descriptions of the great natural wonders of the West and hilarious tales of frontier life. An adventurous and hardy traveler, Carrie was the first white woman to tour the entire Yellowstone Park and one of the first to tell of Alaska's treasures.

The Strahorns not only chronicled the early days of the Pacific northwest but were themselves involved in its settlement. After investigating its possibilities, Robert left his publicity job to build railroads, establish towns, and invest in irrigation and electric power enterprises. Carrie worked to establish such amenities as churches and colleges. Her book, written and published some time after they had settled down, compared the western areas in the 1870s and 1880s with the same places after the settlers had moved in and stagecoaches had been replaced by better modes of transport.

Carrie Adell Green was born in 1854, in Marengo, Illinois. Her father was one of the most noted surgeons of the Mississippi Valley. Her mother, Louise Babcock Green, was a descendant of Aaron Burr. When Carrie met Robert Strahorn, she seemed destined to settle in the midwest to raise a family as warm, loving, and close-knit as her own had been. She had studied music under American and European vocal masters. Robert Strahorn, a reporter for the Denver *Rocky Moun-*

tain News and an Indian fighter, was an out-of-towner. When Carrie sent the copy for her wedding invitations to her uncle, Marengo's printer, he could not believe she had the name of the groom right, and he printed the invitations with the name of another man Dame Rumor had chosen for her. She promptly sent the invitations back, indicating in no uncertain terms that she was going to wed Robert Edmund Strahorn.

The wedding took place on September 19, 1877, and after tearful farewells to the family, the couple set out for Cheyenne, Wyoming Territory. While they were moving into a tiny apartment, Robert received an offer from the Union Pacific Railroad to head up a "library bureau." He had prepared a handbook, *Wyoming Black Hawk and Big Horn Region*, describing in great detail the climate and resources of the territory. A copy fell into the hands of Jay Gould, the railroad president. Seeing it as a perfect way to attract settlers along the routes of his railway, Gould proposed that Robert follow it up with similar handbooks on other northwestern states and territories. It would mean years on the road.

Carrie did not relish the idea of staying alone in Cheyenne, which she thought had little to recommend it, nor of going home to Marengo. No, she would go with Robert—all the way.

As Strahorn's employer had warned, it was rough travel. Roads in many places were vestigial, rocky, dusty, or muddy. At the end of the day they might find nothing but a shack for shelter. Once Carrie was the only woman crowded into a building with twenty-six men, every one of whom chivalrously offered her his blanket. In some places, they could get no food. They had a few scares from Indians, one of whom offered six ponies and two blankets in exchange for Carrie, an offer Robert was not willing to accept. The Strahorns were pestered by mosquitoes and fearful of rattlesnakes; they burned in the sun and froze in the cold nights. But Carrie was no complainer. "Those who take chances in new countries," she wrote, "undergo hardships that would be unendurable at times were it not for the vein of ludicrousness that runs through the experiences" (*Fifteen Thousand Miles*, p. 152).

Pard (her name for Robert) and Dell (his name for her) traveled during each spring and fall, returning home around Christmas time to spend the winter writing. Pard ground out illustrated pamphlets on the mountain west, including Montana, Idaho, and Oregon, to several of which he added a section extolling the attractions of Yellowstone. Carrie sent stories to the *Omaha Republican* and, three times a week, wrote letters to her mother. When she had time to put her book together, she relied on those letters.

In 1880, Carrie totted up the miles they had traveled since their adventurous experiences began:

We had run about the whole gamut of exploration—the great stock ranges, the profoundest forests, the broad grain lands, and the varied attractions for the pleasure or health seeker, with everything else that could have any possible bearing on future transportation interests. . . . By winze and ropes and tunnels we had followed the gold, copper, and lead hidden in rocky rifts or sandy bed, or yet again from its black soft blanket of porphyry, out into the sunlight and through arastra, crusher, amalgamator, or smelter to the bright coins of commerce. The advantage of future rail routes, or even of more stage lines, was nowhere overlooked. (*Fifteen Thousand Miles by Stage*, p. 307)

It had not all been hard work. They visited many beauty spots that became attractions for later tourists. In Montana, they saw the Great Falls of the Missouri, Yellowstone, and the Hot Sulphur Springs. In Idaho they went to Hailey Hot Springs—where they later founded the town of Hailey—Lake Coeur d'Alene, and the lava beds (whose attractions were not at all evident). In Colorado, they toured Estes Park and climbed Pikes Peak. They saw the pueblos of New Mexico. In California, they were delighted by Yosemite and San Francisco. They took a canoe trip up the Fraser and Harrison rivers in British Columbia.

In time they became weary of being migratory birds and living in trunks. "It makes me tired," wrote Carrie, "when I think of the weight of fatigue we often labored under in belonging to the rolling stock of the Union Pacific Railroad Company" (*Fifteen Thousand Miles by Stage*, p. 527). After six years of it, Robert gave up his publicity job and began to build railroad lines himself; he established towns: Hailey, Mountain Home, and Caldwell in Idaho, and Ontario in Oregon. In Caldwell, Carrie was an organizer of the First Presbyterian Society and helped to raise money (a dime at a time) to build its church. She was instrumental in starting the College of Idaho and the music school. Robert founded a Strahorn Memorial Library at the college and another in Carrie's home town.

In 1890 they went East and settled in Boston for seven years, where Pard became an investment banker and Dell devoted herself to music and literary studies. They began to make new friends, but Dell was not happy:

The great hurrying masses of humanity all along the East shore, mostly in the hot race for making or spending money, were a barrier rather than a help to our happiness. We missed the great anthems of the forest and the singing streams, the crisp, cool night air; we missed the elixir from the snowy peaks, we missed the sunny Western skies, and the tent in the Rockies with the hearty spirit of Western good fellowship. (*Fifteen Thousand Miles by Stage*, p. 651)

The Strahorns' last home was in Spokane, Washington. Pard had made a fortune from his investments, and they were able to live in style and offer hospitality to their many friends and acquaintances. Here Carrie wrote her book and took an active interest in the development of the city. She died during a visit to San Francisco on March 17, 1925. Robert married again. He lost his fortune in the Depression, however, and in 1944 he died poor in San Francisco.

BIBLIOGRAPHY

Works by Carrie Adell Strahorn

Articles in the *Omaha Republican*, 1877–1881.

Fifteen Thousand Miles by Stage: A Woman's Unique Experience during Thirty Years of Path Finding and Pioneering from the Missouri to the Pacific and from Alaska to Mexico. New York and London: Putnam, 1911.

Works about Carrie Adell Strahorn

Bean, Margaret. " 'Railway Sphinx' Made Fortune, then Lost It." *Spokesman-Review* (Spokane, Wash.), Feb. 3, 1957. On Robert Strahorn; includes information about Carrie's career.

Durham, N. W. *History of the City of Spokane and Spokane County, Washington.* Spokane: S. J. Clarke, 1912, vol. III, pp. 5–11. Biographies of Robert and Carrie Strahorn.

"The Passing of Mrs. Robert E. Strahorn. A Few of the News Excerpts, Editorial Comments and Sketches of Her Remarkable Career in Pacific Coast Papers." Leaflet, 1925, copy in William Andrews Clarke Library, University of California, Los Angeles.

Newspaper clippings in the Spokane Public Library include a note and a photograph of Carrie from the *Spokane Chronicle*, Jan. 18, 1916, and an unidentified obituary of March 18, 1925.

Some information about Carrie is contained in accounts of Robert Strahorn, including the *National Cyclopedia of American Biography*, vol. 6, p. 252, and current vol. C (1930), p. 445; Oliver Knight, "Robert E. Strahorn, Propagandist for the West," in *Pacific Northwest Quarterly* 59 (Jan. 1968): 33–45; Olive Groefsema, *Elmore County [Idaho]* (n.p., 1949), pp. 277–78, an obituary. A typescript of Strahorn's autobiography, "Ninety Years of Boyhood," is located in the Strahorn Memorial Library, College of Idaho, Caldwell, Idaho. A microfilm is available from the Idaho State Historical Society, Boise, which has other material on Robert Strahorn.

ANNA LOUISE STRONG
1885–1970

Anna Louise Strong traveled to countries undergoing change—Poland in 1921, Russia at various times between 1921 and the late 1940s, Spain during its civil war from 1936 to 1937, and China at various times between 1925 and the end of her life in 1970. She covered political revolutions as a journalist, became involved in the lives of the revolutionists, and tried to explain to American readers and listeners the dynamics of revolution. She produced a steady stream of books and articles as a propagandist for the Soviet Union and the Chinese People's Republic. She published an English-language newspaper in Moscow and later a newsletter giving Westerners information about China · under Mao Tse-tung.

Although Strong had difficulty dealing with the inefficiency and bureaucracy of the Communist regimes, she remained loyal to their socialistic ideals. Unlike many of her American contemporaries, she was not completely disillusioned by the Stalin purges of 1936 and 1937, although she did leave Russia at that time to visit Spain. When in 1949 the Russians accused her of spying and deported her, she remarked that the same thing could happen to any journalist in search of the truth. At last in China, in 1968, when some of her close friends were accused of being "left deviationists," she concluded that her place was no longer among the Chinese. She died while she was planning a return to the United States to work against the war in Vietnam.

Why should a political journalist be counted as a traveler? Most of her moving about—and she was constantly shuttling back and forth between America and Russia or Asia—was part of her work. But now and then she found time to explore parts of the world more remote from the great upheavals that characterize the present century. As a young woman, she had loved the mountains of California and had joined other mountaineering women of the West Coast in climbs up Mount Rainier. When she first left home for Russia in 1921, she was already planning further travels.

> Some day I shall go down by the route of the great deserts to China! Some day I shall strike south over the Khyber Pass to India! Some day I shall go by the world's highest mountains

and most secret wastes, traveling with the nomads in the heart of Asia! (*The Road to the Grey Pamir*, p. 3)

She did all of these things, and she wrote about all of them. Alone or with government expeditions, she went to Mexico, Spain, the Pamirs, Samarkand, Tibet, Laos, and North Vietnam. Her travel writings, which reveal a delight in the color and adventure of strange places, report on the educational and technological advances occurring in the rural villages and among nomadic tribes. When she first traveled through central Asia in 1925, she viewed the continent of Asia in a different light than did most travelers. "Instead of exotic culture of shrines and ancient palaces, amusing laws and quaint religions," she saw "the awakening and industrialization of Asia" (*I Change Worlds*, pp. 227–28).

Despite her long residence in Russia and China and her devotion to the Communist philosophy, Strong remained a patriotic American. Both of her parents came from families who had been among America's earliest pioneers. Her aim was to build a bridge between the peoples of the revolutionary countries and her own country, to spur Americans to end the capitalistic and imperialistic policies she felt so destructive to peace in the world.

Anna Louise Strong was born in a two-room parsonage in Friend, Nebraska, on November 24, 1885. Her father, Sydney Dix Strong, was a Congregational minister. He had met her mother, Ruth Tracy Strong, when the two were students at Oberlin College. After they married, the couple had spent an inheritance of two thousand dollars on a world tour, which seemed to their relatives impractical but to them a rich investment. Anna was their first child. She grew up in the midwest, made remarkably swift progress in school, and graduated from high school too young to enter college. She was the youngest person in her time to earn a Ph.D. from the University of Chicago (at age twenty-three).

Her first years after college were spent in New York and Chicago, where she worked with settlement houses and put on child welfare exhibits. She moved to Seattle, Washington, where her widowed father lived. She worked with him on civic betterment programs and was elected the first woman member of the school board. She and her father were strong pacifists and arranged antiwar rallies, which led to her recall from the board. A Socialist, she was involved in the labor movement and took a leading part in the Seattle General Strike in 1919.

After World War I and the tsarist revolution, Strong's sympathies with labor and socialistic ideals led her to go to Russia—a step encouraged by Lincoln Steffens. In order to get there, she accepted an assignment with the American Friends Service Committee in Warsaw, but after a short time she arranged a transfer to Moscow. There she was horrified by the devastation wrought by war: "My utopia to which I had been admitted was in ruins; famine and pestilence swept the land." Seven years of war had been followed by two years of drought in the Volga valley, and hundreds of thousands of people fled pestilence and hunger. She saw the refugees in Baranowice, "sleeping, eating, giving birth and dying under the sun and rains of heaven, a miserable louse-ridden horde" (*I Change Worlds*, pp. 97–98). She and her fellow Americans had assumed that, as soon as capitalistic graft and exploitation ceased, widespread comfort would reign. They had not allowed, she thought, for the backwardness of a nonindustrialized country, the huge populations, the lack of surplus goods, and natural disasters.

She was put in charge of two carloads of food being sent to the Volga by the Quakers. During the next years, working half inside and half outside of government agencies, she established the John Reed Children's Colony for young refugees and later a trade school in Moscow. Most of the money for both projects she raised by writing and lecturing in the United States. Both eventually failed because the money was largely diverted by petty officials to other uses. Often disheartened by the obstacles put in her way, Strong retained her admiration for Trotsky, to whom she gave English lessons, and she supported Lenin's policies.

She visited China in 1925 and again in 1927, "a traveler now," she said, "roving to revolution" (*I Change Worlds*, p. 251). The Chinese Nationalist Party was rent by dissension; the Soviet-backed Kuomintang was fighting the right wing under Chiang Kai-shek. Strong's Russian friend, Borodin, served as an advisor to the Kuomintang. When he found it advisable to leave the country in a hurry and by a northern route, Strong got permission to go with his party by auto across the northwest provinces of China to Mongolia and the Trans-Siberian Railway. It was a trip full of difficulties and excitement. Crossing the Gobi desert was a "confused jumble of wonder, a medley of black hills and pinky-grey landscapes, of weird reds and buttes and awe-inspiring mountains of white sand cutting the heavens, of the excited flight of wild goats or the ghastly shrieks of dying camels" (*China's Millions*, 1936 edition, p. 298).

On her way out of China, she spent three days at a Buddhist monastery where she finished writing *China's Millions*, which was published in 1928. (In 1936 she wrote a second part of the book, and the whole appeared under the same title. The second part contains the account of her trip by the old camel route out of the country.)

Feeling isolated and depressed in Moscow, she undertook a horseback trip over the ridge of the Caucasus. When she saw Mt. Kasbek, she was seized with a hunger for high peaks, but she had no climbing gear. She found a guide and borrowed a torn pair of pants; with a dark veil to shield her face and a sheepskin to protect her from the cold, she was ready to go, except for her feet. The guide made shoes of knotted thongs, filled with hay. "The knots kept me from slipping on the ice, the straw gave padding, and the netted form allowed glacier water and the drying wind to pass with equal freedom through these 'shoes.' " They climbed to within 244 feet of the summit, when a blizzard forced them back. "We spent the night at 13,000 feet elevation sheltered by rock and partly buried in snow. Shaking all night with cold, exhaustion and elevation I thrilled with a fiery exaltation. . . . I had renewed my strength like the great land around me" (*I Change Worlds*, pp. 272–73).

Two months later, she was in the rich agricultural basin at the foot of the mountains in Soviet central Asia, visiting Samarkand, the ancient capital of

Turkestan. Few Americans were allowed to enter the region, but Strong had managed to get permission to attend the Women's Conference of Central Asia in Tashkent. Land was being confiscated from farmers and divided up among the peasants. Women were being encouraged to discard the veil, and some had been murdered for their flouting of Moslem law. Everywhere great changes were occurring: "The struggle was as complex and difficult and the ignorance and darkness even greater than they had been in China" (*I Change Worlds*, p. 274). She wrote lyrically of Samarkand:

> I shall always be glad that I first saw Samarkand in the golden glow of her beauty, when frosty November dawns melted swiftly into gorgeous sunny days; when the first rains had sapphired the sky and turned desert hills into snow peaks and laid the dust of the plains, but had not yet made mud. Then I learned that having loved and left many cities, one can still fall in love with a new one; that sheer blue-gold weather can be as intoxicating to the critical senses as champagne, or as youth. (*Red Star in Samarkand*, p. 77)

She visited cotton farms, schools, a silk factory, and hospitals. Some of the most significant changes brought by Sovietization were in the field of health. Strong went about with a sanitary inspector who was supervising the food supply of restaurants and bakeries. "In the jumbled filth of those old bazaars it seemed incredible to think of health laws; but she had enforced the ruling that new baked bread must be wrapped in a clean sheet and not in a dirty coat" (*Red Star in Samarkand*, p. 315). The seemingly insoluble problems of malaria, venereal disease, infant mortality, and poor sanitation were being tackled.

A year after her Samarkand trip, Strong decided to make the long-dreamed-of pilgrimage south through Asia. An opportunity arose to go to the Pamirs, known as the Roof of the World, "that high mid-Asian plateau whence start the three great mountain barriers of the world—the Himalayas into Tibet, the Hindu Kush into Afghanistan, and the Tien Shan, dividing Russia and China." It was "the mystery land of the explorer" (*The Road to the Grey Pamir*, p. 6). She joined a detachment of the Red Army going to Osh (supposedly the spot where Adam lived when expelled from Paradise). From there, she went with a geological expedition searching for a nomadic "pasture soviet," which might be anywhere near Sary Tash. She found the soviet, sat in on a people's court, and then rejoined the army for the journey into the Pamirs.

Her difficulties began with the horse she bought, which was "spooky," shying at everything along the trail. Not an experienced rider, she had difficulty controlling her mount. It threw her once into mud and later onto rocks, injuring and incapacitating her for days. After a journey of seventeen days, the party reached Murgab; Anna was so bruised, chilled, and sunburned that she was unable to appreciate the Pamirs at all.

At Murgab the troop detachment went on, and plans were made for Anna to accompany a Kirghiz official, Mamashef, back to Osh. With them went a caravan man from Kashgar, who began by stealing all the horses. He was captured but allowed to travel with her, so that Anna was stuck with a man who disliked her and a horse thief. Mamashef wanted to travel with all possible speed, and Anna did not enjoy the trip at all:

> Yet in looking back at the mad three days I was driven along by the once-hospitable Kirghiz, I cannot really blame him. He came of a race whose women work harder than men and rank lower; no Western tradition of chivalry had marred that view. (*The Road to the Grey Pamir*, p. 267)

At length she was rescued by an expedition of young men from the University of Central Asia, with whom she took a trail out of the Alai. She looked back at the Pamirs: "I was through with them at last, and glad to be through with them. There was one pathway to India I should never try again" (*The Road to the Grey Pamir*, p. 268).

She returned to Russia exhausted, having lost thirty pounds, but after a time she resumed her journalistic work. She was on the first train to run on the Turkestan-Siberian Railway. She started an English-language newspaper, *The Moscow News*. She met Joel Shubin, a Communist party member and editor of a Moscow paper, with whom she entered into a common-law marriage in 1932. After Stalin's rise to dictatorship, Anna felt less comfortable in Russia. In America the anti-Russian feeling was rising. The FBI had accumulated a large file on Strong; the Daughters of the American Revolution attacked her.

Anna happened to be in the United States when Germany invaded the Soviet Union in 1941. Joel died in 1942, while she was in America unable to leave and with almost no communication. She did not even hear of his death for months. Back in Russia in 1944, she went with the Red Army while it drove the Germans back.

Her interest in the Chinese revolution and her sympathy with Mao Tse-tung were unpalatable to the Soviets, and in 1949 they deported her as a spy. In the United States her old Communist friends believed the accusation and avoided her. In 1955 she learned by chance that the Soviet case against her had been dropped for lack of evidence, but it was 1958 before she could get a new passport. During the interim she tried to settle in the United States, bought several houses, and spent time with her family. She went to Hollywood to work on a movie script, and she wrote a novel. But she longed to return to China.

In 1958 she visited Russia once again and then moved permanently to China. For the last dozen years of her life, she made her home in Peking, where, most of the time, she lived in the Peace Compound where she received respect and care. From 1962 until her death in 1970, she published a weekly *Letter from China*, reporting on Sino-Soviet relations and Chinese life. Mao Tse-tung honored her on her eightieth birthday, and she was made an honorary member of the Red Guard. For years she suffered from Paget's disease, a painful bone disorder which made walking difficult. She died in a Peking hospital on March

29, 1970, and was buried in Peking's National Memorial Cemetery of Revolutionary Martyrs. A day of public mourning was observed in the city.

BIBLIOGRAPHY

Works by Anna Louise Strong

The First Time in History: Two Years of Russia's New Life. New York: Boni & Liveright, 1924.

Children of Revolution: The Story of the John Reed Children's Colony on the Volga. Seattle, Wash.: Pigott, 1925.

"Three Men of Japan." *Asia* 26 (Mar. 1926): 228–31, 256–58.

"New Women of Old Canton." *Asia* 26 (June 1926): 493–95.

"Women of Nationalist China." *Woman Citizen* n.s. 12 (Nov. 1927): 18–19.

"Woman Citizens of the Soviet Union." *Asia* 28 (Apr. 1928): 294–99.

"Old and New Gods in Mongolia." *Asia* 28 (July 1928): 564–69.

"Motoring out from China." *Asia* 28 (Sept. 1928): 703–713.

"Some Hankow Memories." *Asia* 28 (Oct. 1928): 794–97.

China's Millions. New York: Coward-McCann, 1928. An expanded version published 1936.

"Red Holidays in Central Asia." *Travel* 53 (June 1929): 7–17.

"Soviet Outpost in Asia." *Asia* 29 (June 1929): 460–66.

"Profane Invasion of Holy Bokhara." *Atlantic* 144 (July 1929): 103–110.

"Romance of Radio in Turkestan." *Travel* 53 (July 1929): 24–26.

"Samarkand Returns to Power." *Atlantic* 144 (Aug. 1929): 255–63.

"Red Rule in Golden Samarkand." *North American* 228 (Sept. 1929): 309–315.

Red Star in Samarkand. New York: Coward-McCann, 1929.

"Pioneering on the Roof of the World." *Travel* 54 (Apr. 1930): 7–11.

"Economic Paradox in Uzbekistan." *Contemporary Review* 138 (Aug. 1930): 218–24.

"Grasshoppers, Soldiers, and Silk Weavers." *Atlantic* 146 (Nov. 1930): 673–81.

"Soviet of the High Pastures." *Atlantic* 146 (Dec. 1930): 817–27.

"At the Edge of Civilization." *Contemporary Review* 140 (Oct. 1931): 504–8.

The Road to the Grey Pamir. Boston: Little, Brown, 1931.

"We Soviet Wives." *American Mercury* 32 (Aug. 1934): 415–23.

I Change Worlds: The Remaking of an American. New York: Holt, 1935. Autobiography.

"Birobidjan." *Asia* 36 (Jan. 1936): 41–43.

"Arctic Sea Route Is Open." *Asia* 36 (Feb. 1936): 44–49.

"Free Women." *Asia* 36 (May 1936): 326–31.

China's Millions: The Revolutionary Struggles from 1927 to 1935. London: V. Gollancz, 1936. This incorporates the 1928 volume, *China's Millions.*

This Soviet World. New York: Holt, 1936.

"Children of the Spanish War." *Survey Graphic* 26 (Sept. 1937): 458–62.

Spain in Arms. New York: Holt, 1937.

One-Fifth of Mankind. New York: Modern Age, 1938.

My Native Land. New York: Viking, 1940.

The New Lithuania. New York: National Council of American-Soviet Friendship, 1941.

"With the Red Army in Minsk." *Nation* 159 (July 29, 1944): 121–22.

"Poles Take Over." *Nation* 159 (Aug. 12, 1944): 183–84.
I Saw the New Poland. Boston: Little, Brown, 1946.
Dawn over China. Bombay: People's Publishing House, 1948.
"Jailed in Moscow." *New York Herald Tribune*, Mar. 27–Apr. 1, 1949.
When Serfs Stood up in Tibet. Peking: New World Press, 1960.
Tibetan Interviews. Peking: New World, 1961.

Note: Strong wrote many books and pamphlets and about a hundred periodical articles. All combine history, description, and political comment. Those listed are primarily autobiographical or travel.

Works about Anna Louise Strong

Alsterlund, B. Biographical sketch. *Wilson Library Bulletin* 15 (Feb. 1941): 460.
Contemporary Authors. Detroit: Gale Research, 1922–date, 1st revision, vol. 29, p. 678.
Cowley, Malcolm. "Fellow Traveler." *New Republic* 82 (May 1, 1935): 345.
Current Biography. New York: H. W. Wilson, 1940–date, annual vol. 1949.
Duke, David T. "Anna Louise Strong and the Search for a Good Cause." *Pacific Northwest Quarterly* 66 (July 1975): 123–37.
International Dictionary of Women's Biography. Edited by Jennifer S. Uglow and Frances Hinton. New York: Continuum, 1982.
Jaffe, Philip. "The Strange Case of Anna Louise Strong." *Survey* 53 (Oct. 1964): 129–39.
Notable American Women: The Modern Period. Edited by Barbara Sicherman and others. Cambridge, Mass.: Harvard University Press, 1980.
Pringle, Robert. "The Making of a Communist: Anna Louise Strong, 1885–1925." Master's thesis, University of Virginia, 1967.
"Some Memories of Anna Louise Strong." *Eastern Horizon* 9 (1970).
Strong, Tracy B., and Helene Keyssar. *Right in Her Soul: The Life of Anna Louise Strong*. New York: Random House, 1983. Tracy Strong was a great-nephew of Anna Strong. The authors used family archives, manuscript material, interviews, an unpublished autobiography, and newspaper sources for this definitive biography.
Willen, Paul. "Anna Louise Strong Goes Home Again." *The Reporter* (Apr. 7, 1955): 28–29.
Obituaries appeared in the *New York Times*, on Mar. 30, 1970; the *Washington Post*, on Apr. 12, 1970; and papers of other countries (except in the Soviet Union).

Strong manuscripts and documents are located in the Peking Library; the Suzzallo Library at the University of Washington, Seattle; and the Hoover Library at Stanford University, Stanford, California.

ELLA CONSTANCE SYKES
18??–1939

Ella Constance Sykes discovered the fascination of Persia in 1894 when she accompanied her brother, Percy (later Sir Percy) Molesworth Sykes, on a journey to Kerman and Baluchistan, where they remained for two and a half years. She is believed to have been the first European woman to visit these parts of Persia, and for her it was an unforgettable experience. "I was under a spell throughout my stay," she wrote, "a spell that endowed me with rose-coloured spectacles, and which . . . fills me with a strange yearning for the country which became a much-loved home to me, and where I spent the happiest years of my existence" (*Through Persia on a Side-Saddle*, pp. 2–3).

Some years later, in 1915, she and her brother returned to the East and spent nine months crossing the Russian Pamirs and traveling in Chinese Turkestan. Ella was the first Englishwoman to cross the dangerous passes leading to and from the Pamirs. Again, she thoroughly enjoyed the travel and meeting the people in what was then a little-known backwater of Asia.

Although the Sykes expeditions were full of adventure, and not without danger, the hardships of travel were mitigated by the status of Percy Sykes as a British official. His caravan was well supplied with food, shelter, and all the amenities needed for comfortable and "civilized" camping, including plenty of servants to do the work. Ella had enough energy and time to observe the country and the peoples met on the way, and she described her adventures with such immediacy that readers can share them. She was rewarded by election as a Fellow of the Royal Geographical Society. Her brother, who was knighted in 1915, was an author and a member and gold medalist of the R.G.S.

Ella was the daughter of Mary Molesworth Sykes and her husband, the Reverend William Sykes, a chaplain to the British forces. Little biographical information about her is recorded. She speaks of having had a university education, followed by study in Germany. She had traveled in Scotland and Europe, but despite a strong interest in the "gorgeous East" she was resigned to being no more than an armchair traveler until a sudden invitation came from her brother in 1894 to accompany him to Persia. He had recently returned from that country and was to go again to found a British consulate in the districts of Kerman and Baluchistan, which had not before had British representation.

Sykes gave his sister only ten days to prepare for the journey. "Although I felt somewhat uncertain as to how I should adapt myself to an uncivilised existence, never having quitted Europe before," she wrote, "I was delighted at the prospect" (*Through Persia*, p. 1). The household worked hard to collect clothing, camp equipment, and the furniture, linen, glass, and crockery needed for the new consulate. These necessities included a piano, which did not reach the consulate until three days before Ella left it! Ella engaged a Swiss maid, Maria, who could not ride; after they reached the end of the roads, she had to be carried in a chair, along with Ella's dog. Before the expedition was over, Maria had been sent back to England.

When Ella arrived at Enzeli, the harbor of Persia, she was immediately under its spell.

> I can never forget my feelings of joy and exultation when I realised that I was at last in Persia, on the threshhold of a new life, . . . The glamour of the East penetrated me from the first moment of landing on its enchanted shores, and although many a time I encountered hard facts, quite sufficient to destroy the romantic illusions of most folk, yet they struck against mine powerlessly. (*Through Persia*, pp. 2–3)

They were met at Enzeli by Percy's Indian syce, or groom, Fakir Mahomet, who proved to be an invaluable servant, even taking over, at the last, the duties of lady's maid for Ella. A sizeable number of Persian servants had been engaged. On one of their first nights on the road, the travelers were given two rooms in a great bare building. "And now our servants showed to advantage," wrote Ella:

> They unpacked our belongings, covering the floors with carpets, hanging up curtains before the draughty doors and windows, setting up our folding wrought-iron bed-steads, removing the leather covers from the enamelled basins which contained all our washing apparatus, and mounting the aforesaid basins on wooden tripods. . . . By the time we had washed in our folding indiarubber baths, the servants had prepared us an excellent dinner of soup, *pillau*, woodcocks, stewed fruit and custard, everything done so briskly and willingly that it was a pleasure to be served by such men. (*Through Persia*, pp. 7–8)

Part of the road toward Tehran wound steeply, and the narrow trail was a sea of mud over which the horses had to pick their way. At the worst parts, the dangers were brought home to them by the sight of dead mules and donkeys who had fallen. After a couple of days of riding over this rough terrain, Ella found herself able to ride easily down places she never imagined she could, for she "had always been a timid horsewoman" (*Through Persia*, p. 11). Before long she was enjoying long rides and spirited canters with her sportsman brother. She was, of course, using a woman's sidesaddle. The Persians could not understand how she could sit on a horse sideways and not fall off.

> The more I rode, the more I saw the disadvantages of the saddle to which I was condemned. The side-saddle is by no means an ideal invention in my eyes. It is difficult to mount into it from the ground; it is dangerous in riding among hills to be unable to spring off on either side in case of an accident; the habit is very apt to be caught on the pommels if the rider falls, and the position in which she sits cramps her much if persisted in for many hours at a slow walk, which is the usual thing in hilly and stony countries. (*Through Persia*, pp. 288–89)

Ella was a Victorian upper-class Englishwoman, and, eager as she was for freedom, she felt bound by custom. She also recognized her brother as her guardian and the head of the expedition. He made the decisions, watched over her, and saw that she upheld the honor of her position as a member of an official family. That she was able to overcome the usual patronizing view of the people of another culture and to sympathize with their joys and sorrows is to her credit. She had one advantage over her brother in that she could talk freely to the women, and she took every opportunity to do so, especially after gaining some proficiency in Persian.

They spent seven weeks in Tehran, where they were guests at the British legation. Ella was rather disappointed in the capital city, which had a tumble-down appearance. She thought the telegraph line, which connected India with Europe, "a wonderful achievement of English energy over Oriental obstructiveness" (*Through Persia*, p. 16). She also praised the climate. To one accustomed to English winters, it was a treat to wake up morning after morning to a world bathed in sunshine. Some of the women complained of the intense dryness of the air, but Ella never felt better in her life and in fact had not a day of illness while in Persia, though often exposed to great heat or cold and long days of hard riding.

Ella sought the advice of the other European women in Tehran on matters of housekeeping in the country, and found it discouraging to hear accounts of the thievish propensities, dirty habits, and other delinquencies of Persian servants. When she became mistress of the consulate at Kerman, she found the stories all too true. In spite of a great many servants, some of whom hired others to do the work, she felt that four good English servants could have done better. Keeping the household running took much of her time. In addition, many of the furnishings sent ahead did not reach Kerman for weeks, but Ella was determined not to let such little things worry her.

Kerman was a small town. No other Europeans lived there until an acquaintance came along who was traveling about buying up treasures. At Kerman he sought to buy an ancient carpet in a nearby shrine. It had been presented to the shrine in the sixteenth century, and "was much worn and cut up into as many as thirty pieces, which the Persians had re-joined with no regard to the pattern," Ella observed. "Now it must be the pride of the museum to which its possessor presented it" (*Through Persia*, p. 84).

The Sykeses, too, bought artifacts, shawls, and carpets. They explored the countryside and collected insects, an interest brother and sister shared. Ella disliked tarantulas, but she gamely pursued some with her net, popping them into her "lethal bottle" and preserving them. "I am unable to give any personal account of the interior of the city," Ella said, "as, during the whole of my stay close to it, I did not go inside its walls, my brother fearing I might be mobbed by the populace who had never seen an Englishwoman before" (*Through Persia*, p. 103).

When their residence at Kerman was over, Percy was appointed to a boundary commission to delimit the last piece of frontier between the Indian and Persian empires. Brother and sister began a journey of 600 miles to the Indian border, much of it across an almost uninhabited desert. They were sorry to leave the consulate, where "we had enjoyed life to the utmost . . . yet we were both glad to be off, for both of us felt strongly the charms of a nomadic existence" (*Through Persia*, p. 225).

They had engaged fifty camels; mules could not travel across Baluchistan because of the intense heat and the lack of vegetation. Since there were few towns, the expedition had to carry all its provisions. Ella had packed dried fruits, tins of "compressed vegetables," jelly packets for making jellies, condensed milk and egg powder for making puddings—even wine and champagne.

They met the boundary commission at Kuhak and traveled with it for twenty days, when the commission finished its work. The Sykes party then traveled to Quetta, 430 miles away. On arrival, Ella unpacked the clothes which had been sent to her from England the previous autumn, and she prepared to live a town life again. They stayed in the residency, where they enjoyed to the full the luxuries of civilization.

While they were on their way to Simla they heard that the shah of Persia had been assassinated. Percy was ordered to the Karun Valley, near the border of Persia and Turkey, to investigate recent attacks on Europeans there. The Sykeses left India by ship bound for the Persian Gulf.

Some uncomfortable weeks were spent in the Karun region, where the hostility of the Arabs and the intense heat kept Ella indoors through most of the day. Percy went to Shushtar to extract indemnity from the governor for outrages against Europeans. He returned suffering from fever. He had planned to escape the heat by going to the high hills of the Bakhtiari country, but because of his illness they had to give this up and make their way to Tehran and thence home.

They reached England in March 1897, after an absence of over two and a half years. They looked back on their Persian sojourn as fruitful and happy. "To the end of my days I shall be ever grateful," said Ella, "for those happy years, so rich in friends and experiences" (*Through Persia*, p. 362).

Eighteen years passed before Ella had another opportunity to visit the East. During that time she published *Through Persia on a Side-Saddle* (1898) and a popular description of Persia, *Persia and Its People* (1910). An article on the women of Persia appeared in the *National Geographic* in October 1910. She went on a mission to Canada for the Colonial Intelligence League for Educated Women and published, in 1912, *A Home-Help in Canada*.

In 1915 Percy, now Brigadier General Sir Percy Sykes, was sent to Chinese Turkestan to replace the consul general, Sir George Macartney, while the latter was on leave. Ella was delighted when he asked her to accompany him. The European war was raging as they left, which meant that they approached Asia by way of Scandinavia and Russia. From Petrograd to Andijan they traveled by train over the limitless steppes, stopping at several cities. When Ella caught sight of camels she realized, "with a leap of the heart," that they were once again in the East. At Tashkent in Russian Turkestan the war was brought home to them by the presence of 15,000 German and Austrian prisoners.

The railway ended at Andijan. Here, she records, they had their last clean resting place until they arrived at Kashgar, their goal. From Osh they set off with a caravan of small ponies and two sorry post horses for the 260-mile journey. Nine out of the twelve stages of their trip were spent crossing the Tien Shan Range. They passed caravans of ponies and camels loaded with bales of cotton, gangs of colorful Kashgaris going to work at Osh, and even a party of wealthy Chinese, their ladies carried in palanquins with mules fore and aft. Since the trail was steep and narrow, Ella pitied the women in their swaying conveyances.

They crossed the Terek Pass at 12,000 feet, having lodged at its foot in a Kirghiz felt tent. Heavy snow lay on each side of the track, and they passed the skeletons of horses and donkeys who had fallen on the cruel pass. At the top they paused to enjoy the view of the great Alai Range, "peak towering above peak of boldly serrated mountains" (*Through Deserts and Oases of Central China*, p. 31).

At Kashgar they were greeted by Sir George Macartney and his children and by a group of Indians who gave them a lavish meal. They rode on to the Russian consulate, where they were given tea, then to a Chinese reception, with more tea; and, when they reached the British consulate, they could not resist a fourth tea, served by Lady Macartney.

Again faced with housekeeping, this time with servants whose language she did not know and whose ideas of cleanliness did not coincide with hers, Ella cheerfully adjusted to the situation. There was little "social dissipation" at Kashgar, but there was a colony of Russians who played tennis and a species of croquet. The little colony reminded Ella of "the Florentines rendered immortal by Boccaccio, who, when the plague was raging, left their city and went to a lovely garden outside its walls, caring nothing for the misery and death they had so skilfully avoided." In this case, it was the war from which the Russians isolated themselves (*Through Deserts and Oases of Central Asia*, p. 49).

Ella was permitted to visit the bazaar, where she delighted in the brightly colored clothing of the Kashgarian women, who, except for the higher classes, went unveiled. In contrast to the subdued Persian women, these peasants "chaffered and haggled" with the men in the bazaar. Ella commented that veiling Islamic women and binding the feet of Chinese girls were masculine devices to keep women in subjection.

During their weeks in Kashgar, brother and sister rode all over the city and its environs. At the beginning of June, it was unpleasantly hot and they set off for a trip to the Russian Pamirs, "that hitherto jealously guarded district." Ella did not look forward to the trip, which her sportsman brother was eager to make. He had heard that the *ovis polis*, the great mountain sheep named for Marco Polo, could be found there, and he hoped to get a specimen. She had read that it took unusual nerve and agility to negotiate the passes by which one reached the Roof of the World. "But I try to make it a rule to see only one lion in my path at a time . . . and naturally my blood was stirred at the thought that I was about to start upon an adventure vouchsafed to very few women" (*Through Deserts and Oases of Central Asia*, p. 105).

Ella, the only woman in the party, was guarded and protected in every possible way. "I rode astride," she mentions casually, "on a native saddle," changing to another horse with a sidesaddle for part of the day and frequently walking. They passed over stony desert, crossed the river, and climbed passes by narrow, slippery tracks. They slept in tents, prepared ahead of them by the servants. They always had afternoon tea and, at the end of the day's ride, a warm bath. They saw many Kirghiz, "peaceful pastoral people," whom they found to be friendly and hospitable. Whenever they stopped near an encampment, the women visited Ella, bringing offerings of pastry.

Ella took great pride in the fact that she was the first Englishwoman to negotiate the Katta Dawan Pass and actually to reach the Roof of the World. She paid for the pleasure by being half-blinded by wind and sand; her face was swollen from snow and sleet. Nor was it a place of beauty, being a treeless region, "a dreary waste," very hot in the daytime and icy cold at night. They stayed several days at Lake Karakul, then they rode on to Pamirsky Post on the Murghab River. While her brother hunted, Ella amused herself collecting flowers and visiting the Kirghiz ladies. Percy returned with a good specimen of *ovis polis* and they left the Pamirs, descending an almost interminable trail down into Chinese Turkestan. Their progress was leisurely, with plenty of time to observe the people. They watched the favorite Kirghiz sport in which mounted riders vied to snatch the carcass of a goat from the one who had possession of it. The riders threw themselves into the game with reckless enthusiasm.

Ella and Percy explored a glacier on Mustagh Ata, with Ella mounted on a yak, and they crossed the difficult Ulughat Pass, again riding yaks. Here, where the pass was over 16,000 feet, Ella suffered an attack of mountain sickness. After a strenuous ride, they reached Kashgar again. It was a relief to be back in a comfortable home with an abundance of vegetables and fruits.

A few weeks later they took another tour, this time to the east, passing from oasis to oasis along the edge of the Takla Makan desert. "If Chaucer could have come to life again," said Ella, "he would have delighted in our caravan." Their party was joined by other travelers, including the chief falconer of the mehtar of Chitral, who was searching for a pair of white hawks; a Hindu trader with a wooden leg; a youth from Gilgit with "the features and limbs of the immortal riders of the Elgin marbles" (*Through Deserts and Oases of Central Asia*, p. 178); and the master of the horse of the rajah of Punial and his groom, who were in search of Badakhshani stallions for their chief. Throughout the journey, with its unsuccessful search, the two eyed the handsome grey and chestnut mounts that Percy and Ella were riding; after they returned to Kashgar, Sykes sold his Badakhshanis to the rajah.

Sykes, as consul general, was greeted ceremoniously in every town. At Yarkand they were treated to a spread of fowls, eggs, and tea laid out in a marquee. The Russian colony provided more food, and then the Chinese held a reception. Ella was glad to escape to the home of the British agent. Yarkand, the richest oasis of the country, was surrounded by fields of rice, maize, wheat, and millet; however, the people seemed to lack energy, and Ella noted that they had a very high incidence of goiter.

Khotan, the farthest east city of Chinese Turkestan, was their goal. Here they visited a silk factory. They also went to a jade pit, where they watched workers turning cups of jade on lathes and polishing them.

A few weeks after their return to Kashgar, the Macartneys returned, and brother and sister traveled homeward through central Asia and northern Europe. Then the war, "with its urgent claims upon every man and woman, took possession of our thoughts and energies" (*Through Deserts and Oases of Central Asia*, p. 231).

Ella's book *Through Deserts and Oases of Central Asia*, including several chapters contributed by Sir Percy on the history and geography of Chinese Turkestan, was published in 1920.

Ella Sykes died on March 23, 1939. Many changes had occurred in her world. World War I had ended, but another global war threatened. The Russian Revolution had been won by the Communists. Persia had become the republic of Iran.

BIBLIOGRAPHY

Works by Ella Constance Sykes

Through Persia on a Side-Saddle. London: A. D. Innes, 1898; Philadelphia: Lippincott, 1898.
"Domestic Life in Persia." *Scientific American* 55 (Apr. 25, 1903): 22830–32.
"A Talk about Persia and Its Women." *National Geographic* 21 (Oct. 1910): 847–66.
Persia and Its People. New York: Macmillan, 1910.
"At a Women's Hostel in Canada." *Cornhill* 105 (May 1912): 668–70.

A Home-Help in Canada. London: Smith, Elder, 1912.

"Simple Life on a Poultry-Ranch in British Columbia." *Cornhill* 111 (Feb . 1915): 214–22. Same article in *Living Age* 284 (Mar. 20, 1915): 730–36.

"At a Y.M.C.A. Hut Somewhere in France." *Cornhill* 115 (Feb. 1917): 204–214. Same article in *Living Age* 293 (May 5, 1917): 282–89.

(With Sir Percy Sykes) *Through Deserts and Oases of Central Asia.* London: Macmillan, 1920.

Work about Ella Sykes

An obituary appeared in *Geographical Journal* 94 (July 1939): 94.

ELIZABETH MARSHALL THOMAS
1931–

Elizabeth Marshall Thomas made several expeditions to the Kalahari Desert of South-West Africa (now Namibia) between 1951 and 1955 to study the Bushmen. Later she spent time with the Dodoth, a tribe of warrior herdsmen in Uganda. She approached these two very different peoples not as a traveler or an anthropologist but as an observing friend. She was accepted as one and grew to know many individuals intimately, drawing from them details of their economic and social lives.

Over a period of thirty years, she and her family kept in touch with their Bushmen friends and wrote of their losing struggle to maintain their culture in a fast-changing world. Thomas's books about the tribes with which she worked are as fascinating as novels, as beautifully expressed as poems. Still a college student when she began her African journeys, she has since made a name for herself as an anthropologist. Turning her attention to animal behavior, she spent a summer alone on Baffin Island observing a pack of wolves. A novel published in 1986, *Reindeer Moon*, combines her interest in animal life and man's relationship with his environment.

The first journey to the Kalahari was arranged by Elizabeth's father, Laurence Marshall, and included her mother Lorna and her brother John. Marshall, founder and president of the Raytheon Company, had recently retired and wished to spend his time pursuing a long-held interest in the Bushmen. Elizabeth, born in Boston, Massachusetts, on September 13, 1931, was at the time only twenty, a student at Smith College. Her brother (later a successful documentary film maker) was nineteen. None of the family members had taken even an introductory course in anthropology, and they had no experience with cameras, but their wish was to make several trips to the Bushmen, study their language, map the country, and take pictures. John hoped to make motion picture films. Elizabeth wanted to explore the lives of primitive people and to write about them.

Before leaving for Africa Laurence Marshall approached the anthropology department of Harvard University for advice. The director of the Peabody Museum appointed a committee to help the family work out aims and procedures. Leonard Carmichael, then secretary of the Smithsonian Institution, also introduced the Marshalls to experts on southern Africa. Several of the men they met accompanied the family on one or more of their expeditions. When they reached Africa, they found others willing to help them.

The assistance offered by scholars, scientists, and field workers was at great variance with the misinformation given the travelers by the white people of South-West Africa. "There are no more Bushmen; lions have eaten them," they were told. Others warned that the tribesmen were hostile and dangerous, armed with poisoned arrows, and that they were difficult to find because they hid in the bush. The last bit of advice was true. It took the family several months to find the Bushmen. They met some, working for a farmer, who were willing to guide them to a place in the interior called Gautscha, which the tribesmen sometimes visited. It was a grassy spot dominated by several baobab trees in a salt flat with one deep water hole.

The visitors drove in trucks for hundreds of miles to reach Gautscha and arrived so weary that they dropped to the ground and fell asleep. The Bushmen guides, meanwhile, built grass shelters, made a fire, and ate a meal. They were heard later "speaking authoritatively" and in the morning the Marshalls learned that their new friends had been telling a lioness to "go away." Close by where their heads had lain, they saw the footprints of the lioness.

A few Bushmen appeared and the Marshalls explained that they wished them no harm but only came to learn about their lives. The men agreed to bring their families to the water hole. They were shy and fearful of outsiders, with good reason. Many had been exploited by farmers, who needed laborers, and cheated by the Bantu, with whom they traded skins for metal and tobacco.

The Kalahari is a hostile land "of thirst, heat and thorns," where rain falls only in three months of the year. It would be completely forbidding, with no landmarks, if not for the baobab tree:

> It is the biggest thing in all the landscape, dominating all the veld, more impressive than any mountain. It can be as much as two hundred feet high and thirty feet in diameter. It has great, thick branches that sprout haphazardly from the sides of the trunk and reach like stretching arms into the sky. The bark is thin and smooth and rather pink, and sags in folds toward the base of the tree. . . . Its trunk is soft and pulpy, like a carrot instead of wooden, and if you lean against it you find that it is warm from the sun and you expect to hear a great heart beating inside. . . . In the Kalahari there is no need of hills. The great baobabs standing in the plains, the wind, and the seasons are enough. (*The Harmless People*, p. 4)

Bushmen, she wrote, were "a naked, hungry people." They have no features in common with the Negro or Bantu peoples living nearby except for "peppercorn curly hair"; they are yellow rather than black; and they have faces very like those of Asians. The Bushmen and the Hottentots belong to the same racial group and are the earliest human inhabitants still living in southern Africa. The Bushmen are short (the men are a little over five feet tall, the women are a little shorter), handsome, and graceful, with soft voices. When Elizabeth visited them, they were wearing the skins of animals; men wore only a leather loincloth, women a small leather apron and a big leather cape in which the babies were carried. Children went naked. They lived in small groups, making grass huts so inconspicuous that a stranger might not be able to perceive them.

The veld determined the way of life. There was not water enough to raise livestock, so the men hunted game, using arrows which were, indeed, poisoned. The arrows seldom killed the animal at once, and the hunters followed it, sometimes for days, until the poison took effect. Bushmen did not work metal and had no weapons other than the bows and arrows. A peaceable people, they avoided conflict with outsiders and with each other. When an animal was killed, every bit of it was used: The meat not used at once was dried, the skin made clothing, the bones became arrow points. No crops could be grown, and the people lived on wild food—melons, roots, grain, and grubs. When they exhausted the supply of wild food in one place, they moved to another, yet each group had a specific territory.

The Marshalls visited four of the Bushmen language groups in 1951 and later— the Naron, the Ko, the Gikwe, and the Kung. Elizabeth was with the family in their 1951, 1952, and 1955 expeditions. Other family members returned several more times; Lorna made further studies of the Kung of the Nyae Nyae area, and John made another trip in 1978.

Elizabeth transferred to Radcliffe College in order to study anthropology, and she graduated in 1954. She married Stephen M. Thomas, a writer. In 1952 she won the *Mademoiselle* college fiction contest with a story, "The Hill People," later reprinted in Martha Foley's *Best Short Stories of 1953*. Her book about the Bushmen, *The Harmless People*, was published in 1959 on the day her second child was born. Acclaimed as an unusually fine travel book, it led to a Guggenheim Fellowship. Lorna Marshall in 1976 published her scholarly *The !Kung of Nyae Nyae*. John Marshall's documentary film, *The Hunters*, won the 1958 Robert J. Flaherty Award, and his *Nai, the Story of a Kung Woman* has been shown on public television.

The Guggenheim fellowship and backing from the *New Yorker* enabled Elizabeth to go to Uganda in 1961 to work with the Dodoth tribesmen and to gather material for her second book, *Warrior Herdsmen*. She was accompanied this time by her husband and children.

The Dodoth are a nation of twenty thousand people, offshoots of the Karamojong, who live in the far northeast corner of Uganda, not far from the source of the Blue Nile. The Thomases and those who worked with them established a camp at Morukore in the district of Lokoki. Morukore consisted of four households, and with the members of these households Elizabeth became closely acquainted.

The Dodoth were conservative pastoralists who had for the last two centuries resisted any change in their customs. As Elizabeth noted, they "paint no pictures, carve no figures, weave no fabrics, and make no dishes, baskets, or jars." They had no music or musical instruments. They had little religion, yet their culture was complex and the people highly imaginative.

> The care and passion, the artistic expression, and the materialism that other people devolve on other things are fixed, by the Dodoth, on their cattle. . . . For the Dodoth, cattle are the warp of life. They are the only wealth, the foundation of economic and social stability, the origin of all human ties. If drought comes, if the gardens and the grain crops fail, cattle provide food. . . . Cowhides make sleeping mats and clothing. Cow dung makes flooring. . . . With cattle, men marry. . . . A man gives twenty or fifty or a hundred and fifty cattle for each wife, wanting to pay as much as he can rather than search for a bargain, for he not only gains a woman to live with him and bear his children but also forms a strong and deep connection with her family. . . . Cattle are part of religious life. During all important ceremonies, an ox or many oxen are speared as sacrifices. (*Warrior Herdsmen*, pp. 6–8)

Other people hostile to the Dodoth lived near them and raided their cattle. When drought and disease depleted their herds, the Jie and the Turkana took the Dodoth cattle. "Thus battles are fought, and crops and dwellings burned, and human lives risked and lost for the little lyre-horned cattle" (*Warrior Herdsmen*, p. 9). Because of these battles, the Thomases were warned that going among the Dodoth was risky for people with white skins. Not so, reported Elizabeth. "We had an eerie immunity from the pastoral wars and came and went like birds in the air" (*Warrior Herdsmen*, p. 10). Their possessions were equally safe. The Dodoths cared nothing for such treasures as trucks and European goods, only for cattle.

Each household, each large family, occupied its own self-contained dwelling. It was made in the form of a great circle, enclosed with upright poles wound with densely woven branches, its doors so tiny that one must crouch and squeeze through. No enemy could enter; spears could not penetrate the walls; and the livestock, which shared the enclosure at night, could not get through the doorways. Inner walls made separate sections to accommodate different groups within the extended family. Elizabeth described a typical scene:

> Early in the morning, when the sky was cold and pale and the morning wind rising, the heavy poles that closed the cattle gate, the one large opening in the outer wall, were moved away and the cattle would emerge in procession . . . followed by its herdboys, three dark-skinned, naked little sons of the household, each carrying the smoldering end of a log, a remnant of his mother's nighttime fire. Warm smoke would blow back over the little boys to mix with the cold, gray mist rising from the earth around them. They were like little boys in clouds. The boys would flourish sticks at the cattle and the cattle, eating as they went, would start their slow procession toward pasture. (*Warrior Herdsmen*, pp. 13–14)

This dwelling was the domain of a fierce old man, Lopore. He built the house, where he lived with four wives, many children, and the relatives of his wives. "His grown sons respected him, his married daughters obeyed him. And of his wives, two loved him, one adored him, and one no longer cared for him and today merely resides in his house" (*Warrior Herdsmen*, p. 17). Elizabeth's group asked his permission to pitch their camp near his dwelling, and Lopore not only gave the permission but became a good friend during the six months the expedition remained. He told Elizabeth of their tribal customs, and she was allowed to see the ceremony of sacrificing an ox before the men went out against cattle raiders.

The raids got so bad that many families were hard up; others moved their cattle into populated areas and the pastures were overgrazed. Refugee families, without cattle, were starving. They suffered from dysentery or pneumonia. Many, especially the children, died. The starving people swarmed into the town, Kaabong, in hopes of getting food and medical care. In exchange for help and protection, the Dodoth, like other independent tribes, were under great pressure to change their ways. After the Thomases left Uganda, knowing that changes would come, they watched for news of their friends there.

Change also overtook their friends among the Bushmen. In the early 1960s, the farmers in South-West Africa demanded more land and wanted to exterminate the animals that preyed on sheep. The mining companies wanted rights in the Kalahari. The government drilled a well at Tsumke and collected the Bushmen to live there, behind a chain link fence, where they cultivate corn. They are allowed to go out to the veld to hunt. When John Marshall visited them in 1978, one of the men told him "We are disappearing. We are as few as fingers" (*Smithsonian*, April 1980).

BIBLIOGRAPHY

Works by Elizabeth Marshall Thomas

The Harmless People. New York: Knopf, 1959; London: Secker & Warburg, 1959.
"Bushmen of the Kalahari." *National Geographic* 128 (June 1963): 866–88.
Warrior Herdsmen. New York: Knopf, 1965; London: Secker & Warburg, 1965.
"American Family's Poignant Sojourn with the Bushmen." *Smithsonian* 11 (Apr. 1980): 86–95.

Works about Elizabeth Marshall Thomas

Contemporary Authors. Detroit: Gale Research, 1922–date, first revision, vol. 17, p. 726.
Marshall, Lorna. *The !Kung of Nyae Nyae*. Cambridge, Mass.: Harvard University Press, 1976. An appendix lists John Marshall's films of the Bushmen.
Steinberg, Sybil. "Elizabeth Marshall Thomas." *Publishers Weekly*, Jan. 19, 1987, pp. 70–71.

ALEXINE TINNE
1835–1869

Alexine Tinne was a Dutch heiress whose several trips up the Nile River between 1856 and 1864 rank her as one of the first explorers determined to discover the source of the river. Certainly she was the most colorful, as well as the most tragic, of the Nile explorers. The last of her trips on the river was a true voyage of exploration—she took the only steamer in the Sudan, went up the White Nile and the Bahr al-Ghazal, and reached the country beyond Wau. She later traveled in the Sahara, where, in her thirty-third year, she was killed by Tuareg tribesmen.

On her Nile voyages Alexine was accompanied by her mother, Harriet Tinne, who took most of the responsibility for the administrative arrangements. Harriet kept a diary, but of Alexine's writings little is left beyond a description of plants she collected and deposited in a herbarium in Vienna. Neither published any accounts, and their travels became known only through her brother's communications, based on their letters, to the Royal Geographical Society, on the comments of other travelers, and on newspaper stories, which were sometimes wildly inaccurate. In 1970 Penelope Gladstone's *Travels of Alexine* for the first time gathered together from Harriet's diary, family letters, and the Royal Archives in The Hague about as much as is now known of the remarkable Tinnes, mother and daughter.

When David Livingstone wrote about the great Nile explorers, he commented that "none rises higher in my estimation than the Dutch lady, Miss Tinne." Samuel White Baker saw the Tinne expedition on the Nile in 1862 and thought they must be demented because they meant to travel among naked Africans.

It was not easy to overlook the Tinnes, for they traveled in the most lavish and leisurely style, with a huge retinue of servants, a number of pet dogs, every convenience in the way of furnishings, and enormous piles of luggage. Popular opinion was that they were foolish to undertake any expedition into wild country without male escorts. As a matter of fact, they did have male escorts much of the way, for they attracted some very interesting companions. They were themselves interesting, gay, and popular. They traveled strictly for the fun of it, and for Alexine the greatest pleasure was to go where no one had preceded her.

Alexine Tinne was the only child of her father's second marriage. When she was born, on October 17, 1835, he was sixty-three and his wife was thirty-seven, and both were overjoyed at her arrival. Philip Tinne came from a long-established Dutch family. He had founded a business in Liverpool, England, where his two sons by his first wife lived. Alexine's mother was Harriet van Capellen, also of a worthy Dutch family with connections at the court. After their marriage, the couple established a home at The Hague, where Alexine was born. She was christened Alexandrina Petronella Francina. When she was nine, Philip died, leaving a large fortune to his family, mostly to his two sons in England and to Alexine, who, at the age of twenty-one, came into possession of about 69,000 pounds.

A love-affair that agitated Alexine seems to have been the catalyst for the beginning of her foreign travels. Adolf Konigsmarck had seemed the perfect match for her, a well-born army officer, in love with her, as she was with him. Something happened that made her never again want to see him. Harriet, who since her husband's death had devoted herself entirely to Alexine, decided to take her away from The Hague on a long trip. It began as a grand European tour, and it lasted for two years. Harriet confided to her diary at its beginning that she was "really too old to travel." She was fifty-seven. The disruption of her daily routine and the change in foods made her uncomfortable. But Alexine was young and eager for adventure, and Harriet felt she must accompany her.

Early in 1856, the two women went to Egypt. There they engaged a ninety-foot *dahabeah* and loaded it with furniture, food, champagne, and livestock. Their entourage included personal servants, a cook, a waiter, an Egyptian guide, a secretary, a captain, and a crew of sailors. A Mr. Van de Velde, a Dutch friend they had met on their way to Egypt, accompanied them. They went up river as far as Aswan, where they stopped to see a monastery at La Pontie, to sightsee around Luxor, and to visit Philae's beautiful ancient buildings. They left the boat to travel across the desert, via camel, to Al Quseir on the Red Sea, before they returned down the river to Cairo, after a journey of ten weeks.

They spent the summer visiting the Holy Land, where they hired as guide, protector, and interpreter Osman Aga, who was to serve them until their last Nile trip. Van de Velde, who had visited the Holy Land before, remained with them. In Beirut they stayed for some time in a monastery, Sainte Roc, where Alexine managed to obtain a piano. They finished up the year again in Egypt and celebrated Christmas at Shepheards Hotel in Cairo. Harriet was weary, but her daughter was taken with the idea of another Nile voyage.

This time she wanted to go as far as Khartoum, which, she was told, would be impossible without a steamer. Since no steamer was available, they fitted up a large *dahabeah* and hired a bigger crew; after a great party—for they had made many friends in Cairo—they started up river toward Asyut. Here, they thought they could get camels and explore the desert to the west. When they reached this point, however, they learned it was too dangerous for desert travel, so they continued up the Nile. At the second cataract they found it impossible to continue and they turned back, arriving at Cairo again in March. The remainder of 1857 they spent in Beirut, Turkey, Italy, Vienna, and finally, home. They took with them their Egyptian cook, Halib, and a big dog Alexine had acquired along the way.

In 1860 they began preparations for a longer Nile journey, for Alexine still wished to explore much farther south. They included in the party Harriet's sister, Adriana van Capellen. Aunt Addy was fourteen years younger than Harriet and had been a lady-in-waiting to the Netherlands queen mother. She had visited Russia with the queen mother, who was a sister of Tsar Alexander I. There, Aunt Addy had had an unhappy love affair, which left her a rather morose companion, not at all like Harriet, who, though she might tire of constant movement, always took a lively interest in everything she saw and did.

They started in the summer of 1861, but, since the Nile voyage could not begin until January, they rented a house in Cairo, had silver and china sent to them, and had a piano brought in for Alexine. They lived in style, adding to their establishment a large number of servants, for whom they ordered uniforms, and entertaining all their old and new friends. They did not discriminate in favor of Europeans; they were glad to make friends from all races and nations. As they were obviously wealthy, the merchants took advantage of them. On the credit side, they met many kind and helpful people, including Ferdinand de Lesseps, who invited them to visit the canal he was building at Suez.

In January they set off from Cairo with three boats, in one of which the Europeans, Halib, two Arab domestics, the pet dogs—now numbering five—and provisions for a year were crowded. Many other groups were sailing up the river, and by the time they reached Aswan the Tinnes had extended their acquaintance to include the other voyagers—Russians, Scandinavians, Italians, Germans, and Sardinians. When the others found that the Dutch ladies were going on south to the Sudan, they were much interested and dubbed Alexine Queen of the Equator. As a matter of fact, she had planned to go up the Blue Nile and explore the interior of Ethiopia.

After a journey of nearly twelve weeks the Tinne party reached Khartoum. The whole expedition had disembarked at Korosko and crossed the desert by horse, donkey, and camel. There were 102 camels for the luggage and the dogs, who rode in panniers. Addy and Harriet found it very uncomfortable riding on camels, and Harriet changed to a donkey. Addy would gladly have quit the party, but there was no turning back.

At Khartoum they found everyone talking about the English explorers who were searching for the source of the Nile. John Speke and James Grant were due to return from an expedition that had been sent out to East Africa by the Royal Geographical Society. In fact, they were overdue, and the society had sent funds to buy a boat and provisions to meet the explorers at Gondokoro, many miles farther up the river. The British consul at Khartoum, John Petherick, had been entrusted with the money and the mission. Somewhat to Harriet's dismay, the talk inspired Alexine to give up the Blue Nile in favor of proceeding up the White Nile. Khartoum is located at the confluence of the two rivers.

Alexine thought they might build a house somewhere up river and live there for a time, so they added building materials to their pile of luggage, and by a lucky chance they found an Italian mason who was willing to go along. Alexine tried to hire a steamer belonging to the governor general, but she was unsuccessful. However, the man in charge of the steamer agreed to tow her boats part of the way. The flotilla left Khartoum on May 11. At the end of a week they reached Jebel Dinka, a trading station used by slavers. The women were horrified at the conditions there, where men, women, and children were kept, some in chains. When a woman begged Alexine to take her baby to save it from starvation, Alexine bought the whole family of six, a gesture more humanitarian than wise, for it caused her to be accused of buying slaves. The family later disappeared, perhaps to escape, perhaps to be recaptured.

Harriet left Alexine and most of the party camped near here to return to Khartoum with the steamer and a leaking *dahabeah* for repairs, more provisions, and more money. Halib, suffering from a throat abscess, went with her to get medical attention. Harriet was fortunate enough to hire the steamer for a year, although at an exorbitant price, and she soon rejoined the rest of the party.

They chugged up the river to Lake No. Here they had a choice of two tributaries, the Bahr al-Ghazal or the Bahr al-Jebel. They took the latter. The narrow stream wound for a hundred and fifty miles through the sudd, a mass of vegetation that greatly hampered their progress. The boats were tied together and the ropes often broke or got tangled. The steamer needed a constant supply of wood, which was hard to find. It took three weeks to get through this lonely and desolate stretch. At last they reached the Holy Cross mission station, where they spent some time with the two priests and eleven laymen, who were only too pleased to offer hospitality to Europeans. John Petherick and his wife, Katherine, had just passed through, on their way to Gondokoro to meet Speke. Alexine tried to catch up with them to offer to take the supplies in her steamer, but she was unsuccessful.

As they neared Gondokoro, Osman Aga, who was trying to capture a boat which had broken away, fell into the river and drowned. He was buried with great ceremony on the shore. His death cast the first shadow over the expedition.

Gondokoro was almost deserted. Except for a few huts, it was occupied only during December and January when the traders brought in ivory and slaves to be sent north. It was considered to be the farthest navigable point on the Nile, but the Tinnes managed to go beyond it as far as Rejaf, where the river became too treacherous. They planned to remain here and to send the steamer back to Khartoum to fetch more provisions before marching into the interior, but after a short stay they changed their minds. The natives were not at all friendly, for the slave traders had made them fearful of all outsiders. Addy wanted desperately to go home. Alexine became ill. The expedition returned to Khartoum. They had spent five months on the White Nile, and Harriet wrote that she had enjoyed the "damn-me don't care sort of life."

Alexine would not admit defeat. She spent the next weeks in Khartoum planning a return trip—this time to ascend the Bahr al-Ghazal and thence to reach the highlands of central Africa, perhaps the Equator. Two Germans, Baron Theodor von Heuglin, an ornithologist, and Hermann Steudner, a botanist, wished to explore the interior and were added to the party. A fellow Dutchman, Baron d'Ablaing, also decided to join them. They set off in February with six boats—the steamer, their *dahabeah*, three luggage *nuggars*, and d'Ablaing's own *dahabeah*. They had six servants, seventy-one soldiers, animals, and supplies and ammunition for six months. Aunt Addy was left in Khartoum.

For eight months the unhappy Addy had no word from the party. She met Speke and Grant on their return from Gondokoro (where Samuel and Florence Baker had given them provisions and transportation before the luckless Pethericks arrived). Speke told her of the dangers they had suffered, and, at Addy's request, he wrote a warning letter, which Addy sent on to Harriet. The letter reached Harriet, but she did not worry. In fact, she wrote a long letter to her stepson, John Tinne, about the success of the expedition, which he communicated to the Royal Geographical Society.

Addy, meanwhile, did worry. She managed to get seventy-five soldiers and porters and provisions, and she sent out a search party. They met Alexine at Wau in January 1864 on her return trip. The provisions and extra porters were desperately needed. The expedition had met with a series of tragedies—tropical storms, floods, hostile traders, illness, and death. The survivors, exhausted and saddened, reached Khartoum at the end of March.

Three coffins were carried out. Harriet had died of fever on July 22, 1863. Her maid of many years, Flora, lived only a month longer. Anna, Alexine's maid, sustained her distraught mistress after the loss of her beloved mother, then she, too, succumbed to fever. Steudner, the botanist, had died at Wau and was buried there. Heuglin and d'Ablaing, both ill, were carried in litters. Alexine was overcome with grief. A further blow fell after they reached Khartoum when Aunt Addy died.

Alexine had succeeded in exploring unknown country. She had brought back a valuable botanical collection, which went to the Imperial Herbarium of the Court of Vienna and was illustrated in a beautiful book, *Plantae Tinneanae*. The book includes an account of the expedition up the Bahr al-Ghazal and a portrait of Harriet.

Alexine never returned to The Hague. Nor did she wish to visit any of the places she and Harriet had enjoyed together. She lived in Cairo for a time. In 1867 she settled in Algiers, where she was well regarded as a generous and friendly resident. She traveled through the Algerian desert and began her final trip across the Sahara in January 1869. Months later, on August 1, according to the best accounts, her party was attacked by Tuareg brigands. Five of her companions survived to tell the distressing story of her murder. Her body was never found.

The family gave a new building to the English Episcopal Church in The Hague as a memorial to Alexine. (It was bombed in the second World War.) At Juba in the Sudan a monument containing the names of African explorers includes that of Alexine Tinne.

BIBLIOGRAPHY

Works about Alexine Tinne

Adams, William Davenport. *Celebrated Women Travellers of the Nineteenth Century*. London: Sonnenschein, 1883.

Gladstone, Penelope. *Travels of Alexine: Alexine Tinne, 1835–1869*. London: Murray, 1970.

Johnston, Harry H. *The Nile Quest*. London: Scholarly Press, 1903; New York: Stokes, 1903, pp. 192–200.

Ladies on the Loose: Women Travellers of the 18th and 19th Centuries. Edited by Leo Hamalian. New York: Dodd, Mead, 1981, pp. 225–28.

Oliver, Caroline. *Western Women in Colonial Africa*. Westport, Conn.: Greenwood Press, 1981, pp. 50–75.

Rittenhouse, Mignon. *Seven Women Explorers*. Philadelphia: Lippincott, 1964, pp. 13–35.

Wells, William. *The Heroine of the White Nile; or, What a Woman Did and Dared. A Sketch of the Remarkable Travels and Experiences of Miss Alexandrine Tinne*. New York: Carlton & Lanahan, 1871. A Sunday School book, undocumented.

Alexine's murder was reported in the *New York Times*, on Aug. 30, 1869.

FANNY BULLOCK WORKMAN
1859–1925

Fanny Bullock Workman spent almost half of her lifetime traveling. An American, she lived abroad much of the time between 1886 and her death in France at the age of sixty-six. With her husband and constant traveling companion, William Hunter Workman, she explored Europe, climbed Alpine mountains, and visited many places around the Mediterranean. In the 1890s, they joined the popular sport of bicycle riding and wheeled their way through Spain and India. They then discovered the form of travel which would make them famous: exploring the Himalayan Mountains.

They made eight expeditions into the Karakoram range, at that time almost entirely unexplored and unmapped. In a day before the invention of lightweight tents and clothing, freeze-dried foods, sun-block cream, and radio transmitters, the couple (who were both past forty) planned and carried out these mountaineering treks with success. They carried scientific equipment to measure altitudes, temperatures, and their own physiological adaptation to mountain conditions. They did some surveying and mapping, took photographs, and, although they made some errors, they also contributed significantly to the world's geographical knowledge.

They reported on their travels in eight large volumes—all, except one, were published under both their names. Fanny, a feminist, was fiercely proud of her record of being the first woman to reach an altitude of over 23,000 feet in 1906; the record was not broken until 1934. Annie Peck, another American climber, thought she had broken the record for women in 1908, but Fanny hired engineers to measure the Andean mountain Annie had climbed and to prove that it was not quite as high as the Nun Kun peak she herself reached. Fanny was also proud of her membership in many geographical and mountaineering societies, listing them on the title pages of her books, as did her husband. The books are valuable contributions to the early literature of travel and mountaineering.

Fanny Bullock was born in Worcester, Massachusetts, on January 8, 1859. Her father, Alexander Hamilton Bullock, was elected governor of Massachusetts in

1866. Her mother, Eliza Hazard Bullock, was the daughter of a wealthy Connecticut manufacturer and merchant. With a background of wealth and position, Fanny was educated by tutors and "finished" in a New York private school and in Paris and Dresden. She came home ready to enter an upper-class social life. In 1881 she married William Hunter Workman, a prominent Worcester physician. She was twenty-two; he was thirty-four, a graduate of Yale and Harvard. After a respectable period they had a daughter, Rachel. Little is known about Rachel, who must have spent all her early years in boarding schools, for the Workmans began to travel two years after her birth. Rachel grew up to graduate as a geologist from London University and to marry Sir Alexander MacRobert, a Scot. Her parents named a mountain in the Himalayas for her.

Dr. Workman continued his Massachusetts practice until 1889, when he resigned his medical posts because of ill health and moved the family to Europe. They had already made trips to Norway and Sweden, and for some years they enjoyed the art galleries and concerts of Germany. They did not live a sedentary life, for they climbed in the Alps, went on walking tours, and bicycled about several European countries. It must have been quite a change and liberation of a sort when, in 1895, they gave up the life of wealthy, socially prominent expatriates for one of carefree but energetic travel. They undertook a long bicycle trip through Algeria and Spain.

As Fanny pedalled along, with a pack behind her seat and a canteen hanging from her belt, she was free from many social restrictions. But she kept to the dress of a lady—hats and veils, sometimes a parasol, white shirtwaists, and long bulky skirts reaching below her ankles. Not until much later did she adopt shorter skirts and wrap her sturdy legs in puttees for climbing. Never, never, did she descend to wearing trousers or bloomers.

According to the Workmans, bicycles were chosen "not to satisfy the spirit of adventure commonly ascribed to Americans" but because it was the best means of conveyance to give them "entire independence of the usual hindrances of the traveller to pass through the country at leisure, stopping where and when we pleased" (*Sketches Awheel*, p. v). They carried from twelve to twenty pounds of luggage and covered an average of seventy-five kilometers a day, slowed by the necessity to mend frequent punctures. They stopped at small inns for food and shelter.

Although bicycling was becoming so popular that it had its own clubs and maps, the Workmans could not learn much in advance about the conditions of the roads. Personal correspondence "only elicited the rather dubious reply that not much could be said for the roads, particularly in the spring" (*Sketches Awheel*, p. xiii). Some were good; others were badly made and poorly kept up; some were abominable. Often they had to push the wheels uphill over mountains.

The country people, wrote the Workmans, "almost invariably took us to be French, never dreaming that the representatives of any more distant nation could be travelling among them." When they said they were from America, "they regarded us with very much the same awe-inspired expression as might have

been called forth had we been inhabitants of one of the heavenly bodies''
(*Sketches Awheel*, pp. 47–48). In Algeria they were delighted with the palms
and flowering trees and Moorish architecture, but they felt the people were rude
and annoying. Near the coast they met mule trains driven by brutish, often
intoxicated drivers. The mules were frightened by the bicycles and ran off the
road, and several times the cyclists were threatened by angry, knife-brandishing
drivers. One muleteer seemed about to chop them up with a mattock, but the
Workmans showed their revolvers, and he retreated.

Even in the city, annoyances awaited them.

> Barcelona is not a pleasant place for a woman to visit with a bicycle on account
> of the great number of rough mechanics and labourers at all times on the streets.
> ... Even in a regulation street gown she cannot walk a block alone without being
> rudely spoken to. (*Sketches Awheel*, p. 19)

On the other hand, they received many courtesies from Spanish gentlemen and
from other cyclists and were invited to attend races. Had they desired, they
might have had escorts from city to city, but they preferred to be free to explore.
In Spain they visited cathedrals and art galleries and attended bullfights. At the
end of their three-and-a-half-month trip, they concluded that ''Spain is not so
far advanced in civilisation but that adventures may still be found without any
great amount of seeking'' (*Sketches Awheel*, p. 6). In Morocco they felt more
like pioneers, and for a time they exchanged their bicycles for horses and rode
into the hills.

The novelty of tourists getting about by bicycle, and especially a woman doing
so, attracted newspaper interest. The papers, wrote Fanny,

> had been heralding our movements and arrival at different cities, garnishing the
> notices with various bits of information suggested by the imaginations of their
> editors regarding us and our bicycles, the most common of which were that we
> were a ''matrimonio ingles'' or English married pair from London, and that we
> were mounted on wonderfully fine bicycles. (*Sketches Awheel*, p. 163)

Two books resulted from these bicycle trips, *Algerian Memories* (1895) and
Sketches Awheel (1897). The Workmans adopted a curious dual, third-person
style that obliged them to speak of ''one of us'' or ''the male member of our
party,'' leading sometimes to the ridiculous: ''one of us'' wore a mantilla. The
books are larded with descriptions of cities and towns, giving little sense of
discovery or adventure. Poor souls, they had no gift for making friends; they
seem never to have carried letters of introduction which might have opened doors
to upper-class Spaniards. Their New England consciences kept them to strict
schedules and routes and the keeping of logs and notes. But their cycling books
were quite popular and no doubt stimulated others to tour by the same means.

The Workmans next tackled a more difficult country, India, for a bicycle tour that covered approximately 14,000 miles. Of course they had a serious purpose: to see as many as possible of the ruins of architecture and art remaining from ancient civilizations. They had boned up on the history of the early societies, religions, and styles of architecture, and they carried cameras and film on which to record their finds so as to make them known to others. "To see even a tithe of the comparatively few [monuments] now left," they wrote, "required extensive travel of a primitive kind and the endurance of much hardship" (*Through Town and Jungle*, p. ix). They went from the southern extremity of India northward far into Kashmir, and from Cuttack on the eastern coast across the breadth of India to the Arabian Sea, with much crossing and circling about the interior. Sometimes they left their bicycles to get about "by rail, steamboat, tonga, tumtum, bullock-cart, palki, and on foot." They traveled many more miles through Burma, Ceylon, and Java, and spent ten days at the temples of Angkor in Siam.

Travel by bicycle in India, they found, was quite a different thing from European journeying. Hotels were to be found only in cities, and the traveler had to depend on finding a *dak* bungalow for shelter. Often dirty, ill equipped, and comfortless, many failed even to supply food and water. The couple solved the problem by taking a route near a railway so that, when no other shelter was at hand, they could always stay in a railroad waiting room, although it offered no more than a straight chair or a hard bench. A servant was sent ahead with their trunks to wait for them at prearranged railway stops. They carried a small supply of food (tea, sugar, biscuits, cheese, and tinned meats), as well as canteens of water, medical kits, repair kits for the bicycles, air pillows, a blanket apiece, and writing materials. Of course they had cameras, and Fanny carried a teakettle bouncing on her handlebars.

The Indian tours occupied parts of three years. After the first tour the Workmans left their kit in a Srinagar hotel while they went off to explore the glaciers and peaks of Baltistan. Because a great flood, which swept over the Kashmir Valley in 1903, destroyed all their Indian photographs and negatives, they went back over some of the same ground to take more photographs before going on to complete the planned trip. In 1904 Fanny and William published the results of their tour in a lavishly illustrated book, *Through Town and Jungle: Fourteen Thousand Miles A-wheel among the Temples and People of the Indian Plain*, which contains much weighty historical and architectural data but little of substance about the people themselves.

Something more significant than a flood, however, had happened to them on the Baltistan trip: They had been introduced to the heady experience of climbing in the highest mountains of the world. The Workmans' pleasure in beholding the frozen wonderland enlivened their book *In the Ice World of Himalaya*, which was published in 1900. It was the first of five books that resulted from their mountain climbing expeditions. They were not the first to explore the mighty Karakoram, but Fanny was one of the first of her sex to do so. She set her first altitude record for women in 1899, when she attained an altitude of 21,000 feet on Mt. Koser Gunge. She pointed out that her climb had come after the cycle trip in tropical Java and after two and a half weeks "lying around inactive on the decks of steamers," certainly not the best training for mountain work. Although she was not light in weight and was a slow climber, she had remarkable powers of endurance and unparalleled determination.

The Workmans used equipment that had been sent from England, including flannel-lined Mummery tents and eider sleeping sacks, and they had heavy cameras and scientific instruments. A huge supply of food had to be carried, which meant a large number of porters. Although the Workmans were good at organizing an expedition, they were not at all good at achieving cooperation with the carriers. A number of times they had very sad experiences; once they were left to their own devices on the trail, and once they had much of their food supply stolen—all because they could not communicate with the headmen and had no rapport with the porters.

They suffered from the bitter cold and from the altitude. They had dangerous moments; once Fanny fell into a crevasse, from which she was extricated by a guide hauling on the rope. But when things seemed discouraging they remembered the former world of social chit-chat, balls, and church attendance, and they rejoiced in their freedom from "utter respectability."

After five expeditions (in 1898, 1899, 1902, 1903, and 1906), all resulting in valuable contributions to the mapping of the mountain areas, the Workmans felt they had done with mountaineering, but, in 1908, they wrote,

> we had breathed the atmosphere of that great mountain-world, had drunk of the swirling waters of its glaciers, and feasted our eyes on the incomparable beauty and majesty of its towering peaks, and, as time passed on, its charms asserted their power anew and called to us with irresistible, siren strains to return yet once again to those regions, the grandeur of which satisfies so fully the sense of the beautiful and sublime. (*The Call of the Snowy Hispar*, p. 1)

This time, they explored the Hispar Glacier and crossed the Hispar Pass to the Biafo Glacier. Fanny had already made her highest ascent, Pinnacle Peak in the Nun Kun massif. She estimated the altitude to be 23,300 feet; it is now determined to be 22,815 feet. A mountain in Baltistan was named Mount Bullock Workman. They had contributed to the mapping of the area.

In 1911 and again in 1912, when Fanny was in her fifties and William in his sixties, they returned to the "abode of snow." On the last trip one of their Italian porters, just ahead of Fanny, fell into an icy, fathomless hole. Fortunately for Fanny, she was not roped and could step back in time. The death threw a pall over the expedition, but instead of turning back they completed the trek and made their scientific measurements. On their return Fanny wrote *Two Summers in the Ice-Wilds of Eastern Karakoram*. One photograph showed Fanny on Silver Throne Plateau reading a paper headed "Votes for Women."

The Workmans had become famous; they received honors from a number of countries and learned societies. Fanny was invited to speak to the Royal Geographical Society in 1905, the second woman to do so (Isabella Bird Bishop was the first), but she was never made a Fellow, though William was. She lectured throughout Europe and was the first American woman to lecture to the Sorbonne.

World War I put an end to travel for the Workmans. They spent the war years in the south of France. In 1917 Fanny's magnificent constitution failed, and, after a long illness, she died in Cannes on January 22, 1925. Dr. Workman took her ashes back to Massachusetts for burial. She left an estate of nearly $500,000 and made bequests to four women's colleges—Radcliffe, Wellesley, Smith, and Bryn Mawr. Bryn Mawr established a Fanny Bullock Workman Traveling Fellowship, to which her husband also contributed. Dr. Workman lived until 1937. The famous couple are remembered in Worcester, where their ashes are buried in the Rural Cemetery beneath a monument reading "Pioneer Himalayan Explorers."

BIBLIOGRAPHY

Works by Fanny Bullock Workman

(With William Hunter Workman) *Algerian Memories: A Bicycle Tour over the Atlas to the Sahara*. London: Unwin, 1895.
———. *Sketches Awheel in Modern Iberia*. New York and London: Putnam, 1897. Also published as *Sketches Awheel in Fin de Siècle Iberia*. London: Unwin, 1897.
———. *In the Ice World of Himalaya: Among the Peaks and Passes of Ladakh, Nubra, Suru, and Baltistan*. London: Unwin, 1900.
"Among the Great Himalayan Glaciers." *National Geographic* 13 (Nov. 1902): 405–6.
"First Ascents of the Hoh Lumba and Sosbon Glaciers in the Northwest Himalayas." *Independent* 55 (Dec. 31, 1903): 3108–12.
(With William Hunter Workman) *Through Town and Jungle: Fourteen Thousand Miles A-wheel among the Temples and People of the Indian Plain*. London: Unwin, 1904.
———. *Ice-Bound Heights of the Mustagh: An Account of Two Seasons of Pioneer Exploration and High Climbing in the Baltistan Himalaya*. London: Constable, 1908.
Peaks and Glaciers of Nun Kun: A Record of Pioneer Exploration and Mountaineering in the Punjab Himalaya. London: Constable, 1909.
"Miss Peck and Mrs. Workman." *Scientific American* 102 (Feb. 12, and Apr. 16, 1910): 143, 319. Letters on the controversy over the mountain heights. Peck's reply appeared in the issue for Feb. 26, 1910.
"Recent First Ascents in the Himalaya." *Independent* 68 (June 2, 1910): 1202–10.
(With William Hunter Workman) *The Call of the Snowy Hispar: A Narrative of Exploration and Mountaineering on the Northern Frontier of India*. London: Constable, 1910; New York: Scribner, 1911.
"Conquering the Great Rose." *Harper* 129 (June 1914): 44–45.
"Exploring the Rose." *Independent* 85 (Jan. 10, 1916): 54–56.
"Four Miles High." *Independent* 86 (June 5, 1916): 377–78.

Two Summers in the Ice-Wilds of Eastern Karakoram: The Exploration of Nineteen Hundred Square Miles of Mountains and Glaciers. London: Unwin, 1917.

Works about Fanny Bullock Workman

Dictionary of American Biography. New York: Scribner, 1927-date, vol. 10 (1936): 533–34.

International Dictionary of Women's Biography. Edited by Jennifer S. Uglow and Frances Hinton. New York: Continuum, 1982.

Kay, A. "Matron of the Mountains." *Coronet* 36 (Oct. 1954): 139–40.

Ladies on the Loose: Women Travellers of the 18th and 19th Centuries. Edited by Leo Hamalian. New York: Dodd, Mead, 1981, pp. 210–22.

Mason, Kenneth. *Abode of Snow.* New York: Dutton, 1955, pp. 131–32, 139–40.

Middleton, Dorothy. *Victorian Lady Travellers.* London: Routledge & Kegan Paul, 1965, pp. 75–89.

Miller, Luree. *On Top of the World: Five Women Explorers in Tibet.* London: Paddington, 1976, pp. 101–29.

Notable American Women, 1607–1950. Edited by Edward T. James and others. Cambridge, Mass.: Harvard University Press, 1971.

"A Record Climb in the Himalayas: Mrs. Bullock Workman, Cyclist and Mountaineer." *The Young Woman* 9 (1900–1901).

Rittenhouse, Mignon. *Seven Women Explorers.* Philadelphia: Lippincott, 1964, pp. 79–101.

Tarbell, Arthur. "Fanny Bullock Workman, Explorer and Alpinist." *New England Magazine,* n.s. 33 (Dec. 1905): 487–90.

"Woman in the Himalayas." *Putnam's* 7 (Jan. 1910): 474–82.

An obituary of Fanny Workman appeared in the *New York Times,* on Jan. 27, 1925; that of Dr. Workman appeared on Oct. 10, 1937.

APPENDIX: BOOKS OF EXPLORATION AND TRAVEL

This is a selected list of exploration and travel books written by women and published in the English language. Intended to supplement the foregoing biographical accounts of women explorers and travelers, it applies the same criteria that determined the choice of those individuals. Anthropological, historical, and geographical accounts are not included, nor are all experiences of residents of foreign countries. Guide books and journalistic accounts of tours are omitted, as are books written mainly for a juvenile audience. Several categories of travelers are excluded, not because they are unworthy but because they deserve special treatment: sea voyagers, mountain climbers, air and space travelers, oceanic explorers, and many round-the-world travelers. All of the books listed are judged to be worthwhile, enjoyable accounts; some will be recognized as literary gems.

Titles attached to the biographical studies are not repeated here.

Ackermann, Jessie A. *The World through a Woman's Eyes*. Chicago: n.p., 1896. By a round-the-world missionary of the Woman's Christian Temperance Union.

Agassiz, Elizabeth, with Louis Agassiz. *A Journey in Brazil*. Boston: Ticknor & Fields, 1868. The Thayer expedition to Brazil in 1865–1866.

Ahl, Frances Norene. *New Zealand through American Eyes*. Boston: Christopher, 1948. Ahl's books include several on aeronautics.

———. *Two Thousand Miles up the Amazon*. Boston: Christopher, 1941.

Akeley, Mary Lee Jobe. *Adventures in the African Jungle*. New York: Junior Literary Guild, 1931. Tales by Carl and Mary Akeley. Before her marriage to Akeley, Mary Jobe explored Canada and published articles under her maiden name.

———. *Carl Akeley's Africa: An Account of the Akeley-Eastman-Pomeroy African Hall Expedition of the American Museum of Natural History*. New York: Dodd, Mead, 1929.

———. *Congo Eden: A Comprehensive Portrayal of the Historical Background and Scientific Aspects of the Great Game Sanctuary of the Belgian Congo*. New York: Dodd, Mead, 1950.

———. *Restless Jungle*. New York: McBride, 1936.

———. *Rumble of a Distant Drum: A True Story of the African Hinterland.* New York: Dodd, Mead, 1946.

———. *The Wilderness Lives Again: Carl Akeley and the Great African Adventure.* New York: Dodd, Mead, 1940.

Akeley, Mary Lee Jobe, with Carl Akeley. *Lions, Gorillas and Their Neighbors.* New York: Dodd, Mead, 1932.

Alexander, Frances. See Cobbold, Lady Evelyn Murray.

Ames, Evelyn Perkins. *A Glimpse of Eden.* Boston: Houghton Mifflin, 1967; London: Collins, 1968. East Africa.

———. *In Time Like Glass: Reflections on a Journey in Asia.* Boston: Houghton Mifflin, 1974.

Anderson, Isabel Weld Perkins. *The Spell of the Hawaiian Islands and the Philippines.* Boston: Page, 1916. Mrs. Larz Anderson accompanied her husband, a diplomat, to the Philippines, Japan, and Europe. She published a series of books on foreign countries between 1914 and 1937.

Anderson, Stella. See Benson, Stella.

Andrews, Cicily. See West, Dame Rebecca.

Anspach, Margravine. See Craven, Elizabeth Berkeley.

Anstee, Margaret Joan. *Bolivia, Gate of the Sun.* New York: Eriksson, 1971. Also published as *Gate of the Sun, a Prospect of Bolivia.* Harlow, England: Longman, 1970. Anstee was head of United Nations programs in Bolivia for six years.

Atkins, Mary. *The Diary of Mary Atkins, a Sabbatical in the 1860's.* Mills College, Calif.: Eucalyptus Press, 1937. A journey to the Far East via Hawaii in 1863.

Ayer, Emma Burbank. *A Motor Flight through Algeria and Tunisia.* Chicago: McClurg, 1911.

Aynsley, Harriet Georgiana Maria (Mrs. J. C. Murray). *An Account of a Three Months' Tour from Simla through Bussahir, Kunowar and Spiti to Lahoul.* Calcutta, India: Thacker, Spink, 1882.

———. *Our Tour in Southern India.* London: White, 1883.

———. *Our Visit to Hindostan, Kashmir and Ladakh.* London: W. H. Allen, 1879.

Ayscough, Florence. *A Chinese Mirror; Being Reflections of the Reality behind Appearance.* Boston and New York: Houghton Mifflin, 1925; London: Cape, 1925.

Bainbridge, Lucy Seaman. *Jewels from the Orient.* New York and Chicago: Revell, 1920. Bainbridge's second trip around the world.

———. *Round the World Letters: Five Hundred and Forty-Two Pages of Charming Pen Pictures by the Way, a Graphic Portrayal of Scenes, Incidents, and Adventures of a Two Years' Tour of the World.* New York: Blackall, 1882; Boston: Lothrop, 1882.

Baïracli-Levy, Juliette de. *As Gypsies Wander; Being an Account of Life with the Gypsies in England, Provence, Spain, Turkey & North Africa.* London: Faber, 1953.

———. *A Gypsy in New York.* London: Faber, 1962.

———. *Spanish Mountain Life. The Sierra Nevada.* London: Faber, 1955.

———. *Summer in Galilee.* London: Faber, 1959; New York: Duell, Sloan & Pearce, 1960.

———. *Wanderers in the New Forest.* London: Faber, 1958.

Baldridge, Caroline. See Singer, Caroline.

Balfour, Alice Blanche. *Twelve Hundred Miles in a Waggon.* London and New York: Arnold, 1895. Across Africa from Cape Town to Zanzibar.

Balneaves, Elizabeth. *Mountains of the Murgha Zerin: Between the Hindu Khush and the Karakoram*. London: Gifford, 1972.

———. *Peacocks and Pipelines: Baluchistan to Bihar*. London: Lutterworth, 1958.

———. *The Waterless Moon*. London: Lutterworth, 1955.

Banning, Margaret Culkin. *Salud! A South American Journal*. New York and London: Harper, 1941.

Barker, Lady. See Broome, Mary Anne Stewart.

Barkly, Fanny Alexandra. *Among Boers and Basutos*. London: Remington, 1893. Fanny, wife of the governor of Basutoland, lived in Mafeting and brought up children here and in the Orange Free State to which she fled in 1878.

———. *From the Tropics to the North Sea*. London: Roxburghe, 1896. A diplomat's wife in the Seychelles and Helgoland.

Barnard, Lady Anne Lindsay. *South Africa a Century Ago: Letters Written from the Cape of Good Hope (1797–1801)*. Edited by W. H. Wilkins. London: Smith, Elder, 1901; New York: Dodd, Mead, 1901. Also published as *The Letters of Lady Anne Barnard*. Cape Town: A. A. Balkema, 1973. Letters by the wife of the first secretary of Cape Colony, first published more than a century after they were written.

Bassett, Marnie. See Freycinet, Rose de.

Bates, Mrs. D. B. *Incidents on Land and Water; or, Four Years on the Pacific Coast*. Boston: French, 1857.

Bates, Katharine Lee. *From Gretna Green to Land's End: A Literary Journey in England*. New York: Crowell, 1907; London: Grant Richards, 1908.

———. *Spanish Highways and Byways*. New York and London: Macmillan, 1900.

Beale, Marie Oge. *Flight into America's Past: Inca Peaks and Maya Jungles*. New York and London: Putnam, 1932.

———. *The Modern Magic Carpet: Air Jaunting over the Ancient East*. Baltimore: J. H. Furst, 1930.

Beauvoir, Simone de. *The Long March*. Translated by Austryn Wainhouse. London: Weidenfeld & Nicolson, 1958; Cleveland and New York: World, 1958. A six-weeks' trip to China in 1955. The title does not refer to Mao's 1930s Long March.

Beckman, Nellie Sims. *Backsheesh: A Woman's Wanderings*. San Francisco: Whittaker & Ray, 1900. Eighteen months in Europe, Asia Minor, Egypt, Syria, and Palestine.

Bedford, Sybille. *A Visit to Don Otavio: A Traveller's Tale from Mexico*. London: Collins, 1953. Also published as *The Sudden View: A Mexican Journey*. New York: Harper and Row, 1953; London: Gollancz, 1953.

Bensly, Agnes Dorothea von Blomberg. *Our Journey to Sinai: A Visit to the Convent of St. Catarina, with a Chapter on the Sinai Palimpsest*. London: Religious Tract Society, 1896. Bensly accompanied Agnes Lewis and Margaret Gibson when they discovered a famous biblical palimpsest.

Benson, Stella (Stella Anderson). *The Little World*. New York and London: Macmillan, 1925. Travel pieces written between 1919 and 1924.

———. *Worlds within Worlds*. London: Macmillan, 1928; New York and London: Harper, 1929. Experiences in China, Japan, and the United States.

Bent, Mabel Virginia Anna, with James Theodore Bent. *Southern Arabia*. London: Smith, Elder, 1900. In 1889, the Bents went from Bahrein to excavate sepulchral mounds near Ali; in 1893–1894, they went to the Hadhramaut (after journeys in South Africa and Abyssinia).

Berenson, Mary Logan Smith. *Across the Mediterranean*. Prato, Italy: Tipografia Giach-
etti, 1935; London: Constable, 1937. By Mrs. Bernard Berenson.

———. *A Modern Pilgrimage*. New York and London: Appleton, 1933. Through Palestine and Syria by three scholars, Mr. and Mrs. Berenson and Elisabetta Mariano,
their librarian.

———. *A Vicarious Trip to the Barbary Coast*. London: Constable, 1938. Travels in
Tripoli and Libya, based on letters from Bernard Berenson and his secretary.

Bertrand, Gabrielle. *The Jungle People: Men, Beasts, and Legends of the Moï Country*.
Translated from the French by E. Brockett. London: Hale, 1959.

———. *Secret Lands Where Women Reign*. London: Hale, 1958. Assam, India.

Betts, Ursula. See Bower, Ursula Graham.

Bewicke, Alicia. See Little, Alicia H. N. Bewicke.

Bigland, Eileen. *Into China*. New York: Macmillan, 1940; London: Collins, 1940.

———. *Journey to Egypt*. London and New York: Jarrolds, 1948.

———. *The Key to the Russian Door*. London: Putnam, 1942.

———. *The Lake of the Royal Crocodiles*. London: Hodder and Stoughton, 1939; New
York: Macmillan, 1939. Rhodesia.

———. *Laughing Odyssey*. London: Hodder & Stoughton, 1937; New York: Macmillan,
1938. Russia.

Billings, Katharine. See Fowler-Lunn, Katharine Stevens.

Bingham, Millicent Todd. *Peru, a Land of Contrasts*. Boston: Little, Brown, 1914.

Bisland, Elizabeth. See Wetmore, Elizabeth Bisland.

Blessington, Marguerite Power Gardiner Farmer, Countess of. *The Idler in France*.
London: Colburn, 1841; Philadelphia: Carey & Hart, 1841. Lady Blessington
went abroad with her husband in 1822; after he died in 1829, she wrote to increase
her income.

———. *The Idler in Italy*. London: Colburn, 1839; Philadelphia: Carey & Hart, 1839.

———. *Journal of a Tour through the Netherlands to Paris in 1821*. London: Longman,
1822.

Bly, Nellie. See Seaman, Elizabeth Cochrane.

Bosanquet, Mary. *Journey into a Picture*. London: Hodder & Stoughton, 1947. A journey
in Italy.

———. *Saddle Bags for Suitcases: Across Canada on Horseback*. New York: Dodd,
Mead, 1942; Toronto: McClelland & Stewart, 1942. Also published as *Canada
Ride: Across Canada on Horseback*. London: Hodder & Stoughton, 1944.

Bowdich, Sarah. See Lee, Sarah Wallis Bowdich.

Bower, Ursula Graham (Ursula Bower Betts). *Drums behind the Hill*. New York: Morrow,
1950. Also published as *Naga Path*. London: Murray, 1950. Nine years among
the barbaric Naga tribes of northeast India.

———. *The Hidden Land: Mission to a Far Corner of India*. New York: Morrow, 1953;
London: Murray, 1953. While married to Col. F. N. Betts, Bower spent a year
with the isolated Apa Tani tribe in Assam, where Betts was the political officer.

Bradley, Mary Hastings. *Caravans and Cannibals*. New York: Appleton, 1926. Belgian
Congo.

———. *On the Gorilla Trail*. New York: Appleton, 1922. In East Africa, Bradley's
first expedition, with Carl Akeley.

———. *Trailing the Tiger*. New York: Appleton, 1929. In British India, the Dutch East
Indies, and French Indochina.

Brassey, Annie Allnutt, Baroness. *In the Trades, the Tropics, and the Roaring Forties.* London: Longman, 1885; New York: Holt, 1885. To the West Indies and Madeira; although Lady Brassey's books are on sea travel, she also did much visiting on land.

————. *The Last Voyage.* London and New York: Longman, 1889. Written on a trip to India, Borneo, and Australia. Lady Brassey died at sea during this trip.

————. *Sunshine and Storm in the East; or, Cruises to Cyprus and Constantinople.* London: Longman, 1880; New York: Holt, 1880.

————. *The Voyage in the Sunbeam, Our Home on the Ocean for Eleven Months.* London: Longman, 1878. Also published as *Around the World in the Yacht Sunbeam*, New York: Holt, 1882; and *Afloat and Ashore; or, A Voyage in the Sunbeam*, n.p.: Juvenile Publishing, n.d. Lady Brassey's first voyage around the world in 1876–1877. Her cruise books appeared in a number of editions, under various titles, and were translated into several languages. Two privately printed books, *The Flight of the Meteor* and *A Cruise in the 'Eothen,'* appeared, respectively, in 1869 and 1872. *Lady Brassey's Three Voyages in the Sunbeam*, London: Longman, 1887, consists of all except the privately printed books and *The Last Voyage*, which was published posthumously, edited by M. A. Broome.

Bremer, Frederika. *Greece and the Greeks: The Narrative of a Winter Residence and Summer Travel in Greece and Its Islands.* Translated by Mary Howitt. London: Blackett, 1863. Bremer, a Swedish writer, traveled much in the United States, Europe, and the Near East. Many of her books were translated into English and published under various titles.

————. *The Homes of the New World: Impressions of America.* Translated by Mary Howitt. London: Hall, Virtue, 1853.

————. *Life in the Old World: or, Two Years in Switzerland and Italy.* Translated by Mary Howitt. Philadelphia: T. B. Peterson, 1860.

————. *Travels in the Holy Land.* Translated by Mary Howitt. London: Hurst & Blackett, 1862.

Bridges, Mrs. F. D. *Journal of a Lady's Travels round the World.* London: Murray, 1883.

Brinley, [Kathrine] Gordon. *Away to the Gaspé.* New York: Dodd, Mead, 1935; Toronto: McClelland & Stewart, 1935. The first of several "Away" books on Canada by Mrs. Putnam Brinley.

Broome, Mary Ann Stewart (formerly Lady Barker). *Colonial Memories.* London: Smith, Elder, 1904.

————. *Letters to Guy.* London: Macmillan, 1885. A new edition published as *Remembered with Affection.* Melbourne and New York: Oxford University Press, 1963.

————. *Station Amusements in New Zealand.* London: Hunt, 1873.

————. *Station Life in New Zealand.* London: Macmillan, 1870.

————. *Travelling about over New and Old Ground.* London and New York: Routledge, 1872.

————. *A Year's Housekeeping in South Africa.* London: Macmillan, 1877. Also published as *Letters from South Africa*, New York: Macmillan, 1877; and *Life in South Africa*, Philadelphia: Lippincott, 1877.

Brown, Demetra Kenneth (Demetra Vaka). *A Child of the Orient.* London: Lane, 1914; Boston: Houghton Mifflin, 1914. A return to the author's native Turkey.

————. *Haremlik: Some Pages from the Life of Turkish Women.* Boston: Houghton

Mifflin, 1909. Also published as *Some Pages from the Life of Turkish Women*. London: Constable, 1909.

———. *The Heart of the Balkans*. Boston and New York: Houghton Mifflin, 1917.

———. *In the Shadow of Islam*. London: Constable, 1911.

———. *The Unveiled Ladies of Stamboul*. Boston and New York: Houghton Mifflin, 1923.

Brown, Lilian. See Richmond Brown, Lilian Mabel Alice Roussel, Lady.

Brown, Margery Finn. *Over a Bamboo Fence: An American Looks at Japan*. New York: Morrow, 1951. Also published as *Behind the Bamboo Curtain*. London: Hurst & Blackett, 1953.

Bulstrode, Beatrix (Beatrix Gull). *A Tour in Mongolia*. London: Methuen, 1920; New York: Stokes, 1920.

Burton, Isabel Arundell, Lady. *Arabia, Egypt, India: A Narrative of Travel*. London: W. Mullan, 1879.

———. *The Inner Life of Syria, Palestine, and the Holy Land*. London: H. S. King, 1875.

Calderon de la Barca, Frances Erskine Inglis. *The Attaché in Madrid: or, Sketches of the Court of Isabella II*. Translated from the German. New York: Appleton, 1856. Published anonymously as by the attaché himself.

———. *Life in Mexico during a Residence of Two Years in That Country*. London: Dent, 1843.

Callcott, Maria Dundas Graham, Lady (Maria Graham). *Journal of a Residence in Chile during the Year 1822, and a Voyage from Chile to Brazil in 1823*. London: Longman, 1824.

———. *Journal of a Residence in India*. Edinburgh: Constable, 1812; London: Longman, 1812.

———. *Journal of a Voyage to Brazil, and Residence There, during Part of the Years 1821, 1822, 1823*. London: Longman, 1824.

———. *Letters on India*. London: Longman, 1814.

———. *Three Months Passed in the Mountains East of Rome, during the Year 1819*. London: Longman, 1820.

———. *Voyage of H.M.S. Blonde to the Sandwich Islands in the Years 1824–1825*. London: Murray, 1826. Published anonymously.

Calverley, Eleanor Jane Taylor. *My Arabian Nights and Days: A Medical Missionary in Old Kuwait*. New York: Crowell, 1958. Calverley spent 1911 to 1929 in Kuwait; she was the first to give medical care to its Moslem women.

Cameron, Agnes Deans. *The New North, Being Some Account of a Woman's Journey through Canada to the Arctic*. New York and London: Appleton, 1910.

Cameron, Charlotte Wales-Almy. *A Cheechako in Alaska and Yukon*. London: Unwin, 1920.

———. *Mexico in Revolution: An Account of an English Woman's Experiences & Adventures in the Land of Revolution, etc*. London: Seeley, Service, 1925; Philadelphia: Lippincott, 1925.

———. *Two Years in Southern Seas*. Boston: Small, Maynard, 1923; London: Unwin, 1923. In Melanesia.

———. *Wanderings in South-eastern Seas*. Boston: Small, Maynard, 1924; London: Unwin, 1924.

———. *A Woman's Winter in Africa, a 26,000 Mile Journey*. London: S. Paul, 1913.

──────. *A Woman's Winter in South America*. London: S. Paul, 1911; Boston: Small, Maynard, 1912.

Candee, Helen Churchill Hungerford. *Angkor, the Magnificent, the Wonder City of Ancient Cambodia*. New York: Stokes, 1924.

──────. *New Journeys in Old Asia: Indo-China, Siam, Java, Bali*. New York: Stokes, 1927.

Candlin, Enid Saunders. *The Breach in the Wall: A Memoir of the Old China*. New York: Macmillan, 1973; London: Cassell, 1973.

──────. *A Traveler's Tale: Memories of India*. New York: Macmillan, 1974.

Canfield, Flavia Camp. *Around the World at Eighty*. Rutland, Vt.: Tuttle, 1925. With an introduction by Canfield's daughter, Dorothy Canfield Fisher.

Carpenter, Mary. *Six Months in India*. London: Longman, 1868. By an English educator and penologist.

Carrington, Dorothy. *Granite Island: A Portrait of Corsica*. London: Longman, 1971. Also published as *Corsica: Portrait of a Granite Island*. New York: Day, 1974.

Carter, Lillian. *Away from Home*. New York: Simon & Schuster, 1977. Two years in the Peace Corps, by the mother of U.S. President Jimmy Carter.

Cary, Amelia, Viscountess Falkland. *Chow-chow; Being Selections from a Journal Kept in India, Egypt, and Syria*. London: Hurst & Blackett, 1857. By the wife of Lord Falkland, governor of Bombay.

Chapman, Olive Murray. *Across Cyprus*. London: Lane, 1937.

──────. *Across Iceland, the Land of Frost and Fire*. London: Lane, 1930; New York: Dodd, Mead, 1930.

──────. *Across Lapland with Sledge and Reindeer*. London: Lane 1932; New York: Dodd, Mead, 1932.

──────. *Across Madagascar*. London: E. J. Burrow, 1943.

Chesterton, Ada Elizabeth (Ada Jones). *My Russian Venture*. Philadelphia: Lippincott, 1931; London: Harrap, 1931.

──────. *Young China and New Japan*. Philadelphia: Lippincott, 1933; London: Harrap, 1933.

Chetwode, Penelope. *Kulu, the End of the Habitable World*. London: Murray, 1972.

──────. *Two Middle-aged Ladies in Andalusia*. London: Murray, 1963. One "lady" was a horse.

Clark, Eleanor. *Baldur's Gate*. New York: Pantheon, 1970.

──────. *Rome and a Villa*. London: M. Joseph, 1953; Garden City, N.Y.: Doubleday, 1956.

──────. *Tamrart: 13 Days in the Sahara*. New York: Stuart Wright, 1984.

Clark, Harriet Elizabeth Abbott, with Francis Edward Clark. *Our Journey around the World: An Illustrated Record of a Year's Travel of Forty Thousand Miles through India, China, Japan . . . with Glimpses of Life in Far-off Lands As Seen through a Woman's Eyes*. Hartford, Conn.: A. D. Worthington, 1894. The last part of the book is by Harriet.

Clarke, Sara. See Lippincott, Sara J.

Close, Etta. *Excursions and Some Adventures*. London: Constable, 1926; New York: Dial, 1927. "Scattered memories" of travel in the lesser-known parts of the world.

──────. *A Woman Alone in Kenya, Uganda, and the Belgian Congo*. London: Constable, 1924.

Cobbold, Lady Evelyn Murray. *Kenya, the Land of Illusion*. London: Murray, 1935.

————. *Pilgrimage to Mecca*. London: Murray, 1934.

————. *Wayfarers in the Libyan Desert*. London: Humphreys, 1912; New York: Putnam, 1912. The American edition was published under the name of Lady Evelyn's traveling companion, Frances Alexander.

Cochrane, Elizabeth. See Seaman, Elizabeth Cochrane.

Collis, Septima M. *A Woman's Trip to Alaska; Being an Account of a Voyage through the Inland Seas of the Sitkan Archipelago in 1890*. New York: Cassell, 1890.

Cran, Marion Dudley. *A Woman in Canada*. Philadelphia: Lippincott, 1910; Toronto: Musson, 1910; London: J. Milne, 1910. By an English writer of garden books.

Craven, Elizabeth Berkeley, Baroness Craven (afterward Margravine of Anspach). *A Journey through the Crimea to Constantinople, in a Series of Letters*. Dublin: H. Chamberlaine, 1789.

Crawford, Minnie Leola. *Seven Weeks in Hawaii*. By an American Girl. Chicago: H. D. Berrett, 1913.

————. *Seven Weeks in the Orient*. Chicago: H. D. Berrett, 1914.

Crocker, Barbara. See Whelpton, Barbara Fanny.

Cumming, Constance. See Gordon Cumming, Constance Frederica.

Curie, Eve. *Journey among Warriors*. Garden City, N.Y.: Doubleday, 1943. A correspondent covering anti-Axis participants in World War II.

Cushman, Mary Floyd. *Missionary Doctor: The Story of Twenty Years in Africa*. New York and London: Harper, 1944. Angola.

Czaplicka, Marie Antoinette Crispine. *My Siberian Year*. London: Mills & Boon, 1916. Thirteen months in Siberia by an ethnographer and sociologist.

D'Arusmont, Frances Wright (Frances Wright). *Views of Society and Manners in America; in a Series of Letters from That Country to a Friend in England, during the Years 1818, 1819, and 1820. By an Englishwoman*. London: Longman, 1821; New York: Bliss & White, 1821.

Davidson, Robyn. *Tracks*. London: Cape, 1980. A young woman's lone ride by camel across western Australia from Alice Springs to the Indian Ocean.

Davies, Hannah. *Among Hills and Valleys in Western China: Incidents of Missionary Work*. With an introduction by Mrs. Isabella Bishop. London: S. W. Partridge, 1901.

De Freycinet, Rose. See Freycinet, Rose de.

De la Barca, Frances. See Calderon de la Barca, Frances Erskine Inglis.

Desmond, Alice Curtis. *Far Horizons*. New York: McBride, 1931. Europe, the Orient, and South America.

————. *South American Adventures*. New York: Macmillan, 1934.

De Watteville, Vivienne. *Out in the Blue*. London: Methuen, 1927. East Africa.

————. *Speak to the Earth: Wanderings and Reflections among Elephants and Mountains*. New York: Smith & Haas, 1935; London: Methuen, 1935.

Dickson, Dame Violet. *Forty Years in Kuwait*. London: Allen & Unwin, 1971.

Dietz, Nettie Fowler. *A White Woman in a Black Man's Country: Three Thousand Miles up the Nile to Rejaf*. Omaha, Neb.: privately printed, 1926 [c. 1914].

Dieulafoy, Jane (Jeanne) Paule. *At Susa, the Ancient Capitol of the Kings of Persia: Narrative of Travel through Western Persia and Excavations Made at the Site of the Lost City of the Lilies, 1884–1886*. Translated by Frank L. White. Philadelphia: Gebbie, 1890. A translation of *A Suse* (1888).

Diver, [Katherine Helen] Maud Marshall. *The Englishwoman in India*. Edinburgh and London: Blackwood, 1909. The writer was born and brought up in India.

———. *Kabul to Kandahar*. London: Davies, 1935. On the Afghan wars.

Duff Gordon, Lucie Austin, Lady. *Last Letters from Egypt. To Which Are Added, Letters from the Cape*. With a memoir by her daughter Mrs. Ross. London: Macmillan, 1875. "Letters from the Cape" was first published in *Vacation Tourists and Notes of Travel in 1862–63*, edited by Francis Galton, London, 1864.

———. *Letters from Egypt, 1862–63*. London: Macmillan, 1865. Lady Duff Gordon spent her last years as a well-loved resident of Egypt.

Dunbar, Ianthe M. *The Edge of the Desert*. Boston: Small, Maynard, 1923; London: P. Allan, 1923. Tunisia.

Dunbar, Ianthe M., with John Walter Hills. *The Golden River: Sport and Travel in Paraguay*. London: P. Allan, 1922.

Duncan, Jane Ellen. *A Summer Ride through Western Tibet*. London: Smith, Elder, 1906. A lone horseback trip in the Himalayas.

Dunham, Katherine. *Katherine Dunham's Journey to the Accompong*. New York: Holt, 1946. Dunham's visit to Jamaica laid the foundation for much of her choreography.

Durack, Elizabeth. *Face Value: Women in Papua and New Guinea*. Sydney: U. Smith, 1970.

———. *Seeing through Papua New Guinea: An Artist's Impressions of the Territory*. Melbourne: Hawthorn, 1970.

———. *Seeing through the Philippines*. Melbourne: Hawthorn, 1971.

Durham, Mary Edith. *The Burden of the Balkans*. London: Arnold, 1905.

———. *High Albania*. London: Arnold, 1909.

———. *Through the Lands of the Serb*. London: Arnold, 1904.

Eames, Jane Anthony. *Another Budget; or, Things Which I Saw in the East*. Boston: Ticknor & Fields, 1855.

———. *The Budget Closed*. Boston: Ticknor & Fields, 1860.

———. *A Budget of Letters; or, Things Which I Saw Abroad*. Boston: W. D. Ticknor, 1847.

Eastlake, Elizabeth Rigby, Lady. *A Residence on the Shores of the Baltic, Described in a Series of Letters*. London: Murray, 1841. Also published as *Letters from the Shores of the Baltic*. London: Murray, 1842.

Eden, Emily. *Letters from India*. London: Bentley, 1872.

———. *Up the Country: Letters Written to Her Sister from the Upper Provinces of India*. London: Bentley, 1866.

Edwards, Amelia Ann Blandford. *Pharoahs, Fellas and Explorers*. London and New York: Osgood & McIlvaine, 1891. Also published as *Egypt and Its Monuments*. New York: Harper, 1891. Edwards was a founder of the Egypt Exploration Fund.

———. *A Thousand Miles up the Nile*. London: Longman, 1877.

———. *Untrodden Peaks and Unfrequented Valleys: A Midsummer Ramble in the Dolomites*. London: Longman, 1873. Also published as *A Midsummer Ramble in the Dolomites*. London: Routledge, 1889.

Ellison, Grace Mary. *An Englishwoman in Angora*. London: Hutchinson, 1923; New York: Dutton, 1923.

———. *Yugoslavia, a New Country and Its People*. London: Lane, 1933.

Elwood, Anne Katharine (Mrs. Colonel Elwood). *Narrative of a Journey Overland from England by the Continent of Europe, Egypt, and the Red Sea to India, Including a Residence There and Voyage Home in the Years 1825, 26, 27, and 28.* London: Colburn & Bentley, 1830.

Epton, Nina Consuelo. *Journey under the Crescent Moon.* London: Gollancz, 1949. The first of a series of books by Epton, who traveled mainly in Europe, the Mediterranean region, and Indonesia.

Fairfield, Cicily. See West, Dame Rebecca.

Falconbridge, Anna Maria. *Two Voyages to the Sierra Leone during the Years 1791-2-3, in a Series of Letters.* London: n.p., 1794. The second edition is entitled *Narrative of Two Voyages to the River Sierra Leone, during the Years 1791–1793 ... and Every Interesting Particular Relating to the Sierra Leone Company, also the Present State of the Slave Trade in the West Indies.* London: L. I. Higham, 1802. Anna Maria accompanied her husband, an agent of the St. George's Bay Company, to West Africa in 1791.

Falkland, Viscountess. See Cary, Amelia, Viscountess Falkland.

Fanshawe, Anne Harrison, Lady. *Memoirs.* London and New York: Lane, 1905. Published in several editions long after her death, which occurred in 1680, Lady Fanshawe's memoirs deal in part with life in European countries where her husband was ambassador.

Fay, Eliza. *Original Letters from India, Containing a Narrative of a Journey through Egypt, and the Author's Imprisonment at Calicut by Hyder Ally. To Which Is Added an Abstract of Three Subsequent Voyages to India.* Calcutta, India, 1817. Also published as *The Original Letters from India, 1779–1815.* Calcutta, India: Thacker, Spink, 1908; London: L. & V. Woolf, 1925. The 1925 edition was the first to be published outside of India.

Fernea, Elizabeth Warnock. *A View of the Nile.* Garden City, N.Y.: Doubleday, 1970. Fernea and her husband spent much time in the Middle East, and she wrote about the Arab people.

Field, Kate. *Ten Days in Spain.* Boston: Osgood, 1875.

Fiennes, Celia. *Through England on a Side Saddle in the Time of William and Mary.* London: Field & Tuer, 1888. Between 1685 and 1702, Fiennes visited every county in England and crossed over briefly into Scotland and Wales. Extracts from the journals first appeared anonymously in 1812 (more than seventy years after her death). A full scholarly edition, based on Fiennes's manuscript, was published as *The Journeys of Celia Fiennes.* London: Cresset, 1947.

Finch, Marianne. *An Englishwoman's Experience in America.* London: Bentley, 1853. Finch attended a women's rights convention in Boston in 1851 and then toured America.

Fisher, Gertrude Adams. *A Woman Alone in the Heart of Japan.* Boston: Page, 1907; London: Sisley's, 1907.

Fisher, Ruth Hurditch. *On the Borders of Pigmy Land.* New York: Revell, 1905; London: Marshall, 1905. By a missionary who lived in Africa from 1900 to 1915.

————. *Twilight Tales of the Black Baganda.* London: Marshall, 1911. A history of the Kingdom of Bunyoro-Kitora.

Fisher, Welthy Honsinger. *Beyond the Moon Gate; Being a Diary of Ten Years in the Interior of the Middle Kingdom.* New York and Cincinnati: Abingdon, 1924; London: Gay & Hancock, 1925. Fisher founded Literacy House, a training center for teachers in Lucknow, India.

————. *The Top of the World.* New York and Cincinnati: Abingdon, 1926. India and Tibet.

Flandrau, Grace C. Hodgson. *Then I Saw the Congo.* London: Harrap, 1929; New York: Harcourt, Brace, 1929. Across Africa along the Equator.

Forbes, [Joan] Rosita Torr (Rosita McGrath). *Adventure; Being a Gypsy Salad.* London: Cassell, 1928; Boston: Houghton Mifflin, 1928. Forbes wrote many books, some of which she called travel books; others, adventure books; and still others, autobiographies. Those listed are primarily travel accounts.

————. *Conflict: Angora to Afghanistan.* London: Cassell, 1931; New York: Stokes, 1931.

————. *Eight Republics in Search of a Future: Evolution and Revolution in South America.* London: Cassell, 1933; New York: Stokes, 1933.

————. *Forbidden Road—Kabul to Samarkand.* London: Cassell, 1937; New York: Dutton, 1937. Also published as *Russian Road to India—by Kabul and Sarmarkand.* Hardmondsworth, England: Penguin, 1940.

————. *From Red Sea to Blue Nile: Abyssinian Adventures.* London: Cassell, 1925; New York: Macaulay, 1925.

————. *India of the Princes.* London: Gifford, 1939.

————. *Islands in the Sun.* London: Evans, 1949. The West Indies.

————. *The Secret of the Sahara: Kufara.* London: Cassell, 1921; New York: Doran, 1921.

————. *Unconducted Wanderers.* London and New York: Lane, 1919.

Fountaine, Margaret. *Love among the Butterflies: The Travels and Adventures of a Victorian Lady.* Edited by W. F. Cater. Boston: Little, Brown, 1980; London: Collins, 1980. From a diary stored away for years after the writer's death in 1940.

Fowler-Lunn, Katharine Stevens (later Fowler-Billings). *The Gold Missus: A Woman Prospector in Sierra Leone.* London: Allen & Unwin, 1938; New York: Norton, 1938. A geologist on Africa's Gold Coast.

Franklin, Jane Griffin, Lady. *The Life, Diaries, and Correspondence of Jane Lady Franklin, 1792–1875.* Edited by Willingham Franklin Rawnsley. London: E. Macdonald, 1923. Lady Franklin was the wife of explorer Sir John Franklin. She visited Van Diemen's Land, Tasmania, New Zealand, the Mediterranean countries, the United States, and the Far East.

Fraser, Mary Crawford. *A Diplomatist's Wife in Many Lands.* London: Hutchinson, 1910; New York: Dodd, Mead, 1910. This book was followed by a number of others consisting of letters and reminiscences of the diplomatist's wife.

————. *Letters from Japan: A Record of Modern Life in the Island Empire.* New York and London: Macmillan, 1899.

Freeth, Zahra Dickson. *Kuwait Was My Home.* London: Allen & Unwin, 1956. Freeth's father, Col. H. R. P. Dickson, was advisor to Kuwait's leading family from 1920 on. See Dickson, Dame Violet.

————. *A New Look at Kuwait.* London: Allen & Unwin, 1972.

————. *Run Softly, Demerara.* London: Allen & Unwin, 1960. Life in a tropical mining town in British Guiana.

Freycinet, Rose de. *Realms and Islands: The World Voyage of Rose de Freycinet in the Corvette Uranie 1817–1820, from Her Journal and Letters and the Reports of Louis de Saulces de Freycinet, Capitaine de Corvette.* By Marnie Bassett. London: Oxford University Press, 1962. Rose dressed as a man in order to embark secretly on the ship with her new husband. Her journals and letters are translated from the French.

Fullerton, Alice Ogston. *To Persia for Flowers*. London: Oxford, 1938. Two women botanists in Persia.

―――. *To Portugal for Pleasure*. London: Grafton, 1945.

Galsworthy, Ada Cooper. *Over the Hills and Far Away*. London: Hale, 1937. Travel with John Galsworthy in Europe, America, and Africa.

Gatti, Ellen Morgan Waddill. *Exploring We Would Go*. New York: Scribner, 1944. Africa in the 1930s.

Gaunt, Mary Eliza Bakewell (later Miller). *Alone in West Africa*. London: T. Werner Laurie, 1911; New York: Scribner, 1912. By an Australian traveler.

―――. *A Broken Journey: Wanderings from the Hoang-ho to the Island of Saghalien and the Upper Reaches of the Amur River*. London: T. Werner Laurie, 1919.

―――. *Reflection in Jamaica*. London: Benn, 1932.

―――. *A Woman in China*. London: T. Werner Laurie, 1914.

Gellhorn, Martha Ellis. *Travels with Myself and Another*. New York: Dodd, Mead, 1979.

Geyer, Georgie Anne. *The New 100 Years War*. Garden City, N.Y.: Doubleday, 1972. The Arab-Israeli conflict.

Giles, Dorothy. *The Road through Czechoslovakia*. Philadelphia: Penn, 1930. Through Bohemian forests to the valley of the Vah and into the High Tatras and the Carpathians.

―――. *The Road through Spain*. Philadelphia: Penn, 1929.

Goldwasser, Janet, with Stuart Dowty. *Huan-Ying: Worker's China*. New York: Monthly Review Press, 1975.

Gordon, Cora Josephine, with Jan Gordon. *A Donkey Trip through Spain*. New York: McBride, 1924. Also published as *Misadventures with a Donkey in Spain*. London: Blackwood, 1924.

―――. *The Luck of Thirteen: Wanderings and Flight through Montenegro and Serbia*. London: Smith, Elder, 1916; New York: Dutton, 1916. Also published as *Two Vagabonds in Serbia and Montenegro*. Harmondsworth, England: Penguin Books, 1939. The Gordons published several other travel books; most were entitled *Two Vagabonds*, etc.

Gordon, Helen Cameron, Lady Russell. *My Tour in Portugal*. London: Methuen, 1932. Lady Russell was a Fellow of the Royal Geographical Society.

―――. *Spain As It Is*. London: Methuen, 1931.

―――. *Syria As It Is*. London: Methuen, 1939.

―――. *West Indian Scenes*. London: Hale, 1942.

―――. *A Woman in the Sahara*. New York: Stokes, 1914; London: Heinemann, 1915.

Gordon, Lucie. See Duff Gordon, Lucie Austin, Lady.

Gordon Cumming, Constance Frederica (Constance Cumming). *At Home in Fiji*. Edinburgh and London: Blackwood, 1881. By one of the most intrepid Victorian globe trotters.

―――. *Fire Fountains: The Kingdom of Hawaii, Its Volcanoes, and the History of Its Missions*. Edinburgh and London, Blackwood, 1881.

―――. *From the Hebrides to the Himalayas: A Sketch of Eighteen Months' Wanderings in Western Isles and Eastern Highlands*. London: S. Low, Marston, Searle & Rivington, 1876. A new edition of part 1 was published as *In the Hebrides*, London: Chatto & Windus, 1883; and an expanded version of part 2 was published as *In the Himalayas and on the Indian Plains*, London: Chatto & Windus, 1883 and 1884.

———. *Granite Crags*. Edinburgh and London: Blackwood, 1884. California.

———. *A Lady's Cruise in a French Man-of-War*. Edinburgh and London: Blackwood, 1882.

———. *Two Happy Years in Ceylon*. Edinburgh and London: Blackwood, 1892.

———. *Via Cornwall to Egypt*. London: Chatto & Windus, 1885.

———. *Wanderings in China*. Edinburgh and London: Blackwood, 1886.

Gornick, Vivian. *In Search of Ali Mahmoud: An American Woman in Egypt*. New York: Saturday Review/Dutton, 1973.

Gough, Mary. *The Plain and the Rough Places: An Account of Archaeological Journeying through the Plain and the Rough Places of the Roman Province of Cilicia, in Southern Turkey*. London: Chatto & Windus, 1954. Also published as *Travel into Yesterday: An Account of Archaeological Journeying through the Plain and the Rough Places of the Roman Province of Cilicia, in Southern Turkey*. Garden City, N.Y.: Doubleday, 1954.

Gourguechon, Charlene. *Charlene Gourguechon's Journey to the End of the World: A Three-Year Adventure in the New Hebrides*. New York: Scribner, 1977. Among the Big Nambas of Malekula.

Graham, Maria. See Callcott, Maria Dundas Graham, Lady.

Greenbie, Marjorie Latta Barstow. *In the Eyes of the East*. New York: Dodd, Mead, 1921.

Greenwood, Grace. See Lippincott, Sara J.

Griffith, M. E. See Hume Griffith, M. E.

Grimshaw, Beatrice Ethel. *Fiji and Its Possibilities*. New York: Doubleday, 1907. Also published as *From Fiji to the Cannibal Islands*. London: Eveleigh Nash, 1907.

———. *In the Strange South Seas*. London: Hutchinson, 1907.

———. *Isles of Adventure: From Java to New Caledonia but Principally Papua*. London: Jenkins, 1930.

———. *The New New Guinea*. London: Hutchinson, 1910.

Gripenberg, Alexandra. *A Half Year in the New World: Miscellaneous Sketches of Travel in the United States*. Translated and edited by Ernest J. Mayne. Newark, Del.: University of Delaware, 1954. Published in Finland in 1889. A Finnish woman, Gripenberg came as a delegate to the 1888 International Woman's Conference in Washington, D.C., and later traveled in the northern states.

Gruber, Ruth. *I Went to the Soviet Arctic*. New York: Simon & Schuster, 1939; London: Gollancz, 1939. Gruber was a foreign correspondent; she wrote on Israel and other countries.

Guinness, Mary Geraldine (later Taylor). *The Call of China's Great North-west; or, Kansu and Beyond*. London and Philadelphia: China Inland Mission, 1923.

———. *In the Far East: Letters from Geraldine Guinness in China*. Edited by her sister. London: Morgan & Scott, 1889; New York and Chicago: Revell, 1889. Guinness married Hudson Taylor, a founder of the China Inland Mission.

Gull, Beatrix. See Bulstrode, Beatrix.

Hacker, Carlotta. *Africa, Take One*. Toronto and Vancouver: Clarke, Irwin, 1974; London: Books Canada, 1974. A modern film safari.

———. *And Christmas Day on Easter Island*. London: M. Joseph, 1968.

Hadley, Leila Elliott Burton. *Give Me the World*. London: Gollancz, 1958; New York: Simon & Schuster, 1958. A two-year voyage around the world.

Hahn, Emily. *Africa to Me: Person to Person*. Garden City, N.Y.: Doubleday, 1964. Hahn traveled and lived in England, Africa, and China; her books combine autobiography, travel, and politics.

———. *China to Me: A Partial Autobiography*. Garden City, N.Y.: Doubleday, 1944.

———. *Congo Solo: Misadventures Two Degrees North*. Indianapolis: Bobbs-Merrill, 1933.

———. *Hong Kong Holiday*. Garden City, N.Y.: Doubleday, 1944.

———. *The Islands: America's Imperial Adventure in the Philippines*. New York: Coward McCann & Geoghegan, 1981.

Hall, Adelaide. *Two Women Abroad, What They Saw and How They Lived while Travelling among the Semi-civilized People of Morocco, the Peasants of Italy and France, as well as the Educated Classes of Spain, Greece, and Other Countries*. Chicago: Monarch, 1897.

Hall, Margaret Hunter. *Aristocratic Journey; Being the Outspoken Letters of Mrs. Basil Hall Written During a Fourteen Months' Sojourn in America 1827–1828*. Edited by Una Pope-Hennessy. New York and London: Putnam, 1931.

Hardy, Iza Duffus. *Between Two Oceans; or, Sketches of American Travel*. London: Hurst & Blackett, 1884.

———. *Oranges and Alligators: Sketches of South Florida Life*. London: Ward & Downey, 1886.

Hardy, Mary Anne McDowell Duffus, Lady. *Down South*. By Lady Duffus Hardy. London: Chapman & Hall, 1883. The southern United States.

———. *Through Cities and Prairie Lands: Sketches of an American Tour*. London: Chapman & Hall, 1881; New York: Worthington, 1881.

Harkness, Ruth. *The Lady and the Panda: An Adventure*. London: Nickolson & Watson, 1938; New York: Carrick & Evans, 1938. In Tibet, finding the first pandas ever brought to the United States.

———. *Pangoon Diary*. New York: Creative Age, 1942. Search for a silver-grey bear in the Peruvian Andes.

Harley, Ethel. See Tweedie, Ethel Brilliana Harley.

Harrison, Juanita. *My Great Wide Beautiful World*. Arranged and prefaced by Mildred Morris. New York: Macmillan, 1936. A black woman who worked her way around the world, visiting twenty-two countries between 1927 and 1935.

Hart, Alice Marian Rowlands. *Picturesque Burma, Past and Present*. By Mrs. Ernest Hart. London: Dent, 1897; Philadelphia: Lippincott, 1897.

Hatch, Olivia Phelps Stokes. *Olivia's African Diary: Cape Town to Cairo, 1932*. Washington, D.C.: distributed by A.C.E. Distribution Center, 1980. From a journal kept by Olivia Stokes (later Mrs. John D. Hatch, Jr.).

Heber, Kathleen Mary, with Adolph Reeve Heber. *In Himalayan Tibet: A Record of 12 Years Spent in the Topsy-Turvy Land of Lesser Tibet, etc*. Philadelphia: Lippincott, 1926. Also published as *Himalayan Tibet*. London: Seeley, Service, 1926. Travels with Theodore and Kermit Roosevelt, the president's sons.

Hillary, Louise. *High Time*. London: Hodder & Stoughton, 1973; New York: Dutton, 1974. A family trek in Nepal by the wife of Sir Edmund Hillary.

———. *A Yak for Christmas: The Story of a Himalayan Holiday*. London: Hodder & Stoughton, 1968; New York: Doubleday, 1969.

Hobbs, Lisa. *I Saw Red China*. New York: McGraw-Hill, 1966.

———. *India, India*. New York: McGraw-Hill, 1967.

Hobson, Sarah. *Family Web: A Story of India*. Chicago: Academy, 1982.

———. *Through Persia in Disguise*. London: Murray, 1973. Also published as *Masquerade: An Adventure in Iran*. Chicago: Academy, 1979. Disguised as a boy, Hobson studied designs and crafts in Iran.

Hore, Annie Boyle. *To Lake Tanganyika in a Bath Chair*. London: Sampson, Low, Marston, Searle, & Rivington, 1886. By the wife of an explorer attached to a mission in Tanganyika.

Hotchkis, Anna M. See Mullikin, Mary Augusta.

Houlson, Jane Harvey. *Blue Blaze: Danger and Delight in Strange Islands of Honduras*. London: Duckworth, 1934; Indianapolis: Bobbs-Merrill, 1934. Jane accompanied a scientist studying under the auspices of the Museum of the American Indian, Heye Foundation.

Houstoun, Matilda C. Jesse Fraser. *Hesperos; or, Travels in the West*. London: J. W. Parker, 1850. An Englishwoman's travel in the United States.

———. *Texas and the Gulf of Mexico; or, Yachting in the New World*. London: Murray, 1844; Philadelphia: G. B. Zieber, 1845.

———. *Twenty Years in the Wild West; or, Life in Connaught*. London: Murray, 1879. Irish travel.

Howard, Winefred Mary, Baroness Howard of Glossop. *Journal of a Tour in the United States, Canada, and Mexico*. London: Sampson, Low, Marston, 1897.

Hoyt, Anne. See Wetmore, Elizabeth Bisland.

Hubbard, Margaret Carson. *African Gamble*. New York: Putnam, 1937. The Transvaal.

———. *No One to Blame: An African Adventure*. London: Putnam, 1934; New York: Minton Balch, 1934. East Africa.

Hubbard, Mina Benson. *A Woman's Way through Unknown Labrador: An Account of the Exploration of the Nascaupee and George Rivers*. By Mrs. Leonidas Hubbard, Junior. London: Murray, 1908; New York: McClure, 1908.

Hulme, Kathryn Cavarly. *Arab Interlude*. Philadelphia: Macrae Smith, 1930. North Africa.

Hume Griffith, M. E. *Behind the Veil in Persia and Turkish Arabia: An Account of an Englishwoman's Eight Years' Residence amongst the Women of the East. With Narratives of Experiences in Both Countries by A. Hume Griffith*. London: Seeley, 1909; Philadelphia: Lippincott, 1909. By the wife of a medical missionary, with some chapters by her husband.

———. *Dust of Gold: An Account of the Work of the C.E.Z.M.S. among the Blind and Deaf of India, China, and Ceylon*. London: Church of England Zenana Missionary Society, 1927.

Humphrey, [Harriette] Zephine. *'Allo Good-by*. New York: Dutton, 1940. Mexico.

———. *Cactus Forest*. New York: Dutton, 1938. Southwest United States.

———. *Green Mountains to Sierra*. New York: Dutton, 1936. Auto tour across the United States.

Hunt, Helen. See Jackson, Helen Maria Fiske.

Hutchison, Isobel Wylie. *North to the Rime-Ringed Sun; Being the Record of an Alaska-Canadian Journey Made in 1933–34*. London and Glasgow: Blackie, 1934. By an English botanist.

————. *On Greenland's Closed Shore, the Fairyland of the Arctic*. Edinburgh and London: Blackwood, 1930.

————. *Stepping Stones from Alaska to Asia*. London and Glasgow: Blackie, 1937. Also published as *The Aleutian Islands, America's Back Door*. London and Glasgow: Blackie, 1942.

Hutchinson, Louisa. *In Tents in the Transvaal*. London: Bentley, 1879. Zululand.

Ichikawa, Haruko. *Japanese Lady in Europe*. London: Cape, 1937; New York: Dutton, 1937.

Ingrams, Doreen. *A Time in Arabia*. London: Murray, 1970. Doreen and Harold Ingrams lived in the Hadhramaut (Yemen) for ten years.

Innes, Emily. *The Chersonese with the Gilding Off*. London: Bentley, 1885. By a resident of Sarawak.

Irvine, Lucy. *Castaway*. New York: Random House, 1983; London: Gollancz, 1983. Lucy and her husband spent a year on the deserted island of Tuin in the South Pacific.

Jackson, Helen Maria Fiske (Helen Hunt). *Bits of Travel*. Boston: Osgood, 1872. The grand tour of Europe.

————. *Bits of Travel at Home*. Boston: Roberts, 1878.

————. *Glimpses of Three Coasts*. Boston: Roberts, 1886.

Jameson, Anna Brownell Murphy. *Winter Studies and Summer Rambles in Canada*. London: Saunders & Otley, 1838. Part reprinted as *Sketches in Canada and Rambles among the Red Men*. London: Longman, 1852. By an Irish archeologist and iconographer.

Jenner, Delia. *Letters from Peking*. London: Oxford University Press, 1967. By a teacher at Peking Broadcasting Institute, from 1963 to 1965.

Jobe, Mary Lee. See Akeley, Mary Lee Jobe.

Johnson, Emilie. *My China Odyssey*. Federal Way, Wash.: Silver Fox, 1981. A return trip to China in 1978 by one who had been a social worker there during World War II.

Johnson, Enid. See Peck, Anne Merriman.

Jones, Ada. See Chesterton, Ada Elizabeth.

Justice, Elizabeth Surby. *A Voyage to Russia, Describing the Laws, Manners, and Customs of That Great Empire, As Govern'd, at This Present, by . . . the Czarina, etc.* York: G. Gent, 1739.

Kandell, Alice. See Salisbury, Charlotte Y.

Keith, Elizabeth, with Elspet K. R. Scott. *Eastern Windows: An Artist's Notes of Travel in Japan, Hokkaido, Korea, China, and the Philippines*. London: Hutchinson, 1928; Boston and New York: Houghton Mifflin, 1928.

————. *Old Korea, the Land of Morning Calm*. London and New York: Hutchinson, 1946; New York: Philosophical Library, 1947.

Kelly, Marie Noëlle, Lady. *Mirror to Russia*. London: Country Life, 1952. Lady Kelly was the wife of the British Ambassador to Russia.

————. *This Delicious Land, Portugal*. London: Hutchinson, 1956; New York: Pitman, 1956.

————. *Turkish Delights*. London: Country Life, 1951.

Kemp, Emily Georgiana. *Chinese Mettle*. London and New York: Hodder & Stoughton, 1921.

————. *The Face of China: Travels in East, North, Central and Western China*. London:

Chatto & Windus, 1909; New York: Duffield, 1909. Travels from 1893 to 1894 and from 1907 to 1908.

————. *The Face of Manchuria, Korea, Russian Turkestan*. London: Chatto & Windus, 1910; New York: Duffield, 1911.

————. *Wanderings to Chinese Turkestan*. London: Wightman, 1914.

Kempe, Margery. *The Booke of Margery Kempe. A Modern Version*. With introduction by R. W. Chambers. London and Toronto: Cape, 1936. Perhaps the earliest woman overseas traveler, Kempe visited Jerusalem and Rome in the fifteenth century. The 1436 manuscript account of her travels was dictated; Kempe could neither read nor write.

Kendall, Elizabeth Kimball. *A Wayfarer in China: Impressions of a Trip across West China and Mongolia*. London: Constable, 1913; Boston and New York: Houghton Mifflin, 1913.

Keyes, Frances Parkinson. *Silver Seas and Golden Cities: A Joyous Journey through Latin Lands*. New York: Liveright, 1931. Spain, Portugal, and South America.

Kirkland, Caroline. *Some African Highways: A Journey of Two American Women to Uganda and the Transvaal*. London: Duckworth, 1908; Boston: D. Estes, 1908.

Knight, Sarah Kemble. *The Journal of Madam Knight, and Rev. Mr. Buckingham. From the Original Manuscripts Written in 1704 and 1710*. New York: Wilder & Campbell, 1825. Knight's journal of a trip alone by horseback from Boston to New York City in 1704 was published for the first time almost a century after the author's death.

A Lady of Quality. See Schaw, Janet.

Lamb, Ginger (Virginia Lamb). *Quest for the Lost City*. New York: Harper, 1951; London: Gollancz, 1952. On the Mexican-Guatemalan border.

Lamont, Margaret, with Corliss Lamont. *Russia Day by Day: A Travel Diary*. New York: Covici Friede, 1933.

La Motte, Ellen Newbold. *Peking Dust*. New York: Century, 1919. An American nurse, La Motte traveled in the Far East, joined the Society of Woman Geographers, and wrote books on the opium trade.

Landon, Margaret. See Leonowens, Anna Harriette Crawford.

Lansbury, Violet (afterward Dutt). *An Englishwoman in the U.S.S.R.* London: Putnam, 1940.

Larymore, Constance Belcher. *A Resident's Wife in Nigeria*. London: Routledge, 1908; New York: Dutton, 1908. Based on a journal of five years in northern Nigeria, where Larymore was the first Englishwoman to reside.

Lattimore, Eleanor Holgate. *Turkestan Reunion*. New York: J. Day, 1934; London: Hurst & Blackett, 1935. Mrs. Owen Lattimore was a member of the Society of Woman Geographers.

Laurence, [Jean] Margaret. *The Prophet's Camel Bell*. London: Macmillan, 1963. Observations on the nomads of the former Somaliland Protectorate, by the wife of an engineer constructing water reservoirs. Also published as *New Wind in a Dry Land*. New York: Knopf, 1964.

Lee, Sarah Wallis Bowdich (Sarah Bowdich), with Thomas Edward Bowdich. *Excursions in Madeira and Porto-Santo, during the Autumn of 1823, While on His Third Voyage to Africa, by the Late T. Edward Bowdich . . . To Which Is Added, by Mrs. Bowdich, I. A Narrative of the Continuance of the Voyage to Its Completion*

...*II. A Description of the English Settlements in the River Gambia*. London: G. B. Whittaker, 1825. After her husband died, Sarah married Robert Lee.

———. *Stories of Strange Lands, and Fragments from the Notes of a Traveller*. London: E. Moxon, 1835.

Leith-Ross, Sylvia (Sylvia Ross). *African Conversation Piece*. London and New York: Hutchinson, 1944.

———. *Beyond the Niger*. London: Lutterworth, 1951.

———. *Stepping Stones: Memoirs of Colonial Nigeria, 1907–1960*. London: P. Owen, 1983.

Leonowens, Anna Harriette Crawford. *The English Governess at the Siamese Court; Being Recollections of Six Years in the Royal Palace at Bangkok*. London: Trubner, 1870; Boston: Fields, Osgood, 1870. This and *The Romance of the Harem* were the basis for Margaret Landon's *Anna and the King of Siam* and the film *The King and I*.

———. *Life and Travel in India; Being Recollections of a Journey before the Days of Railroads*. Philadelphia: Porter & Coates, 1884.

———. *The Romance of the Harem*. Philadelphia: Porter & Coates, 1872. Also published as *The Romance of Siamese Harem Life*, London: Trubner, 1873; Boston: Osgood, 1873; and as *Siamese Harem Life*, with an introduction by Freya Stark, London: Barker, 1952.

Le Plongeon, Alice Dixon. *Here and There in Yucatan: Miscellanies*. New York: J. W. Bouton, 1886.

Levy, Juliette. See Baïracli-Levy, Juliette de.

Lippincott, Sara J. (Sara Clarke; Grace Greenwood). *Haps and Mishaps of a Tour in Europe*. Boston: Ticknor, Reed, & Fields, 1854.

———. *New Life in New Lands: Notes of Travel*. New York: J. B. Ford, 1873.

Little, Alicia H. N. Bewicke (Alicia Bewicke). *Intimate China: The Chinese As I Have Seen Them*. London: Hutchinson, 1899; Philadelphia: Lippincott, 1899.

———. *The Land of the Blue Gown*. London: Unwin, 1902. Also published as *In the Land of the Blue Gown*. New York: Appleton, 1909. By an early missionary in China.

London, Charmian Kittredge. *The Log of the Snark*. New York: Macmillan, 1915. By the wife of Jack London.

———. *Our Hawaii*. New York: Macmillan, 1917.

———. *Voyaging in Wild Seas: A Narrative of the Voyage of the Snark in the Years 1907–1909*. London: Mills & Boon, 1908. Also published as *A Woman among the Head Hunters*. London: Mills & Boon, 1915.

Londonderry, Frances Ann Vane Tempest, Marchioness. *A Journal of a Three Months' Tour in Portugal, Spain, Africa, etc.* London: J. Mitchell, 1943.

———. *Narrative of a Visit to the Courts of Vienna, Constantinople, Athens, Naples, etc.* London: Colburn, 1844.

———. *Russian Journal of Lady Londonderry, 1836–7*. Edited by W. A. L. Seaman and J. R. Sewell. London: Murray, 1973. From a manuscript in the Londonderry family archives.

Lott, Emmeline. *The English Governess in Egypt: Harem Life in Egypt and Constantinople*. London: Bentley, 1866. A governess in the household of Ismail Pasha, viceroy of Egypt.

————. *The Grand Pacha's Cruise on the Nile in the Viceroy of Egypt's Yacht*. London: Newby, 1869.

————. *The Mohaddetyn in the Palace. Nights in the Harem; or, The Mohaddetyn in the Palace of Ghezire*. London: Chapman & Hall, 1867.

Loviot, Fanny. *A Lady's Captivity among the Chinese Pirates in the Chinese Seas*. Translated from the French by Amelia B. Edwards. London: Routledge, 1858.

Lunn, Katharine. See Fowler-Lunn, Katharine Stevens.

Lyon, Jean. *Just Half a World Away: My Search for the New India*. New York: Crowell, 1954; London: Hutchinson, 1955.

McCarthy, Mary Therese. *Medina*. New York: Harcourt Brace Javonovich, 1972.

————. *The Stones of Florence*. London: Heinemann, 1959.

————. *Venice Observed*. London: Heinemann, 1956.

McGrath, Rosita. See Forbes, Rosita Torr.

Mackenzie, Jean Kenyon. *Black Sheep: Adventures in West Africa*. Boston and New York: Houghton Mifflin, 1916. Letters written during ten years as a Presbyterian missionary in West Africa.

Macleod, Olive (Olive Temple). *Chiefs and Cities of Central Africa: Across Lake Chad by Way of British, French, and German Territories*. Edinburgh and London: Blackwood, 1912.

Maitland, Louise. *Forest Venture: Conquering the Deserts of the Middle East*. London: Hale, 1960.

Mannin, Ethel Edith. *An American Journey*. London: Hutchinson, 1967.

————. *Aspects of Egypt: Some Travels in the United Arab Republic*. London: Hutchinson, 1964.

————. *Bavarian Story*. London: Jarrolds, 1949; New York: Appleton, 1950.

————. *Bitter Babylon*. London: Hutchinson, 1968.

————. *The Country of the Sea: Some Wanderings in Brittany*. London: Jarrolds, 1957.

————. *The Flowery Sword: Travels in Japan*. London: Hutchinson, 1960.

————. *Forever Wandering: Impression of Travel*. London: Jarrolds, 1934; New York: Dutton, 1935.

————. *German Journey*. London and New York: Jarrolds, 1934.

————. *An Italian Journey*. London: Hutchinson, 1974.

————. *Jungle Journey*. London and New York: Jarrolds, 1950.

————. *A Lance for the Arabs: A Middle East Journey*. London: Hutchinson, 1963.

————. *Land of the Crested Lion: A Journey through Modern Burma*. London: Jarrolds, 1955.

————. *The Lovely Land: The Hashemite Kingdom of Jordan*. London: Hutchinson, 1965.

————. *Mission to Beirut*. London: Hutchinson, 1973.

————. *Moroccan Mosaic*. London and New York: Jarrolds, 1953.

————. *South to Samarkand*. London: Jarrolds, 1936; New York: Dutton, 1937.

Manning, Ella Wallace. *Igloo for the Night*. London: Hodder & Stoughton, 1943. In Baffin Land.

Marsden, Kate. *My Mission in Siberia: A Vindication*. London: E. Stanford, 1921.

————. *On Sledge and Horseback to the Outcast Siberian Lepers*. London: Record, 1892; New York: Cassell, 1892.

Martin, Monica. *Out in the Mid-Day Sun*. Boston: Little, Brown, 1949; London: Cassell, 1951. India.

Martineau, Harriet. *Eastern Life, Present and Past*. London: E. Moxon, 1848; Philadelphia: Lea & Blanchard, 1848. Egypt and Palestine.

————. *Letters from Ireland*. London: J. Chapman, 1852.

————. *Retrospect of Western Travel*. London: Saunders & Otley, 1838; Cincinnati, Ohio: U. P. James, 1838. The diary on which *Society in America* was based.

————. *Society in America*. London: Saunders & Otley, 1837.

Matches, Margaret. *Savage Paradise*. New York and London: Century, 1931. Several months in New Guinea and other islands.

Maury, Sarah Mytton Hughes (Mrs. William Maury). *An Englishwoman in America*. London: Richardson, 1848.

Max Müller, Georgina Adelaide Grenfell. *Letters from Constantinople*. London, New York, and Bombay: Longman, 1897.

Meakin, Annette M. B. *Galicia, the Switzerland of Spain*. London: Methuen, 1909.

————. *In Russian Turkestan: A Garden of Asia and Its People*. London: G. Allen, 1903.

————. *A Ribbon of Iron*. Westminster, England: Constable, 1901; New York: Dutton, 1901. A trip on the Great Siberian Railway from Moscow to Vladivostok, then to Japan, and home to England via Canada and the United States.

————. *Russia: Travels and Studies*. London: Hurst & Blackett, 1906; Philadelphia: Lippincott, 1906.

————. *What America Is Doing: Letters from the New World*. Edinburgh and London: Blackwood, 1911. The eastern seaboard of America, visited just prior to World War I.

Mears, Helen. *The First Book of Japan*. New York: Watts, 1953.

————. *Year of the Wild Boar: An American Woman in Japan*. Philadelphia and New York: Lippincott, 1942.

Mehdevi, Anne Sinclair. *Persian Adventure*. London: Gollancz, 1953; New York: Knopf, 1953. A visit to Iran by an American woman who married an Iranian.

Melville, Elizabeth. *A Residence at Sierra Leone, Described from a Journal Kept on the Spot, and from Letters Written to Friends at Home*. By a lady. Edited by Mrs. Norton. London: Murray, 1849.

Merrick, Henrietta Sands. *Caucus-Race*. New York and London: Putnam, 1938. Iran and Syria.

————. *In the World's Attic*. New York and London: Putnam, 1931. Himalaya and Ladakh.

————. *Spoken in Tibet*. New York and London: Putnam, 1933.

Michaud, Sabrina, with Roland Michaud. *Caravans to Tartary*. New York: Viking, 1978. Husband and wife artist team who travel and produce outstanding color photographs.

————. *Mirror of the Orient*. Boston: New York Graphic Society, 1980.

Miles, Beryl. *Attic in Luxembourg*. London: Murray, 1956.

————. *Candles in Denmark*. London: Murray, 1958.

————. *Islands of Contrast: Adventures in New Zealand*. London: Murray, 1955.

————. *Spirit of Mexico*. New York: McBride, 1961; London: Murray, 1961.

————. *The Stars My Blanket*. London: Murray, 1954. Australia.

Miller, Christian. *Daisy, Daisy: A Journey across America on a Bicycle*. Garden City, N.Y.: Doubleday, 1981.

Miller, Janet. *Camel-bells of Baghdad: An Adventurous Journey to the City of the Arabian*

Nights, etc. Boston and New York: Houghton Mifflin, 1934; London: Putnam, 1935.

———. *Jungles Preferred.* Boston and New York: Houghton Mifflin, 1931; London: Putnam, 1931. By an American doctor who spent three years in the Belgian Congo.

Miller, Mary. See Gaunt, Mary Eliza Bakewell.

Mitchison, Naomi Haldane. *Mucking Around: Five Continents over Fifty Years.* London: Gollancz, 1981.

———. *Naomi Mitchison's Vienna Diary.* New York: Smith & Haas, 1934.

Mitton, Geraldine Edith (afterward Scott), Lady. *Austria Hungary.* London: A. & C. Black, 1914.

———. *A Bachelor Girl in Burma.* London: Hutchinson, 1898.

———. *The Lost Cities of Ceylon.* London: Murray, 1916.

———. *Round the Wonderful World.* London: T. C. & E. C. Jack, 1914; New York: Putnam, 1914.

Modiano, Colette. *Turkish Coffee and the Fertile Crescent: Wanderings through the Lebanon, Mesopotamia, Israel, Jordan and Syria.* London: Joseph, 1974.

———. *Twenty Snobs and Mao: Travelling De Luxe in Communist China.* Translated from the French by Jacqueline Baldick. London: Joseph, 1969. Also published as *Chairman Mao and My Millionaires; or, Through China with Twenty Snobs.* New York: American Heritage, 1970.

Moir, Jane F. *A Lady's Letters from Central Africa, a Journey from Mandala, Shire Highlands, to Ujiji, Lake Tanganyika, and Back.* Glasgow: J. Maclehose, 1891. Jane's husband ran a steamer on Lake Nyasa.

Mons, Barbara Hilda. *High Road to Hunza.* London and New York: Faber, 1958. A journey by car, plane, and ponies to visit the mir of Hunza.

Montagu, Lady Mary Wortley. *Letters of the Right Honourable Lady M—y W—y M— e.* London: n.p., 1763. So-called *Embassy Letters*, a compilation of letters written during Lady Mary's years in Turkey from 1716 to 1717. Montagu was the first Christian woman to penetrate the heart of the Islamic world; her letters have appeared in many editions since her death in 1762.

Montefiore, Judith Cohen, Lady. *Private Journal of a Visit to Egypt and Palestine, by Way of Italy and the Mediterranean.* London: Rickerby, 1836.

Mordaunt, Evelyn May (Evelyn May Clowes Wiehe; Elinor Mordaunt). *The Further Venture Book.* London: Lane, 1926; New York: Century, 1927. Travel in the Dutch East Indies.

———. *Purely for Pleasure.* London: Secker, 1932. Also published as *Rich Tapestry.* New York: Farrar & Rinehart, 1932. Central America, Equatorial Africa, and Indochina.

———. *The Venture Book.* London: Lane, 1926; New York: Century, 1926. The Pacific islands.

Morrell, Jemima. *Miss Jemima's Swiss Journal.* London: Putnam, 1963. From a typewritten copy entitled "The Proceedings of the Junior United Alpine Club, 1863. The Journal by Miss Jemima." Written for private circulation. The first Cook's tour of Switzerland.

Morris, Elizabeth Keith. *An Englishwoman in the Canadian West.* Bristol, England: Arrowsmith, 1913; London: Marshall, 1913.

———. *Hungary, the Land of Enchantment.* London: H. Hartley, 1931.

Morris, Jan (James Morris). *Cities.* London: Faber, 1963; New York: Harcourt, Brace

& World, 1964. Before a sex change in 1972, the writer's books were signed James Morris.

———. *Coast to Coast*. London: Faber, 1956. Also published as *As I Saw the USA*. New York: Pantheon, 1956.

———. *The Great Port: A Passage through New York*. New York: Harcourt, Brace & World, 1970; London: Faber, 1970. A journey commissioned by the Port of New York Authority.

———. *Journeys*. New York and Oxford: Oxford University Press, 1984.

———. *Places*. London: Faber, 1972.

———. *The Presence of Spain*. New York: Harcourt, Brace & World, 1964; London: Faber, 1964. Also published as *Spain*. New York: Oxford University Press, 1979.

———. *Venice*. London: Faber, 1960. Also published as *The World of Venice*. New York: Pantheon, 1960.

Morton, Rosalie Slaughter. *A Doctor's Holiday in Iran*. New York and London: Funk & Wagnalls, 1940.

Motley, Mary (Mary Motley de Renville). *Devils in Waiting*. London: Longman, 1959; New York: Viking, 1960. French Congo.

———. *Home to Numidia*. London: Longman, 1964.

———. *Morning Glory*. London: Longman, 1961; New York: St. Martin's, 1963. The Sahara.

Mott-Smith, May. *Africa from Port to Port*. New York: Van Nostrand, 1930.

Mueller, Georgina. See Max Müller, Georgina Adelaide Grenfell.

Mullikin, Mary Augusta, with Anna M. Hotchkis. *The Nine Sacred Mountains of China: An Illustrated Record of Pilgrimages Made in the Years 1935–1936*. Hong Kong: Vetch and Lee, 1973.

Munson, Arley Isabel. *Jungle Days; Being the Experiences of an American Woman Doctor in India*. New York and London: Appleton, 1913.

———. *Kipling's India*. Garden City, N.Y.: Doubleday, 1915; London: Eveleigh Nash, 1916.

Murphy, Grace Emline Barstow. *There's Always Adventure: The Story of a Naturalist's Wife*. New York: Harper, 1951; London: Allen & Unwin, 1952. Travels in the south Atlantic with Robert C. Murphy, an ornithologist.

Murray, Amelia Matilda. *Letters from the United States, Cuba and Canada*. London: Parker, 1856; New York: Putnam, 1856. The Hon. Amelia Murray was a Lady of the Bedchamber to Queen Victoria.

Murray, Mrs. J. C. See Aynsley, Harriet Georgina Maria.

Mytinger, Caroline. *Headhunting in the Solomon Islands around the Coral Sea*. New York: Macmillan, 1942. With Margaret Warner, Mytinger set out to paint the portraits of primitive negroids living in the South Pacific.

———. *New Guinea Headhunt*. New York: Macmillan, 1946.

Ness, Elizabeth Wilhelmina. *Ten Thousand Miles in Two Continents*. London: Methuen, 1929. Travels in Africa and Persia by Mrs. Patrick Ness, a Fellow of the Royal Geographical Society and the first woman member of its council.

Nicolson, Victoria. See Sackville-West, Victoria Mary.

Oakley, Amy Ewing. *Behold the West Indies*. New York and London: Appleton-Century, 1941.

———. *Cloud-Lands of France*. New York: Century, 1927. The first of several books on travel in France, illustrated by Thornton Oakley.

O'Brien, Kate. *Farewell Spain*. Garden City, N.Y.: Doubleday, 1937; London and Toronto: Heinemann, 1937.

Pardoe, Julia. *The Beauties of the Bosphorus*. London: G. Virtue, 1838.

———. *The City of the Magyar; or, Hungary and Her Institutions in 1839–1840*. London: G. Virtue, 1840.

———. *The City of the Sultan, and Domestic Manners of the Turks*. London: Colburn, 1837.

———. *Pilgrimages in Paris*. London: W. Lay, 1857.

———. *The River and the Desert; or, Recollections of the Rhone and the Chartreuse*. London: Colburn, 1838.

———. *Traits and Traditions of Portugal, Collected during a Residence in That Country*. London: Saunders & Otley, 1833.

Parks, Fanny (Mrs. Parlby). *Wanderings of a Pilgrim, in Search of the Picturesque, during Four-and-Twenty Years in the East; with Revelations of Life in the Zenana*. London: Richardson, 1850.

Peary, Josephine Diebitsch. *My Arctic Journal: A Year among Ice-Fields and Eskimos*. New York and Philadelphia: Contemporary, 1893; London: Longman, 1893. Josephine accompanied her husband, Admiral Robert Peary, to the Arctic from 1891 to 1892 and again in 1893.

Peck, Anne Merriman, with Enid Johnson. *A Vagabond's Provence*. New York: Dodd, Mead, 1936. Peck wrote a number of books combining travel and history, many of them for young people.

Peck, Ellen Mary Hayes. *Travels in the Far East*. New York: Crowell, 1909. Through Egypt, India, Burma, and Ceylon.

Pelzer, Dorothy West. *Trek across Indonesia*. Singapore: C. Brash, 1982.

Pender, Rose, Lady. *A Lady's Experiences in the Wild West in 1883*. Lincoln: University of Nebraska Press, 1978.

———. *No Telegraph; or, A Trip to Our Unconnected Colonies*. London: privately printed, 1879.

Penn, Lucie. See Street, Lucie.

Pennell, Elizabeth Robins. *French Cathedrals, Monasteries and Abbeys, and Sacred Sites of France*. New York: Century, 1909; London: Unwin, 1909.

———. *Italy's Garden of Eden*. Philadelphia: Pennell Club, 1927.

———. *Nights: Rome, Venice, in the Aesthetic Eighties; London, Paris, in the Fighting Nineties*. Philadelphia and London: Lippincott, 1916.

———. *Over the Alps on a Bicycle*. London: Unwin, 1898.

Pennell, Elizabeth Robins, with Joseph Pennell. *A Canterbury Pilgrimage, Ridden, Written, and Illustrated*. London: Seeley, 1885. The husband and wife team, best known as artists, made many of their trips by bicycle.

———. *An Italian Pilgrimage*. London: Seeley, 1887.

———. *Our Journey to the Hebrides*. New York: Harper, 1889.

———. *Our Sentimental Journey through France and Italy*. London and New York: Longman, 1888.

———. *Two Pilgrims' Progress from Fair Florence to the Eternal City of Rome*. Boston: Little, Brown, 1899.

Petherick, Katharine, with John Petherick. *Travels in Central Africa and Explorations of the Western Nile Tributaries*. London: Tinsley, 1869. Petherick was British consul in Khartoum, where Katharine lived with him in the early 1860s.

Phelan, Nancy Creagh. *Atoll Holiday*. Sydney: Angus & Robertson, 1958. The Gilbert Islands.

———. *The Chilean Way: Travels in Chile*. London: Macmillan, 1973.

———. *Pillow of Grass*. London: Macmillan, 1969; Elmsford, N.Y. and London: House & Maxwell, 1970. Japan.

———. *Some Came Early, Some Came Late*. South Melbourne: Macmillan, 1970. Australia.

———. *Welcome the Wayfarer: A Traveller in Modern Turkey*. London: Macmillan, 1965; New York: St. Martin's, 1965.

Piozzi, Hester Lynch Salusbury Thrale. *Observations and Reflections Made in the Course of a Journey through France, Italy, and Germany*. London: Strahan & Cadell, 1789; Dublin: Chamberlaine, 1789. Mrs. Thrale, long-time friend of Dr. Samuel Johnson, married Gabriel Piozzi and with him traveled for two and a half years on the Continent.

Ponafidine, Emma Cochran. *My Life in the Moslem East*. Indianapolis: Bobbs-Merrill, 1932. Mrs. Pierre Ponafidine also translated her husband's *Life in the Moslem East*, New York: Dodd, Mead, 1911. An American born in Persia in 1863, Emma married Ponafidine, a Russian nobleman, and lived in Russia until she escaped from the Bolsheviks in 1922.

———. *Russia, My Home: An Intimate Record of Personal Experiences before, during & after the Bolshevist Revolution*. Indianapolis: Bobbs-Merrill, 1931.

Poole, Sophia Lane. *The Englishwoman in Egypt: Letters from Cairo Written during a Residence There in 1842, 3, & 4 with E. W. Lane . . . by His Sister*. Also a second series, from 1845 to 1846. London: C. Knight, 1844–1846.

Pringle, M. A. *Towards the Mountains of the Moon: A Journey in East Africa*. Edinburgh and London: Blackwood, 1884. Also published as *A Journey in East Africa*. Edinburgh: Blackwood, 1886.

Putnam, Anne Eisner, with Allan Keller. *Madami: My Eight Years of Adventure with the Congo Pygmies*. New York: Prentice-Hall, 1954. Also published as *Eight Years with Congo Pygmies*. London: Hutchinson, 1955.

Rama Rau, Santha. *East of Home*. New York: Harper, 1950; London, Gollancz, 1951. Travels in the Far East.

———. *Home to India*. London: Gollancz, 1945; New York: Harper, 1945.

———. *My Russian Journey*. New York: Harper, 1959; London: Gollancz, 1959.

———. *View to the South East*. New York: Harper, 1957; London: Gollancz, 1958. Southeast Asia.

Richmond Brown, Lilian Mabel Alice Roussel, Lady. *Unknown Tribes, Uncharted Seas*. London: Duckworth, 1924; New York: Appleton, 1925. With Mitchell Hedges, on an expedition to Central America. Lady Richmond Brown was a Fellow of the Royal Geographical Society.

Rickover, Ruth Masters. *Pepper, Rice, and Elephants: A Southeast Asian Journey from Celebes to Siam*. Annapolis, Md.: Naval Institute Press, 1975. A journey made before World War II.

Rigby, Elizabeth. See Eastlake, Elizabeth Rigby, Lady.

Ripley, Eliza Moore Chinn McHatton. *From Flag to Flag: A Woman's Adventures and Experiences in the South during the War, in Mexico, and in Cuba*. New York: Appleton, 1889. Experiences as a refugee during the American Civil War.

Roberts, Emma. *Hindostan: Its Landscapes, Palaces, Temples, Tombs, the Shores of the*

Red Sea, and the Sublime and Romantic Scenery of the Himalaya Mountains. London: Fisher, 1845–47. Roberts, an Englishwoman, lived in India in the 1830s and earned her way as a newspaper editor.

————. *Notes on an Overland Journey through France and Egypt to Bombay.* London: W. H. Allen, 1841.

————. *Scenes and Characteristics of Hindostan with Sketches of Anglo-Indian Society.* London: W. H. Allen, 1835.

Robeson, Eslanda Goode. *African Journey.* New York: J. Day, 1945; London: Gollancz, 1946. By Mrs. Paul Robeson.

Romer, Isabella Frances. *The Bird of Passage; or, Flying Glimpses of Many Lands.* Paris: Galignani, 1849. Impressions of Europe and Turkey from 1844 to 1848.

————. *A Pilgrimage to the Temples and Tombs of Egypt, Nubia and Palestine in 1845– 46.* London: Bentley, 1846.

————. *The Rhone, the Darro, and the Guadalquivir: A Summer Ramble in 1842.* London: Bentley, 1843.

Roosevelt, [Anna] Eleanor. *India and the Awakening East.* New York: Harper, 1953; London: Hutchinson, 1954.

Roper, Myra. *China, the Surprising Country.* Garden City, N.Y.: Doubleday, 1966; London: Heinemann, 1966.

Ross, Sylvia. See Leith-Ross, Sylvia.

Russell, Lady. See Gordon, Helen Cameron, Lady Russell.

Ryan, Margaret G. *African Hayride.* New York: Rand McNally, 1956.

Sackville-West, Victoria Mary (Vita; Victoria Nicolson). *Passenger to Teheran.* London: L. & V. Woolf, 1926; New York: Doran, 1927.

————. *Twelve Days: An Account of a Journey across the Bakhtiari Mountains in South- western Persia.* London: L. & V. Woolf, 1928; Garden City, N.Y.: Doubleday, Doran, 1928.

St. Albans, Suzanne Marie Adele Beauclerk, Duchess of. *Green Grows the Oil.* London and New York: Quartet, 1978. In the United Arab Emirates.

————. *A Portrait of Oman.* London and New York: Quartet, 1980.

Salisbury, Charlotte Y. *Asian Diary.* New York: Scribner, 1968.

————. *China Diary.* New York: Walker, 1973.

————. *China Diary, after Mao.* New York: Walker, 1974.

————. *The Long March Diary: China Epic.* New York: Walker, 1986. Retracing Mao's Long March, the retreat from Chiang Kai Shek's army from 1934 to 1935.

————. *Russian Diary.* New York: Walker, 1974.

————. *Tibetan Diary: Travels Along the Silk Route.* New York: Walker, 1981.

Salisbury, Charlotte Y., with Alice Kandell. *Mountaintop Kingdom: Sikkim.* New York: Norton, 1971?

Savage, Barbara. *Miles from Nowhere: A Round-the-World Bicycle Adventure.* Seattle, Wash.: Mountaineers, 1983.

Savory, Isabel. *In the Tail of the Peacock.* London: Hutchinson, 1903. Two women tour Morocco.

————. *The Romantic Roussillon: In the French Pyrenees.* London: Unwin, 1919; New York: Scribner, 1920.

————. *A Sportswoman in India: Personal Adventures and Experiences of Travel in Known and Unknown India.* London: Hutchinson, 1900; Philadelphia: Lippincott, 1900.

Schaw, Janet. *Journal of a Lady of Quality; Being the Narrative of a Journey from Scotland to the West Indies, North Carolina, and Portugal, in the Years 1774 to 1776*. Edited by Evangeline Walker Andrews in collaboration with Charles McLean Andrews. New Haven, Conn.: Yale University Press, 1921. From a manuscript in the British Museum.

Schreider, Helen, with Frank Schreider. *The Drums of Tonkin: An Adventure in Indonesia*. New York: Coward McCann, 1963.

———. *Exploring the Amazon*. Washington, D.C.: National Geographic, 1970.

———. *20,000 Miles South: A Pan American Adventure*. Garden City, N.Y.: Doubleday, 1957. Also published as *La Tortuga: A Pan American Adventure*. London: Secker & Warburg, 1957.

Scidmore, Eliza Ruhamah. *Alaska, Its Southern Coast and the Sitkan Archipelago*. Boston: Lothrop, 1885.

———. *China, the Long-Lived Empire*. New York: Century, 1900.

———. *Java, the Garden of the East*. New York: Century, 1898.

———. *Jinrikisha Days in Japan*. New York and London: Harper, 1891.

———. *Winter India*. London: Unwin, 1903; New York: Century, 1903.

Scott, Elspet. See Keith, Elizabeth.

Seaman, Elizabeth Cochrane (Elizabeth Cochrane; Nelly Bly). *Nelly Bly's Book: Around the World in Seventy-Two Days*. New York: Pictorial Weeklies, 1890. An investigative journalist sent by the *New York World* to beat the fictional 80-day around-the-world record of Jules Verne's Phileas Fogg.

Selby, Bettina. *Riding the Mountains Down*. London: Gollancz, 1984. Travel by bicycle in Pakistan, India, and Nepal.

———. *Riding to Jerusalem*. London: Sidgwick & Jackson, 1985; New York: P. Bedrick, 1986.

Shalom, Sabina. *A Marriage Sabbatical*. New York: Dodd, Mead, 1984; London: Muller, 1984. India, Australia, and the South Seas.

Sheil, Mary Leonora Woulfe, Lady. *Glimpses of Life and Manners in Persia, with Notes on Russia, Koords, Toorkomans, Nestorians, Khiva, and Persia*. London: Murray, 1856.

Sheldon, Louise Vescelius. *Yankee Girls in Zulu Land*. London: F. Warne, 1888; New York: Worthington, 1888. Also published (revised) as *Yankee Girls in Oom Paul's Land*. London: Henderson, 1899; New York: Street & Smith, 1900.

Shor, Jean Bowie. *After You, Marco Polo*. New York: McGraw Hill, 1955. Also published as *The Trail of Marco Polo*. London: Muller, 1956.

Singer, Caroline (Caroline Baldridge), with Cyrus LeRoy Baldridge. *Half the World Is Isfahan*. New York and London: Oxford University Press, 1936.

———. *Turn to the East, by Two Who Seek Here to Intimate the Richness of Their Adventure*. New York: Minton, Balch, 1926.

———. *White Africans and Black*. New York and London: Allen & Unwin, 1929; New York: Norton, 1929; Lagos, Nigeria: C. M. S. Bookshop, 1929.

Skene, Felicia Mary Frances. *Wayfaring Sketches among the Greeks and Turks, and on the Shores of the Danube*. London: Chapman & Hall, 1847. Skene lived near Athens from 1838 to 1845.

Smythe, Emily Ann. See Strangford, Emily Ann Smythe, Viscountess.

Speed, Maude. *A Scamper Tour to Rhodesia and South Africa (with a Sketch-book)*. London and New York: Longman, 1933.

————. *Through Central France to the Pyrenees*. London: Longman, 1924.

Stanford, Doreen Napier. *Sun and Snow, a Siberian Adventure*. London: Longman, 1963. Also published as *Siberian Odyssey*. New York: Dutton, 1964.

Stokes, Olivia. See Hatch, Olivia Phelps Stokes.

Stone, Julia A. *Illustrated India, Its Princes and People. Upper, Central and Farther India, up the Ganges, and down the Indus. To Which Is Added an Authentic Account of the Visit to India of His Royal Highness the Prince of Wales*. Hartford, Conn.: American, 1877.

Storm, Marian. *Enjoying Uruapan: A Book for Travelers in Michoacan*. Mexico: Editorial Bolivar, 1945. By a writer principally interested in botany.

————. *Hoofways into Hot Country*. Mexico: Bland, 1939.

————. *Prologue to Mexico: The Story of a Search for a Place*. New York: Knopf, 1931. Also published as *Little Known Mexico*. London: Hutchinson, 1932.

Strangford, Emily Anne Smythe, Viscountess. *The Eastern Shores of the Adriatic in 1863, with a Visit to Montenegro*. London: Bentley, 1864.

————. *Egyptian Sepulchres and Syrian Shrines, Including Some Stay in the Lebanon, at Palmyra, and in Western Turkey*. London: Longman, 1861.

Street, Lucie (later Penn). *The Tent Pegs of Heaven: A Journey through Afghanistan*. London, Hale, 1967. An automobile journey as a guest of the royal family of Afghanistan.

Stuart-Wortley, Emmeline Charlotte Elizabeth Manners, Lady. &c. [Sketches of Travel in America]. London: Bosworth, 1853. "My book of American travels was called, 'Travels in the United States &c.' and that &c. I propose now . . . to take up again."

————. *Travels in the United States etc. during the Years 1849 and 1850*. New York: Harper, 1851; London: Bentley, 1851.

————. *A Visit to Portugal and Madeira*. London: Chapman & Hall, 1854.

Sutherland, Louise. *The Impossible Ride*. London: Southern Cross, 1982. A bicycle trip through the Amazon jungle on the newly made Trans-Amazon Highway.

Taylor, Annie Royle. "The Diary of Miss Annie R. Taylor's Remarkable Journey from Tau-Chau to Ta-Chien-Lu through the Heart of the Forbidden Land." In William Carey, *Adventures in Tibet, Including the Diary of Miss Annie R. Taylor's Remarkable Journey* . . . Boston and Chicago: United Society of Christian Endeavor, 1901. Also published as *Travel and Adventure in Tibet, Including the Diary*. . . . London: Hodder & Stoughton, 1902.

————. *Pioneering in Tibet: The Origin and Progress of the Tibetan Pioneer Mission*. London: n.d. Ascribed to Taylor.

————. *Tibetan Pioneer Mission, together with Some Facts about Tibet. (My Experiences in Tibet, by Miss A. R. Taylor)*. London: Morgan & Scott, 1894.

Taylor, Jane, with Laurens van der Post. *Testament to the Bushmen*. New York and Harmondsworth, Middlesex: Viking, 1984.

Taylor, Mary Geraldine Guinness. See Guinness, Mary Geraldine.

Temple, Olive, See Macleod, Olive.

Templeton, Edith. *The Surprise of Cremona*. London: Eyre & Spottiswoode, 1954.

Thomas, Tay (Mary P. Thomas). *Follow the North Star*. Garden City, N.Y.: Doubleday, 1960.

————. *In the Shadow of the Rising Sun*. Singapore: Maruzen Asia, 1983.

————. *Only in Alaska*. Garden City, N.Y.: Doubleday, 1969.

————, with Lowell Thomas, Jr. *Our Flight to Adventure*. Garden City, N.Y.: Doubleday, 1956.

Thompson, Era Bell. *Africa, Land of My Fathers*. Garden City, N.Y.: Doubleday, 1954.

Tinling, Christine Isabel. *Bits of China: Travel Sketches in the Orient*. Introduction by Anna A. Gordon. New York and Chicago: Revell, 1925.

————. *From Japan to Jerusalem: Personal Impressions of Journeyings in the Orient*. New York: Revell, 1926.

Todd, Mabel Loomis. *Corona and Coronet; Being a Narrative of the Amherst Eclipse Expedition to Japan, in Mr. James's Schooner-Yacht Coronet, to Observe the Sun's Total Obstruction, 9th August, 1896*. Boston and New York: Houghton Mifflin, 1898.

————. *Tripoli the Mysterious*. Boston: Small, Maynard, 1912; London: Grant Richards, 1912.

Topping, Audrey. *Dawn Wakes in the East*. New York: Harper & Row, 1973; Adelaide, Australia: Rigby, 1973. Travel in China.

————. *The Splendors of Tibet*. New York: Sino, 1980.

Toy, Barbara. *Columbus Was Right! Rover around the World*. London: Murray, 1958.

————. *A Fool in the Desert: Journeys in Libya*. London: Murray, 1956.

————. *A Fool on Wheels: Tangier to Baghdad by Land Rover*. London: Murray, 1956.

————. *A Fool Strikes Oil: Across Saudi Arabia*. London: Murray, 1957.

————. *The Highway of the Three Kings: Arabia—From South to North*. London: Murray, 1968.

————. *In Search of Sheba: Across the Sahara to Ethiopia*. London: Murray, 1961.

————. *Rendezvous in Cyprus*. London: Murray, 1970.

————. *The Way of the Chariots: Niger River—Sahara—Libya*. London: Murray, 1964.

Trautman, Kathleen. *Spies behind the Pillar, Bandits at the Pass*. New York: McKay, 1972. Afghanistan.

Tremlett, Mrs. Horace. *With the Tin Gods*. London and New York: Lane, 1915; Toronto: Bell & Cockburn, 1915. In Nigeria, where Horace was prospecting for tin.

Tristan, Flora. *Peregrinations of a Pariah, 1833–1834*. Translated and edited by Jean Hawkes. London: Virago, 1986. The first English translation of Tristan's *Mémoires et pérégrinations d'une paria* (1838). On Peru.

Trollope, Frances Milton. *Belgium and Western Germany in 1833, Including Visits to Baden-Baden, Wiesbaden, Cassel, Hanover, the Harz Mountains, &c. &c.* Philadelphia: Carey, Lea, & Blanchard, 1834; London: Murray, 1834.

————. *Domestic Manners of the Americans*. London: Whittaker, Treacher, 1832; New York: Dodd, Mead, 1832.

————. *Italy and the Italians*. London: Bentley, 1842.

————. *Paris and the Parisians in 1835*. London: Bentley, 1836; New York: Harper, 1836.

————. *Vienna and the Austrians, with Some Account of a Journey through Swabia, Bavaria, the Tyrol, and the Salzbourg*. London: Bentley, 1838.

————. *A Visit to Italy*. London: Bentley, 1842.

Turnbull, Jane M. C., with Marian Turnbull. *American Photographs: Travels*. London: T. C. Newby, 1859. Photographic trip of 26,000 miles through the United States, Canada, and Cuba between 1852 and 1857.

Tweedie, Ethel Brilliana Harley (Mrs. Alec Tweedie; Ethel B. Harley). *A Winter Jaunt to Norway, with Accounts of Nansen, Ibsen, Bjornson, Brandes and Many Others.*

London: Bliss, Sands, & Foster, 1894. Mrs. Alec Tweedie wrote a number of popular travel books.

Ullens de Schooten, Marie-Thérèse. *Lords of the Mountains: Southern Persia and the Kashkai Tribe*. London: Chatto & Windus, 1956.

Urrutia, Virginia. *Two Wheels and a Taxi: A Slightly Daft Adventure in the Andes*. Seattle, Wash.: Mountaineers, 1987.

Vaka, Demetra. See Brown, Demetra Kenneth.

Vane, Frances Ann. See Londonderry, Frances Ann Vane Tempest, Marchioness.

Vassall, Gabrielle Maud. *In and round Yunnan Fou*. London: Heinemann, 1922.

———. *Life in French Congo*. London: Unwin, 1925.

———. *On and off Duty in Annam*. London: Heinemann, 1910; New York: Appleton, 1910. Gabrielle lived in the lower Mekong Delta, Vietnam, as the bride of a French army doctor.

Waldron, D'Lynn (Diane Lynn Waldron-Shah). *Far from Home*. London: Redman, 1962. A correspondent, sketch artist, and photographer in Asia, Arabia, Africa, and Indonesia.

———. *Further Than at Home*. New York: Harper, 1959. A round-the-world trip by an American woman who met the Shah of Nepal and subsequently married him.

Walker, Mary Adelaide. *Eastern Life and Scenery, with Excursions in Asia Minor, Mytilene, Crete, and Roumania*. London: Chapman & Hall, 1886. Changes in Turkish life after the Crimean war.

———. *Old Tracks and New Landmarks: Wayside Sketches in Crete, Macedonia, Mitylene*. London: Bentley, 1897.

———. *Through Macedonia to the Albanian Lakes*. London: Chapman & Hall, 1864.

———. *Untrodden Paths in Roumania*. London: Chapman & Hall, 1888.

Wallace, Susan Arnold Elston. *Along the Bosphorus, and Other Sketches*. London: Unwin, 1898; Chicago and New York: Rand McNally, 1898. By the wife of Lew Wallace, minister to Turkey from 1881 to 1885.

———. *The Land of the Pueblos*. New York: J. B. Alden, 1888. The Wallaces lived in New Mexico from 1878 to 1881, while he was governor.

———. *The Repose in Egypt, a Medley*. New York: J. B. Alden, 1888. Includes *Along the Bosphorus*.

———. *The Storied Sea*. Boston: Osgood, 1883.

Ward, Harriet. *Five Years in Kaffirland, with Sketches of the Late War in That Country to the Conclusion of Peace*. London: H. Colburn, 1848. An abridged version was published as *The Cape and the Kaffirs*, London: H. G. Bohn, 1851. Ward went to southeastern Africa with her husband in 1842 and remained for several years. The book includes a history of the War of the Axe, 1846–1848.

West, Dame Rebecca (Cicily Isabel Fairfield; Mrs. Henry Maxwell Andrews). *Black Lamb and Grey Falcon: The Record of a Journey through Yugoslavia in 1937*. London: Macmillan, 1941.

Wetmore, Elizabeth Bisland (Elizabeth Bisland). *A Flying Trip around the World*. New York: Harper, 1891; London: Osgood & McIlvaine, 1891. An American journalist tried to beat Elizabeth Seaman's trip around the world.

———, with Anne Hoyt. *Seekers in Sicily, being a Quest for Persephone by Jane and Peripatetica*. London and New York: Lane, 1909.

Wharton, Edith Newbold. *In Morocco*. New York: Scribner, 1920. One of several travel books by the novelist.

Whelpton, Barbara Fanny (Barbara Crocker), with Eric Whelpton. *Calabria and the Aeolian Islands*. London: Hale, 1957. The Whelptons worked together on several travel books; Barbara is the illustrator.

Whishaw, Lorna. *As Far As You'll Take Me*. New York: Dodd, Mead, 1958. The Alaska Highway.

———. *Mexico Unknown*. London: Hammond, Hammond, 1962. In Mexico and Central America.

Whiting, Lilian. *Athens, the Violet-Crowned*. Boston: Little, Brown, 1913.

———. *Canada, the Spellbinder*. London and Toronto: Dent, 1917; New York: Dutton, 1917.

———. *Italy, the Magic Land*. Boston: Little, Brown, 1907.

———. *The Land of Enchantment, from Pike's Peak to the Pacific*. Boston: Little, Brown, 1907.

———. *Paris, the Beautiful*. Boston: Little, Brown, 1908; London: Hodder & Stoughton, 1909.

Wiehe, Evelyn. See Mordaunt, Evelyn May.

Willcox, Faith Mellen. *In Morocco*. New York: Harcourt Brace Jovanovich, 1971; London: Longman, 1972.

Winternitz, Helen. *East along the Equator: A Journey up the Congo and into Zaire*. New York: Atlantic Monthly, 1987.

Woodin, Ann Snow. *In the Circle of the Sun*. New York: Macmillan, 1971. A year in the Sahara-Sindian desert.

Woolson, Constance Fenimore. *Mentone, Cairo and Corfu*. New York: Harper, 1896.

Wordsworth, Jill. *Follow the Sun*. London: Hale, 1958. Also published as *I Follow the Sun*. New York: Morrow, 1959. Africa.

———. *Gorilla Mountain*. London: Lutterworth, 1961. Eight months among gorillas in Uganda.

Wright, Frances. See D'Arusmont, Frances Wright.

SELECTED BIBLIOGRAPHY

ANTHOLOGIES AND COLLECTIVE BIOGRAPHIES

Adams, William Davenport. *Celebrated Women Travellers of the Nineteenth Century*. London: Sonnenschein, 1883.

All True! The Record of Actual Adventures That Have Happened to Ten Women of Today. New York: Brewer, Warren & Putnam, 1981.

Allen, Alexandra. *Travelling Ladies*. London: Jupiter, 1980.

A Book of Travellers' Tales. Assembled by Eric Newby. New York: Viking, 1985.

Branch, Lesley. *The Wilder Shores of Love*. New York: Simon & Schuster, 1954.

Courtney, Janet. *The Adventurous Thirties, a Chapter in the Women's Movement*. Freeport, N.Y.: Books for Libraries, 1967.

Dole, Gertrude E. *Vignettes of Some Early Members of the Society of Woman Geographers in New York*. Closter, N.J.: Society of Woman Geographers, 1978.

Explorers' and Travellers' Tales. Edited by Odette Tchernine. London: Jarrolds, 1958.

The Great Travellers. A Collection of Firsthand Narratives of Wayfarers, Wanderers, and Explorers in All Parts of the World from 450 B.C. to the Present. Edited by Milton Rugoff. New York: Simon & Schuster, 1960.

Holmes, Winifred. *Seven Adventurous Women*. London: Bell, 1953.

La Bastille, Anne. *Women and Wilderness*. San Francisco: Sierra Club. 1980.

Ladies on the Loose: Women Travellers of the 18th and 19th Centuries. Edited by Leo Hamalian. New York: Dodd, Mead, 1981.

Land, Barbara. *The New Explorers: Women in Antarctica*. New York: Dodd, Mead, 1981.

Middleton, Dorothy. *Victorian Lady Travellers*. London: Routledge & Kegan Paul, 1965.

Miller, Luree. *On Top of the World: Five Women Explorers in Tibet*. London: Paddington Press, 1976.

Mozans, H. J. (pseud. of John A. Zahm). *Woman in Science*. New York and London: Appleton, 1913.

Niles, Blair. *Journeys in Time, from the Halls of Montezuma to Patagonia's Plains: A Treasury Gathered from Four Centuries of Writers*. New York: Coward-McCann, 1946.

Olds, Elizabeth Fagg. *Women of the Four Winds*. Boston: Houghton Mifflin, 1985.

Oliver, Caroline. *Western Women in Colonial Africa*. Westport, Conn.: Greenwood Press, 1982.

Rittenhouse, Mignon. *Seven Women Explorers*. Philadelphia: Lippincott, 1964. Written for young people.

Roberts, Brian. *Ladies in the Veld*. London: Murray, 1965.

Robson, Isabel. *Two Lady Missionaries in Tibet*. London: Partridge, 1909.

Russell, Mary. *The Blessings of a Good Thick Skirt: Women Travellers and Their World*. London: Collins, 1986.

Stevenson, Catherine Barnes. *Victorian Women Travel Writers in Africa*. Boston: Twayne, 1982.

Tabor, Margaret E. *Pioneer Women*. London: Sheldon Press, 1930.

Van Thal, Herbert. *Victoria's Subjects Travelled*. London: A. Barker, 1951.

BIBLIOGRAPHICAL SOURCES

Bevis, Richard W. *Bibliotheca Cisorientalia: An Annotated Checklist of Early English Travel Books on the Near and Middle East*. Boston: G. K. Hall, 1973.

Cox, Edward G. *A Reference Guide to the Literature of Travel*. Seattle: University of Washington, 1935–1949.

Dulles, Foster Rhea. *Americans Abroad: Two Centuries of American Travel*. Ann Arbor, Mich.: University of Michigan, 1964.

Foster, Barbara. *Memoirs of the Travelling Ladies*. Bulletin of the Special Libraries Association, Geography and Maps Division, 99–100 (Mar.–Dec. 1975, Mar.–June, 1976).

Selected Guide to Travel Books. Edited by Susan Nueckel. New York: Fleet, 1974.

Travel Literature through the Ages: An Anthology. Collected and edited by Percy G. Adams. New York and London: Galland, 1988.

Traveler's Reading Guides: Background Books, Novels, Travel Literature and Articles. Edited by Maggy Simony and others. Bayport, N.Y.: Freelance, 1981–1984.

INDEX

Page references to whole chapters appear in *italics*.

About the Author

MARION TINLING is a freelance writer based in Sacramento, California. She is the author of *Women Remembered: A Guide to Landmarks of Women's History in the United States* (Greenwood Press, 1986). The editor of *The Correspondence of the Three William Byrds of Westover, Virginia*, she has published articles in such journals as *The William and Mary Quarterly*, *The Historian*, and *Historic Preservation*.